ELMER L. TOWNS

365

WAYS TO

KNOW

GOD

Regal

From Gospel Light
Ventura, California, U.S.A.

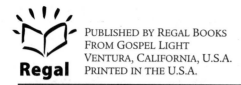

PUBLISHED BY REGAL BOOKS
FROM GOSPEL LIGHT
VENTURA, CALIFORNIA, U.S.A.
PRINTED IN THE U.S.A.

Regal Books is a ministry of Gospel Light, a Christian publisher dedicated to serving the local church. We believe God's vision for Gospel Light is to provide church leaders with biblical, user-friendly materials that will help them evangelize, disciple and minister to children, youth and families.

It is our prayer that this Regal book will help you discover biblical truth for your own life and help you meet the needs of others. May God richly bless you.

For a free catalog of resources from Regal Books/Gospel Light, please call your Christian supplier or contact us at 1-800-4-GOSPEL *or* www.regalbooks.com.

Cover design by David Griffing
Interior design by Stephen Hahn
Edited by Anita Palmer

Library of Congress Cataloging-in-Publication Data
Towns, Elmer L.
   365 ways to know God / Elmer L. Towns.
      p. cm.
   ISBN 0-8307-3341-8
   1. Devotional calendars. I. Title: Three hundred sixty-five ways to know God. II. Title.
   BV4811.T68 2004
   242'.2—dc22   2004020992

1 2 3 4 5 6 7 8 9 10 11 12 13 14 15 / 10 09 08 07 06 05 04

Rights for publishing this book in other languages are contracted by Gospel Light Worldwide, the international nonprofit ministry of Gospel Light. Gospel Light Worldwide also provides publishing and technical assistance to international publishers dedicated to producing Sunday School and Vacation Bible School curricula and books in the languages of the world. For additional information, visit www.gospellightworldwide.org; write to Gospel Light Worldwide, P.O. Box 3875, Ventura, CA 93006; or send an e-mail to info@gospellightworldwide.org.

CONTENTS

TALKING TO GOD ON A FIRST-NAME BASIS

Elmer Towns knows a lot about the names of God. He has lectured on the names of each of the three Persons of the Godhead and has written three best-selling books on them: *The Names of Jesus, My Father's Names* and *The Names of the Holy Spirit*. *The Names of the Holy Spirit* won the Gold Medallion award from the Christian Booksellers Association in 1995. He also has compiled the most extensive lists of the names of God (see the appendices at the back of the book). Now he has written this daily devotional on 365 names of God in the Bible.

Elmer wrote the first three books to give us information on God's names and to help us understand the nature of God from His names. Many people have used them in their Bible studies or Sunday School classes. Now, in this devotional, he writes to our hearts so that we can feel and apply God to our everyday living. Through the names of God, we can touch God each day in a new and different way; but most important, God can touch us daily.

This book could be called *Talking to God on a First-Name Basis*, because it contains prayers for you to talk to God with—using one of His personal names each day. This book can be an exciting journey into knowing God more intimately through His many names.

Elmer prayed that he would be anointed to write a book through which readers could feel the presence of God. I believe God has answered his prayer, because I felt the presence of God as I read these devotionals and talked personally to each Person of the Godhead.

Tim LaHaye
Coauthor, the Left Behind Series

INTRODUCTION

The Bible has more than a thousand names, titles and metaphors for God. Why does God have so many names? For the same reason we do. Each name and title represents a different position, function or characteristic. For instance, I am called husband, father, grandfather, dean, faculty, golfer, author, Sunday School teacher and so on. The more you are and do, the more names and titles you have. Since God is greater than anyone in the universe, wouldn't you expect Him to have the most titles and names?

Every time you learn a new title or name of a person, you learn more about that person. As you read through this devotional, you'll learn more about God than you ever have before, because you will explore 365 of His names, one for every day of the year. So be prepared to know God intimately this year. And when you learn about God and His relationship to you, you'll learn more about yourself. Be prepared to live closer to God than ever before.

There's one reading for each day of the year. Also, there's a suggested daily Bible reading to expand your understanding of the name assigned for that day. Get ready to be transformed this year as you experience 365 ways to know God.

Elmer L. Towns
Written from my home
at the foot of the Blue Ridge Mountains
2004

JANUARY

THE TRINITY: THE LORD, MY SHEPHERD (JEHOVAH ROI)

The LORD is my shepherd; I shall not want.
PSALM 23:1

The Lord is your Shepherd; He can lead you to green pastures where you can lie down for rest. There you can feed on green grass to regain your strength. He will lead you beside still water so you can moisten your dry tongue. Will you follow Him today? The Lord is your Shepherd; He will lead you in the right paths, for His name's sake. He will guide you through the valley of the shadow of death. Don't be afraid of shadows, for they are only dark eclipses created by threatening mountains. The Shepherd will be with you in danger and will lead you through dark valleys but not leave you there.

Shepherd, there are many paths calling to me. What is the right
path for me today? Guide me. The mountain trails through
life's valleys are filled with dead-end canyons.
When I get lost, come help me.

Your Shepherd will prepare a table of food for you after you get through your dark valley. Your favorite cup is full and running over. Eat, drink, and rejoice in His provision. The Shepherd has two "sheep dogs" that will pursue you if you stray. The first is His goodness, which will keep you following Him. The second is His mercy, which will forgive any of your future wayward steps.

Shepherd, it feels good to happily rest beside You. When my eyes get
distracted by the things of this world, come draw me back with goodness
and mercy. Shepherd, I want to dwell with You in Your house forever.
Amen.

Reading: Psalm 23
Key Thought: The Lord wants a relationship with you.

2 · JESUS: A MORE EXCELLENT NAME

*Having become so much better than the angels, as He has by inheritance
obtained a more excellent name than they.*
HEBREWS 1:4

Jesus has a *More Excellent Name* than the angels. The angels were ministering spirits sent to help the heirs of salvation (see Hebrews 1:14), but Jesus was sent to purchase salvation. He has a *More Excellent Name* than Moses, who led Israel out of Egypt and gave them the Israelites the Law (see 3:3). Jesus fulfilled the Law and died to take it out of the way (Colossians 2:13-15). Jesus has a *More Excellent Name* than the high priest, who interceded for Israel (see Hebrews 4:14-16). Jesus gives us grace, for which the high priest prayed. Jesus has a *More Excellent Name* than Melchizedek, because Jesus obtained a better salvation and a new covenant (see 7:22-24). Because of the excellence of His name, you can go to the Father though Jesus at any time. Will you pray to the Father through the name of Jesus?

*Jesus, I love Your name. Your name calms my fears and guides me each
day. Jesus, Your name saved me and Your name keeps me safe.*

Because Jesus has a *More Excellent Name*, you can pray in His name (see John 14:13-14). Because the name of Jesus has power, you can break addiction and cast out demonic powers in His name (see Acts 16:18). Because the name of Jesus sets prisoners free, you can have a powerful witness to the unsaved in His name (see:10-14). One day, every knee will bow to recognize and worship the name of Jesus (see Philippians 2:9-11). Will you do it now?

*Jesus, I worship at the sound of Your name. You are worthy to receive all
honor, praise, and thanksgiving. Amen.*

Reading: Hebrews 1
Key Thought: The name of Jesus is the key to God's power.

3 JESUS: WORTHY

*You are worthy, O Lord, to receive glory and honor and power; for You created
all things, and by Your will they exist and were created.*
REVELATION 4:11
*Worthy is the Lamb who was slain to receive power and riches and wisdom,
and strength and honor and glory and blessing!*
REVELATION 5:12

Jesus is *Worthy* to receive our worship for two extraordinary reasons:
First, we should worship Jesus because He is the omnipotent Creator,
and "without Him nothing was made that was made" (John 1:3). Jesus
has given us life, purpose and existence, because we were created in His
image. Because of His creative act at the beginning of the world, all created beings—angels and redeemed souls—cry out praise and adoration to
Jesus. Have you given Him praise and adoration on Earth?

*Lord Jesus, I cry, "Holy, holy, holy," for Your awesome power
that created me. You are Worthy to receive my praise for
Your saving grace, which redeemed me.*

Jesus is *Worthy* for another reason—His sacrificial death for all people and His pardon of your sin specifically. Jesus was not worthy of a
cruel death, but still He chose to die for you. The One who had great
glory and power in Heaven became *Worthy* of even more adoration
because He purchased redemption on the cross. John wept because he
thought no one was *Worthy* to open and read the scroll—in other words,
the scroll was the title deed to Heaven and Earth. But the Lord stepped
forth to do it, because He was qualified to do so (see Revelation 5:4,8-
10). That makes Jesus *Worthy* of all praise in Heaven and Earth.

*Lord Jesus, I fall down at Your feet to cry, "Worthy is the Lamb,"
because You created all things. You are Worthy to open the scroll
because You redeemed me. Amen.*

Reading: Revelation 4
Key Thought: As Creator and Redeemer, Jesus is *Worthy* of our praise.

4 THE FATHER: THE GOD OF MY FATHERS

*But this I confess to you, that according to the Way which they call
a sect, so I worship the God of my fathers, believing all things which are
written in the Law and in the Prophets.*
ACTS 24:14

Paul worshiped the *God of His Fathers*, the God of Abraham, Isaac, Jacob
and Joseph. The God of all true believers in the Old Testament is the
God we worship today. When the Lord called Abraham and Abraham
obeyed, the Lord became his God. When Isaac lived in the Promised
Land, the Lord was his God. When Jacob had 12 sons, the Lord was his
God, and each of his sons made the Lord his God. Just as the Lord was
the God who protected and guided Israel in the Old Testament, He will
be your God to help you today.

*O Lord, I've always believed in You, but when I became a Christian,
You became my personal God. Now I worship You.*

Just as the Jews wandering in the wilderness worshiped the Lord in
the Tabernacle, the Lord wants you to worship Him from the sanctuary
of your body. Just as the Lord entered the Old Testament Temple in a
Shekinah glory cloud, so He entered your body when you were saved.
The Lord's presence makes any dwelling a sanctuary; today He'll make
your body His temple.

*O God of My Fathers, come make Your home in my body. I worship You
as did Paul; come be with me as You were with Paul. Be glorified
through my body today. Amen.*

Reading: 2 Corinthians 6:14-18
Key Thought: The Lord will dwell in your body just as He dwelt in the
Temple.

5 JESUS: A NAME ABOVE EVERY NAME

Therefore God also has highly exalted Him and given
Him the name which is above every name.
PHILIPPIANS 2:9

The name of Jesus is a *Name Above Every Name*. It is more excellent than that of Adam, the first man, because Jesus is the Alpha and the Omega. Jesus' name is more excellent than that of Noah, who saved the world from the flood, because Jesus will save the world from fire in the future. Jesus' name is more excellent than that of Abraham, the friend of God, because Jesus was God's Son. Jesus' name is more excellent than that of Moses, who delivered Israel from slavery in Egypt, because Jesus' name is powerful to deliver any from addictive slavery to sin. Jesus' name is more excellent than that of any judge who defeated Israel's enemies, because Jesus defeated sin, lust and the devil on the cross. What has Jesus done for you?

Lord, when I'm in trouble, I whisper, "Jesus." When I want to
break a habit or overcome an enemy, I say, "Jesus." When
I need anything, I pray, "Jesus."

The name of Jesus is greater than that of every Old Testament prophet, priest or king, because Jesus was the focus of their ministry. The name of Jesus is greater than that of every apostle, including Paul, because Jesus called them, empowered them, commissioned them and used them. What Jesus has done for these people, He can do for you.

Jesus, Your name is sweet to me, for it saved me from sin. Your
name is powerful to me, for it gives me strength and hope.
Your name is above every name. Amen.

Reading: Acts 5:22-42
Key Thought: The name of Jesus is above every name on Earth.

6   JESUS: THE NAME OF JESUS

Whatever you do in word or deed, do all in the name of the Lord Jesus.
COLOSSIANS 3:17

There's power in the *Name of Jesus*. Remember that signs and wonders are done through the *Name of Jesus* (see Acts 4:30). The *Name of Jesus* cleansed the lepers and opened the eyes of the blind, and He can do what you need done today. Don't forget you can get your prayers answered in the *Name of Jesus*: "If you ask anything in My name, I will do it" (John 14:14).

Jesus, give me discipline to overcome my weaknesses, power to overcome opposition and strength to overcome disappointments. Jesus, I claim the strength of Your name to rid my life of all evil lusts. By Your name, deliver me from the Evil One (see Matthew 6:13).

The *Name of Jesus* can fix broken lives and can heal sickness. A man had never walked, but Jesus' name made him strong (see Acts 3:16). The *Name of Jesus* can dispel evil powers. A girl was released from a demon when Paul said, "In the name of Jesus Christ come out" (see 16:18). The *Name of Jesus* can transform your life and ministry. So, do everything today in the *Name of Jesus*. Remember, "Whatever you do in word or deed, do all in the name of the Lord Jesus" (Colossians 3:17). What can the *Name of Jesus* do for you?

Jesus, Your name is sweet; it gives me joy. Jesus, Your name is comforting; it gives me assurance. Jesus, Your name is powerful; I claim Your strength to overcome barriers. Jesus, Your name is awesome; I worship Your name. Amen.

Reading: Acts 4:1-12
Key Thought: The *Name of Jesus* is powerful.

THE HOLY SPIRIT: THE SPIRIT OF THE LIVING GOD

*Clearly you are an epistle of Christ, ministered by us, written
not with ink but by the Spirit of the living God, not on tablets of stone
but on tablets of flesh, that is, of the heart.*
2 CORINTHIANS 3:3

The third Person of the Trinity is the *Spirit of the Living God* who writes the message of Christ upon your life. There are many who will not read the Bible, but they may read the pages of your life. So let the *Spirit of the Living God* write the message of Christ in your attitudes and actions. Let Him embed the principles of Christ into your life. Just as the *Spirit of the Living God* puts His influence in the Bible, so He can put His influence into you; then, non-Christians can see Christ in the pages of your life and come to salvation. You may be the only Bible they read.

*Holy Spirit, I open the pages of my life to You. Erase everything
that is a poor testimony. Write on the empty pages of my heart
Your message of grace and forgiveness.*

The Holy Spirit does not write on pages with ink, as the New Testament was written. He does not write on stone, as the Ten Commandments were chiseled; but He writes the message of Jesus on your heart when He makes you like Jesus. Will you yield to Him today, so He can write His message on your life? Then, the world can see Jesus in you. And in time, you will be given an opportunity to share your life story with people.

Holy Spirit, I want to be an open letter that tells of Jesus; I want non-Christians to see Jesus in my life. Amen.

Reading: 2 Corinthians 3:1-5
Key Thought: The Holy Spirit writes about Christ on our lives for others to read.

I will get opportunities to share, will I yield to Jesus today?

8 JESUS: THE LIGHT

Then Jesus spoke to them again, saying, "I am the light of the world. He who follows Me shall not walk in darkness, but have the light of life."
JOHN 8:12

Jesus is the *Light*; He can show you where to walk today. He was the *Light* that shined into your heart before you were saved so that you were convicted of your sin and repented. He was the *Light* that pointed you to salvation. Today, He'll be your *Light* to show you what to do as you walk through the many decisions that you face. Jesus is a bright, shining *Light*. He can enlighten you through the Scriptures, but you must study them. He can help you see clearly as you pray, but you must seek His presence. He can give you light to make better decisions, but you must make time for communion with Him.

Lord, take away my spiritual blindness. Help me see what I must do today. Don't let me stumble or get lost. Shine light on my path.

Jesus is the *Light* of salvation. You may stumble when you walk outside the perimeter of light, so always take Jesus, the *Light*, with you. Let His light shine, giving you illumination when you don't know what to do. You can always have the blessings of *Light* when you take Jesus with you.

Lord, help me make better choices; keep me from making mistakes. Be Light to help me understand my friends and associates at work. Shine on me when I walk through dark, threatening valleys. Lord, thank You for the warmth of Your light. I feel comfortable in Your presence. Keep me from stumbling in the night. Keep me in the Light. Amen.

Reading: John 8:1-12
Key Thought: Jesus is the *Light* to guide you.

9 JESUS: THE TRUTH

*Jesus said to him, "I am the way, the truth, and the life. No one
comes to the Father except through Me."*
JOHN 14:6

Jesus is the *Truth*; He cannot lie. He will always tell you what is right; He will not deceive you. When you read His Word, it will always give you an accurate record of the past, and it will give you an honest description of what people are like today. When the Word of God predicts the future, its predictions will come about. Jesus said God's Word "is truth" (John 17:17). Whether you are referring to the words Jesus spoke on the earth or His words written in Scripture, both are true. Because He is the *Truth*, He wants you to be truthful.

*Lord, it's hard to be truthful, because I have a deceitful heart
that always wants to put me in the best light. Forgive my sins and
help me always to tell the truth.*

Truth never contradicts itself; it is always consistent. What Jesus said on Earth was always true. Jesus' words were consistent with the rest of Scripture, and the Scripture is consistent within itself. "The Scripture cannot deny itself" (see 10:35). Because the Bible is consistent, you can trust its message. Because Jesus is the *Truth*, you can believe in Him.

*Lord, I believe that everything You've said in the Bible is true. I will base
my life on the Scriptures, because I believe they work. I will read the
Scripture, because I believe it is consistent. The more I know about the
Bible, the more I realize that it's consistently true in itself and that its
influence is true in my experiences. Amen.*

Reading: John 8:13-36
Key Thought: The words of Jesus are true.

10 ⬧ THE TRINITY: HIS VOICE

The Lord thundered from heaven, and the Most High uttered His voice.
PSALM 18:13

God speaks in many ways. In the Bible, some audibly heard His voice, and others inwardly heard it. At other times He spoke through prophetic utterances. He also spoke through intermediate means such as miracles and providence; once He spoke through Balaam's ass. But notice how many times God spoke through nature. David said, "Each day utters a new voice" (see Psalm 19:2). David the shepherd boy declared, "The voice of the LORD is powerful; the voice of the LORD is full of majesty" (29:4). The powerful wind was the voice of the Lord breaking cedars (see v. 5). He described the lightning as "the voice of the LORD [dividing] the flames of fire" (v. 7). God speaks in many ways; let Him speak to you today.

Lord, I am quiet before You. I am listening for Your instructions for today. Speak, Lord, for Your servant waits.

God uses the weather to accomplish His will. No one can make a storm; no one can control the wind, temperature or rain. God uses the storms; it is His voice in the world. Never again will God destroy the world through a flood (see Genesis 9:11), but He'll use floods to punish the disobedient, to move those who will not listen or to redirect lives. God will even use emotional floods in your life for a purpose. When the storms come, listen to His voice, for He speaks through them.

Lord, I don't like storms, but I accept them. Help me to learn Your will from the storms of life. Amen.

Reading: Psalm 18:1-14
Key Thought: God can use many ways to speak to you.

11 JESUS: THE BREAD OF GOD

For the bread of God is He who comes down from heaven and gives life to the world.
JOHN 6:33

Jesus is the *Bread of God*. Just as bread gives us strength for our daily activities, so Jesus gives us mental and spiritual strength to live for Him. Just as bread is enjoyable to eat, so Jesus is our joy and satisfaction in life. Just as bread keeps us alive (without food we would die), so Jesus keeps us living. We eat the bread of Jesus when we read and study the Word of God. We eat the bread of Jesus when we think on Him and meditate on the Word of God (see Joshua 1:8; Luke 2:19). We eat the bread of Jesus when we attend church and listen to the Word being preached. And of course, we could never give out the bread of Jesus to a hungry world unless we first eat it for ourselves and experience His goodness.

Lord Jesus, You are the Bread of life. Just as I enjoy warm bread right
from the oven, I look forward to fellowship with You more.

Jesus is the *Bread of God* who comes down from Heaven. When we taste Him, we begin munching on the good things of God. "Oh, taste and see that the LORD is good" (Psalm 34:8). Jesus is satisfying Bread, healthful Bread, life-giving Bread, and resurrection Bread. "Whoever eats My flesh and drinks My blood has eternal life, and I will raise him up at the last day" (John 6:54).

Jesus, You have good bread. I could fellowship with You forever.
Could I have more? Amen.

Reading: John 6:32-44
Key Thought: Jesus is the *Bread of God* who gives life to the world.

You must first know the bread of God before you pass it out to other people.

18

JESUS: THE DOOR OF THE SHEEP

Then Jesus said to them again, "Most assuredly, I say to you,
I am the door of the sheep."
JOHN 10:7

During the time of Jesus, a sheepfold was an enclosure to keep sheep from wandering or getting lost. It usually had rock walls, and sometimes it was enclosed with thick thorn bushes to keep out thieves or predators, who would steal or kill the sheep. A sheepfold usually didn't have a roof, and it had only one door. The shepherd would sleep across the opening of the door to keep intruders out and the sheep in. Thus, the shepherd became the door of the sheep. Sometimes, several flocks were kept in the same sheepfold. In the morning, the shepherd would call "his own sheep by name" and would lead them out of the fold (John 10:3). Each shepherd had a different whistle, and the sheep knew their master's call: "When he brings out his own sheep, he goes before them; and the sheep follow him, for they know his voice" (v. 4). Jesus is the Shepherd of the sheep, and He knows you by name. Do you recognize the Lord's voice when He calls you?

Jesus, thank You for calling me and protecting me.
I will follow where You lead.

When a shepherd becomes the door of the sheep, he puts his life on the line. The shepherd will fight to protect his sheep because each one is precious to him. The key is relationship; the shepherd knows, calls, leads and protects his sheep. Jesus wants that kind of relationship with you.

Lord Jesus, I am Your sheep. Thank You for giving Your life
for me. I want to go in and out of the sheepfold to
"find pasture" (John 10:9). Amen.

Reading: John 10:1-13
Key Thought: The Shepherd wants a protective relationship with you.

13 THE FATHER: THE FATHER OF LIGHTS

Every good gift and every perfect gift is from above, and comes down from the Father of lights, with whom there is no variation or shadow of turning.
JAMES 1:17

God is the *Father of Lights* who originally created physical light, including the sun and all stars. But more than physical light, God is the Father of spiritual light. When you come to Him, He will enlighten your life and give you spiritual understanding. When you walk near the *Father of Lights,*, there is no darkness, so you'll never get lost. When you're close to the Light, there are no shadows, so you'll not be surprised or afraid of unseen fears. When you walk near the *Father of Lights*, you'll see where you're going, so you can walk in confidence.

O Father of Lights, I often stumble in the dark, and it hurts to fall. Shine more light on my path; give me eyes to see so I can walk.

The light from a burning candle makes a shadow; it is impossible to get next to a light without causing shadows. But when you get close to God, something impossible happens. There are no shadows. There is no "variation or shadow" (James 1:17) in the *Father of Lights*. When you get close to God, He gets close to you. He surrounds you on every side; there'll be no twilight zones and no dim shadows. You'll be surrounded by Light. Isn't that where you want to live?

I come to You, Father of Lights, in whom there is no variation or shadow. I will walk close to You, in Your light. I will be comfortable in the warmth of Your presence. I will be safe where there is no threatening darkness. I will stay as close to You as possible. Amen.

Reading: James 1:16-21
Key Thought: When you get close to God, you'll have fewer shadows.

14 JESUS: THE VINE

I am the vine, you are the branches. He who abides in Me, and I in him, bears much fruit; for without Me you can do nothing.
JOHN 15:5

Jesus is the *Vine*, the source of your spiritual life. Abide in Him, and you'll have a fruitful life. You are the branches where His life grows and His fruit is produced. The key to fruitfulness is relationship; you must constantly remain attached to (abiding in) Him, or the opposite will happen. If you become detached, your spiritual life will not be fruitful; no fruit will grow, and the branches of your life will begin to die.

Lord, when I was small, I was constantly growing; but when I became an adult, I stopped growing. I sometimes feel the same thing has happened to me spiritually. Now that I've reached spiritual adulthood, don't let me stop growing as a Christian.

Jesus is the *Vine*, and you are the branches. You will continue to grow as you are attached to Him. You must do more than talk about Jesus, sing about Jesus or even learn facts about Jesus. You must abide in Him in order to grow and be fruitful. You must be totally dependent on Jesus, just as a branch is totally dependent on the vine for everything. Just as energy (life) flows through the vine to the branches, your energy flows through Jesus to you. The *Vine* must become your life; yield to Him. The *Vine* has the fruit you desire; let Him grow it in you.

Jesus, since You are my Vine, produce optimism and spiritual expectation in me. Help me become like You, just as a branch is like the vine. Amen.

Reading: John 15:1-8
Key Thought: The life of Jesus flows through us when we abide in Him.

15 JESUS: THE WAY

Jesus said to him, "I am the way, the truth, and the life.
No one comes to the Father except through Me."
JOHN 14:6

Jesus is the *Way* to Heaven; there is no other way to get there. Will you follow the *Way* today? Because Jesus is the *Way*, He invited some fishermen, "Follow Me, and I will make you become fishers of men" (Mark 1:17). He invited Matthew, the tax collector, "Follow Me" (2:14). Because Jesus is the *Way*, He still wants people to follow Him today.

Lord, I've always been independent. As a child, I'd pull at my parent's
hand to run ahead. When I got mad, I'd pout and refuse to keep up. But
today, I submit my will to You. Teach me to follow You.

Just as Jesus left His footprints on the sandy beach of Lake Galilee, today He wants to leave His influence in every place in life. Jesus will do it through you. Are your "footprints" leaving an influence for Jesus in the places you walk? When you help another, Jesus wants them to realize that He's been there. When you share the gospel with another, He wants the listeners to realize He's been there. Jesus is the *Way*; when you don't know where to walk or how to walk, look to Him for direction. His way on Earth was not always easy; neither will your way always be comfortable, but it's worth it. Let Him walk through your life. As you follow His way, you will leave His footprints in the lives of others.

Lord, I'll follow You through ease or difficulty. I only ask that You go
with me and help me. Amen.

Reading: Mark 1:16-20; 2:13-17
Key Thought: Jesus asks you to follow His way.

16 ◆ THE HOLY SPIRIT: RAIN

He shall come down like rain upon the grass before mowing,
like showers that water the earth.
PSALM 72:6

The Holy Spirit is *Rain* to those who are famished; He gives refreshing life. He is *Rain* to those who have stopped growing; He can replenish their leaves and roots. He is *Rain* to those who have stopped producing fruit; He can make them fruitful again. Let Him rain on you.

Lord, rain on my parched soul. Rain on the dry ground that surrounds
me. Revitalize my branches, let my leaves soak up Your life-giving water,
and make me fruitful again. Let the streams overflow their banks.

The Holy Spirit is *Rain* to you who are thirsty; He will satisfy your thirst. You don't have to die in the desert for lack of water. But you must come to Him as empty pots, because only He can fill you. Drink of the Holy Spirit; that's an active choice you must make. "If anyone thirsts, let him come to Me and drink" (John 7:37). The Holy Spirit is *Rain* to signify the blessing of God on His people. The opposite is also true; when God's people reject Him, God shuts up Heaven. The streams of living water no longer flow. Crops don't grow, and there's nothing to eat. When God's people reject Him, the Holy Spirit will not rain on them. He is *Rain.* Why wouldn't everyone want *Rain*?

Lord, I've been thirsty long enough; I'll not suffer through another day.
Show me any sin that's hidden in my heart. I repent of all my
transgressions. I'm coming to You for life-giving water. Rain refreshes
me. A cool drink of water is even better. Amen.

Reading: 1 Kings 17—18
Key Thought: The Holy Spirit is *Rain* to refresh God's people.

PUT FIRST THINGS FIRST
17 JESUS: THE PREEMINENCE

And He is the head of the body, the church, who is the beginning, the firstborn from the dead, that in all things He may have the preeminence.
COLOSSIANS 1:18

"Preeminence" means "first," and Jesus wants to have first place in your life. Put Him first in your thoughts, your choices and your relationships. When you do everything that Jesus would have you do, He becomes preeminent in your life. "Preeminence" also means "the best in quality and character." When you let Jesus control your life, you give Him the *Preeminence* in all that you do. "Preeminence" also means "the highest." There is nothing higher in Heaven than Jesus, so lift Him up in your prayer life. Give Him the *Preeminence* in your home. When Jesus has His rightful place, He can lead you, protect you and cause you to grow.

Lord, I pause to recognize Your greatness and give You first place in my life. I exalt You to your rightful place. Come, be preeminent in my life.

Today, Jesus is not preeminent in the affairs of the nations; but in the end of the age, He will rule all ethnic peoples and nations. Also, Jesus is not preeminent in the lives of many peoples; but one day, every tongue (including the unsaved) will confess Jesus, and every knee (including the God-haters) will bow to recognize His *Preeminence*. Those who make Jesus preeminent on Earth will be rewarded by Him in Heaven.

My tongue confesses that You are Lord. My knee bows to Your sovereign rule of my life. I make You preeminent in all I do. Amen.

Reading: Luke 9:28-36
Key Thought: Make Jesus preeminent in your life.

18 ◆ JESUS: WONDERFUL

*For unto us a Child is born, unto us a Son is given; and the government will be
upon His shoulder. And His name will be called Wonderful.*

ISAIAH 9:6

Jesus is called *Wonderful*, a noun in the Hebrew language that Isaiah used
as His name. Throughout the Scriptures, the word "wonderful" is used
to describe miracles; it's a word that suggests the supernatural. Jesus is
called *Wonderful*, the source of miracles; all supernatural expressions
come from Him. Jesus is called *Wonderful*, describing the mysterious or
secretive attributes of God. Jesus has all the attributes of God, both
those seen and unseen. His name *"Wonderful"* expresses those things
about God that we don't know. His name *"Wonderful"* reflects His
incomprehensible nature. Jesus is so *Wonderful*; we have difficulty finding words to express it. Jesus also has a name written that no one knows
but Him (see Revelation 19:12). It's a *Wonderful* name.

*Lord, I praise You for Your wonderful nature, and I stand in awe of the
wonderful things You do for me. Lord, when I don't know what to say
in prayer, I simply worship in Your wonderful presence.*

Jesus is called *Wonderful*, a name that separates Him from the common things of life and lifts Him into the realm of majestic deity. Also,
His name *"Wonderful"* expresses the concept of glory. Jesus has God's
glory, and He brings more glory to the Godhead. His name *"Wonderful"*
puts Him in a class all by Himself. Call Him *Wonderful*, the separated
One, the distinguished One, the noble One, and the only One.

*Lord, I call You Wonderful because of all I know about You in
Scriptures, and I worship You for all the wonderful things You have
done for me. Amen.*

Reading: Colossians 1:16-20
Key Thought: Jesus is too *Wonderful* to describe.

THE TRINITY: THE GOD OF THE BEGINNING (*ELOHIM KEDEM*)

The God of the beginning is your refuge, and His eternal arms are under you.
SEE DEUTERONOMY 33:27

God is the *God of the Beginning*. He started time. Before the events of the first verse in the Bible, there was nothing but God. "In the beginning God created the heavens and the earth" (Genesis 1:1). You measure time by the sequence between events, but before the beginning, there were no human events to measure; there was only God. If God hadn't begun everything, there would be no abstract thing like time. You'd never be late; you'd never waste time, because you wouldn't know what it was. If God hadn't created time, you might never accomplish anything, because there'd be no starting time or quitting time or overtime.

God, I'm glad You made time; You give meaning to my minutes.
I know I'm using my hours and eventually I'll die. "My times
are in Your hand" (Psalm 31:15).

God made a choice to begin everything. Can you follow His example? Do you have something you need to start today? Head knowledge doesn't usually move us to begin something. Sometimes our emotions move us to begin a project. But knowing and feeling are not enough. You must exercise your will; you must choose to begin. Isn't that what the *God of the Beginning* did? Just as He chose to begin everything, you must choose to begin today what you put off yesterday.

O God of the Beginning, teach us to understand how
many days we have (see Psalm 90:12). Help me
begin today what I must do. Amen.

Reading: Deuteronomy 33:26–34
Key Thought: Just as God began everything, so I must learn to begin my projects.

20 ◆ JESUS: A COLUMN OF SMOKE

*And the LORD went before them by day in [a column of smoke] to lead the way,
and by night in [a column of fire] to give them light.*
EXODUS 13:21

*God did not lead them by way of the land of the Philistines,
although that was near [closer].*
EXODUS 13:17

Jesus was the *Column of Smoke* and the Column of fire that led Israel out of Egyptian bondage. He did not lead them the short way, directly from Egypt to the Promised Land. He led them the long way, through the desert where there was no water or food. He wanted them to learn to trust Him in the wilderness in spite of these obstacles. In the same way, Jesus will sometimes lead you the long way, which may seem to you the wrong way. Sometimes, He'll lead you where there seems to be no outward food or water, and where there are obstacles. He may be leading to see if you'll trust Him. However, there are no wrong ways when the Lord leads; just long ways, with more time to teach you the lessons to make you strong.

*Lord, Israel murmured in the wilderness; help me not complain when I
don't understand where I'm going. Israel refused to acknowledge You,
but I submit to the circumstances You bring into my life.*

Jesus led Israel in both the daylight and at night; so look to Him so that you won't get lost. Stop when He stops and follow Him when He starts. Follow Him in good days and bad; follow Him when you're hungry and when you're full. Where He guides, He will provide.

*Lord, I want to stay as close as possible to the light in the Column.
I want Your personal presence to guide me. Amen.*

Reading: Exodus 14:1-3; 15:22-26
Key Thought: Learn God's purpose when He leads You through any difficulties.

21 ❖ JESUS: PRECIOUS

Therefore, to you who believe, He is precious.
1 PETER 2:7

Jesus is *Precious*. A diamond is called a precious stone. As the best diamond in the world would cost you everything to purchase, so Jesus is *Precious*, because His death cost Him everything. "You were not redeemed with corruptible things such as silver and gold, but with My precious blood" (see 1 Peter 1:18-19). As an item is precious because it is scarce or the only one of a kind, so Jesus is *Precious* because He is the only Son of God—there is none other like Him. He is *Precious* because He is the only hope for those who are dying. Saints hang on to Jesus because He is their guarantee of life after death. No one else promises to be with them.

Lord Jesus, I want to walk with You and talk with You. You are my
Friend, my Guide, my Protector and my God. Lord, I value my
salvation; it is the most precious thing in my life. You are Precious to me.

Just as some items are sentimental or have precious memories, Jesus is *Precious* to us because we remember how He saved us. We remember how Jesus has helped us so many times in our lives. But He is also *Precious* to us as we contemplate spending eternity with Him.

Jesus, You are Precious to me; You are my Savior and Friend. I treasure
You in my heart for saving me, for keeping me and for answering all my
prayers. I look forward to spending eternity with You. Amen.

Reading: John 12:1-11
Key Thought: Jesus is more valuable to us than the most precious thing in life.

YOU ARE TIMELESS, PRICELESS.

Thank you Jesus for giving me peace.

22 ◆ THE FATHER: THE VERY GOD OF PEACE

*And the very God of peace sanctify you wholly; and I pray God your whole
spirit and soul and body be preserved blameless unto the
coming of our Lord Jesus Christ.*

1 THESSALONIANS 5:23, *KJV*

When you search for peace, you'll find its source in God the Father. You won't find it in peace treaties, police protection or the United Nations. True peace, the *Very God of Peace,* must be poured into the hearts of individuals before it spreads to communities or nations. True peace happens when each person places God on the throne of his or her heart. When God rules the heart, a person gets peace over the compulsive lust of the flesh, the lust of the eyes and the pride of life. Then the *Very God of Peace* spreads throughout your life as you make peace with others. When you find inner peace, it can spread to families, communities and countries. Also, a nation will experience peace to the degree that the *Very God of Peace* controls the hearts of all its citizens.

*Lord, I want inner peace; come rule my heart. Help me influence others
around me the way You've influenced me.*

There will be wars and racial turbulence in the world. There will be interpersonal friction because people live for themselves. The *Very God of Peace* does not rule the hearts of the vast majority of individuals. But while people may not be able to change the whole world, they can change their own world. Some think they cannot change their families; but when they change their relationships to their loved ones, their loved ones are changed. Experience God's peace, and then spread it to others.

*Father, help me live Your plan of peace for my family and community.
Help me do my part to be an influence for peace today. Amen.*

Reading: Psalm 122
Key Thought: Your experience of peace can influence others.

23 JESUS: RABBI

Then Jesus turned, and seeing them following, said to them,
"What do you seek?" They said to Him, "Rabbi"
(which is to say, when translated, Teacher).
JOHN 1:38

Jesus is *Rabbi*. The title is a transliteration (the letters cross over into English, letter for letter) of the Aramaic word for "teacher." Just as you respect teachers for what they know and reveal to their hearers, so you revere Jesus as *Rabbi*, because He is the revelation of the Father to the world. Those who saw Jesus saw the Father (see John 14:9). Jesus instructs us about who the Father is and what He is like. Jesus is your *Rabbi*.

Jesus, You are more than a spiritual teacher; You are the Son of God, the
only One who can teach us salvation. Be my Rabbi; teach me all I need
to know. Teach me how to walk in grace and how to live for You.

A rabbi was also called master, because he was the master of his students; in other words, he was a change agent in the life of his students. Jesus is your *Rabbi*, not only because of what He knows, but also because He is the Change Agent of your heart. Jesus will help you know the Scriptures, and He will help you do the will of God. Just as there is an intimate relationship between a teacher and a pupil, so your passion should be to know your *Rabbi* better (see Philippians 3:10). Jesus wants to influence your life and to be your Lord; will you let Him do it?

Rabbi, I will learn Your teachings and let the Scriptures control my life.
Be the Master of my life. Guide me and direct me this day. Amen.

Reading: John 1:29-42
Key Thought: Jesus will teach you what you need to know.

24 JESUS: THE LORD JESUS CHRIST

The Revelation of Jesus Christ, which God gave Him to show His servants—
things which must shortly take place.
REVELATION 1:1

Our Savior's composite name is "Jesus Christ," the name Christians called Him at the end of the first century when John wrote the book of Revelation. However, in the Gospels He is mostly called by His Greek name "Jesus," which reflects His earthly life. "Jesus" is "Joshua" in Hebrew, from the root meaning "Jehovah saves." In the book of Acts, He is mostly called by His title "Lord," which emphasized that He was the second Person of the Trinity and which reflected His deity. In the Epistles, He is mostly called by His office title "Christ." Put them all together, and He is the *Lord Jesus Christ.*

I come to You as Savior, thanking You for salvation, but I worship
before You as my God. I marvel at the depth of Your person that is
reflected in Your many names and titles.

When His title "Lord" appears first in sequence (the *Lord Jesus Christ*), it is emphasizing that He is God. When His office title "Christ" appears first in sequence (Christ Jesus, the Lord), it is emphasizing His accomplishment on Calvary. When His name "Jesus" (Jesus Christ, the Lord) appears first, it is emphasizing His earthly humanity. The book of Revelation is about Him; thus, it is called the Revelation of Jesus Christ. The emphasis is not on judgment, symbols or Satan. It is the revelation of who Jesus is and why He is returning to Earth. Study to see His many names in the first chapter of Revelation.

Lord, open the pages of Your Word to reveal Yourself to me. Help me to
understand You as I understand Your many names and titles. Amen.

Reading: Revelation 1
Key Thought: The names and titles of Jesus reveal His nature.

25 THE HOLY SPIRIT: OIL

Therefore God, Your God, has anointed You with the oil of gladness.
HEBREWS 1:9

The Holy Spirit is the *Oil* of gladness. The Lord said, "I see the oppression of My people. I hear their cry. I know their sorrows" (see Exodus 3:7). Just as the Lord knew and identified with the suffering of His people in Moses' day, He knows your troubles today. He is *Oil*, pouring Himself into your wounds; He can make you rejoice.

*Lord, Your healing Oil is good. Rejuvenate my Spirit and take
away the scars of my mind. Just as Your Oil takes away physical
pain, I also want You to take away mental and spiritual memories.
Let Your Oil wash away the impurities in my wounds and
cleanse me physically and mentally.*

The Holy Spirit is *Oil*; when He pours His presence on your discouragement, you'll have new zeal to live for God and new strength to serve Him—you'll rejoice! The Holy Spirit is *Oil*; when He pours His presence on your failures, you'll see new opportunities in your life—you'll grow. He is *Oil*, washing away your impurities that fester and breed germs; you can be whole again. He is *Oil*, giving you a second chance and a new opportunity. Let the *Oil* of the Holy Spirit give you a new challenge this day.

*Lord, Your Oil has made me a new person. My hurt is gone; my body is
renewed for service; and my soul is again made whole. Thank You for
today's anointing. I'll need a new one tomorrow. Amen.*

Reading: Hebrews 1:1-9
Key Thought: The anointing of the Holy Spirit gives happiness and healing.

◆ 26 ◆ JESUS: CARPENTER'S SON

Is this not the carpenter's son? Is not His mother called Mary?
And His brothers James, Joses, Simon, and Judas?
MATTHEW 13:55

Jesus was a *Carpenter's Son*; Joseph, His stepfather, was His legal guardian. Jesus was born of the virgin Mary, but it was Joseph whose occupation provided His food, clothing and shelter. Joseph was the human father who guided Jesus' growth and taught Him a trade. Since there is dignity in work, Jesus became a carpenter, as was Joseph. When Jesus was 12 years old, He went to the Temple for His bar mitzvah, to be declared as "Son of the Law." It was then that Joseph had to declare his son would take up his trade: "He shall be a carpenter." Jesus worked as a carpenter in Nazareth until He was baptized by John the Baptist, at approximately 30 years of age (see Luke 3:23). He then began His earthly ministry. What can we learn from Him?

Lord, thank You for submitting to the limitations of a human
body. You gave us an example of how to work for a living.
Help me follow Your example.

Even though Jesus is God, He became a *Carpenter's Son* to grow as we must grow, to learn as we must learn and to gain favor with God and man, as we must do. But let's not forget that Jesus left us an example of how we should work. Let's follow His example.

Lord, I want to walk through life as You walked. I want to be
successful at an occupation as You were. I want to learn obedience
as You did (see Hebrews 5:8). I want to please the heavenly
Father as You did Help me today. Amen.

Reading: Luke 2:40-52
Key Thought: Jesus gave us an example of earthly work.

27 JESUS: RABBONI

Jesus said to her, "Mary!" She turned and said to Him,
"Rabboni!" (which is to say, Teacher).
JOHN 20:16

Jesus is *Rabboni*, an unusual descriptive term for the usual word "Rabbi," or "teacher." The title *"Rabboni"* was not used by just anyone or any student; those who had a special relationship to the rabbi used the title *"Rabboni."* Because Jesus had to cast demons out of Mary Magdalene, she called Him *Rabboni*. Because Jesus had given sight to blind Bartimaeus, he too called Jesus *Rabboni* (see Mark 10:51). You should be as grateful as Mary Magdalene, who called Him *Rabboni* because she was grateful for the forgiveness of sin. You should be as grateful as Bartimaeus, who called Him *Rabboni* because he was grateful for the work of God in his life.

Jesus, You are my special Rabboni because You have forgiven my sins
and revealed Yourself to me. You have worked in my life.

Jesus is *Rabboni;* but not everyone can call Him by this unique title because not everyone has a saving relationship to Him. But because you believe in Christ, you have a special relationship to Him. He becomes *Rabboni* to those who desire to know Him intimately (see Philippians 3:10). Paul said, "For to me, to live is Christ, and to die is gain" (1:21). If that's your passion, you can call Him *Rabboni*.

You are my Rabboni. I am grateful for the new life You gave me. You
are the resurrected Christ, the One whom Mary saw on that first Easter
morning. And like Mary, I call You Rabboni with deepest
love and lasting commitment. Amen.

Reading: John 20:11-16
Key Thought: Jesus is *Rabboni* to those who have a special relationship to Him.

THE TRINITY: THE GOD WHO IS NEAR (*ELOHIM MIKAROV*)

28

"Am I a God near at hand," says the LORD, "and not a God afar off? Can anyone hide himself in secret places, so I shall not see him?"
JEREMIAH 23:23-24

Do you act as if God were far off? If you understood the *God Who Is Near,* it would influence all your life. God is present to hear every conversation at work and within your family. He's not just with you when you're at church or when you pray; He is near to you as you play sports and as you drive the car. "In Him we live and move and have our being" (Acts 17:28).

Lord, I know You are everywhere. You are in Heaven and everywhere in the world, and You are in my heart. Let me feel Your presence, so I can live for You.

It would be hard to stretch the truth if you fully realized God was near when you spoke, because God is truth. It would be hard to sin if you realized God was near, because God is pure. It would be hard to gossip about people or rip them up if you realized God is near, because God loves all. If you realized that God is near, you would be more honest with money, more forgiving of others and more disciplined in prayer and church attendance. A father who was channel surfing stopped at a sexy scene, when suddenly he sensed that someone was in the room. Looking around, the father saw his young son and changed the channel. What would you change if you experienced God's presence?

Lord, I know You are here when I pray; help me feel Your presence in all that I do. When I feel Your presence, it changes my actions. Amen.

Reading: Jeremiah 23:1-24
Key Thought: You will change when you realize God is near.

29   JESUS: SAVIOR

For there is born to you this day in the city of David a Savior,
who is Christ the Lord.
LUKE 2:11

Jesus is the *Savior*, a title that means "deliverer" and "preserver." Jesus has many names, but the most important name may be *"Savior,"* because He is the only One who can save you. "Salvation is of the LORD" (Jonah 2:9). Jesus is the *Savior* who will deliver you in many ways. He has saved you from the guilt of past sin and from the present bondage of sin, and He will save you from the future penalty of sin when you are taken to Heaven.

Lord, You have done so many things for me—things I don't even realize. But Your most important gift was saving me; thank You. I feel confident in Your salvation, yet I want more. I want to enjoy all the benefits possible that come from salvation.

Jesus is the *Savior* (see 2 Peter 1:1). John referred to Him as "Savior of the world" (1 John 4:14). The Caesars of the Roman Empire called themselves the saviors of the world, but they could only give military deliverance. Jesus came to save you from damnation and eternal death. He will save you from weaknesses, temptations, attacks from Satan and addiction to sin. He will save in all ways those who come to Him.

I praise You, Savior, for "so great a salvation" (Hebrews 2:3). You have saved me in so many ways; continue to save me to the very end. Amen.

Reading: Luke 2:8-20
Key Thought: Jesus saves you completely in every way.

30 ◆ JESUS: SHILOH

The scepter shall not depart from Judah, nor a lawgiver from between his feet,
until Shiloh comes; and to Him shall be the obedience of the people.
GENESIS 49:10

Jesus is *Shiloh*, which means "peacemaker." He can give you peace about
any and all decisions this day. He is called *Shiloh*, a name given in the Old
Testament more than 1,800 years before Christ was born. This name was
reflective of His coming to make peace between the Father and all sinners by His death on the cross (see Ephesians 2:14). Because of your sins,
He is your *Shiloh*.

> *Shiloh, You gave me peace with God when You came into my heart at*
> *conversion. Thank You for giving me "peace through the blood of*
> *[Your] cross" (Colossians 1:20). I yield to You; come fill my*
> *heart with Your strength, direct my thoughts, and give me*
> *courage to choose Your will for my life.*

Jesus is *Shiloh*, bringing peace to troubled hearts. "In Me you may
have peace. In the world you will have tribulation; but be of good cheer,
I have overcome the world" (John 16:33). *Shiloh* will give you inner peace
when you let Him control your heart. Jesus is *Shiloh*, the Prince of Peace
for your job, for your home, for your nation and for the world. One day
there will be a millennium of peace when Jesus rules the world. For now
Jesus is *Shiloh*, the One who brings inner peace to the human heart when
people invite Him into their lives. Then we who know His peace must
spread it into our world and our friends.

> *Shiloh, come rule in my life, and then influence my job,*
> *my home and my friends. Amen.*

Reading: John 16:23-33
Key Thought: Jesus can give you peace.

31 THE FATHER: THE FATHER OF MERCIES

Blessed be the God and Father of our Lord Jesus Christ, the
Father of mercies and God of all comfort.
2 CORINTHIANS 1:3

When you call God Father, it's not just His name that you're calling upon. "Father" indicates a relationship; you are relying on your relationship with Him. It began with a relationship between Jesus and the Father, who loved each other throughout eternity. Jesus died for your sins so that the Father could forgive you and receive you into God's Heaven. When you accepted Jesus as your Savior, you were born again into God's family. Now you can enjoy an intimate relationship in the family with both the Father and the Son. Now you are God's child (see John 1:12). Why don't you thank Him for making you His child?

Father, thank You for allowing me to have a relationship with You. You
are the Father of my Lord Jesus Christ and the God of all comfort.

When you call God your Father, you're not just using a name; you're entering a spiritual relationship. When you became God's child, He established a relationship of mercy with you. He no longer looked at you as an alien or a sinner, but in mercy He forgave all your sin. He no longer had to punish your disobedience. Instead He accepted you into His family, so He can love you, protect you and guide you. He is the *Father of Mercies* and the God of all comfort. Now you can enjoy all the blessings of the heavenlies, and you can enter the intimacy of God's presence. Will you enjoy the Father today?

Father, thank You for allowing me to have an intimate
relationship with You. Amen.

Reading: 2 Corinthians 1:1-7
Key Thought: You can be intimate with the heavenly Father.

FEBRUARY

1 Jesus: The Unspeakable Gift

Thanks be unto God for his unspeakable gift.
2 Corinthians 9:15, *KJV*

Jesus is the *Unspeakable Gift*; receive Him as you would receive any gift. Remember, a gift is free; if you have to work for it, it's not a gift. You can't pay for a gift; you can't work for a gift, and you can't put it on your credit card. All you can do is receive a gift. Jesus is the *Unspeakable Gift* of salvation; receive Him freely.

Lord, I receive You into my heart. I am saved by grace through faith, not by works; salvation is Your gift to me (see Ephesians 2:8-9). This gift is greater than anything in life. Teach me to appreciate my salvation and to live accordingly.

Jesus is the *Unspeakable Gift*; words are not adequate to describe Him. He is greater than the human mind can conceive and more precious than the human heart desires. Human words can't adequately express the worth of the salvation He gives. Jesus is the *Unspeakable Gift*, greater than anything on Earth. Any fun you have in the world cannot compare to His joy. Any financial gain does not compare to His riches. Any good for which you strive cannot compare to the satisfaction of finding Jesus and making Him the center of your life. Thank God today for the *Unspeakable Gift* of Jesus.

Lord Jesus, my words are not adequate to express my feelings, so look within my heart to receive the worship that is there. And when my words of worship are not adequate, look deeper in my heart to discover my love for You. Amen.

Reading: Luke 19:1-27
Key Thought: Jesus is greater than any way you can describe Him.

2   JESUS: THE TRIUMPHANT LAMB

And I looked, and behold, in the midst of the throne . . . stood a
Lamb as though it had been slain.
REVELATION 5:6

Jesus is the *Triumphant Lamb* who was slain to give you victory. When no one else could open the Book of Life, His death gave Him authority to unveil the mysteries of life and of the future. He stands in Heaven with seven crowns, which symbolize His ruling power. He stands complete in the Father's plan. Because the *Triumphant Lamb* will complete the Father's purpose in the last day, He can complete the Father's purpose in your life for this day. The question is not why sin seems to be so triumphant in the world today; the question is whether you will let Jesus defeat the sin that you face.

O meek and tender Lamb of God, I come to You for forgiveness. Take
away my sin. Give me victory!

Jesus is the Lamb who stood silently before His accusers. "He was oppressed and He was afflicted, yet He opened not His mouth; He was led as a lamb to the slaughter" (Isaiah 53:7). Jesus was the sacrificial yearling Lamb who took away the sins of the world (see John 1:29). He understands your frailty and weakness; He can take away your sin because He took it upon Himself. He died for you that you might not die for your sin.

O Lamb, out of Your weakness comes strength; out of Your
meekness comes honor. I sing a new song with those in Heaven,
"Thou art worthy, O Lord, to receive glory and honor and power"
(Revelation 4:11). I marvel at Your greatness and sing again,
"Worthy is the Lamb that was slain to receive . . . wisdom,
and strength, . . . and blessings" (5:12). Amen.

Reading: Revelation 5:13—6:1
Key Thought: The *Triumphant Lamb* can give you victory.

3 THE HOLY SPIRIT: A DOVE

And immediately, coming up from the water, He [Jesus] saw the heavens parting and the Spirit descending upon Him like a dove.
MARK 1:10

The Holy Spirit is like a *Dove*, coming to rest gently on you this day, just as He rested on Jesus at His baptism. He is a *Dove* to light gently upon you to take away your anxieties. He is a *Dove* to give you peace. But, it's not just the feeling of peace you need; you need the Holy Spirit, for He is Peace. Remember the promise of Jesus, "Peace I leave with you, My peace I give to you" (John 14:27). When Jesus sends peace, the Holy Spirit delivers it. When the Holy Spirit comes into your life, receive His gentle presence as a *Dove* that is gently coming to rest on you.

O holy Dove, gently rest upon me to give peace at the center of my storm. Settle my emotions, and become the controlling peace to every area of my life. Be a Dove to bring gentleness to my soul. I yield my feelings to You.

The third Person of the Trinity is like a *Dove*, lighting upon you so carefully that you won't even feel it until you experience His peace in your life. He is like a *Dove*; He does not always come with violent manifestations or emotional outbursts. Sometimes He comes with a quiet voice and a whispered conversation. Be still; get quiet; and wait for Him.

Holy Spirit, I receive You as a gentle Dove. Guide me to be gentle with my words and gentle with my actions. Transform me to be like You.
Amen.

Reading: Luke 3:21-22; John 1:25-33; 14
Key Thought: The Holy Spirit comes to make you gentle.

4 JESUS: THE YOUNG CHILD

And when they had come into the house, they saw the young Child with Mary His mother, and fell down and worshiped Him. And when they had opened their treasures, they presented gifts to Him: gold, frankincense, and myrrh.
MATTHEW 2:11

Jesus was a *Young Child* when the wise men came to Bethlehem to give Him gifts and to worship Him. The title *"Young Child"* means more than a baby in arms. Jesus was an infant, perhaps crawling or maybe even walking. This suggests that there was a period of time between the shepherds' visit and the wise men's visit. It shouldn't surprise us that the *Young Child* grew (see Luke 2:40,52), for that's what children do. It shouldn't surprise us that the wise men of understanding and position would do what they did. "They saw the young Child . . . and fell down and worshiped Him" (Matthew 2:11). Most people only cuddle young children or enjoy their antics; but if it's Jesus, you worship Him as God. What is your response to Jesus, the *Young Child*?

Lord Jesus, I worship at the feet of the Child Jesus, because He is God. But I also worship at Your feet in Heaven for what You did on the cross.

The wise men worshiped the *Young Child* with gifts.; "And when they had opened their treasures, they presented gifts to Him: gold, frankincense, and myrrh" (Matthew 2:11). Today, when you visit a newborn baby and family, you take a gift. What the wise men did is what you should do. What are you taking to Jesus today?

Lord Jesus, I come to worship, giving You my time, my talent and my treasure. But beyond those things, I give You my greatest gift; I give You myself. Amen.

Reading: Matthew 2:1-12
Key Thought: The greatest gift of all is giving yourself to the *Young Child*.

5 ▸ JESUS: THE ALL AND IN ALL

Where there is neither Greek nor Jew, circumcised nor uncircumcised, barbarian,
Scythian, slave nor free, but Christ is all and in all.
COLOSSIANS 3:11

Jesus is the *All and in All*. When you become a member of His Church—the Body—you are equal with all other believers. He indwells all believers, no matter who they are. He is ready to answer all prayers equally, no matter who prays. He protects, guides, blesses and uses all believers, no matter their ethnic or economic background. All who are members of His Body have equal rights, and to each Jesus is the *All and in All*. No one is lost or overlooked. You'll always have access to all that Jesus wants to give you. Will you claim it? You'll never be left behind, nor will He exalt anyone over another. You are special to Jesus and He loves you eternally. Jesus is all you would want, in all situations, at all times. Will you be satisfied with Him?

> *Lord, forgive me when I whine over things that don't matter and that*
> *aren't necessary. Help me see clearly Your care for me, and help me*
> *experience deeply Your love.*

Jesus is all you have ever needed; and when you trust Him, He'll be all you'll ever want. To find satisfaction in life, look to the things that are important, and forget about the things that are not important.

> *Lord, You are the most important one in my life. Forgive me*
> *when I've given You second place. You are my All and in All.*
> *Teach me to look beyond people, things and places, so*
> *I can have satisfaction in You. Amen.*

Reading: Psalm 149
Key Thought: Jesus should be the most important Person in your life.

6 · JESUS: THE LIGHT OF THE CITY

The city had no need of the sun or of the moon to shine in it, for the glory of God illuminated it. The Lamb is its light.
REVELATION 21:23

When we get to Heaven, we won't need the sun that shines in our solar system. Jesus will be the *Light of the City*. Jesus will be everything that we look for in light. Jesus will be abundantly present—everywhere, all the time—so we don't need to worry about stumbling in the dark or bumping into things or getting lost. Jesus will show us everything we need to know, so we don't need to look for a reading light or for a lighted room in order to learn. Heaven will be a perfect place, so we won't need a fire to keep us warm. And there'll be no dangers in Heaven, so we won't need protection in the dark from predators. Heaven will not need the sun, because the glory of God will shine in it and Jesus will be its Light.

Lord, I know what Your light does for me now, so I look forward to Your light in Heaven.

Light, in contrast to darkness, is a trademark of civilizations. Walk in the light on Earth for a better life, because you can do more in the light; it's safer and it's more comfortable. But primarily walk in the light because you'll be closer to Jesus, who is the Light.

Lord, remind me that when my path gets dark, it's because I'm not close to You. Help me see the Light, walk closer to the Light and learn from the Light. Amen.

Reading: Revelation 21:22-27
Key Thought: Jesus will be your Light in Heaven.

7 ⬥ JESUS: THE AUTHOR OF OUR FAITH

*Looking unto Jesus, the author and finisher of our faith, who for the
joy that was set before Him endured the cross, despising the shame, and has
sat down at the right hand of the throne of God.*
HEBREWS 12:2

Jesus is the *Author of Our Faith*. He not only began writing the story, but
He also finished the manuscript. A book is usually good because an
author put it all together. Just as an author sees a problem and scripts a
solution, Jesus saw the sin problem of humanity and scripted a solution.
Just as an author develops the story line or plot, Jesus saw what He had
to do and developed a plan to save humanity. Just as an author chooses
the right words to express his story, Jesus is the Word who expressed the
story of salvation in His life (see John 1:1). Just as an author develops
characters or actors to live out the story, Jesus became the central character of salvation. Not only is Jesus the *Author of Your Faith*, but also He
has finished your story. Most people say, "I could never write a book." In
the same way, others say, "I could never hang on to salvation." But it's
not about your ability to finish, for He's the Finisher of your faith.

*Lord Jesus, I am in You—the Author—so I know my
salvation story will be completed.*

Jesus can finish your salvation story because He finished His own
story. He went all the way to the cross, endured suffering and took all the
ridicule. Because He finished His task, He will help you finish yours.

*Lord Jesus, I look to You for strength when I am weak. I look to
You to carry me through to the end. Amen.*

Reading: Matthew 27:15-34
Key Thought: Because Jesus finished His task in providing salvation, He
can see you through to the end.

8   JESUS: A NAZARENE

*And he came and dwelt in a city called Nazareth, that it might be fulfilled which
was spoken by the prophets, "He shall be called a Nazarene."*
MATTHEW 2:23

Two cities are especially important to the baby Jesus. He was born in
Bethlehem, as predicted in Micah 5:2. But God led Mary and Joseph to
return to their hometown of Nazareth so that Jesus could be called a
Nazarene. There is no written record of any prophets who wrote that
Jesus would come from Nazareth. Rather, look carefully at the text; it
says "prophets," meaning more than one. Also, this prophecy was spoken; it was not written. This means that several prophets had predicted
that Jesus would be a *Nazarene.* Since everyone had to come from some-
place, Jesus didn't just appear as an angel, nor did He invade the earth as
a grown man. Jesus was born in Bethlehem and grew up in Nazareth.
Jesus was a *Nazarene.*

*Lord Jesus, thank You for coming to the earth and choosing
one specific spot to be born and to grow up.*

The word "Nazareth" comes from the root *nazar,* meaning "to separate," as in the Nazarite vow. The people of Nazareth were more conser-
vative than those of most Jewish towns. They separated themselves from
other people and from sin. In social, religious and moral customs, they
were extremely separated to God. Jesus was as separated as the people of
Nazareth because He was God. Jesus was separate from worldly and secular trends because He was raised in a town called Separated Ones. Jesus
was a *Nazarene.*

*Lord Jesus, Your hometown must have been special for God to choose it
for Your boyhood. Thank You for becoming flesh for me. Amen.*

Reading: Matthew 2:19-23
Key Thought: God had a special hometown for Jesus.

THE TRINITY: THE SHADOW OF THE ALMIGHTY

*He who dwells in the secret place of the Most High shall abide
under the shadow of the Almighty.*
PSALM 91:1

A shadow can be both good and bad. A threatening shadow may warn of an approaching storm. When we see a shadow in the night, we are scared because we think someone has broken into our home. We are frightened of walking through the shadow of death because no one enjoys pain and no one wants to die. Little children are afraid of shadows because they haven't yet learned that a shadow creates illusions. Don't let shadows frighten you. Remember that those who live in fellowship with the Lord dwell securely under His shadow. This means that the Lord is between you and any evil that would harm you.

*Lord, I will walk happily with You through the sunshine,
and I'll not change when I walk in shadows, because You are with
me in the valley of the shadow of death.*

A shadow is good when you're hot and tired, and you think you can't go on. A shadow will cool you down and restore your energy and let you get off your aching feet. You can even take a restful nap in the shadow. A shadow is good when God blocks out harm. When God is your Shadow, it means He's near and He's protecting you.

*Lord, I need some relief. Life is tough. Meet me in the shadow of Your
presence to renew my determination and replenish my energy. Watch
over me while I rest. Amen.*

Reading: Psalm 91
Key Thought: Get under the Shadow of God, so He'll be near.

10 JESUS: THAT SPIRITUAL ROCK

For they drank of that spiritual Rock that followed them,
and that Rock was Christ.
1 CORINTHIANS 10:4

Jesus was that *Spiritual Rock* from which the Jews Israelites drank when they thirsted in the wilderness as they traveled from Egypt. The spring at Horeb was dry. God told Moses to take his rod and strike the rock. In obedience to God's command, water flowed from the rock and the people drank (see Exodus 17:1-6). When God's people looked to Him, Christ supplied their need. He can take care of your needs in the same way.

Jesus, I'm not physically lost in the desert like the Israelites.
I have a suitable life, but sometimes I wander in a spiritual desert. I'm
hot and thirsty. I need water; come quench my thirst.

Jesus is that *Spiritual Rock* that followed Israel throughout their desert wanderings. He was not a granite stone that followed them; He was their Lord who protected them (see Exodus 17:8-16). He was their daily Manna who fed them (see 16:14-22); and He was their God who supplied them with spiritual water when they thirsted. He was their Light to guide them through their night; He was the Column of fire, the Shekinah glory cloud. Jesus met every spiritual need of Israel. Just as Jesus was with His people in the desert, so He can be with you in your spiritual desert. Call on Him today for help.

Jesus, I need You to follow me this day, just as You followed Israel in the
desert. I need spiritual protection when tempted. I need manna when
I'm hungry. I need spiritual water when I'm thirsty and fainting. I need
You, my Spiritual Rock. Amen.

Reading: 1 Corinthians 10:1-15
Key Thought: Depend on Jesus because He is with you.

11 Jesus: The Son of the Highest

*He will be great, and will be called the Son of the Highest; and the Lord
God will give Him the throne of His father David.*
LUKE 1:32

Jesus is the *Son of the Highest*, as no human can be. The name "Most High"
in the original Hebrew language is *El Elyon*, which means "Possessor of
heaven and earth" (Genesis 14:19). Originally, Lucifer wanted to be "like
the Most High [God]" (Isaiah 14:14), the ruler of Heaven and Earth.
Notice the word "like." Lucifer could never have become the actual Most
High God; that is a title and position that only God can possess. Since
Jesus is the Father's Son, He is the *Son of the Highest* or the Son of the
Most High. One of the many reasons to worship the Father is because
He possesses Heaven and Earth. Therefore, worship Jesus, because He is
the *Son of the Highest*.

*Jesus, I worship You as the Son of the Highest. Rule my heart today,
just as You rule Heaven and Earth.*

The heavenly Father is El Elyon; He possesses all things, which He
gives to Jesus. When Jesus sent His disciples out to serve, He said, "All
authority has been given to Me in heaven and on earth" (Matthew
28:18). He sends you to serve Him today with the same authority: "Go
make disciples" (see v. 19). His promise to you is "I am with you always"
(v. 20). So serve the Lord with confidence, knowing You have the Lord's
power and presence with you today.

*Jesus, it is thrilling to know that You, the Son of the Highest,
will be with me today. Use me in Your service; give me the power of
Your authority and presence. Amen.*

Reading: Luke 1:26-33
Key Thought: You have the backing of Jesus' authority as you serve Him.

12 THE HOLY SPIRIT: A SOUND FROM HEAVEN

And suddenly there came a sound from heaven, as of a rushing mighty wind,
and it filled the whole house where they were sitting.
ACTS 2:2

The Holy Spirit was like a *Sound from Heaven* when He came upon the disciples at Pentecost. A loud sound may surprise you; a sweet sound may entice you; an unexpected sound may startle you; and familiar sounds may make you feel comfortable. When Christians were praying in the Upper Room, they didn't know what to expect. Jesus had promised to send the Holy Spirit to them (see Acts 1:8). He came upon them as a loud "sound from Heaven, as of a rushing mighty wind" (2:2). Because He was like a mighty wind, He can do mighty things in your life. The sound filled the whole house, so He can influence your whole world. Those who prayed "were all filled with the Holy Spirit" (v. 4); you are included in that "all." The Holy Spirit can enter your life to transform all you do.

Holy Spirit, I need to hear from You. Let me hear the sound of Your
presence coming into my life.

The Holy Spirit is a *Sound from Heaven*. He doesn't sound anything like what you hear on Earth. A *Sound from Heaven* is optimistic and filled with hope. It is sweet and good. When you focus your ears on Heaven, you'll hear eternal things. A *Sound from Heaven* will make you want to worship, so stop what you're doing. Be quiet and listen for Heaven's Sound. The Sound you'll hear will be God Himself.

Holy Spirit, I need You today. My mind is clear and I'm quiet.
I'm waiting for Your voice. Speak, for Your servant will hear and do
what You say. Amen.

Reading: Acts 2:1-8
Key Thought: You will hear a new and different sound from the Holy Spirit.

13 JESUS: THE SON OF JOSEPH

Philip found Nathanael and said to him, "We have found Him of whom Moses in the law, and also the prophets, wrote—Jesus of Nazareth, the son of Joseph."
JOHN 1:45

Jesus is called the *Son of Joseph* because Joseph was His earthly stepfather and legal guardian. Therefore we are technically right calling Jesus the *Son of Joseph*. Jesus was conceived by the Holy Spirit in the virgin Mary when Joseph was engaged to her. Joseph could have legally annulled the engagement, but when an angel explained the supernatural birth, he married Mary (see Matthew 1:18-25). Joseph endured the embarrassing rumors that Jesus had been conceived out of wedlock (see John 8:41). As an earthly father, Joseph protected Jesus, provided for Him, taught Him the trade of carpentry and guided His youth into manhood.

Jesus, You are the Son of Joseph. You are the Son of God.
I will follow You and worship You.

Philip told his friend that Jesus was the *Son of Joseph* (see John 1:45). Are you willing to tell others who He is? Because Philip was a faithful witness, his friend Nathaniel became one of the 12 disciples. When Nathaniel had questions about Jesus, Philip simply said, "Come and see" (v. 46). Tell your friends about Jesus. When they have questions, tell them to look at Jesus and He will answer their questions. When your friends see who Jesus is, they will follow Him as you do.

Jesus, I know You are human, born of a virgin, the Son of Joseph.
But I also know You are the eternal Son of God. I will learn from
You and tell my friends what I've learned. I will worship You
and be transformed by Your presence. Amen.

Reading: John 1:43-51
Key Thought: Tell others who Jesus really is.

14 ◆ JESUS: THE ROCK

And I also say to you that you are Peter, and on this rock I will build My church,
and the gates of Hades shall not prevail against it.
MATTHEW 16:18

Jesus is the *Rock* on which the Church is built. Some have mistakenly thought that in Matthew 16:18 Jesus was applying the word "rock" to Peter. The name "Peter" is *Petros*, a reference to a small stone, perhaps like a pebble. The word "rock" in this verse is *petra*, a large rock, actually like a rock ledge that sticks out of a mountain. The confusion has come because both words came from the same root. Actually, the Church is built on Peter's statement "You are the Christ, the Son of the living God" (v. 16). The Church is not a dead institution, though some churches are dead. The Church is alive because it's built on Jesus, the Son of the living God. The Church is alive because it's made up of individuals who believe that Jesus is the Son of God and who have accepted Him into their hearts.

Lord Jesus, I know that the Church is grounded on You; You are the
Rock. I get stability from You.

When the Church is built on Jesus, it is as solid as a rock. Jesus is the original church planter and church builder, for He said, "I will build." Also, the Church is continually being built, for the statement "I will build" contains a future tense verb that means "continually being built." He's doing it today. Finally, the Church belongs to Jesus; He called it "My church." When you're in Jesus, you're in the Church; and when you're in Jesus, you're on the *Rock*.

Jesus, I know that the Church is growing because it is continually
being built. I know I am secure in You because the gates of Hades
can't prevail against Your work. Amen.

Reading: Matthew 16:13-28
Key Thought: The Church is being built by Jesus.

15 THE TRINITY: THE KING (*JEHOVAH MELEK*)

Woe is me, for I am undone! Because I am a man of unclean lips, and I dwell in the midst of a people of unclean lips; for my eyes have seen the King, the LORD of hosts.
ISAIAH 6:5

The Lord is *Jehovah Melek*, the *King* who sovereignly rules. He rules Heaven and the universe, exercising His will over the earth. Just as our earthly kings rule kingdoms, so the Lord determines the laws by which everything happens. Just as our earthly kings guide the lives of those in their kingdoms, the Lord can direct your life only if you yield it to His control. Just as earthly kings expect obedience from their followers, the Lord wants heart obedience; He shouldn't have to coerce you into loving Him, because coercive love is not love. The *King* wants willing love, willing obedience and willing worship.

> *O Jehovah Melek—my King—come rule in my heart. Overcome my rebellious and selfish heart. Make me always do things Your way.*

Jehovah Melek will not force people to serve Him on the earth. Each person must either submit to His rule and live for Him, or refuse His rule. Those who will not submit to the *King* in this life will appear before Him—the *King* of the universe—to be judged in the future. Then they will be forced to recognize His authority and be forced to bow before Him in worship. But that worship will be ineffective, because it will be coerced and come too late—after our time of testing on this earth is over.

> *O King, sit upon the throne of my heart. Rule my life today. Let Your will override my stubborn pride. Amen.*

Reading: Isaiah 6
Key Thought: The *King* wants to rule from the throne of your heart.

16 ◆ JESUS: THE SAME YESTERDAY, TODAY AND FOREVER

Jesus Christ is the same yesterday, today, and forever.
HEBREWS 13:8

Just as Jesus was present in New Testament times to lead His disciples, so He is ready to guide you today. Jesus is the Beginning and the End, so He'll not lead you for a little while and then forsake you. He dealt with fearful disciples when they faced a storm, so He can give you peace. He helped Joshua face the obstacles of Jericho, so He can pull down barriers in your life. He saw the world reject the preaching of Noah, so He can send an ark of safety when judgment floods come. Yesterday is gone, and you can do nothing about it. Tomorrow is not here, and most people fear the future. But you can do something about today. Will you live for Jesus today?

Lord, I put the past under Your blood, so forgive all my debts.
I commit my future to You. Give me courage to face what is coming.
Today I will do Your will.

The best thing you can do today is to find the heart of Jesus, who is the *Same Yesterday, Today and Forever,* and trust Him. It's good for you to know what Jesus has done in the past; that's a basis to guide today's activity. But don't love Jesus just for what He did for you in the past; love Him for who He is today. Jesus is the eternal God who is near you to help you.

Lord, I know You can do the same things today that You did in the past.
Help me today. Prepare me for tomorrow. Amen.

Reading: John 21:15-25
Key Thought: Live for Jesus today.

17 JESUS: REDEEMER

For I know that my Redeemer lives, and He shall stand at last on the earth.
JOB 19:25

Jesus is the *Redeemer*. Before you were saved, you were owned by sin and the Devil, but Jesus bought you with a special redemptive price. "You were not redeemed with . . . silver and gold, . . . but with the precious blood of Christ, as of a lamb" (1 Peter 1:18-19). Jesus is your *Redeemer*, and now you belong to Him.

> *Lord, I sometimes forget what I was before You saved me. Never let me forget how You redeemed me. Thank You for releasing me from the prison house of sin. I am no longer a slave of the Devil. How can I serve You?*

Jesus is your *Redeemer* because He took your curse: "Christ has redeemed us from the curse of the law, having become a curse for us" (Galatians 3:13). He was punished for your sin; you are no longer in bondage to sin—you are free! But as your *Redeemer*, Jesus did more than pay the price to release you from bondage; He made you a son of God: "To redeem those who were under the law, that we might receive the adoption as sons" (4:5). Now you're a part of God's family; now you have a privileged position in His family. Your *Redeemer* has taken you from being a slave to sin and made you a part of God's family.

> *Thank You, Redeemer, for not leaving me stranded in sin. Thank You for bringing me into Your family and making me Your child. "Redemption" is a wonderful word. I enjoy my new position in You. Amen.*

Reading: Galatians 4:1-7
Key Thought: Jesus redeemed you and made you a member of God's family.

18 THE FATHER: CREATOR

Have you not known? Have you not heard? The everlasting God,
the LORD, the Creator of the ends of the earth, neither faints nor is
weary. His understanding is unsearchable.
ISAIAH 40:28

The Lord is the *Creator;* without Him nothing exists (see Colossians 1:16). No person is able to create another human. No one can create life, a soul or the ability to think. God is the *Creator* who formed man and woman, so He knows all about you.

Lord, thank You for making me the way that I am. Thank You for
making me after Your image. Help me to reflect Your nature to others.

The Lord is the *Creator.* Some people think that higher things evolved out of lower life, but they face an unexplainable gap between the first molecule and nothing. The first atom came from the *Creator.* There are two particles of an atom—a proton and a neutron—with an electron swirling around these two. His power holds them together. Break apart an atom and you'll get a massive nuclear explosion. But there are trillions upon trillions of atoms in the universe. Consider the immeasurable nuclear destruction of the universe possible if all were to be split at the same time. The power of that explosion is held in check by the greater power of God's nature. Since He is in every atom, think how close He is to you. The Lord is the *Creator* who made atoms out of nothing. He is powerful enough to know your needs and close enough to help you.

Creator, forgive my unbelief when I doubt Your existence. Forgive
my stubborn will for not trusting Your power to work things out in my
life. I worship You as Creator and God. Amen.

Reading: Psalm 19; 29
Key Thought: The powerful *Creator* knows your need.

19   JESUS: THE SHADOW OF A GREAT ROCK

A man will be as a hiding place from the wind, and a cover from the tempest, as rivers of water in a dry place, as the shadow of a great rock in a weary land.
ISAIAH 32:2

Just as a person struggling through the desert needs escape from the blistering sun, so you need protection from burning trials and temptations in your spiritual desert. Jesus will be your *Shadow of a Great Rock* to protect you. Just as a weary traveler needs a resting place in the shadows before journeying on, so you need to be to revitalized for the next part of your journey. Jesus is the *Shadow of a Great Rock* to revitalize you. Look to Him for protection and comfort. You can walk again on the highway of life after resting in His shadow.

> *Lord, today I need a little rest. Also, I need encouragement to get up and walk again in the heat of the day. Ah, it's good to relax in Your presence.*

Jesus is the *Shadow of a Great Rock*. There are no trees in the desert for shade. If there were trees, they would die in the heat. But rocks are much more durable. Only a big rock—big enough to create a shadow—can help you. Jesus' shadow is big enough for you and other pilgrims. Did you notice that He's located at the exact place in your journey where you need Him most? Come rest a while, take off your shoes and cool down. Take a nap before you have to go on your way.

> *Lord Jesus, You are my Rock of renewal; I get strength from You. But also, You are my Rock of stability. You give me purpose in life! Amen.*

Reading: Isaiah 32
Key Thought: Jesus will shadow you from burning trials.

20 JESUS: KING OF KINGS AND LORD OF LORDS

And He has on His robe and on His thigh a name written:
KING OF KINGS AND LORD OF LORDS.
REVELATION 19:16

Jesus is the *King of Kings and Lord of Lords*, the absolute, sovereign Ruler of the universe. Today He has given people and nations the freedom to choose or to deny His rule. Those who choose Him will live, and those who deny Him will die. One day He will return to Earth to examine what choice each person has made. When Jesus returns, written on His garments will be His title *"King of Kings and Lord of Lords."*

Lord, I pray, "Thy kingdom come," and in anticipation of Your rule,
I worship Your majesty. O King of kings, I want You to rule in my heart
today, just as You'll rule the universe in the future.

As *King of Kings and Lord of Lords,* Jesus will return to Earth on a white horse, followed by the armies of Heaven. There will be multitudes following Him, and the saints and angels will come with Him. He will come to rule on Earth, but today He's asking to rule your heart. Jesus is the Lord of lords. When He comes, all false religions will be destroyed and all false gods will be eliminated. Idols, just as the false gods they represent, will be burned with fire. Jesus will be the only Lord in that day, for He will be Lord of lords. The kings of this world will all be gone. Jesus will be the only King in that day, for He will be King over all.

O Lord of lords, I bow to worship You for personal salvation.
I know that You saved me and transformed me. I know You're
coming again for me. I am waiting. Amen.

Reading: Revelation 21:1-8
Key Thought: One day, Jesus will be the ultimate and only King.

THE HOLY SPIRIT: THE SPIRIT OF THE LORD GOD

21

The Spirit of the Lord GOD is upon Me, because the LORD has anointed Me to preach good tidings to the poor; He has sent Me to heal the brokenhearted, to proclaim liberty to the captives, and the opening of the prison to those who are bound.

ISAIAH 61:1.

The Holy Spirit is the *Spirit of the Lord God* who anointed Jesus to preach the gospel. Therefore, He can anoint you to effectively share the good news of salvation. Just as the Holy Spirit sent Jesus to do miracles of mercy, so He can send you to show mercy to needy people. Just as the Holy Spirit helped Jesus proclaim liberty to captives, so He can use you to give the message of spiritual liberty to all. You can open the prison of sin to those who are in bondage to Satan. Just as the Holy Spirit anointed Jesus for ministry, He can also anoint you for ministry.

Holy Spirit, I believe in You. What You have done in ministry through Jesus, do the same for me. I want to be used by You.

The *Spirit of the Lord God* led Jesus while He was upon Earth (see Luke 4:1,14). They had perfect harmony because Jesus was one with the Father and the Holy Spirit. When you yield completely to the Holy Spirit, He can lead you every step of each day. He can help you accomplish much more with your life. The world has yet to see what can be accomplished through any person who is completely surrendered to the Father, Son and Holy Spirit.

Holy Spirit, I yield my life to You. Help me see areas of my life that are not yielded, so I can yield them to You. I want to be completely filled with Your presence. Amen.

Reading: Luke 4:1-20
Key Thought: The more you yield to the Holy Spirit, the more you can do for Him.

22 ▸ JESUS: THE SON

> *All things have been delivered to Me by My Father, and no one knows*
> *the Son except the Father. Nor does anyone know the Father except the Son,*
> *and the one to whom the Son wills to reveal Him.*
> MATTHEW 11:27

Jesus is the *Son*. He's the *Son* of man, the *Son* of God, the *Son* of the morning and the *Son* of Mary, but His most eternal relationship is the *Son* of the Father. Just as, on Earth, a son has the nature of his father, so Jesus has the divine nature of His heavenly Father: "I and My Father are one" (John 10:30). Just as an earthly son gets life from his father, so Jesus gets life from the heavenly Father: "For as the Father has life in Himself, so He has granted the Son to have life in Himself" (5:26). Just as a son wants fellowship with his earthly father, so Jesus constantly spent time in prayer with His Father.

> *Jesus, I want to fellowship with You and the Father, just as You and the*
> *Father had fellowship with one another when You lived on Earth.*

Notice how an earthly son is like Jesus. A: a son obeys his father just as Jesus obeyed the heavenly Father; a son pleases his father just as Jesus pleased the Father; a son usually looks forward to spending time with his father just as Jesus longed to return to His Father in Heaven (see John 17:11,13); a son is usually concerned about the reputation of his father just as Jesus was (see vv. 4-6).

> *Jesus, You are a wonderful example of what a son should be to the*
> *heavenly Father. I want to be obedient and respectful, and I want to*
> *please the Father just as You pleased Him. Amen.*

Reading: John 5:19-24
Key Thought: In His relationship to the Father, Jesus reflects the characteristics of a son.

23 ▸ JESUS: THE WORD

*In the beginning was the Word, and the Word was with God,
and the Word was God.*
JOHN 1:1

Jesus is called the *Word* because He expressed the true idea of the Father, just as a written word represents the ideas of an author. Jesus is also called the *Word* because He is the One who communicated the Father's desires to the people, just as a written word communicates an author's intent. Jesus is also the *Word* because He interprets the Father to the world, just as a human author interprets a theme to readers. Words are symbols of meaning, and Jesus is the symbol that showed the world what God was like in the flesh.

Jesus, I look to You to show me what God is like. I will study the Word of God to better understand God and know what He expects of me.

Jesus was the powerful *Word* who lived in the flesh. Jesus' spoken words were also powerful, for His words raised the dead, calmed the storms and comforted the hurting. And the written Word of Christ is just as powerful as His spoken words. The written Word can save, heal, cast out demons and become the basis for answered prayer (see Colossians 3:16; Hebrews 4:12). Jesus elevated His words to a supernatural level when He said, "The words that I speak to you are spirit, and they are life" (John 6:63). Peter agreed with Him: "You have the words of eternal life" (v. 68).

Lord, I love Your Word, because You tell me about the Father. I love Your words because they are spirit and life. Amen.

Reading: John 1:1-14
Key Thought: Jesus is the *Word* who communicates the Father to us.

24 THE TRINITY: THE UNKNOWN GOD

As I was passing through and considering the object of your worship, I even found an altar with the inscription: TO THE UNKNOWN GOD.
ACTS 17:23

God is the *Unknown God*. He is the real God, who is the prototype of all false gods, which are crafted by those who don't know the real God. Just as there is a real object from which imitations are made, so God is the real One whom the world doesn't know, yet they make imitations of Him. He is not like the false gods of gold or silver or stone, carved with human hands. The world doesn't know the God of Heaven—the *Unknown God*—but He is everywhere present at the same time.

*Lord, I know You, even though the world does not recognize You.
I know You in salvation, and I know You in fellowship. I want
to make You known to others.*

The world may think that God doesn't exist and that He's unknown, but it is still accountable to Him because He created "the world and everything in it" (Acts 17:24). We are all offspring of God, and we live and move and have our being in Him (see v. 28). We are all responsible to seek God because He is not far from any of us (see v. 27). It is our task to let the world see God in us.

*Lord, I will not let anything substitute for You, nor will I worship
anything in Your place. I will make room for You at the center of
my life. I will worship You only. Amen.*

Reading: Acts 17:16-34
Key Thought: The real God of Heaven is the prototype of all false gods.

25 JESUS: THE TRUE VINE

I am the true vine, and My Father is the vinedresser.
JOHN 15:1

Jesus is the *True Vine*. In the Old Testament, Israel was called God's vine, but the nation was an unfaithful vine (see Isaiah 5:1-7). In contrast, Jesus is the *True Vine*. Israel was disobedient to the Father, but Jesus was true to the Father's mission for Him. Jesus was truthful in character and speech. On the night before He was arrested, He said, "I am the true vine" (John 15:1). Just as a vine gives life and energy through its fruit, so Jesus gives eternal life to those who believe Him. Just as a vine gives satisfying drink, so Jesus gives joy and contentment to those who follow Him. Just as a vine gives shade to the weary traveler, so Jesus gives shelter from the burning sun of opposition and trouble. What do you need from Jesus?

> *Lord Jesus, You are true. You have kept every promise concerning forgiveness, eternal life, happiness and protection. You are the True Vine who keeps Your word.*

Jesus said, "I am the vine, you are the branches" (John 15:5). Looking at a vine, you can't tell which is the original stem and which is a branch. This is what Jesus meant when He said, "You in Me, and I in you" (14:20). We must stay connected to Him because "the branch cannot bear fruit of itself, unless it abides in the vine" (15:4).

> *Lord Jesus, You are the Vine; let Your energy flow through me. You are the Source of Life; let Your fruitfulness grow through me. You are the Vine; I am the branches. Amen.*

Reading: Isaiah 5:1-7; John 15:1-7
Key Thought: You must be attached to the Vine to get life and fruit.

26 ◆ JESUS: PROPITIATION

> *My little children, these things write I unto you, that ye sin not. And if*
> *any man sin, we have an advocate with the Father, Jesus Christ the*
> *righteous: And he is the propitiation for our sins: and not for ours*
> *only, but also for the sins of the whole world.*
> 1 JOHN 2:1-2, *KJV*

Jesus is the *Propitiation*—His title that means "full satisfaction." Idol worshipers use the word "propitiation" when offering sacrifices to their idols to appease their supposed wrath. Jesus is your *Propitiation*—the full satisfaction—to satisfy God's punishment of your sins.

> *Lord, thank You for paying the price to satisfy my sin debt. But You paid*
> *not just for my sin; You died for the whole world.*

Jesus is your *Propitiation*, meaning your sins are fully forgiven. "He [God] loved us and sent His Son to be the propitiation for our sins" (1 John 4:10). Now when the Lord looks at you, He doesn't see your sin; He sees the ledger marked "Paid in full." Because Jesus has satisfied your debt, you are now free in Christ. The word "propitiation" is also translated "mercy seat," which is the lid on the Ark of the Covenant. The mercy seat was the place of propitiation—satisfaction—where the blood was sprinkled for forgiveness. The mercy seat also was the place where the presence of God came to rest in the Tabernacle. God does not have a throne on Earth; He sits on the mercy seat. Because blood is sprinkled there, it is a seat of mercy. Now, because of propitiation, Jesus can come to you, and His presence can abide with you.

> *Lord, thank You for forgiving all my sin debt and satisfying the*
> *indictments against me. Help me enjoy Your forgiveness; I need Your*
> *presence in my life this day. Come. Amen.*

Reading: 1 John 2:1-11
Key Thought: Jesus has satisfied every debt you owe because of sin.

27   THE FATHER: GOD THE FATHER

*Paul, an apostle (not from men nor through man, but through Jesus Christ
and God the Father who raised Him from the dead).*
GALATIANS 1:1

God the Father is equal in nature to God the Son and God the Holy Spirit.
Because God is three Persons—the Trinity—each Person is separate from
the others, yet God has one nature. Each Person in the Godhead is all-
wise, all-powerful and equally present everywhere. Each Person is totally
holy, completely loving and innately good. So, you must worship each
Person of the Godhead with all your heart. *"God the Father"* is a title of
relationship to His beloved Son and to the Holy Spirit. Just as there is a
loving relationship between the members of the Godhead, so you can
have a loving relationship with others who belong to God. When you
were born again, you became a child of God; you became a member of
God's family. Now you shall love others as the Father loves you.

*Father, I praise You for Your powerful acts of creation and Your love for
me. Jesus, thank You for dying for my sins. Holy Spirit, I am grateful for
Your transforming power in my conversion.*

"God the Father" is a favorite name used by Paul. His readers were
mostly idol worshipers before conversion, so they believed in a deity. But
they didn't know God as their Father until Paul taught them who He was.
Paul exhorted them to know *God the Father* in a personal relationship.

*O God my Father, You are first among equals in the Trinity.
You are first in my life without equal. I exalt You to the throne of my
life. Let me know You better. Amen.*

Reading: Galatians 1:1-12
Key Thought: God is the Father whom you can know intimately.

28 JESUS: THE LAMB OF GOD

Behold! The Lamb of God who takes away the sin of the world!
JOHN 1:29

On the banks of the Jordan River, John the Baptist announced to the world, "Behold! The Lamb of God." For hundreds of years, thousands of faithful Israelites sacrificed millions of lambs—all looking forward to the coming of the Messiah, who would forgive their sins. Because Jesus was the *Lamb of God*, all the drudgery of sacrifice finally came to an end. Now, every new day should be exciting because Jesus, the *Lamb of God*, has taken away the sin of the world—including all of yesterday's mistakes. He has taken away your sins because you believed in Him. Today is a new opportunity to serve the Lord. Thank God for the Lamb who has taken away your sins.

O Lamb of God, forgive me for the willful sins I do, and look deeply to see my repentance. Purge me of the ignorant sins that I don't realize I do.

Learn to worship the Lamb. Learn to do on Earth what you'll do in Heaven. Worship should be your passion now, since you will worship once you arrive in Heaven. When you get to Heaven, you will join many others who are worshiping "Him who sits on the throne, and to the Lamb, forever and ever!" (Revelation 5:13). In Heaven you will cry out with others, "Worthy is the Lamb who was slain" (v. 12).

Jesus, Lamb of God, at Your name I join every knee bowing and every tongue confessing that You, Jesus Christ, are Lord"
(see Philippians 2:10-11). Amen.

Reading: Revelation 5:6-12
Key Thought: Jesus is worthy of our worship.

29 ⬧ JESUS: THE ONE WHO HAS THE KEY OF DAVID

These things says He who is holy, He who is true, "He who has the key of David,
He who opens and no one shuts, and shuts and no one opens."
REVELATION 3:7

Jesus is the *One Who Has the Key of David*. It was given to Him by His heavenly Father. The key gives Jesus the authority to determine who will enter the Kingdom. He alone determines who will be given access to the Father, for Jesus said, "I am the way, the truth, and the life. No one comes to the Father except through Me" (John 14:6). Jesus is the *One Who Has the Key of David* whereby all shall be saved. Now you must share this key—the message—with others. "I have set before you an open door, and no one can shut it" (Revelation 3:8). You have an open door to share the message of salvation with those you know. Jesus said, "I am coming quickly! Hold fast what you have, that no one may take your crown" (v. 11). Don't let the door of witnessing shut.

Lord, I need wisdom to grasp all the opportunities I have to serve You.
I need Your wisdom to know what to say, and I need Your courage to
help me speak to others about salvation.

Jesus is the One who can open and shut the door of opportunity. When He opens up an opportunity to witness, you must take that opportunity, or that door may be shut to you in the future.

Jesus, You have the key. I ask You to help me use my
opportunities so that others may believe. Don't let me lose
my chance to witness for You. Amen.

Reading: Acts 8
Key Thought: Jesus opens doors for you to witness to others.

MARCH

1 ◆ THE HOLY SPIRIT: DEW

I will be like the dew to Israel.
HOSEA 14:5

The Holy Spirit is *Dew* who can refresh your spirit with His presence today. Feel Him! He is *Dew,* coming gently to leave refreshment, even when you can't see with your physical eyes. Do you feel the spiritual moisture? He is *Dew* who leaves your spiritual face damp when it's not raining. Experience Him! He is *Dew,* coming silently, invisibly and softly; let His presence work in your life.

> *Lord, be Dew to refresh me when I'm tired. The unsaved don't understand spirituality, nor do they believe in You. Be Dew to moisten my arid soul, to refresh my spirit this day.*

The Holy Spirit is *Dew* to reinvigorate your vision; open up your soul to see more things from God. He is *Dew* to reignite those who are about to give up the battle; let Him reequip you for spiritual warfare. He is *Dew* to reinvigorate those who quit working. He can reenlist you this day. He is *Dew,* like the early morning dampness that makes the grass and plants grow, even when there's no rain. Let Him be *Dew* who gives you new purpose in life.

> *Lord, sometimes I feel like I can't go forward; I want to give up. My spirit needs a new start; I need refreshment in my life. Come let me feel Your refreshing moisture in my soul. I worship and praise You for the fresh challenge of this new day. Come, Dew, let me live anew. Amen.*

Reading: Hosea 14
Key Thought: The Holy Spirit refreshes our hearts like morning dew.

JESUS: THE LORD WHO IS, WHO WAS AND WHO IS TO COME

I am . . . [the Lord] who is and who was and who is to come, the Almighty.
REVELATION 1:8

Jesus is the *Lord Who Is, Who Was and Who Is to Come.* He is eternal, without beginning and without end. This description reflects Jesus' preexistence. He lived before being born as a baby in Bethlehem. From eternity past to eternity future, Jesus is the eternal God. You can trust Him with your life, for He has always existed; He knows all about you; He knows your trouble; and He knows your need.

Lord, I know You helped people in Bible times, because You lived back then; help me today. I believe You are eternal.

Jesus will not change the way He relates to His own. The writer of Hebrews declares, "Jesus Christ is the same yesterday, today, and forever" (13:8). He will do for you—and all believers—what He has done in the past. He can't change His nature, and He will not change His mind. Jesus can be to you today what He has always been in the past. Moses said, "From everlasting to everlasting, You are God" (Psalm 90:2). Before time began, He was eternal God; after time on Earth is finished, He will still be God. You can trust His promises and His care.

Lord, I am blinded by my self-absorption; help me fully see Your love and care. I am human and frail; help me look beyond my doubts to clearly see Your presence in my life. When I only see my needs, help me to see Your eternal nature and to worship You. Amen.

Reading: Matthew 17:14-21
Key Thought: Jesus can help you today as He helped people in Bible times.

3 ◆ JESUS: THE SON OF MARY

Is this not the carpenter, the Son of Mary, and brother of James, Joseph, Judas,
and Simon? And are not His sisters here with us?
MARK 6:3

Jesus is the *Son of Mary*, born as a human baby; yet Mary was a virgin. Because Mary had not known a man, Jesus was born sinless, without a sin nature. He lived His entire life without sin (see 2 Corinthians 5:21), so He could be the unblemished, substitute Lamb of God for the sins of the world. Jesus, the *Son of Mary*, came to His own people—the Israelites—but they did not receive Him (see John 1:11). Even some members of His family were blinded to who He was (see 7:5). When Jesus preached to the people of His hometown Nazareth, "they were offended at Him" (Mark 6:3). What is your response to Jesus? Will you be His disciple; will you live blamelessly for Him?

Jesus, I believe You were 100 percent human, born of Mary; yet
You are 100 percent God. Thank You for becoming human so You could
understand us. I worship You, and I will follow Your
example and strive to live godly.

Jesus, the *Son of Mary*, grew as a child and had favor with God and man (see Luke 2:52) Mary taught Him lessons that a mother teaches her child. Now He wants you to grow to please God as He did. "And the Child grew and became strong in spirit, filled with wisdom; and the grace of God was upon Him" (v. 40).

Jesus, I want You to live in my heart (see Galatians 2:20) to strengthen
me, so I can please the Father. Amen.

Reading: Mark 6:1-6
Key Thought: The human Jesus is your example of how to live.

THE TRINITY: THE LORD IS THERE (JEHOVAH SHAMMAH)

4

The city from that day shall be: THE LORD IS THERE [Jehovah Shammah].
EZEKIEL 48:35

The name *Jehovah Shammah* means the *Lord Is There*. The Lord is already in Heaven, where you will spend eternity. Ezekiel described the city where you shall live as *Jehovah Shammah*, a city of His presence. The most wonderful thing about Heaven is that the Lord will be there with you. *Jehovah Shammah* will meet you in the valley that has the shadow of death. From there, He'll take you to the other side. We fear what we can't see. So most fear death because they can't see the other side. But remember, a shadow can't hurt you; it can only make you hurt yourself. Don't forget the promise, "I'll be with you in the shadow of death" (see Psalm 23:4). You'll step into darkness and come out in the light on the other side. He'll be there with you because He's *Jehovah Shammah*. A shadow is the absence of light. The city where you're going—the Eternal City—is constantly bright because God is its light. There will be no night there, which means no shadows. Neither will there be sorrow or death. To get there, you will step into the shadow of death and come out on the other side with the Lord.

Lord, give me confidence to live for You on this side of death's shadow. Then help me step confidently through the shadow with You to the other side. There I'll be with You, and it will be eternal light. Amen.

Reading: Revelation 21:9-27
Key Thought: The Lord will be with you in both death and Heaven.

5 JESUS: OUR HIGH PRIEST

So also Christ did not glorify Himself to become High Priest, but it was He who said to Him: "You are My Son, today I have begotten You."
HEBREWS 5:5

There were many priests in the Old Testament assigned to small groups of people. Each priest was responsible to sacrifice for those under his care. Over all the priests was the high priest, who was responsible to sacrifice for the entire nation. On the Day of Atonement, the high priest offered a sacrifice for the whole nation. Jesus is our *High Priest* who sacrificed for the sins of the world (see 1 John 2:1-2). Human priests had to sacrifice first for their sins, before they could sacrifice for the nation. But Jesus was without sin. "We have a great High Priest who . . . was in all points tempted as we are, yet without sin" (Hebrews 4:14-15). So Jesus, the perfect *High Priest,* offered the perfect sacrifice for your sins.

Lord Jesus, I come to You for forgiveness. Thank You
for the perfect sacrifice for my sins.

Every time an Israelite sinned, he or she had to come back to sacrifice again because each sacrifice only took care of past sins. But the sacrifice of Jesus, our *High Priest,* is different. He doesn't have to make continual sacrifices for us (see Hebrews 9:24-25); Jesus died once "to put away sin by the sacrifice of Himself" (v. 26). Now "He is also able to save to the uttermost those who come to God through Him, since He always lives to make intercession for them" (7:25).

Lord Jesus, You are my High Priest who has taken away all my sins for-
ever. Now You live in Heaven for me. Amen.

Reading: Hebrews 5:5-10
Key Thought: Jesus, our *High Priest*, has forgiven all our sins once and for all.

6 ◆ JESUS: THE FINISHER OF OUR FAITH

Looking unto Jesus, the author and finisher of our faith, who for the joy that was set before Him endured the cross, despising the shame, and has sat down at the right hand of the throne of God.
HEBREWS 12:2

Jesus is the *Finisher of Our Faith*. If you are good at beginning new projects, but you are a poor finisher, look to Jesus, the *Finisher of Our Faith*. He completed salvation. The blood of Jesus completely forgave your sins; you now stand forgiven before God. Jesus finished everything you need for spiritual growth, but you must take advantage of His completed work. All the power you need to live the Christian life He supplied through the cross. Every advantage of eternal life is supplied to you through the sacrifice of His life for you. All the spiritual riches of the heavenlies are now available to you.

Jesus, thank You for finishing the work of salvation.

Jesus is the *Finisher of Our Faith*; there's nothing more He needs to do for you to go to Heaven. When He cried, "It is finished" (John 19:30), the plan of salvation was complete. The work of Messiah that was predicted in the Old Testament was ended. The task of satisfying God's wrath was done. He finished what was assigned to Him; there is nothing you can do to add to His work. But you must come boldly to His throne of grace to get help to live the Christian life (see Hebrews 4:16). You must run with patience the race that is set before you (see 12:1). He has finished His task; will you finish yours?

Jesus, You finished Your task, now help me finish my task. You have provided a completed plan of salvation; help me to take advantage of spiritual power that is mine in the Cross. Amen.

Reading: Mark 15:7-24
Key Thought: Jesus has finished everything you need for your salvation.

7 THE FATHER: GOD OUR FATHER

To all who are in Rome, beloved of God, called to be saints: Grace to you and peace from God our Father and the Lord Jesus Christ.
ROMANS 1:7

God Our Father, God is Your Father—He is the One who knows you personally and cares for you. When Paul used the phrase *"God Our Father,"* he was telling his readers that God was not like the idols in the temples of false religions. He was not callous and brittle; He had the warmth of a father. Just as an earthly father has emotional feelings for his children, the heavenly Father has deeper feelings because He has pure emotions of love and He desires to do good things for His children. You can never love Him with the same depth of feeling because you are finite and your heavenly Father is infinite.

O God My Father, I love You with all my heart, with all my soul and with all my mind (see Matthew 22:37). I worship You in Your greatness and praise You for Your personal care for me.

He is both God and your Father. Being a Father makes Him no less God than being the all-powerful Creator makes Him less personal. He is both Creator God and your personal Father. He is a Father who protects His children from evil. Will you let Him be your Protector today? He is a Father who provides for the needs of His children. Will you accept His provision today? He is a Father who instructs and guides. Will you listen to His direction today?

O God My Father, I have many needs; give me this day my daily bread. I will study Your Word; teach me Your desires. Amen.

Reading: Romans 1:1-12
Key Thought: The powerful Creator is also your Father who cares for you.

8   JESUS: THE SERPENT IN THE WILDERNESS

And as Moses lifted up the serpent in the wilderness, even so
must the Son of Man be lifted up.
JOHN 3:14

The serpent in the wilderness was a sign of the people's sin. It was a brass sculpture of a snake that was placed on a pole so all could see. Israel rebelled by speaking against God and Moses. The people were complaining, "There is no food and no water, and our soul loathes this worthless bread" (Numbers 21:5). Of all their sin, perhaps ingratitude was the worst, for the Lord had given them manna—bread from Heaven—and Israel called it "worthless bread." "So the LORD sent fiery serpents among the people, and they bit the people; and many of the people of Israel died" (v. 6). It was after the serpents began killing the people that they repented for their sin. God instructed Moses to make a brass serpent and put it on a pole. "Everyone who is bitten, when he looks at it, shall live" (v. 8), He declared. The snake was a sign of their sin, and looking at the serpent was an outward evidence of repentance. When Jesus was lifted up on the cross, Jesus became our sin (see 2 Corinthians 5:21). Just as Israel was saved from physical death when they looked upon the sign of their sin, so our looking upon Jesus is our looking on the sign of our sin.

Jesus, I thank You for becoming my sin in Your death for me.
Thank You that the poison of my sin does not destroy me as it did the
unbelieving Israelites in the wilderness. I look and live. Amen.

Reading: Numbers 21:1-9
Key Thought: Those who look on Jesus as their Sin Bearer will live.

9 JESUS: THE CHILD JESUS

The parents brought in [to the Temple] the Child Jesus. . . .
And the Child grew and became strong in spirit, filled with wisdom;
and the grace of God was upon Him.
LUKE 2:27-40

Jesus did not enter the world as a spirit; nor did He appear instantly, as an angel may appear. Jesus was supernaturally conceived of a virgin and was born nine months later. His development followed the growth pattern of other children: "And the Child grew and became strong in spirit, filled with wisdom" (Luke 2:40). His parents had to teach Him to walk and talk and develop motor skills. His parents brought the *Child Jesus* to the Temple to dedicate Him. Then at age 12, Jesus was brought into the Temple for His bar mitzvah and became a "son of the law." The parents of the *Child Jesus* raised Him according to the Scriptures, just as parents should raise children today. Jesus, the Son of God, was "born under the law, to redeem those who were under the law" (Galatians 4:4-5).

Lord Jesus, I marvel that You became a child and grew according
to the growth pattern of children. I praise You for becoming flesh to
redeem us who were under the Law.

God the Father sent the Son to become a child who would grow into manhood. God the Holy Spirit guided Jesus as an adult: "Jesus, being filled with the Holy Spirit, returned from the Jordan and was led by the Spirit into the wilderness. . . . Then Jesus returned in the power of the Spirit to Galilee" (Luke 4:1-14). Both the Father and the Holy Spirit were active in bringing Jesus to maturity.

Lord Jesus, You gave me a role model to follow; give me power to follow
Your example. You died for my sins; I worship You for salvation. Amen.

Reading: Luke 2:25-35
Key Thought: The *Child Jesus* was like us so that He could redeem us.

10 THE HOLY SPIRIT: THE HAND OF GOD

And I told them of the hand of my God which had been good upon me. . . . So they said, "Let us rise up and build." Then they set their hands to this good work.
NEHEMIAH 2:18

The Holy Spirit is the *Hand of God*. Just as a person can give you a hand when you need help, so the Holy Spirit can give you a hand. Let Him be the *Hand of God* that helps you today. He is nearby; all you need to do is ask for His help. But the Holy Spirit can't help you unless you want Him to; ask for Him, and allow Him to work in your life.

Holy Spirit, I need Your hand in my life. I need Your help today. Come help me now.

The *Hand of God* works for you in two ways. First, the Holy Spirit works directly in your life. When you pray for money, for a solution or for a healing, the *Hand of God* may give it directly to you. But the Holy Spirit also works indirectly, when people don't realize He's working. Did you notice in Nehemiah 2:18 that the Holy Spirit's hand was upon the work of building the wall in Jerusalem? The Holy Spirit worked when the people "set their hands to do this good work." God's hands work through your hands. Look at your hands and consider what your hands can do for God today. Yield your hands so that the Holy Spirit can work through you this day.

Holy Spirit, I yield my hands to You. I will work as hard as I can to accomplish Your will. I will use all my intellect and energy to complete all the jobs that I have to do today. Come use my hands as Your hands. Amen.

Reading: Nehemiah 1—2
Key Thought: The Holy Spirit can work directly or indirectly in your life.

JESUS: THE DAYSMAN BETWEEN US

Neither is there any daysman betwixt us, that might lay his hand upon us both.
JOB 9:33, KJV

Job was looking for a daysman to be a neutral arbitrator between God and him. A daysman is an umpire, an advocate or an impartial judge. God had removed the hedge of protection from Job, and Satan had stripped Job of his family, possessions and health. In Job 9:27-31, Job suggested that no matter how hard he had tried to vindicate himself, nothing worked. He wanted someone who was neutral to judge between God and him. Job wanted someone who was powerful enough to be separate from God and to stand against Him. Of course, such a thing would be impossible unless the daysman were equal to God or, as in this case, were God Himself. Jesus is the *Daysman* who stands equal with the Father and yet stands for Job. Jesus is our *Daysman* who takes our case and pleads it to the Father.

Jesus, thank You for taking my side when I didn't deserve anything. Jesus, thank You for being my Arbitrator with the Father.

Jesus is the *Daysman* because He is equal with the Father, yet He came to Earth to take on flesh. He lived in our shoes, so He understands our weaknesses. Because Jesus died to forgive our sins, He now stands between the Father and us. He asks the Father to forgive us because He has paid the ransom for our sins. Jesus the *Daysman* asks the Father to receive us into Heaven and to make us His child.

Jesus, thank You for being my Mediator. Thank You for going to the Father to plead my case. Amen.

Reading: Job 9:21-35
Key Thought: Jesus is the neutral Umpire who gets the heavenly Father to accept us.

12 ◆ JESUS: PRINCE OF PEACE

For unto us a Child is born, unto us a Son is given; and the government will be upon His shoulder. And His name will be called . . . Prince of Peace.
ISAIAH 9:6

Jesus is the *Prince of Peace*. A prince is one who anticipates becoming a king who will rule sovereignly. One day Jesus will be the King of kings. (see Revelation 19:16). But now Jesus is the *Prince of Peace* who can secure your inner "peace with God" (Romans 5:1). Jesus is the *Prince of Peace* because He "made peace through the blood of His cross" (Colossians 1:20). Jesus is the *Prince of Peace* who can take away your fears and give you inner confidence. He can meet the deepest needs of the human heart because He is Peace and He gives peace. He is "the peace of God, which surpasses all understanding" (Philippians 4:7). He can guard your hearts and minds so that you won't lose the peace you now have in Him.

Lord, take away the strife in my life. Come fill my life with Your presence and let Your peace flood my thinking. I claim peace and contentment for this day.

There are wars and rumors of wars among nations and strife among people because each person is ruled by selfish interest. One day Jesus will rule all people, and they will want to please Him, not themselves. The *Prince of Peace* will bring what the angels promised at His birth: "On earth peace, goodwill toward men" (Luke 2:14).

Lord, I pray that Your kingdom will come and that You will rule on Earth, as You now rule in Heaven. But until that day comes, may Your peace control my life and work. Amen.

Reading: Isaiah 11
Key Thought: We have peace when Jesus rules our hearts.

THE TRINITY: THE LORD OF HOSTS (JEHOVAH SABAOTH)

13

The LORD of hosts is with us; the God of Jacob is our refuge.
PSALM 46:11

The *Lord of Hosts* is *Jehovah Sabaoth*. His title "Sabaoth" means "a host ready to serve or ready to fight." The Lord is ready to help you today; He knows about your problems. They do not catch Him by surprise. He is *Jehovah Sabaoth*, ready to come to your defense. *"Jehovah Sabaoth"* can be translated "the God of the fighting angels." The Lord has a numberless company of "ministering spirits" (Hebrews 1:14) who will defend you from the Evil One. He can dispatch them to your assistance, "for he orders his angels to protect you wherever you go. They will hold you with their hands" (Psalm 91:11-12, *NLT*). However, you must ask for help and trust Him when He comes alongside to fight for you.

O Lord of Hosts, give me wisdom to know what to do, and give me courage to face my troubles. Help me win over them. O Lord of Hosts, come quickly with Your fighting angels to defend me. The Enemy has almost overwhelmed me. I need You right here, right now.

You have heavenly power available to you. Don't focus your eyes on the Enemy or on your weakness. If you do that, you will get discouraged and fail. Look to the *Lord of Hosts—Jehovah Sabaoth—*for your strength. He can give you victory.

Jehovah Sabaoth, come with Your fighting angels to give me victory over the world, the flesh and the Devil. I believe in Your power and trust Your protection. Amen.

Reading: Psalm 24
Key Thought: The Lord is ready to help you win over your troubles.

14 ◇ JESUS: RESURRECTION

*Jesus said to her, "I am the resurrection and the life. He who believes
in Me, though he may die, he shall live."*
JOHN 11:25

Jesus is your *Resurrection*, which means that He gave new life to you when
you were saved. You can know that Jesus gave this eternal life to you
when He came out of the grave, because He said, "I am the resurrection."
Now you are raised in Jesus; you will live forever. Your old body may die
at your death (if the Rapture doesn't come first), but your soul goes to
live with God. At the Rapture, your soul will be rejoined to your new glorious body. One day you'll have a new body like Christ's.

*Lord of the resurrection, thank You for saving me. Thank You
for the promise of raising me in the future.*

When Jesus died, your sin died with Him. When Jesus arose from the
dead, you were in Him, rising from the dead. Jesus is the *Resurrection*.
Now you are in Him, and He is in you (see John 14:20). You are seated in
the heavenlies (see Ephesians 2:6). So let your life on Earth reflect your
new heavenly position. Because Jesus is the *Resurrection*, His life-giving
power can indwell you and give you new desires to live a godly life.
Because Jesus is the *Resurrection*, you can be strengthened in your inner
person by His indwelling presence (see 3:16). Because of Jesus' resurrection, He can give you spiritual victory today.

*Lord, I marvel at Your resurrection and worship You for what you've
done for me. I claim Your resurrection power to help me live for You this
day. Help me overcome my problems and be victorious today. Amen.*

Reading: John 11:1-44
Key Thought: You can be victorious because of Jesus' resurrection.

15 ▸ JESUS: OUR PASSOVER

Therefore purge out the old leaven, that you may be a new lump, since you truly are unleavened. For indeed Christ, our Passover, was sacrificed for us.
1 CORINTHIANS 5:7

Jesus is our *Passover*. Once each year, Jewish families celebrated their deliverance from Egypt by eating a special Passover meal and by sacrificing a lamb to make atonement for the sins of the family. The father would place his hands on the head of the lamb to confess the sins of the family members. That was symbolic of transferring the family sins to the lamb; then the blood of the lamb was shed, a prototype of Jesus' becoming the Lamb of God to take away our sin. Jesus became the fulfillment of the Passover. The lamb had to be perfect, without blemish, which is a picture of the perfect life of Jesus. Because Jesus did not sin, He was qualified to take away the sin of the world. (see John 1:29; 1 Peter 2:22).

*Jesus, You are my Passover Lamb; You became sin for me
(see 2 Corinthians 5:21), and Your blood is the basis for my forgiveness.
Jesus, I praise You for Your sacrificial death. Thank You for dying
for me and for the world.*

Jesus is your *Passover.* Just as each Jewish family looked back in gratitude for deliverance from the death angel that passed over their home, you should look back in gratitude that judgment has passed over you. Then you should look forward to the return of Jesus to take you home to live with Him. His future coming is just as sure as His past sacrificial death. You can have faith in both of them.

*Lord, I look back and remember Your death, and I look forward,
waiting for Your return. Amen.*

Reading: Exodus 12:1-13
Key Thought: The benefits of Passover are ours because of Jesus.

16 ◆ THE FATHER: ONE GOD AND FATHER

One God and Father of all, who is above all, and through all, and in you all.
EPHESIANS 4:6

There is *One God and Father* of all people. Many people deny God's existence, reject His invitation to salvation or even refuse to recognize Him; but the God of the Bible is still the only God powerful enough to create the universe yet loving enough to redeem fallen mankind. But God is not just the Father of those who believe in Him; He is the Father of all. He created mankind and gave life to all. As the *One God and Father* of all, He wants a relationship with those He created. He's a Father who loves all and wants all to come to Him. He's a Father who loves to give gifts to His children. He wants to protect them, guide them, teach them and enjoy them. Let God be your Father today.

Father, I need Your presence in my life. Teach me how to be a good child.

God is the Father of all, even to those who refuse to recognize His ownership of the world and His authority over their lives. Those who reject God's ownership of their lives will be punished in the last Day of Judgment. It is then that all—saved and unsaved—will recognize Him as the *One God and Father*, but then it will be too late. So today, recognize His control over your life, because the one God of the universe is also your personal Father.

O God, help me understand that You are the powerful Creator of the universe, yet You are as intimate to me as a father. Help me understand Your greatness, and yet enjoy intimacy with You.

Reading: Deuteronomy 6:1-5
Key Thought: The sovereign God of the universe can be as intimate to you as a father.

17 ◆ JESUS: MY BELOVED SON

*And suddenly a voice came from heaven, saying, "This is My
beloved Son, in whom I am well pleased."*
MATTHEW 3:17

Jesus is the *Beloved Son* of the Father. When Jesus was baptized, the Father spoke from Heaven, "This is My beloved Son" (Matthew 3:17). The heavenly Father could have called Jesus Mary's son or Joseph's son, because these descriptions would have been accurate. But Jesus is the unique Son of the Father in Heaven, i.e., the second Person of the Godhead. Just as Jesus is the Beloved of the Father's *Beloved Son*, so He should become your Beloved.

*Jesus, just as the Father said that You belong to Him, I too claim
You as my own. You are my Savior, and I am Your servant.
Help me carry out Your purpose today.*

The Father spoke audibly to the crowd when John baptized Jesus. That was the formal induction of Jesus into ministry. The Father was telling the world that He approved of Jesus' baptism and His ministry in the world. The Holy Spirit also came upon Jesus to show the total approval of the Godhead. The heavenly Father called Jesus Beloved. The Father had always loved Jesus throughout eternity, but the Father especially loved Jesus because He became flesh as the divine representation to the world. Because the Father loves the world, He especially loved Jesus for coming to redeem the world.

*Jesus, I accept You as the Beloved Son of the Father. Thank You for
becoming flesh to live among humanity and to die for our sins. Today,
live through my life, so I can show salvation to everyone I meet. Amen.*

Reading: Mark 1:1-11
Key Thought: Jesus is the *Beloved Son* of the Father.

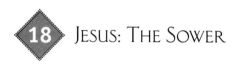

18 ◆ JESUS: THE SOWER

> *Behold, a sower went out to sow. . . . He who sows the good*
> *seed is the Son of Man.*
> MATTHEW 13:3-37

Jesus is the *Sower* of the seed of the Word of God into the hearts of people. Yet, the *Sower* in the parable is an application of every Christian who spreads God's Word. There is no contradiction, because Jesus sows the gospel through His believers. Jesus loves all because He sows the seed on all kinds of ground: He sows on the hard-hearted, wayside hearts. He sows on the shallow, rocky-soil heart. He sows on the thorn-infested, sinful hearts. And He sows into the good ground of receptive hearts. How receptive is your heart?

> *Jesus, give me a receptive heart to receive and believe Your Word.*
> *Forgive me for when I was not quick to seek Your presence or when I*
> *was slow to believe.*

The *Sower* must choose seed to match the soil. Just as peanuts should be planted in soft, sandy soil (not thick, clay soil), so Jesus sows a judgmental message against sin to break a hard heart. Jesus sometimes sows a tender message of forgiveness to mend a broken heart. Just as seeds planted too closely together will choke out sunlight and seeds planted too far apart will reduce profits, so Jesus knows how often and how long the gospel message must be presented. Jesus, the *Sower,* knows how and when to plant, as well as how and when to harvest.

> *Jesus, I've tried to reach others but have not been as successful*
> *as I could be. Teach me how to sow the gospel into others,*
> *and teach me how to harvest. Amen.*

Reading: Matthew 13:1-23
Key Thought: Jesus sows the gospel through us.

THE HOLY SPIRIT: THE DOWN PAYMENT

The Holy Spirit of Promise is the down payment on our inheritance until God redeems us at the Rapture as the possession He has purchased.
SEE EPHESIANS 1:13-14

The Holy Spirit is the *Down Payment* that guarantees you will one day be redeemed from corruption. So, don't give up and don't get discouraged. Every time you feel the Holy Spirit working in your life, realize you aren't forgotten. Your spiritual happiness is only a foretaste of the joy to come. That's a promise of the Holy Spirit.

Lord, I know I am Your child because You work in my life in so many ways. You enlighten me, You guide me, You give me spiritual gifts, and You give me assurance. Thank You for these down payments, which guarantee greater future blessings to me.

The Holy Spirit is the *Down Payment* of what you will experience once you get to Heaven. Right now you get satisfaction from eating the Bread of life and drinking the Water of life. Think of the unimaginable happiness you'll experience in Heaven. Your future experiences in Heaven will be as real as your present experiences on this earth. The Holy Spirit is the earnest money that guarantees a future delivery on what God has promised. If you ever doubt the realities of Heaven, just look within your heart to the work of the Holy Spirit. He will do for you in the future (when you get to Heaven) what He has done for you in the past.

Lord, help me look beyond the mundane issues of this life to see the spiritual realities You have for me. Lord, help me live confidently, because You are my Guarantee for blessings to come. Amen.

Reading: 2 Corinthians 1:18-22
Key Thought: The Holy Spirit is your Guarantee of Heaven.

20 JESUS: THE STONE WHICH THE BUILDERS REJECTED

The stone which the builders rejected has become the chief cornerstone.
PSALM 118:22

Jesus is the chief Cornerstone of God's plan, but He is also the *Stone Which the Builders Rejected*. There are many reasons why the world rejects Jesus. Some are spiritually blind (see 2 Corinthians 4:3-4); they can't see who Jesus is. Some are hard-hearted; "they willingly are ignorant" (2 Peter 3:5, *KJV*). Some love their sin and won't give it up to receive Jesus. How will you choose?

> *Lord, I receive You even though others reject You. I willingly believe in You when the world rejects Your claims in their lives.*

Jesus came to His people—the Jewish people—but they rejected His claims of deity. They charged Jesus with blasphemy at His trial. He offered them salvation (see Matthew 4:17); but they charged Him with treason (see John 19:12), saying that Jesus wanted to be king in place of Caesar. "He came to His own, and His own did not receive Him" (1:11). But the unbelief of that day is no different from that of those who reject Him today. The unbelieving heart will not receive Jesus, because "men [love] darkness rather than light, because their deeds [are] evil" (3:19). Jesus is the *Stone Which the Builders Rejected*. Will you build your life on Him?

> *Lord, I will not deny You, no matter how the world reacts. I will build on You, the Stone. You are my Master and Lord. Amen.*

Reading: Psalm 118
Key Thought: You must receive Jesus even though the world rejects Him.

21 ◆ JESUS: THE SON OF DAVID

And when he heard that it was Jesus of Nazareth, he began to cry out and say,
"Jesus, Son of David, have mercy on me!"
MARK 10:47

Jesus is the *Son of David*, His human ancestry and authority for ministry. God the Father had promised David that his son would sit eternally on the throne. Jesus was born to fulfill that prediction. Therefore, Jesus had authority that was originally given to David. Blind Bartimaeus recognized that Jesus could help him, so he called Him, first, Jesus (Jesus' name and address) and, second, *Son of David* (Jesus' legal name) (Mark 10:47). Jesus healed Bartimaeus because of his faith. Do you have faith to call out to Him for your need today?

Jesus, Son of David, I call out to You. I cannot make it
through this day without You. Come heal my spiritual blindness;
help me see Your path for me this day.

Jesus is the *Son of David*; He can meet your need this day. But realize there will be opposition to your faith, just as there were individuals who tried to quiet Bartimaeus when he cried out for help. But Bartimaeus would not be quieted; he cried out even louder. Jesus was motivated by the faith of Bartimaeus to give him help. Do you have that kind of faith that would motivate God to help you? If you do, Jesus will say to you what He said to Bartimaeus: "Your faith has made you well" (Mark 10:52).

Jesus, You are the Son of David. One day You will rule the world from
David's throne. Today, I need You to rule my life from the throne of my
heart. Like Bartimaeus, I need You; come help me today. Amen.

Reading: Mark 10:46-52
Key Thought: Jesus wants to rule your life.

22 ▸ JESUS: THE FIRSTFRUITS

But now Christ is risen from the dead, and has become the
firstfruits of those who have fallen asleep.
1 CORINTHIANS 15:20

The Jews brought an offering to God during the Feast of Firstfruits. It was the first they harvested. Some even say they gave God the first (in quality) from their first harvest (in sequence). God was given the best of their lives and God was put first in their lives. They brought the first-fruits on Sunday, the first day of the week (see Leviticus 23:9-10). There is a lesson to us; we ought to give God the first of our time (Sunday), the first of our energy (early), the first of our money (tithes) and make Him the *Firstfruits,* first in every part of our lives.

Jesus, I give You first place in my schedule, in my
strength and in my love.

The Jewish nation was called a firstfruits offering to God out of all the nations of the earth (see Jeremiah 2:3). The first converts in a new church were called firstfruits (see Romans 16:5). When the 144,000 arrived in Heaven, they were the firstfruits of martyrs to be offered to God (see Revelation 14:4). When Jesus was raised from the dead on the first Easter Sunday morning, He was the *Firstfruits* of the dead (see 1 Corinthians 15:20,23). When the Jews brought a firstfruits offering to God, it was a promise that there was more to follow. When Jesus was raised as the *Firstfruits* of the dead, it was a promise that all who were in Christ would also be raised.

Lord, I don't offer You things or money or time; I give myself to You as a
sacrifice of firstfruits. Be glorified in me. Amen.

Reading: Deuteronomy 26:1-11
Key Thought: God always wants to be first in our lives.

23 ▷ JESUS: THE BELOVED

To the praise of the glory of His grace, by which He made us accepted in the Beloved.
EPHESIANS 1:6

Jesus is the *Beloved*, the object of His Father's love. Throughout His life on the earth, Jesus acknowledged His Father's love for Him (see John 3:35; 5:20; 17:23). And in return, His Father said, "This is My beloved Son" (Matthew 3:17). Jesus could not have done what He did without the Father's love and support. Now Jesus wants to teach you His love.

You are my Beloved Lord Jesus; I love You. The most important
focus in my life is to love You with all of my heart and soul and strength.
How can I love You more?

Jesus is your *Beloved*; and because you are in Him, you are "accepted in the Beloved" (Ephesians 1:6). When the Father loves Jesus, He also loves you, because Jesus said, "You [are] in Me, and I in you" (John 14:20). Therefore, every benefit Jesus has with the Father is yours. So let the knowledge of His love deepen your love for Him. When you know that the Father loves you, you will begin to conform to His desires and to do the things He wants to do. When you begin to live in His love, you will get a passion to love others as the Father and Jesus love you.

O my Beloved, I accept Your love to me. I yield my life to
be filled with Your presence. Let Your love flow to me
and through me to others. Amen.

Reading: Ephesians 1:1-12
Key Thought: You are loved as much as Jesus is loved by the Father.

24 ◆ JESUS: THE HOPE OF ISRAEL

Because for the hope of Israel I am bound with this chain.
ACTS 28:20

Jesus is the *Hope of Israel*. God's people—the Jewish people—have suffered throughout history. Because God has promised to bless the people of Israel, the Evil One hates them, because he hates God. The Jews have been targeted for persecution by many human enemies: Nebuchadnezzar, Haman, Adolph Hitler, just to name a few. The Evil One has used human instruments against them, like King Herod, who tried to destroy Jesus as a baby. But in spite of everything, Jesus is still the *Hope of Israel*. He died to forgive the sins of the world, including the sins of the Jews.

> *Lord Jesus, I marvel at the scope of history. You were born
> into this world to a Jewish virgin and grew up in a Jewish
> home and lived in the Jewish culture. In spite of all that
> Satan has done, You are still the Hope of Israel.*

Jesus will be the *Hope of Israel* in the future. There is coming a future tribulation aimed at the people of Israel, but Jesus will return to save them and all those who believe in Him. In that future day, He'll still be the *Hope of Israel*. Just as Jesus is their Hope, He is also your Hope. Look to Him today.

> *Lord, not only are You the Hope of Israel, You are my Hope. You
> have come to help me through many trials in the past. I trust You for
> continual deliverance in the future. Amen.*

Reading: Genesis 12:1-3
Key Thought: Jesus is both your Hope and the *Hope of Israel*.

25 THE FATHER: THE WITNESS OF GOD

If we receive the witness of men, the witness of God is greater; for this is the witness of God which He has testified of His Son.
1 JOHN 5:9

The *Witness of God* was the words the Father spoke at the baptism of Jesus: "This is My beloved Son, in whom I am well pleased" (Matthew 3:17; 17:5). The Father wanted everyone to know that He sent Jesus into the world and that He approved what Jesus did. But the Jewish leaders wouldn't believe that it was the Father who had spoken. They rejected His witness. Today, the Father speaks in many ways, including through the Scriptures. But many people won't believe His witness any more now than the Jewish leaders did while Jesus was on Earth. Yet, the *Witness of God* is still true; the Father is pleased with all Jesus was and accomplished.

Jesus, because I am pleased with all You've done for me, I worship You.
I cry, "Worthy is the Lamb" (Revelation 5:12).

The Father has witnessed to Jesus. Are you willing to do the same thing? Will you witness to those around you about Jesus? The Bible commands, "You shall be witnesses to Me [Jesus]" (Acts 1:8). Just as some did not believe what the Father had spoken, so some will not listen to you. But you must witness about Jesus anyway, because the message about Him is true. Witnesses tell what they have seen, heard and experienced. That's what you must do; tell others how Jesus has changed your life.

Jesus, I will witness for You today. I will tell people how You
saved me and how You constantly guide me. Without You, I would
not have a life worth living. Amen.

Reading: 1 John 5:1-13
Key Thought: You should witness to others about Jesus.

26 JESUS: THE FOUNDATION WHICH IS LAID

*For no other foundation can anyone lay than that
which is laid, which is Jesus Christ.*
1 CORINTHIANS 3:11

Some young people today ask, "WWJD?" (What Would Jesus Do?). There is no other foundation on which anyone can build a life than on the example of Jesus' life. There is no other foundation for salvation than Jesus' death. Now He stands in Heaven at the right hand of the Father as your Intercessor. He pleads forgiveness for your sins and asks for help for you to resist temptations. Jesus is the Foundation upon which you now relate to God the Father. Will you build your life upon Him?

*Jesus, I build my life upon Your teaching, for no one else gives me
truth. I stake my salvation upon Your death, for You are the
only forgiveness of sin. I live my life in the power of Your indwelling,
for You are my only protection against evil.*

Jesus is the *Foundation Which Is Laid*. He has done everything for you that needs to be done. When He cried, "It is finished," on the cross, He completed salvation for you and for all who call upon His name. Salvation has been completed, and the Foundation is now laid. Your responsibility is to build your Christian life on that solid Foundation. You can trust Him, for the Foundation is trustworthy.

*Jesus, I will look beyond my doubts and fears. I will stand securely
upon the Foundation Which Is Laid; I rest securely in You. I will look to
You as my example; I will live for You as my Lord. Amen.*

Reading: 1 Corinthians 3
Key Thought: Jesus is the Foundation for a successful life.

27 JESUS: THE KING ETERNAL

Now to the King eternal, immortal, invisible, to God who alone is wise,
be honor and glory forever and ever. Amen.
1 TIMOTHY 1:17

Jesus is the *King Eternal*. Just as an earthly king rules his kingdom through his laws, so Jesus rules the universe by His laws. Jesus controls the natural world through natural laws, and He allows earthly rulers to control the social and political life of people through their judicial laws. Jesus recognizes earthly judicial laws and calls on all people to obey them (see Romans 13:1-7). Jesus controls the spiritual world through spiritual laws; it is through these laws that He wants to direct your life.

Lord, be my King; I want You to direct my life. Come sit
upon the throne of my heart to rule it.

Jesus is the *King Eternal*. He has always ruled the universe. Look at one of His natural laws, such as the law of gravity; break this law and you'll suffer the consequences. Because He allows the Evil One to act contrary to His spiritual laws does not mean that Jesus is not in control. He wants all people to serve Him out of love, not coercion. Those who choose to follow Jesus will be rewarded. Those who reject His rule will be punished. Today, Jesus is Lord of those who yield to Him; but in the future "every knee should bow, . . . every tongue should confess that Jesus Christ is Lord" (Philippians 2:10-11). Will you recognize Him today?

Lord Jesus, I bow to worship You as my King. I accept Your rule
upon this earth and will serve You gladly. Amen.

Reading: Romans 13:1-7
Key Thought: Jesus wants to rule your life as your King.

28 THE HOLY SPIRIT: THE BREATH OF THE LORD

The grass withers, the flower fades, because the breath of the LORD
blows upon it; surely the people are grass.
ISAIAH 40:7

The Holy Spirit is the *Breath of the Lord*; He breathes life into all living things. It is the *Breath of the Lord* that determines how long each thing shall live. This means that it is the Spirit's breath that determines when things will die. Originally, He breathed a life cycle into every kind of tree, plant and grass. And through intermediate forces—wind, cold and nature's forces—it is the Spirit's breath that determines when each dies. The Spirit has breathed a life cycle of 70 years into the normal human body; and by reason of strength, some live into their 80s or beyond (see Psalm 90:10). The Spirit knows the length of the days of your life, but you'll not know which is the last day. So live this day to its fullest potential; live for God.

Holy Spirit, I accept each day You give, and I will live each
one as though it is my last. I'll live this day to the fullest. May
I glorify You throughout this day.

The Holy Spirit is the *Breath of the Lord,* so He gives you the Lord's life. Since the Lord lives forever, He gives eternal life to those who believe in Christ. Since the Lord is holy, He helps you live a holy life. Since the Lord is righteous, He gives you the Spirit to do the right things.

Holy Spirit, breathe on me. Renew Your life in me so that I'll rise up to
shake off the chains that keep me from doing Your will. Amen.

Reading: Isaiah 40:1-11
Key Thought: The Holy Spirit gives life to all living things.

[handwritten: I WILL HAVE TO GIVE AN ACCOUNT OF MY FAITHFULNESS & WORKS]

29 JESUS: THE JUDGE OF THE LIVING AND THE DEAD

And He commanded us to preach to the people, and to testify that it is He who was ordained by God to be Judge of the living and the dead.
ACTS 10:42

Jesus is the *Judge of the Living and the Dead*. This means that He is the Judge of believers and nonbelievers, those who are living and those already dead. Those who believe in Jesus are saved (they have eternal life); and those who don't believe in Him are dead in trespasses and sins (see Ephesians 2:1). Jesus will judge believers to give them their rewards, and He will judge the unsaved to determine their punishment (see Revelation 20:11-12). Jesus is the Judge of all people; none can escape His scrutiny. Because you believe in Him, your sins have been forgiven. Jesus will not punish you in judgment, but you will have to give an account of your faithfulness and works (see 1 Corinthians 3:12-17).

> *Lord, thank You for eternal life. Help me to serve You faithfully so that I can look forward to seeing You, not to receive Your anger, but to receive Your rewards.*

Jesus is the *Judge of the Living and the Dead;* no one can escape His judgment throne. Some think that only those living when He returns will be judged. No, Jesus will raise all the dead to appear before Him with the living. He is the Judge of all souls in the universe; no one will be exempt. Plead His mercy today, so you won't meet His anger in the future.

> *Lord, I know You have judged my sins on the cross; in appreciation I worship You. I know You will judge all unsaved people, so in gratitude I thank You for salvation. I know all people will appear before You; I am not perfect, so I will be judged. My only plea is Your righteousness. Amen.*

Reading: Acts 10:34-43
Key Thought: Jesus will judge all people, both saved and unsaved.

[handwritten margin, right side: Am I worthy of this (Kingship?) WHAT CAN HE SAY ABOUT ME, ONE DAY]

[handwritten bottom: WE WILL ALL BE JUDGED]

JESUS IS THE MEDIATOR BETWEEN ME + GOD!

30 JESUS: THE MAN CHRIST JESUS

*For there is one God and one Mediator between God and
men, the Man Christ Jesus.*
1 TIMOTHY 2:5

Jesus was human because He was born of the virgin Mary. He is the *Man Christ Jesus*; therefore He understands your desires and dreams, and He knows the weaknesses of the human body. He knows what it means to be tired; He suffered on Calvary until He lost consciousness. You do not have any natural human weakness that Jesus doesn't understand. Therefore, the *Man Christ Jesus* can intercede to the Father for you. He can ask for help for your weaknesses. Because Jesus is a man, He can be your Mediator.

*Christ Jesus, I come to You as my Mediator. You know my
weaknesses and You understand my failures; ask the Father to give me
strength to stand against temptation. You understand my dreams and
ambitions; help me reach my life goals.*

Jesus is the *Man Christ Jesus*. When the title "Christ" appears before the human name "Jesus," it emphasizes His work on the cross as our Redeemer. When the name "Jesus" appears first, it emphasizes the man who died on the cross. So in today's verse, the *Man Christ Jesus* stands at the right hand of the Father as your Intercessor and Mediator (see Hebrews 7:24-25). He is pleading with the Father to forgive your sins. Confess all your sins now and ask for forgiveness, because the *Man Christ Jesus* is interceding to the Father for you.

*Christ Jesus, I come asking for forgiveness of sins. Be my
Mediator with the Father for me. Cleanse me and make me
useable to serve You this day. Amen.*

Reading: 1 Timothy 2:1-7
Key Thought: The *Man Christ Jesus* is your effective Mediator to the Father.

[handwritten: HELP ME To SERVE you FAITHFULLY!!]

31 THE TRINITY: THE FAITHFUL GOD (*EL EMUNAH*)

Therefore know that the LORD your God, He is God, the faithful God who keeps covenant and mercy for a thousand generations with those who love Him and keep His commandments.

DEUTERONOMY 7:9

[handwritten: willing sacrifice to each other]

The Lord is *El Emunah*, the faithful God of the future. Some people make gods with their hands and worship them. But idols are not able to do anything that God can do. They can't think, feel or act. But the Lord in Heaven knows all about you, thinks of you and loves you. The Lord has promised to guide you, protect you and work all things together for His own good (see Romans 8:28). Because the Father is the *Faithful God*, He will keep His promises. The Lord is *El Emunah*, the *Faithful God* of the past. He was faithful to bless His people when they kept past covenants, and He was faithful to punish them when they disobeyed His commandments. You can see His faithfulness when He judged His people, and you can see His faithfulness when He forgave them of their sins. As the Father has been faithful to Israel, so He will be faithful to you. Because of His mercies, we are not destroyed. His compassion is new every morning. Great is His faithfulness (see Lamentations 3:22-23). The Lord is *El Emunah*, the *Faithful God* of the present. Your present is grounded in God's past; because He has faithfully kept His word in the past, He will be faithful to you today.

Lord, forgive me when I doubt Your Word and don't believe Your promises. Thank You for Your reminder that You're El Emunah—the Faithful God. Help me to walk confidently today and to serve You faithfully. Amen.

Reading: Deuteronomy 7
Key Thought: You can trust God today because He was faithful in the past.

[handwritten: My present is grounded in Christ's past. He has remained faithful & has kept His promise to me.]

APRIL

JESUS: THE LORD OF PEACE

Now may the Lord of peace Himself give you peace always in every way.
2 THESSALONIANS 3:16

Jesus is the *Lord of Peace*. As Lord, He is Master, so Jesus is the Master of peace. His nature is peace, so when He awoke in a boat in the middle of a violent storm, Jesus commanded the winds, "Peace, be still" (Mark 4:39). When Jesus died on the cross for your sins, He made peace between God and sinners. Now, because of Jesus, you can have peace with God (see Romans 5:1). Since you are a Christian, Jesus can calm your fears and soothe your anxieties. He can give you the peace of God (see Philippians 4:7). Do you need peace in your heart today?

Lord, I come to You. Thank You for saving me and giving me
peace with God. Thank You for living in my heart to give me the peace
of God. Come be the Master of my heart.

Jesus is the *Lord of Peace*. No other religious leader can give peace as Jesus gives, because peace of heart doesn't come from humans; it comes from God. No activity can give heart peace, unless it has Jesus as its focus. Money, fame and earthly power cannot give you peace in this life or in the life to come. If you want contentment, satisfaction and deep inner joy, come to Jesus. He is the *Lord of Peace*.

Lord Jesus, I need Your peace to settle my fears for this day.
Take control of my thinking and settle my mind. Help me look
at life through Your perspective. Amen.

Reading: Ephesians 2:11-22
Key Thought: Jesus can give you peace because He is the *Lord of Peace*.

JESUS: THE LORD OF GLORY

*None of the rulers of this age knew; for had they known, they
would not have crucified the Lord of glory.*
1 CORINTHIANS 2:8

Jesus is the *Lord of Glory*.; He left Heaven and its glories to be born as a babe in Bethlehem. Heaven was magnified by the presence of Jesus, but He gave up its luster and glory to be born in a humble stable and to be part of a poor family. When He left the side of the Father to come to Earth, He was the Lord *from* Glory. He gave it all up because of His love for fallen humanity. Jesus is the *Lord of Glory* who came to die for the world.

*Jesus, thank You for giving up Your heavenly home to come
to Earth for sinners. Thank You for giving up Your glory to
suffer the agonies of Calvary for me.*

Jesus left the glories of Heaven, knowing He would return. The night before He died, Jesus prayed, "Glorify thou me with thine own self with the glory which I had with thee before the world was" (John 17:5, *KJV*). Jesus was the Lord *from* Glory, but when He returned to Heaven, He had more glory than when He left. Jesus had added His glorious victory over sin, death and the Evil One. Now, Jesus is truly the *Lord of Glory*. Jesus has more glory now than before He came to the world.

*Jesus, I want my life to add even more glory to You, for all You've
done for me. I can't fully understand Your love, but I accept it. I glorify
You because You alone are worthy of glory. Amen.*

Reading: Philippians 2:1-11
Key Thought: Jesus receives additional glory for His accomplishments on Calvary.

3 ◆ THE FATHER: OUR FATHER IN HEAVEN

When you pray, say: "Our Father in heaven, hallowed be Your name. Your
kingdom come. Your will be done on earth as it is in heaven."
LUKE 11:2

You should pray, *"Our Father in Heaven."* This is the phrase Jesus used to
teach you how to pray. Notice that He didn't use the singular possessive
pronoun "my." The plural possessive "our" includes Jesus and you. So
when you pray, "Our Father," you are coming to the Father with Jesus.
That means the Father will hear and answer your prayers because Jesus
is your Intercessor (see Hebrews 7:24-25). It also means you are coming
through the blood of Jesus' cross (see 4:14-16). Jesus is near to the
Father's heart, so when you pray "Our Father" with Jesus, you get immediate intimacy with the Father. By coming to the Father with Jesus, you
can be as close to the Father as Jesus is.

Our Father, I come to You with Jesus, so I pray, "Our Father, may Your
name be holy in my life today as Your name is revered in Heaven."

Because you were identified with Jesus in His death, burial and resurrection, you can pray "Our Father." Because you've invited Christ to
live in your heart, you can pray "Our Father" (see Ephesians 3:17). You
can have confidence when you come to the Father with Jesus.

Our Father in Heaven, rule Your kingdom from the throne
of my heart. May I obey Your will in my life today on Earth, as Your
will is obeyed in Heaven. Amen.

Reading: Luke 11:1-13
Key Thought: You must come with Jesus to the Father.

4 JESUS: THE LION OF THE TRIBE OF JUDAH

One of the elders said to me, "Do not weep. Behold, the Lion of the tribe of Judah,
the Root of David, has prevailed to open the scroll and to loose its seven seals."
REVELATION 5:5

Jesus is the *Lion of the Tribe of Judah*. He fulfilled the Old Testament prediction that the King-Messiah (see Genesis 49:8-9) would come from the tribe of Judah. Just as the lion is called the ruler of the jungle, so the lion symbol is used to describe earthly rulers. Jesus is pictured as a lion because He will rule all mankind. Let Him rule your heart and lead you to a better life.

Lord, come rule my heart, because I cannot rule it. Sometimes
I don't do the things I want to do, and sometimes I do the things
I don't want to do (see Romans 7:15).

Jesus is the *Lion of the Tribe of Judah* who will prevail in the future to open the book and loose the seals (see Revelation 5:5), so He can prevail against your unruly heart. He can rule your life and help you control your desires. He can keep you from excesses and lawlessness. But you must yield to Him so that He can control your life. Just as John was counseled not to weep because he couldn't open the book, so you shouldn't despair because of your weaknesses. Jesus is the *Lion of the Tribe of Judah*; He has strength to help control your life today.

Lord, I surrender my rebellious spirit to You, but I also want
You to give me the power to do the will of God. When I lack inner
strength and fortitude, I look to Your great strength. I yield to
Your rule for this day. Amen.

Reading: Revelation 5:1-5
Key Thought: Jesus can give you strength to control your weaknesses.

JESUS: THE LIGHT OF THE KNOWLEDGE OF THE GLORY OF GOD

For it is the God who commanded light to shine out of darkness,
who has shone in our hearts to give the light of the knowledge of the
glory of God in the face of Jesus Christ.
2 CORINTHIANS 4:6

Jesus is the *Light of the Knowledge of the Glory of God.* Just as the Father shined out of darkness to give the world physical light, so Jesus will shine into darkened hearts to give spiritual light concerning Himself and His kingdom. Those who are blinded by sin live in a darkened world. They can't find their way to Heaven; they live in a black, cold and threatening world. Blinded people are shut up to their own limited experience; they are lost and without hope. But Jesus came to give them the light of salvation. "[He] was the true Light which gives light to every man coming into the world" (John 1:9).

> *Lord, it feels good to live where there's spiritual light. I can see*
> *spiritual things because of You. You have shown me how to live and*
> *what will happen to me when I die. Your light is warm and*
> *comfortable, and I am confident of the future.*

Jesus is the *Light of the Knowledge of the Glory of God.* He shines light on unredeemed cultures, which are lost in the darkness of self-worship and greed. Jesus helps spiritually blinded people see the plan of salvation. He shines light on the pathway to guide His followers. He puts a fire in their souls to give them hope for eternity.

> *Lord, I love to walk in the Light, because I remember how*
> *awful I felt walking in darkness. I will walk in Your light for the*
> *rest of my life. Amen.*

Reading: 2 Corinthians 4
Key Thought: Jesus is the Light who shows people where to walk.

6 THE HOLY SPIRIT: THE FINGER OF GOD

Then the magicians said to Pharaoh, "This is the finger of God." But Pharaoh's heart grew hard, and he did not heed them.
EXODUS 8:19

The Holy Spirit is the *Finger of God*. He is the One used by the Father and Son to carry out divine work in the world. The Holy Spirit was the *Finger of God* that wrote the Ten Commandments on tablets of stone. He was the judgmental Finger that brought 10 plagues upon Egypt (see Exodus 8:16-19). He is the weather Finger that controls storms and drought. He can be the *Finger of God* to touch your life today. The Holy Spirit wants to direct your actions and control your destiny. With God's Finger, you can touch your world. Will you yield to the control of the Holy Spirit today?

Holy Spirit, touch me. Just as I touch things in this world, I want You to touch me today. Use me. Give me new purpose and new energy.

The *Finger of God* can touch you with power so you can do the will of the Father. The Holy Spirit is the *Finger of God* who can touch your circumstances to solve problems and put things in order. The *Finger of God* can point you in the direction you should go. Look to the Holy Spirit for direction; trust Him for spiritual power; and yield to His control.

*Holy Spirit, I need Your presence today. Come live in my body.
I want to touch You with my prayers, but most important, I want to touch You with my heart. Amen.*

Reading: Exodus 8:16-19; Luke 11:14-23
Key Thought: God uses the Holy Spirit to get things done.

JESUS: THE LIGHT OF THE GLORIOUS GOSPEL

*The god of this world hath blinded the minds of them which believe
not [the unsaved], lest the light of the glorious gospel of Christ, who is the
image of God, should shine unto them.*
2 CORINTHIANS 4:4, *KJV*

Jesus is the *Light of the Glorious Gospel.* Did you see those two words:
"Light" and "Glorious"? He is both the Light of the gospel and the Glory
of the gospel. In a world where people are blinded by sin and where people are lost in the blackness of eternal night, Jesus is the Light of salvation; He is the Light of the gospel.

*Lord Jesus, when I saw the Light, I believed. When the Light
appeared in my life, I followed it. Give me more illumination today
so that I'll know where to walk.*

Jesus is the Glory of the gospel. When the Shekinah glory cloud rested on the Ark of the Covenant, the priest had to leave the holy of holies
(see Exodus 40:35; 2 Chronicles 5:14). Humans couldn't remain in the
presence of the glory of God. Just as the Lord Jesus came to dwell among
Israel, now He comes to live in the lives of His people. It is through His
followers that He brings the light of the gospel to the world. It is not just
a dazzling light that God wants unsaved people to see. He wants to bring
the light of His presence into the hearts of unsaved people, so they can
believe the glorious gospel. Remember that Jesus said, "I am the light of
the world" (John 8:12).

*Lord Jesus, thank You for living in my heart. Shine Your light to
the world through me. I want to shine You, the Light of the Glorious
Gospel, to all people. Amen.*

Reading: 2 Corinthians 4:1-6
Key Thought: Jesus is the Light that gets people saved.

8   JESUS: THE ONLY BEGOTTEN OF THE FATHER

And the Word became flesh and dwelt among us, and we beheld His glory, the glory as of the only begotten of the Father, full of grace and truth.
JOHN 1:14

Jesus is the *Only Begotten of the Father,* which means He comes from the Father and is the unique personification of the Father. Jesus' being begotten of the Father means that He is the expression of the Father. John 1:14 emphasizes Jesus' characteristic of being "the Word," which means that the message and meaning of the Word reflects the Father. When the Father wants to make an utterance to the world, He does it through Jesus, the Word.

> *Lord Jesus, I come asking You to teach me what the Father in Heaven is like. I want to love the Father more than ever, but I must know Him better to love Him better.*

Jesus is the *Only Begotten of the Father,* which means that He is just like the Father. If you want to see what the Father is like, look at Jesus in the Scriptures. If you want to know how the Father relates to you, look at how Jesus related to people. If you want to approach the Father, go to Him through His Son. To know the Father better, know Jesus.

> *Lord Jesus, I look to You to see the Father. I know that the Father is loving, because I see how You loved people. I know the Father is powerful, because I see Your awesome power in creating the universe and in transforming individuals. I know the Father is kind and gentle, because You are patient with me and forgiving toward me. Amen.*

Reading: John 1:14-28
Key Thought: To better know the Father, learn about Jesus.

THE TRINITY: ALMIGHTY GOD (*EL SHADDAI*)

The LORD appeared to Abram and said to him, "I am Almighty God [El Shaddai]; walk before Me and be blameless."
GENESIS 17:1

The Lord is *Almighty God* (*El Shaddai*), a name that carries two opposite ideas—sympathy and power. The name *"El Shaddai"* means "the powerful One," but it also means "the tender One." The name "Almighty" comes from the Hebrew word *shad*, meaning "the breast," which is tender to nourish children. *El Shaddai* is tender to those who are hurting and needy. He tenderly listens to your problems, and He will comfort you. But remember, the chest is also the symbol of power and might. *El Shaddai* also has awesome power to solve problems. *El Shaddai* comes to you as He came to Abraham, asking you to trust and obey Him. *El Shaddai* is both tender to forgive your sin and powerful to deliver you from problems and oppression from sin.

> *El Shaddai, You are Almighty God. I confess and repent of my sins. Be powerful to forgive them through the blood of Christ (see 1 John 1:7), but also be tender to hold me close to Your amazing grace.*

The name "Almighty" means "all sufficiency." *El Shaddai* will be everything you need; trust Him and obey Him. Your needs or emergencies will not surprise Him. He has faced them before in others. He will comfort you in your pain when you cry to Him. But *El Shaddai* is also powerful; He can deliver you and give you victory. What do you need from Him today?

> *El Shaddai, I will be close to You. Be my intimate Companion to encourage me, and be my powerful God to provide for me. Amen.*

Reading: Genesis 17:1-8
Key Thought: *Almighty God* can comfort or deliver you.

10 ◆ JESUS: THE RIGHTEOUS JUDGE

Finally, there is laid up for me the crown of righteousness, which the Lord,
the righteous Judge, will give to me on that Day.
2 TIMOTHY 4:8

Jesus is the *Righteous Judge*. When you come into future judgment, He will not punish you for your sins, because He died for your sins. Your sins were judged on the cross (John 12:31-32; 16:11), and all your iniquities were covered by the blood. When you appear before the *Righteous Judge*, He will reward you for your faithfulness and service. Every good thing you've ever done will be evaluated by Him (see 1 Corinthians 3:13; 2 Corinthians 5:10). Then He'll give you your rewards, also called crowns (see James 1:12).

Lord, You are the Righteous Judge. Thank You for forgiveness of sins.
Thank You for mercy and grace. I don't deserve it, but I accept it.

The *Righteous Judge* will not make mistakes when He judges people at the end of this age. Because He is omnipotent, with all power, He can bring every person and all facts into His presence. Because He is omnipresent and omniscient, He knows all things; He understands everyone's actions and motivations. Because He is God, you can count on Him to be a *Righteous Judge*. Whereas some corrupt judges can be bribed on this earth, Jesus will give the right judgment in the right way. He will look at all the merits of your case when you appear before Him. You will get the appropriate rewards from the *Righteous Judge*.

Lord, I know You are righteous, so I rest securely in Your presence.
I know You will judge me rightly. Amen.

Reading: 2 Timothy 4:1-16
Key Thought: Jesus will give the right judgment in the right way.

JESUS: THE PRINCE OF THE KINGS OF THE EARTH

And from Jesus Christ, . . . the prince of the kings of the earth.
REVELATION 1:5, *KJV*

Jesus is the *Prince of the Kings of the Earth*. A prince is one who is waiting for the throne that he will formally assume in the future. Jesus is the Prince who will assume His throne at His second return. Then He'll be the King of kings and the Lord of lords (see Revelation 19:16). However, His future reign doesn't deny His present rulership in the hearts of His followers or His sovereignty in Heaven. He wants to sit on the throne of your heart.

Jesus, I pray, "Your kingdom come" (Matthew 6:10), for the future millennium. But for today, I want You to rule my heart.

Jesus is the *Prince of the Kings of the Earth*; but now, in His sovereign plan, He allows each earthly ruler to rule. Whereas many earthly leaders ignore Christ and violate His laws, still "the powers [rulers] that be are ordained of God" (Romans 13:1, *KJV*). Those who rebel at His authority will be punished when they stand before the judgment throne. Even when rulers rebel against God, He works His plans through them. Many rulers think that they're doing whatever they want, but the Bible teaches, "The king's heart is in the hand of the LORD; . . . He turns it wherever He wishes" (Proverbs 21:1).

Jesus, You have all power in Heaven and Earth. I marvel at Your patience and I praise You for working all things together for good to us who love You (see Romans 8:28). Amen.

Reading: John 17:1-19
Key Thought: Let Jesus rule your heart today, because one day He'll rule all things.

12 ◆ THE FATHER: MY FATHER

My Father, who has given them to Me, is greater than all; and no one is able
to snatch them out of My Father's hand. I and My Father are one.
JOHN 10:29-30

The Father has a special relationship to Jesus Christ: Jesus is His Son. We can never understand their relationship, because we are human. But we can enjoy the results of that relationship. Because Jesus and the Father are one and because you are in Christ and He is in you, you can have access to the Father through Jesus (see John 14:20; 15:4-5). You have great security because you are in Jesus. Jesus said, "I give them eternal life, and they will never perish. No one will snatch them away from me" (10:28, *NLT*).

Jesus called the Father *My Father*, reflecting a unique relationship (see 5:16-18). Jesus was closer to the Father's heart than anyone else, because the Father and Son were one (see 17:11,21). Yet because you are in Christ, you can be as close as Jesus is to the Father's heart.

I come to You, Father, because I am in Christ. I want to be as close to
You as Jesus is. Accept me and bless me because of Jesus.

Because Jesus referred to God as "*My Father*," so can you. God is your Father, who protects His children because they were given to Him by Christ. "I give them eternal life, and they will never perish. No one will snatch them away from me, for my Father has given them to me, and he is more powerful than anyone else. So no one can take them from me" (John 10:28-29, *NLT*).

Father, I rest confidently in Your presence, knowing that Jesus gave me
access to Your heart. Thank You for this peace. Amen.

Reading: John 10:22-39
Key Thought: You can be as close as Jesus is to the Father.

13 Jesus: The Only Wise God

*Now to the King eternal, immortal, invisible, to God who alone is wise,
be honor and glory forever and ever. Amen.*
1 TIMOTHY 1:17

Jesus is the *Only Wise God*. Idols can't speak and leaders of false religions don't know anything. But because the Lord Jesus created people, He knows what people think; He even knows their motives and desires. He knows everything about all people, so He knows all about you. Jesus knows your temptations and your strengths. He knows your spiritual dreams and your secret sins. He knows what is best for you for this day. Will you let Jesus, the *Only Wise God*, guide you?

*Lord Jesus, You know everything about me. You know
I am not as strong as I want to be. Stand by me and help me today.
You know what is best for this day.*

Jesus is the *Only Wise God* who knows everything that's ever happened. He knows things that haven't yet happened and "calleth those things which be not as though they were" (Romans 4:17, *KJV*). Jesus knows what will happen to you before it happens, and He knows the things that could have happened to you but didn't. Trust Him to guide you and protect you. Let Him help you make good decisions to keep you from physical harm and spiritual danger.

*Lord Jesus, You know the future, and I don't know what will happen to
me. So guide me this day. You have kept me from making mistakes in
the past, and You've protected me from evil. You are the Only Wise God.
I need Your wise guidance to keep me from making mistakes. I will
depend on Your guidance this day. Amen.*

Reading: Psalm 39
Key Thought: The wisdom of Jesus can help you make good decisions.

14 · JESUS: FAITHFUL AND TRUE

Now I saw heaven opened, and behold, a white horse. And He who sat on him was called Faithful and True, and in righteousness He judges and makes war.
REVELATION 19:11

Jesus is called *Faithful and True*. These names were not given to Him until the end of the book of Revelation. When John saw the second coming of Jesus in power, he called Him *Faithful and True*. This compound name reflects His character. He is faithful to do all He promised, and Jesus promised, "I will come again" (John 14:3). Jesus is true and consistent to all that is established in the universe. Jesus' second coming is the appropriate climax to all He did since creation. Jesus will be *Faithful and True* throughout the great tribulation in Revelation, so He'll be *Faithful and True* in your hour of trial. Right to the end, He'll be the same, regardless of circumstances, regardless of pressures, regardless of others' disappointments; Jesus will prove Himself to be *Faithful and True*.

Lord, how long will my troubles last? The Evil One is strong, and it's been so long. It's easy to get my eyes on tribulation and not on You. Help me look beyond my problem to see Your victorious triumph. How long?

Jesus will always be *Faithful and True* to the plan He established when He created all things. He will allow sin to run its course, and He will allow the Evil One to do His work. But then He'll return, just as He promised, to judge sin and evildoers and to reward those who obey Him.

Lord, thank You for Your faithfulness to keep Your word and for being truthful about the reality of sin. Because I have trusted You for salvation, I will continue to trust You today. Amen.

Reading: Revelation 19:11-21
Key Thought: Jesus will be *Faithful and True* to the end.

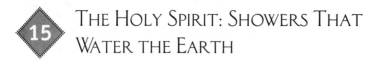
15 ◆ THE HOLY SPIRIT: SHOWERS THAT WATER THE EARTH

He shall come down like rain upon the grass before mowing,
like showers that water the earth.
PSALM 72:6

The Holy Spirit is like *Showers That Water the Earth.* He will come upon His people like the necessary showers that give life to things on the earth. Sometimes He is like a pouring rain that drenches the earth and produces a flood. Sometimes He is like a gentle shower—a mist—that lightly sprinkles droplets upon the leaves and grass. Sometimes the ground doesn't need a downpour; it's already saturated. Sometimes on a hot sweltering day, you need a few rain showers to cool you off. You need a light drizzle to refresh your spirit. Let the Holy Spirit be your Shower of refreshment today.

Holy Spirit, I'm waiting for a Rain Shower. Lately it's been hot, and I'm exhausted. Refresh me so I can continue walking by faith.

The Holy Spirit is like *Showers That Water the Earth.* Showers come when it's been too hot; He'll come when you're tempted and tired. Most people stop working during showers; would this be a good time for you to get some rest? When the rain is gently falling, it's a time to think and to enjoy the natural surroundings. Isn't this a good time to look around, take stock of your work and prepare for the next task?

Holy Spirit, rain on me. I need Your gentle presence to refresh me. I've done a lot of things, and I'm tired. I've got some big tasks ahead of me, and I need some rest. Holy Spirit, refresh me today. Amen.

Reading: Psalm 72:1-19
Key Thought: The Holy Spirit will refresh you like a rain shower.

16 ▶ JESUS: THE TRUSTWORTHY WITNESS

And from Jesus Christ, the trustworthy witness.
REVELATION 1:5, *MLB*

Jesus is the *Trustworthy Witness*; He came to witness the message of the Father. You can trust Jesus, for He perfectly witnessed to the world what the Father wanted said. When Jesus identified Himself as being one with the Father, the Jewish religious leaders "sought all the more to kill Him, because He not only broke the Sabbath, but also said that God was His Father, making Himself equal with God" (John 5:18). Jesus did what He was trusted to do, and He said what needed to be said. Jesus was a *Trustworthy Witness* in the face of death.

> *Lord, thank You for faithfully witnessing about the Father*
> *while on Earth. Thank You for faithfully witnessing to my*
> *heart the love of the Father for me.*

Remember that the word "witness" is translated from the Greek word for martyr. Those who are killed for their faithful witness are called martyrs. The religious leaders accused Jesus of blasphemy because He faithfully witnessed to them about the Father—He was killed for His witness. Now He wants you to be a faithful witness for Him to the world: "You shall be witnesses to Me" (Acts 1:8). How will you witness for Him today?

> *Lord, because You died for me, the least I can do is to be a trustworthy*
> *witness for You. Help me be worthy of the trust you placed in me. I will*
> *faithfully tell others what You have done for me. You can trust me to be*
> *a witness of You and the Father who sent You. Amen.*

Reading: John 7:40-53
Key Thought: Jesus wants you to be a trustworthy witness for Him.

17   JESUS: THE TRIUMPHANT SON OF MAN

Then I turned to see the voice that spoke with me. And having turned I saw . . .
One like the Son of Man, clothed with a garment down to the feet and girded
about the chest with a golden band.
REVELATION 1:12-13

Jesus is the *Triumphant Son of Man* who stood glorified and transfigured before John on the Isle of Patmos. His hair was "as white as snow" (Revelation 1:14), a symbol of His purity. His eyes were "like a flame of fire" (v. 14), a symbol of His ability to accurately discern the nature of people. His feet, which were "as if refined in a furnace" (v. 15), were quick to burn away impurities and sin. Jesus wants you to be pure and truthful in all you do.

Lord Jesus, I bow before Your majesty; forgive my sin.
Receive honor and glory from my life. Guide me to do things
that will bring praise to You today.

Jesus is the *Triumphant Son of Man* who stood before John in priestly garments. His voice was compared to "the sound of many waters" (Revelation 1:15), emphasizing His authority. "Out of His mouth went a sharp two-edged sword" (v. 16), symbolizing the Word of God that gives life. The brilliance about His countenance was "like the sun shining in its strength" (v. 16), reflecting His glory and transforming power. Jesus, the *Triumphant Son of Man,* can transform your life. He can help you triumph over all your spiritual problems.

Lord, when John saw You, he fell at Your feet. I follow his example to
worship at Your feet. Since You are the glorified Son of God in my life,
I praise You for becoming all things for me. Help me see perfectly Your
glory so that I can reflect it to the world. Amen.

Reading: Matthew 17:1-13
Key Thought: The *Triumphant Son of Man* can make you victorious.

THE TRINITY: YOU ARE THE GOD WHO SEES (*EL ROI*)

She called the name of the LORD that spake unto her, Thou God seest me. . . . Wherefore the well was called Beerlahairoi.
GENESIS 16:13-14, KJV

The Lord's name is *El Roi*, the God who sees everything you do. Therefore, you cannot hide anything from Him, and He knows everything you are. Just as He saw Hagar running from her master (see Genesis 16), He sees you struggling with problems. Just as He appeared to Hagar to encourage her, He will come to support you. He sees your problems and knows your weaknesses. Just as He sent Hagar back to raise her son Ishmael, so He has a task for you to do.

Lord, my sins are many; they can't be hidden from You. Forgive my sin; cleanse me so that I can walk before You in integrity. You, God, see that my struggles are great; they discourage me. Come help me get through this day. Lord, look at my talents; they are few. O God, see my ability; I am weak. How can I ever serve You?

Because the Lord is *El Roi*, His ever-seeing presence should give you encouragement. Just as Hagar had to return to face conflict and problems, so you must face your problems; you can't keep trouble out of your life. But the good news is that you can solve your problems—*El Roi* will help you through them. You must face the difficulties from which you run; then you must call upon the Lord, *El Roi*, to help you and to be with you in your difficulties.

Lord, You see me and You know my weakness. Come to me and help me. Give me strength to face my problems and wisdom to solve them. Let me get victory from Your presence. Amen.

Reading: Genesis 16
Key Thought: The Lord sees your problems and will help you.

JESUS: THE TESTIMONY OF GOD

And I, brethren, when I came to you, did not come with excellence of speech or of wisdom declaring to you the testimony of God. For I determined not to know anything among you except Jesus Christ and Him crucified.

1 CORINTHIANS 2:1-2

Jesus is the *Testimony of God* to the world. Do not look for deep truths elsewhere; Jesus is the Personification of truth. Do not look for mysterious wisdom; Jesus is the Wisdom of God. Do not look for sparkling speeches or cleverly written words; Jesus is the *Testimony of God*. You'll not find anything deeper in understanding than Christ, nor will you find anything simpler to understand than Jesus. Everything that God wants you to know, you'll find in Jesus.

Jesus, I learn of You in the pages of Scripture. There is no grace greater than Your grace; there is no love greater than Your love. You walked humbly among men to show us what God was like; now I bow at Your feet to exalt You in my life.

Jesus is the Testimony that God would have you know. Do not search for deep wisdom apart from Him. Do not seek to understand spiritual things that are complicated or confusing apart from Him. If you think you've found truth but Jesus is not there, you are lost in the jungle of error. God has testified what you need to know. You'll find the answers to your questions in Jesus, for He is the *Testimony of God*.

When I look into the crystal waters of a pond, I see the calm surface of a pool. Yet the water beneath the surface is deep, so deep that I'll never reach the bottom. Jesus is like that pond. He is easy to understand, yet so deep that I'll never completely comprehend all He is and does. Amen.

Reading: 1 Corinthians 2:1-5
Key Thought: Jesus has told us what the Father wants us to know.

JESUS: THE WORD OF LIFE

*That which was from the beginning, which we have heard, which we
have seen with our eyes, which we have looked upon, and our hands
have handled, concerning the Word of life.*

1 JOHN 1:1

Jesus is the *Word of Life;* His words give eternal life to all who believe Him. Spokesmen for false religions speak words of death, and idols cannot speak at all. As the *Word of Life,* Jesus communicates the life-giving message of the Father to the world. No one had seen the Father until Jesus came as the *Word of Life* to express what the Father was like. He spoke the message of salvation, and in His death He provided life to all who would believe. His words of life give the message of His death, burial and resurrection.

*Jesus, I know You have the words of life; sing them over
again to me so that I never forget their message. Sing them
often to me, because I love to hear them.*

Jesus is the *Word of Life* that you must hear and understand to know how to go to Heaven. Then you must act on His words in order to be saved. No other words have eternal life embedded in their message. Peter asked a question, telling us that only Jesus has life-giving words: "To whom shall we go? You have the words of eternal life" (John 6:68). Only Jesus has the words that give you eternal life. He is the *Word of Life;* take Him into your life.

*Jesus, I will believe Your words of life and will walk daily according to
Your message. I will love Your words and cherish their message. I will
share Your words of life with those who don't know You. Amen.*

Reading: 1 John 1:1-4
Key Thought: The words of Jesus give life.

21 ◆ THE FATHER: ONE FATHER

Then [the Jews] said to [Jesus], "We were not born of
fornication; we have one Father—God."
JOHN 8:41

There is *One Father*—the God of the universe. No other god can compare to Him. He created all things; idols cannot make anything. The Father sustains all life and order in the universe; false gods have no power to do anything. The Father is the personal God, in whose image the first man was created; everyone who is born has His likeness. That's why He is also the Father of all mankind—the Father-God of all. Because the Father has the power of personality, He knows people, loves people and wants to have fellowship with them. Will you seek Him today?

You are my Father-God because You created me and also because
You saved me and made me Your child. You are the only God in my life.
You are the One Father-God to whom I owe everything.

The one Father-God transcends high above all Heaven and Earth. He is the sovereign Ruler of everything. Yet He is as close to you as a father is to his child because He is your Father. Just as a child owes its parents everything, so you must obey and honor Him. Just as a child must answer to its parents for its disobedience, so He is the one Father-God who will judge all people. Come to Him as a Father, so you won't have to answer to Him as the God of judgment.

I depend on You as my Father to care for me and guide me.
Help me to glorify You today. Amen.

Reading: James 1:17-27
Key Thought: Knowing God is like knowing a father.

22   Jesus: The Son Who Is Consecrated For Evermore

For the law maketh men high priests which have infirmity; but the word of the oath, which was since the law, maketh the Son, who is consecrated for evermore.
HEBREWS 7:28, *KJV*

As an Intercessor, Jesus doesn't need to be consecrated every day, as the Old Testament priests had to sacrifice daily for their sins. They had to be consecrated time and again because they sinned. It was impossible for them to enter God's presence unless they were cleansed each time they approached God. Jesus is the *Son Who Is Consecrated For Evermore.* He was eternally consecrated—prepared—to continually enter God's presence for you. Jesus was perfect—without sin—so He could be our Sin Bearer. So now Jesus is the constant Intercessor for our sins. All day and every day, He stands ready to intercede to the Father for us.

> *Jesus, I constantly need You to intercede for me, because*
> *I constantly fail. I sin innocently; intercede to the Father for me.*
> *I give in to temptation; pray to strengthen me.*

Jesus has an "unchangeable priesthood" (Hebrews 7:24). No matter what sin you commit and no matter why you sin, He will intercede to the Father for you. Remember, "The blood of Jesus Christ His Son cleanses us from all sin" (1 John 1:7). Did you see that word "all"? He cleanses you totally from sin; so confess it, repent and ask Jesus to forgive it. Then seek His power to overcome it. Jesus wants to give you victory. He stands in the Father's presence for you.

> *Jesus, I am amazed at Your grace and forgiveness. Thank You for*
> *cleansing my sin. Now make continued intercession for me. Amen.*

Reading: Mark 14:32-42
Key Thought: Jesus makes constant intercession for your sin.

23 JESUS: THE SON OF THE LIVING GOD

Simon Peter answered and said, "You are the Christ, the Son of the living God."
MATTHEW 16:16

Jesus is the *Son of the Living God*. All false gods have no life in them. False gods don't think or love; nor do they answer the prayers offered to them. They may be carved from wood or stone; they can't communicate with you, and they can't give life to those who worship them. Jesus is the *Son of the Living God*; both Jesus and the Father are alive and have always lived. There was never a time when the living God didn't exist. Perhaps the Father's greatest creative act was when He breathed into Adam's nostrils the breath of life. And in that creative act, life was given to Adam; and through generations of procreation, life was given to you.

I come to You, living God, thanking You for creating me in Your image. Because I have a mind, I think about You. Because I have emotions, I love You. Because I have a will, I choose to follow You.

Jesus is the *Son of the Living God*. He gave you spiritual life through His death, burial and resurrection: "I have come that they may have life, and that they may have it more abundantly" (John 10:10). You have two kinds of life: (1) You received eternal life by believing in Jesus, and (2) you can enjoy satisfying life more abundantly by magnifying Jesus in all you do.

I cling to You, Son of the Living God, for without You I don't have life. But with You in my heart, I have eternal life. Today, help me enjoy Your abundant life. Amen.

Reading: Matthew 16:13-16
Key Thought: Jesus gives you all types of life.

24 ❖ THE HOLY SPIRIT: THE BREATH OF LIFE

*The breath of life from God entered them, and they stood on their
feet, and great fear fell on those who saw them.*
REVELATION 11:11

The Holy Spirit is the *Breath of Life*. When God breathed into the nostrils
of Adam, the Holy Spirit was the *Breath of Life* that gave him physical life.
Through the continual miracles of procreation, the *Breath of Life* has
reached you and has given you existence. "For in him we live and move
and exist" (Acts 17:28, *NLT*). When you were born again, the life of God
entered you; the *Breath of Life* gave you spiritual life. You have life—physical and spiritual—because of the Holy Spirit. Now live for Him today.
Because He is holy, He wants you to live a holy life. Because He is Spirit,
He wants you to live a spiritual life.

*Holy Spirit, thank You for life, both physical and spiritual.
I will live for You today.*

The Holy Spirit is the *Breath of Life* that resurrected the two witnesses back to physical life (see Revelation 11:11). But instead of returning to
their old bodies, they were given resurrected, glorified bodies. They will
live forever in those transformed, renewed bodies. Just as the two witnesses were transformed because the Holy Spirit is the *Breath of Life*, so
you will be resurrected in the last days. You will receive a new resurrected body from the Spirit, because He is the *Breath of Life*.

*Holy Spirit, I know You will give me new life in the future, but today I
need help. Blow Your Spirit into me. Encourage me, strengthen me,
guide me and help me accomplish all I have to do. Amen.*

Reading: Revelation 11:1-12
Key Thought: The Holy Spirit gives life to all you do.

Jesus: The Son of the Father

Grace, mercy, and peace will be with you from God the Father and from the Lord Jesus Christ, the Son of the Father, in truth and love.
2 JOHN 3

Jesus is the *Son of the Father*, sent by the Father to save a sinful world. He is the constant object of the Father's love (see John 5:19-20). The Father and the Son are one in nature (see 10:30), but they are separate Persons. They talk to each other, love each other and work together to save the world.

O Son of God, I magnify You for Your power and love. I know You can do all things, so work in my life today.

The *Son of the Father* wants you to know Him and honor Him, as He honors the Father. Those who do not honor the Son offend the Father (see John 5:23). Just as the Father raised the dead, so Jesus gives spiritual life to those who believe in Him (see v. 21). Those who are spiritually dead in sin can have eternal life through the words of the Son (see v. 24), and believers who have physically died will be raised to resurrection life in the future through the words of the Son (see vv. 25,28). The Father has given the Son the power to give life to all who believe and the authority to judge sinners at the end of the age (see v. 27).

Jesus, I want Your power in my life today. I want Your words to give me strength and optimism to meet the challenges I face. I want Your indwelling presence to encourage me for all I do. Amen.

Reading: 2 John
Key Thought: The *Son of the Father* can give energy to your Christian life.

26 JESUS: THE SON OF GOD

*But these are written that you may believe that Jesus is the Christ, the
Son of God, and that believing you may have life in His name.*
JOHN 20:31

Jesus is the *Son of God*, the second Person of the Godhead. That the
description "Son" is used of Jesus does not mean that He is less than the
Father. They are coequal and coeternal, and they share these attributes
equally with the Holy Spirit. The phrase *"Son of God"* means that Jesus
has the same nature as the Father and that He is the personification of
all the character qualities of deity. Jesus is God; can you trust Him?

*Jesus, I know that You are God, for only God can forgive my sins and
transform my life. But I am concerned when the world doubts who You are.*

People have always doubted the deity of Christ. Even a man on a
cross mocked His claims of deity: "If You are the Son of God, come down
from the cross" (Matthew 27:40). But Jesus didn't respond to doubting
criticism in the way that the world wanted. He showed His deity by per-
forming miracles of compassion and by forgiving sin. The Holy Spirit
will work in human hearts to show them who Jesus is (see John 16:7-15).
God expects people to respond to His love. Jesus expects people to
respond to His invitation to be saved. Jesus is the *Son of God*, Creator and
Lord, and in the final day, He'll be our Judge.

*Jesus, I bow at Your feet, recognizing You as God. You are the
Lord of the ages. I recognize you as my Lord this day. I worship
You as the Son of God. Amen.*

Reading: John 20:24-31
Key Thought: You must recognize Jesus as the *Son of God*.

27 THE TRINITY: MOST HIGH GOD (*EL ELYON*)

But Abram said to the king of Sodom, "I have raised my hand to the LORD, God Most High, the Possessor of heaven and earth."
GENESIS 14:22

The Lord is *El Elyon*, the *Most High God*, a name that means He owns Heaven and Earth. He invites you, "Make the Lord your Refuge. Make the Most High your Habitation. Then no plan by the Evil One shall overcome you" (see Psalm 91:9-10). Then you can respond, "I will dwell in the secret place with the Most High. I will abide under His almighty shadow" (see v. 1). The Lord is *El Elyon*, the *Most High God*, who can take care of you as He provided for His servants in the Scriptures. Look beyond your daily issues to heavenly things. He knows what will happen today and tomorrow and in the future. When you can't see what's happening, trust Him—His plans are much greater than yours.

Lord, I feel threatened, and sometimes I'm scared to death. Evil seems so strong in the world. Help me.

The Lord is *El Elyon*, "the Possessor of heaven and earth"; nothing happens without His knowledge. No one can take away your life until the time the Lord has appointed. Although He allows evil to run its course, the *Most High God* has a plan for your life. He's fashioning you according to His purpose. Behind the scenes He works all things together "for good to those who love God, to those who are the called according to His purpose" (Romans 8:28).

Most High God, I give my life to you; I yield to Your plans for this day. I look for Your protection; help me today. Amen.

Reading: Genesis 14:17-24
Key Thought: The *Most High God* can take care of you.

28 THE FATHER: MY FATHER AND YOUR FATHER

*Jesus said to her, "Do not cling to Me, for I have not yet ascended to My Father;
but go to My brethren and say to them, 'I am ascending to My Father and your
Father, and to My God and your God.'"*
JOHN 20:17

Jesus called on *My Father and Your Father* while He was on Earth. Jesus said He would ascend back to Heaven to His Father, but Mary Magdalene tried to hang on to Him with a view of keeping Him on Earth (see John 20:17). If Mary had kept Jesus on Earth, He would not have been intimate with all believers, nor with His heavenly Father. But Jesus ascended to Heaven so that both He and the Father could indwell all believers (see John 14:21; Galatians 2:20).

*Father, I need Your presence in my life. It will be difficult to make it
through this day if I don't have Your help. Let me come close to talk with
You before I go to meet the world.*

God is your intimate Father, just as He is intimate with all His children who come to Him through Jesus Christ. Because the Father is God, He is omnipresent throughout His universe, which means He is equally present at all places at all times—now, in the past and in the future. Because you have come to the Father through Jesus, He can be intimate with you and with all other believers (see John 14:6). Because you have been born again by the Holy Spirit, He is your intimate Father (see 3:3-7). What do you need from Him today? He is here for you; go to Him.

*You are my Father; I need You, I love You, and
I worship You for all You've done for me. I obey Your instructions
and come to You. Amen.*

Reading: John 20:17-18
Key Thought: You can be as intimate with the Father as Jesus is.

29 ◈ JESUS: UNDEFILED

For such a High Priest was fitting for us, who is holy, harmless, undefiled,
separate from sinners, and has become higher than the heavens.
HEBREWS 7:26

Jesus is the perfect Son of God. Just as the sacrificial lamb had to be
without blemish, so Jesus was the *Undefiled,* sinless Substitute who died
for your sin. Satan tempted Jesus to sin, but He rejected the enemy's
temptation (see Matthew 4:1-11). So He can help you overcome your
temptation or bad habits. Some Jewish people accused Jesus of sin; but
when He challenged them to name one sin, they were not able to do it
(see John 8:46). In the same way, you should have a blameless reputation
before your enemies. On the night before Jesus died, He didn't want to
drink the cup of punishment, but He drank it willingly, submitting to
the suffering of the Cross (see Matthew 26:39-42). Just as Jesus was perfectly obedient to the Father, will you willingly become obedient to the
will of God?

> *Lord Jesus, You are my example for godly living; give me the*
> *power to resist sin. You are my High Priest, who prays for me in*
> *Heaven; intercede to the Father for me.*

"Undefiled" means "the absence of sin." But Jesus is more than One
who never sinned; He has all the positive attributes of holiness. Jesus is
as holy as the Father is, so He can be your perfect High Priest.

> *Lord Jesus, I know You are my perfect High Priest, so I come*
> *asking You to help me in my struggles. Keep me from sin, make me*
> *holy, and use me this day. Amen.*

Reading: Hebrews 10:26-39
Key Thought: Jesus can be your Intercessor because He was *Undefiled.*

30   THE FATHER: YOUR FATHER IN HEAVEN

Let your light so shine before men, that they may see your good works
and glorify your Father in heaven.
MATTHEW 5:16

Your Father in heaven . . . makes His sun rise on the evil and on
the good, and sends rain on the just and on the unjust.
MATTHEW 5:45

Be perfect, just as your Father in heaven is perfect.
MATTHEW 5:48

Your *Father in Heaven* is more than a powerful Creator; your *Father in Heaven* is Lord. But He's more than the sovereign Ruler of the universe; He's your personal *Father in Heaven.* Just as a child has immediate access to the intimacies of his father, so you have that relationship to Your heavenly Father. The Father gives you eternal life, and no one is able to snatch you out of His hand (see John 10:28-29). He has prepared a home for you in Heaven and will work all things in your life for good (see John 14:2; Romans 8:28). The Father will give you His grace and peace (see 1 Thessalonians 1:1).

Father, I rest secure in Your presence. Thank You for receiving me and
giving me a new position in the heavenlies.

Now you belong to Your *Father in Heaven.* You can call on Him for answers to prayer, and He will give you illumination to learn the Word of God. Because the Father belongs to you, you are special. You are His child, so you have access to Him at any time for any plea. Because you are the Father's child, all of Heaven is ready to help you.

Father, thank You for my special place near Your heart. I want to serve
You with power so that I can extend Your kingdom on Earth. I want to
know You intimately so that I can be like You. I want to worship You so
that You will be glorified. Amen.

Reading: John 17:20-26
Key Thought: You received a special relationship to the Father when you became a Christian.

MAY

1 JESUS: THE ZEAL FOR YOUR HOUSE

*Because zeal for Your house has eaten me up, and the reproaches of those who
reproach You have fallen on me.*
PSALM 69:9

*Then His disciples remembered that it was written,
"Zeal for Your house has eaten Me up."*
JOHN 2:17

The disciples remembered Jesus as one with *Zeal for God's House*. They observed how Jesus went to the synagogue each Sabbath "as His custom was" (Luke 4:16). They remembered how Jesus went up to Jerusalem and entered the Temple, as was required of a Jewish male. They remembered how Jesus cleansed the Temple at the beginning (see John 2:13-22) and at the end (see Luke 19:45-46) of His three-year ministry (Luke 19:45, 46). Jesus wanted God's house to be reverent and clean: "My house is a house of prayer, but you have made it a 'den of thieves'" (v. 46). Jesus "was teaching daily in the Temple" (v. 47). Why did Jesus have such extraordinary zeal for the Temple? Because the Father was there.

*Jesus, I confess that I don't treat my church as reverently as You
treated God's house. Forgive my shortcomings. Give me a holy zeal for
God's house, as You demonstrated on Earth.*

When Jesus was on Earth, the *Zeal for the Father's House* demanded His loyalty. That's what the phrase "eaten up" means. Does the church you attend demand your loyalty? Do you attend its meetings, and do you give financially to its causes? Jesus felt an obligation to God's house; He was eaten up with its demands. Why? Because God was present there on the day of worship.

*Lord, I renew my loyalty to my church. I will fulfill my
obligations to You through my church. Amen.*

Reading: 1 Corinthians 10:1-24
Key Thought: Christ would have You fulfill your obligations to your church.

2 ▸ Jesus: The Firstborn

But when He again brings the firstborn into the world, He says:
"Let all the angels of God worship Him."
HEBREWS 1:6

Jesus was the *Firstborn* child of Mary; she had no children before Him. She was a virgin when Jesus was conceived in her of the Holy Spirit. She had not known a man (see Luke 1:34). It was the Father's plan for Jesus to be her *Firstborn,* because most mothers give more love and care to their first child. Because of this care, "the Child grew and became strong in spirit, filled with wisdom; and the grace of God was upon Him" (2:40). Jesus was the God-Man, perfect to be your Savior.

Lord Jesus, I praise You for Your birth and Your growth to full manhood.
Just as the angels in Heaven worship You as the God-Man, so do I.

Jesus was also the *Firstborn* of every creature (see Colossians 1:15), which means He gave life to everything in the world. Jesus is "the Beginning of the creation of God" (Revelation 3:14). Not only was Jesus the source of physical life, but He is also "the firstborn from the dead" (Colossians 1:18), the first one to rise from the dead. Now Jesus is the source of all your spiritual life. Because you're in Him, you have resurrection life (see Galatians 2:20). Because Jesus is the *Firstborn,* He gives you a hope of future Heaven.

Lord, thank You for being the Firstborn of the virgin Mary—to live and
die on the cross for me. Thank You for being the Firstborn from the
dead—to give me resurrection life. Thank You for the hopes of future
resurrection and Heaven. Amen.

Reading: Hebrews 1:1-9; Colossians 1:13-19
Key Thought: Jesus is the *Firstborn* of the resurrection—to give us life.

3   THE HOLY SPIRIT: THE HOLY ONE

I have not concealed the words of the Holy One.
JOB 6:10

The Holy Spirit is the *Holy One,* sent from the Father to help you live in a godly manner. He is called the *Holy One* because His nature is holy. "Holy" is a word that means "separated to God" or "cut off from sin or rebellion against God." "Holy" is a word that means "pure" or "pristine." The Holy Spirit is sent to get sinful people ready to live with a holy God. He does that by convicting people of their sin, leading them to live godly lives and living in them as the *Holy One.* He will sanctify you to "set you apart" from iniquity. What do you want from the Holy Spirit today?

Lord, I recognize my sin; cleanse me from all iniquity.
I want to be holy; come live within my body to separate me from
all that harms my Christian life.

The Holy Spirit is the *Holy One.* He will convict you of sin (see John 16:7-11) and help you live close to God. He will give you a deep desire to get rid of sin. He will guide your steps to walk separated from sin. He will give you a passion to live for God (see 7:37-38). He will help you become holy when you have a deep desire to live for God.

I come to You, Holy One; keep me from the temptations of the
world, the flesh and the Devil. I want to be godly; help me become
more holy. Draw me closer to You. Amen.

Reading: Romans 8:1-17
Key Thought: The Holy Spirit was sent to make you holy.

4 ◇ JESUS: THE FORERUNNER

*Where the forerunner has entered for us, even Jesus, having become High Priest
forever according to the order of Melchizedek.*
HEBREWS 6:20

Jesus is the *Forerunner* who has gone to Heaven first for us. Just as a delegation used to send a runner ahead of them to a city to announce their
arrival, so Jesus is the *Forerunner* who went into Heaven to announce the
arrival of the Church. He is your *Forerunner* who has announced your
coming to Heaven. Just as a forerunner allows the people of a city to get
ready for a delegation, so our *Forerunner* allows all of Heaven to prepare
for our arrival. The Father has prepared a mansion for you (see John
14:1-3), and Jesus is interceding to the Father for you. The angels are
waiting for you. Everything is ready because Jesus is the *Forerunner* who
prepared the way.

*Lord Jesus, I face death with more confidence, knowing that
You've gone before me to Heaven. My doubts fade when I realize You're
waiting for me. I don't want to die, but at least I can look
beyond death to see You waiting for me.*

Not only has Jesus gone as the *Forerunner* to prepare Heaven, but He
also is now your Intercessor who stands at the right hand of the Father,
interceding for you to overcome temptation and to make the trip triumphantly. So live confidently this day, because Jesus is preparing
Heaven for you. He is praying for you as you journey homeward.

*Lord Jesus, I know You stand at the right hand of the Father, making
intercession for me. Because You are in Heaven, I pray confidently and
I live with assurance. Amen.*

Reading: Hebrews 6
Key Thought: Jesus is preparing Heaven for you.

5 JESUS: THE FOUNTAIN OF LIFE

For with You is the fountain of life; in Your light we see light.
PSALM 36:9

When you've been on a long, hot walk, what you want is water. Sometimes the heat gets to be too much, and you're in danger of a heat stroke. You need some cool water on your tongue and something wet on the back of your neck. If you're in really bad condition, you stick your whole head in the water. When you need water to keep from fainting, Jesus is your *Fountain of Life* who will give you a new presence of mind and a new focus. Do you need to cool down your anger, frustration or bitterness?

Lord, I need some cool water before I leave home, because it's pretty hot out there. And when I get home at the end of the day, I'll need more water to refresh my life for the evening duties.

Sometimes at work you need a drink of water to refresh your work habits. Sometimes you need a drink of water in the middle of the night because you wake up and your mouth is dry and you can't sleep. Sometimes a drink of water makes you think well, play better, talk better or perform better. For whatever you need, pause to drink of Jesus. Just as water energizes the body, so the renewed presence of Jesus revitalizes your life. Remember, Jesus, the *Fountain of Life,* called Himself "a fountain of water springing up into everlasting life" (John 4:14).

Jesus, I come to drink of You. Ah, water is good when you're thirsty. I'll keep coming back, because I need You daily. Amen.

Reading: Psalm 36
Key Thought: Jesus is a Fountain of water to refresh your life.

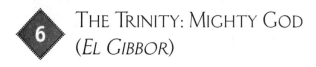

6 THE TRINITY: MIGHTY GOD (*EL GIBBOR*)

For the LORD your God is God of gods and Lord of lords, the great God, mighty and awesome, who shows no partiality nor takes a bribe.
DEUTERONOMY 10:17

The Lord is *El Gibbor*, the *Mighty God* of strength; He can give you endurance. He is *El Gibbor*; He can protect you in danger. He is also *El Gibbor*, the firm rock; He can give you stability. Pray the words of the hymn "Rock of Ages" ("Rock of Ages, cleft for me, let me hide myself in thee"), because He gives you strength, protection and stability. Some people treat God's name like a good-luck charm, holding to a crucifix or repeating the name word "God" when they are in danger. But they're taking His name in vain, because they don't use it rightly. The mighty protection of *El Gibbor* begins with an intimate relationship. You can't use His name as a rabbit's foot to protect you from harm. You must know Him personally and rest in Him intimately.

Mighty Lord, I want to know You personally. Rock of Ages, I will hide in You. El Gibbor, let Your power and protection flow into my life.

El Gibbor can't protect what you don't give to Him, so you must trust *El Gibbor*. When you are busy seeking your own glory and doing your own thing, how can He fit into your life? *El Gibbor* can't be your strength if you don't use Him.

Mighty God, I surrender everything to You. Mighty Lord, I yield my ambition and my possessions; guide me this day and deliver me from the Evil One. Amen.

Reading: Deuteronomy 10
Key Thought: God can only protect what you give to Him.

JESUS: THE SAVIOR OF THE WORLD

*Then they said to the woman, "Now we believe, not because of
what you said, for we have heard for ourselves and know that this is
indeed the Christ, the Savior of the world."*
JOHN 4:42

*And we have seen and testify that the Father has sent the
Son as Savior of the world.*
1 JOHN 4:14

Jesus is the *Savior of the World*, but He's also the Savior of one—the individual. Notice how the circle begins large and gets smaller. Jesus is the *Savior of the World* (see John 4:42); then Jesus is the Savior of the Church (see Ephesians 5:23); and finally, Jesus is your Savior (see 1 Timothy 2:3). He is the Savior of people, one at a time. Jesus loves all the people in the world, but then the scope narrows to you: Jesus loves you and died for you.

*Jesus, thank You for personal attention and for personal salvation.
Thank You for being my personal Savior.*

Since Jesus is the *Savior of the World*; He died for all—all who are alive now, all who were alive in the past and all who will live in the future. Jesus is the Savior from the penalty of past sin; have you asked Him to forgive every past sin? Jesus is also our Savior from the power of this evil world; has He delivered you? Jesus will be our Savior from the presence of sin at the coming day with "the appearing of our Savior Jesus Christ" (2 Timothy 1:10). Are you ready to meet your Savior?

*Jesus, You are my Savior; thank You for saving me from
past sins. I claim Your daily power to save me from daily sins.
I look forward to Your personal coming to save me in the
future from the presence of sin. Amen.*

Reading: Titus 3:1-8
Key Thought: The *Savior of the World* must also be your personal Savior.

JESUS: THE SEED OF ABRAHAM

Now to Abraham and his Seed were the promises made. He does not say,
"And to seeds," as of many, but as of one, "And to your Seed," who is Christ.
GALATIANS 3:16

Jesus is the *Seed of Abraham*. The heavenly Father promised a son to Abraham who would bless "all the families of the earth" (Genesis 12:3). Jesus was born the Messiah, the One who would take "away the sin of the world" (John 1:29) and bring in a Kingdom of righteousness (see Luke 1:33). Because Abraham believed God's promise, Isaac was born (see Genesis 15:6). Eventually, millions of Jews were born into the world; Jesus was one of those Jews. By faith, Abraham knew that the Messiah would come from his seed. "Abraham rejoiced to see My day" (John 8:56), Jesus said. But Jesus didn't come to bring salvation just to the Jews; He came to bring salvation to all the world. He brought salvation to you.

Jesus, thank You for fulfilling prophecy. Thank You for coming to Earth
as a Jew. Thank You for dying for my sins.

Because Abraham was a man of faith who believed the promises of God, he looked forward to the birth of Jesus. But you too can be a person of faith. How? You must first look back on the history of Abraham to believe that the Father's promises apply to you. Then you must look back to the work of Jesus on the cross and apply salvation to your life. Finally, by faith you must study the Scriptures and apply all its promises to your life.

Jesus, I believe what the Bible says about You. I trust my future to You. I
know that You will guide my life and bless me this day. Amen.

Reading: Galatians 3:13-18
Key Thought: God's promise of a Messiah, made to Abraham, applies to me.

THE FATHER: ABBA FATHER

For you did not receive the spirit of bondage again to fear, but you received the Spirit of adoption by whom we cry out, "Abba, Father."
ROMANS 8:15

The Lord is your *Abba Father*. The title "Abba" means that He is your intimate "Papa" in Heaven. The unbeliever only knows the Lord through the greatness of His power and judgment. Some believers only relate to the Lord as the Father of Heaven who answers their prayers. Other believers worship the Father because, as Jesus said, "The Father is seeking such to worship Him" (John 4:23). But you can know the Father personally by His intimate name, *Abba Father.* Just as an earthly father welcomes his child to his lap and hugs him, so you can go to your intimate "Papa" for fellowship.

O my Father, originally I loved You for forgiving my sin.
Now I love You for Your intimate love to me. Thank You for
accepting me into Your family.

Because the Lord is your *Abba Father*, you don't relate to Him by just keeping commandments or obeying orders. You were not given an impersonal legal adoption. You are a member of the Father's family; you belong to Him, and He belongs to you. As your heavenly Father's child, you have all legal rights to His heavenly family. As your Father's child, you are hugged by His arms. Don't worry; don't strive; just rest.

Lord, it feels good to feel good in Your arms. I feel comfortable
to have the security of Your protection. But I don't want to know You
just to feel good; I want to know You—Abba—for Yourself. I want to love
You and spend time with You. Amen.

Reading: Romans 8:14-17
Key Thought: You can be intimate with the heavenly Father.

10   JESUS: THE SENT ONE

> *I must work the works of Him who sent Me while it is day;*
> *the night is coming when no one can work.*
> JOHN 9:4

Jesus is the *Sent One*. Jesus was sent by the Father from Heaven to Earth for several reasons. First, Jesus was the *Sent One* from the Father to reveal to people what God was like. "No one has seen God at any time. . . . [Jesus] has declared Him" (John 1:18). Will you learn about Jesus to know God? Jesus was the *Sent One* to let us know what Heaven was like (see 14:1-3). Will you learn what Jesus said about your future home? Jesus was the *Sent One* to demonstrate God's love to the world (see 3:16). Will you accept the love of God in Christ? Jesus was the *Sent One* to redeem the world. "But when the fullness of the time had come, God sent forth His Son . . . to redeem those who were under the law" (Galatians 4:4-5). Will you receive the redemption Jesus offers?

> *Lord Jesus, I know You were sent into the world to tell us about the Father. I worship the Father for sending You, and I worship You for obeying His instructions.*

Jesus is the *Sent One*; He obeyed the Father's directions. In the same way, Jesus is sending you into the world to tell people the gospel. Will you obey? Just as Jesus was sent as a true witness, will you be a witness for Him?

> *Lord Jesus, send me into the world, just as the Father sent You. I will go to my friends and family to "tell them what great things the Lord has done for [me]" (Mark 5:19). Amen.*

Reading: John 9
Key Thought: Just as Jesus was sent into the world, He now sends you.

11 · Jesus: The Sun of Righteousness

But to you who fear My name the Sun of Righteousness shall arise with healing in His wings; and you shall go out and grow fat like stall-fed calves.
MALACHI 4:2

The name *"Sun of Righteousness"* applies to Jesus in His second coming. Jesus is likened to the sun, which has two functions; the sun burns up things, but also the sun's warmth gives life and healing. When Jesus comes, His judgment will be "burning like an oven, and all the proud, yes, all who do wickedly . . . shall burn . . . up" (Malachi 4:1). Jesus is like the sun; He sears and scorches in judgment. But Jesus is also likened to the therapeutic sunlight, which relieves pain and dispels sickness. It is the same Jesus, and it is the same sunlight, but each can have opposite effects. When Jesus comes, will He deal with you in judgment or in healing fellowship?

Lord Jesus, I look to You for some heat on my pain and troubles. In this life there are accidents and sicknesses; shine some healing on me.

Jesus, the *Sun of Righteousness*, will return with healing for those martyrs who have died for the faith. He'll completely restore those whose bodies are eaten with cancer or maimed in an accident. The blind will see, the lame will walk, and all sickness will be healed. Jesus is the righteous One, meaning He will do the right thing for us, and He will do it in the right way. Jesus is the Source of righteousness because He is the *Sun of Righteousness*.

Lord Jesus, one day You will make all things right. Until that day, give us a little warm therapy for the hurts of this life. Amen.

Reading: Malachi 4
Key Thought: Jesus is the *Sun of Righteousness* who will heal our pains and diseases.

THE HOLY SPIRIT: THE GIFT OF THE HOLY SPIRIT

Repent, and let every one of you be baptized in the name of Jesus Christ for the remission of sins; and you shall receive the gift of the Holy Spirit.
ACTS 2:38

The Holy Spirit is a Gift to you. Jesus said, "I will pray the Father, and He will give you another Helper" (John 14:16). The Holy Spirit was given to enter into the heart of every Christian. Rather than giving you just forgiveness or eternal life or access into Heaven, the Father gave you a Person of the Godhead. The Gift is the Holy Spirit. When this Gift enters your heart, He brings the spiritual riches of Heaven into your life. You have the Gift; now unwrap the present and take Him out of the box. When you receive an earthly gift from a friend, you either try it on or see how it works. Do the same with your *Gift of the Holy Spirit*. Use Him to see how He works.

Holy Spirit, I don't seek spiritual things; I seek You. I don't seek spiritual power or blessings. I need You in my life. I receive You as a free gift.

The Holy Spirit is the Helper whom Jesus promised (see John 15:26). He helps the Father carry out His will on Earth. He helps Jesus by delivering eternal life to all who believe in Him. He is the Gift to help every believer. Will you open this Gift and try Him out?

Holy Spirit, come into my heart and help me live for You. I don't have spiritual power. So come, my Gift; I receive You freely. Amen.

Reading: Acts 2:38-42
Key Thought: The Holy Spirit is the Father's gift to you.

13 · JESUS: A SWEET-SMELLING AROMA

And walk in love, as Christ also has loved us and given Himself for us, an
offering and a sacrifice to God for a sweet-smelling aroma.
EPHESIANS 5:2

A sin offering in the Old Testament was a sweet-smelling aroma. It was not sweet just because it was pleasing to the smell, as a person is pleased with the aroma of a cooking steak. The Father was pleased because the sacrifice symbolized the repentant cry of a sinner to God. In death, Jesus became that *Sweet-Smelling Aroma.* He made it possible for you to be saved. Just as the sweet-smelling aroma of the altar of incense in the Tabernacle symbolized the continued prayers going up to God, so the present-day priesthood of Jesus is a symbol of His continual intercession to the Father for you. Is the sacrifice of Jesus pleasing to you?

Jesus, thank You for Your sacrificial love for me. I have learned
from Your example of love. I have experienced Your love
firsthand, so I will walk in love.

Jesus is a *Sweet-Smelling Aroma;* His death pleased the Father (see Isaiah 53:10). Now Jesus wants you to please the Father by your godly living. Yield your heart to Jesus, and He will help you do it. Jesus wants you to please the Father by yielding your time, talent and treasure in service. He will help you accomplish much in your service for the Kingdom. Jesus wants you to please the Father with your worship, because the Father seeks worshipers (see John 4:24). Magnify the Father and Son today with praise, exaltation and thanksgiving.

Jesus, because You are my Sweet-Smelling Aroma to the Father, I
worship the Father though Your intercession. Amen.

Reading: Mark 15:42—16:1
Key Thought: Jesus is our *Sweet-Smelling Aroma* to God.

JESUS: A TEACHER COME FROM GOD

[Nicodemus] came to Jesus by night and said to Him, "Rabbi, we know that You are a teacher come from God; for no one can do these signs that You do unless God is with him."
JOHN 3:2

Nicodemus called Jesus a *Teacher Come from God* because he wanted to compliment Jesus. Nicodemus was the most outstanding teacher of his day. Jesus—who spoke accurately—called Nicodemus "the teacher of Israel" (John 3:10). In the original Greek, the words Jesus chose suggested that Nicodemus was the most outstanding teacher in Israel. In our terminology, it might be parallel to the title "Teacher of the Year." Yet Nicodemus recognized that Jesus was superior to Him, because Nicodemus said that Jesus was a *Teacher Come from God.* What do you need to learn from Jesus?

Jesus, teach me everything I need to know to be more godly and effective in service. I will become Your student.

Jesus was often called Teacher. Just as a teacher gives you information you don't know, Jesus will teach you what you don't know about the Father. Just as a teacher helps solve problems and makes you more effective in life, Jesus can lead you out of your troubles and make you effective in Christian service. Just as a teacher is a role model, so Jesus personifies the truth and lived a perfect live on Earth. Just as a teacher loves and helps students, Jesus loves you and will come to help you in your hour of need. Jesus can meet your deepest need because He is a *Teacher Come from God.*

Jesus, there is so much I don't know; let me sit in Your classroom. I will listen to You and learn from You. Teach me what I need to know. Amen.

Reading: Matthew 21:23-32
Key Thought: Jesus can teach you what you need to know.

THE TRINITY: THE LORD WILL PROVIDE (JEHOVAH JIREH)

15

And Abraham called the name of the place, The-LORD-Will-Provide [Jehovah Jireh]; as it is said to this day, "In the Mount of the LORD it shall be provided."
GENESIS 22:14

The Lord is *Jehovah Jireh*, a name that means *"The Lord Will Provide."* The Lord asked Abraham to do the most difficult thing he could have done: to sacrifice his son Isaac. Abraham was ready to do it, but the Lord stopped him, explaining that He was *Jehovah Jireh*. The Lord provided a ram for Abraham to sacrifice, and He'll provide for you when you obey Him, just as the Lord did for Abraham. *Jehovah Jireh* will provide for you when you step out in obedience, as did Abraham. How can you receive the same blessings as Abraham received? "So it is: All who put their faith in Christ share the same blessing Abraham received" (Galatians 3:9, *NLT*). Remember, begin every task by asking for His blessings, and complete every task by claiming the promise of His help to provide for you. The secret of spiritual prosperity is the name *"Jehovah Jireh."*

> *Jehovah Jireh, give me spiritual victories, as well as financial blessings, today. Help me overcome my difficulties. Lord, provide for my needs today. Jehovah Jireh, step into my life with Your presence and power.*

Claim the power of *Jehovah Jireh* to help defeat your enemies, as did Joshua, David and Gideon. Just as you must claim blessings, you must also claim victory for your life. He will provide for you when you trust Him completely.

> *Jehovah Jireh, I surrender to Your leadership and trust Your protection. I claim Your provision and depend on Your presence. Be near me today. Amen.*

Reading: Genesis 22:1-18
Key Thought: Ask *Jehovah Jireh* to provide for your needs.

16 JESUS: THE BEARER OF SIN

So Christ was offered once to bear the sins of many. To those who eagerly wait for Him He will appear a second time, apart from sin, for salvation.
HEBREWS 9:28

Jesus carried the cross of Calvary until He was no longer physically able to do so. Another carried the cross to Calvary for Him. But there, Jesus was nailed to the cross and bore the sins of the world. No one else was able to take His place as the *Bearer of Sin*. Jesus had to do it alone—totally and until the end. He bore the sins of many until the sacrifice was accepted and redemption was complete. Then Jesus cried, "It is finished!" (John 19:30). He has done it all for you; what will you do for Him?

Lord Jesus, since You died for me, I will live for You. My sacrifices are small compared to Your great sacrifice, but I will bear my sacrifice for You.

Jesus didn't bear only part of your sin; He bore all of it. So you shouldn't walk in guilt nor live tentatively. Be a bold Christian, because there is no sin charged against you. Jesus, the *Bearer of Sin*, bore your sin with the right concern for others, for He said of His executioners, "Father, forgive them" (Luke 23:34). Then He took time to welcome the repentant thief to Paradise (v. 43). So be positive when you suffer for Him, and be concerned for others as you bear reproach for Him.

Lord Jesus, in appreciation for all You've done for me, I will live joyfully this day. I will not complain when things don't go my way, nor will I gripe over irritations. Any suffering is a privilege, considering how much You suffered for me. Amen.

Reading: Luke 23:46-49
Key Thought: Endure suffering, because Jesus suffered for you.

17 JESUS: THE SALVATION OF GOD

For my eyes have seen Your salvation.
LUKE 2:30

All flesh shall see the salvation of God.
LUKE 3:6

Jesus is called the *Salvation of God*, a title first given to Him in Isaiah 52:10. Simeon, an old man waiting in the Temple for the Messiah, called the baby Jesus the *Salvation of God* (see Luke 2:30). Then John the Baptist, when preaching in the wilderness, called Jesus the *Salvation of God* (see 3:6). Notice, Jesus "had come from God" (John 13:3); therefore, Jesus brings salvation from God to Earth.

Lord Jesus, I thank You for coming into this world with salvation from the Father. I thank You for bringing salvation to me.

Jesus is the *Salvation of God* from your past sins; they cannot be charged against you. Jesus is the *Salvation of God* from your present sins; so don't be an addict to sin nor let the power of sin keep you in bondage. Jesus is the *Salvation of God* for your future sins. "The blood of Jesus Christ His Son cleanses us from all sin" (1 John 1:7). You must deal with all sin—past, present and future—according to 1 John 1:9, which shows the progression from confession to forgiveness to cleansing. And finally, Jesus is the *Salvation of God* who will remove us from the presence of sin in eternity. There is coming a day when we'll live in Heaven, never to struggle with sin again.

Jesus, You are my Salvation of God. I claim You for total salvation in every area of my life. Save me now, and save me in the future. Amen.

Reading: Luke 3:2-6
Key Thought: Jesus comes from God for your complete salvation.

THE FATHER: THE LIVING FATHER

As the living Father sent Me, and I live because of the Father,
so he who feeds on Me will live because of Me.
JOHN 6:57

The Lord is the *Living Father.* All idols are lifeless images and are often carved from stone or wood; they neither have life nor give life. Idols are nothing more than the desires of their maker. But the Father is alive in Heaven and has great desires for you today. Buddha, Mohammed and all creators of false religions have died, but the *Living Father* will exist forever to give you eternal life. Will you receive it? The Lord is the *Living Father.* He did not have to create life—He is life. He created every living thing in the universe. The *Living Father* gives spiritual life to those who call on Him and believe in Him.

O Lord, I tend to take my life for granted, except when I get sick or am
threatened. Help me find meaning in my life, and give me happiness.

The Lord is your *Living Father* who gave life to Adam and, through the continuous miracle of birth, gave life to you. He originally blew breath into Adam, who then became a living soul (see Genesis 2:7); so He can breathe new spiritual life into you every day. The *Living Father* can make this a wonderful day if you will let Him.

O Living Father, I know that both my physical life and spiritual
life come from You. I am grateful for another day to live for You.
May my life glorify You today. Amen.

Reading: John 6:53-59
Key Thought: The *Living Father* can make your life meaningful.

19 JESUS: STRONG CONSOLATION

That by two immutable things, in which it is impossible for God to lie, we might have strong consolation. . . . This hope we have as an anchor of the soul, . . . which enters the Presence behind the veil, where the forerunner has entered for us.
HEBREWS 6:18-20

Jesus is your *Strong Consolation* to overcome doubts. Don't worry about your eternal destiny; Jesus is your Hope. Doubts come from the heart, because believers still have an old sin nature (see 1 John 1:8-10). So don't look within your heart when you have doubts; look to Jesus, the *Strong Consolation*. You can be sure of Heaven, because He is already there for you. Just as a boat is anchored in the harbor to keep from drifting out to sea with the tide, Jesus, your Anchor, is already securely grounded in Heaven; He'll keep you from drifting. Just as a royal delegation will send a forerunner into a city so its citizens can prepare for the dignitaries, so Jesus is your Forerunner who has gone to prepare Heaven for you because He knows you are coming. Your doubts will disappear when you look to Jesus, who is standing in Heaven and waiting for you.

Lord Jesus, I have doubts when I rely on my ability to reason things out. But when I look to You, my doubts go away; then I know that Heaven is sure.

When you have Jesus in your heart, He is your *Strong Consolation* to take away doubts. He is standing in Heaven waiting for you. So walk in this life with assurance, play with confidence, serve without any doubts, and lay hold of the Hope set before you.

Lord Jesus, I know intellectually about Heaven, but I also know You in my heart; so I know I am going to Heaven. You are my Strong Consolation, my Anchor, my Forerunner. Amen.

Reading: Hebrews 6:13-20
Key Thought: Looking to Jesus takes away doubts.

20 JESUS: A STRONGHOLD IN THE DAY OF TROUBLE

*The LORD is good, a stronghold in the day of trouble; and
He knows those who trust in Him.*
NAHUM 1:7

Ever since Eve disobeyed the command of God, there has been trouble on Earth. There have been political troubles, financial troubles, family troubles and inner troubles. Just as Eve didn't have the power to say no, so all people struggle with the power of self-discipline. Because we can't say no, we bring trouble upon ourselves, just as Eve brought it upon herself and all her posterity. No one can escape trouble. "Man who is born of woman is of few days and full of trouble" (Job 14:1). But God knows our trouble, so He promised to be a *Stronghold in the Day of Trouble.*

*Lord, You know the troubles I face; help me. You know the future
troubles that are coming—troubles I don't know about; prepare me.*

The reference in Nahum 1:7 to "the day of trouble" has a twofold application. It applies to the future day of God's judgment. When you're in Jesus, He will be your Stronghold to protect you in the Day of Judgment. It also applies to all kinds of present-day troubles. He will protect you inwardly by giving you courage, patience and hope. He will help you outwardly when you follow the principles of Scripture. He will give you victory through prayer and His divine sovereign work. Don't worry about getting lost and not finding your way; He knows where you are, and He'll come get you.

*Lord Jesus, teach me how to solve troubles when I can have victory.
Teach me how to live with troubles when I can't eliminate them. Amen.*

Reading: Nahum 1:1-7
Key Thought: Jesus will help us with our troubles.

21 ◆ THE HOLY SPIRIT: RIVERS OF LIVING WATER

If anyone thirsts, let him come to Me and drink. He who believes in Me,
as the Scripture has said, out of his heart will flow rivers of living water.
JOHN 7:37-38

The Holy Spirit is *Rivers of Living Water*; He quenches your thirst. When you're dehydrated and close to death, He is Water to restore your life. When you're tempted to drink at a polluted fountain of the world, He is the only Water that will give you health. When you've spent all your energy working too hard, He is Water that will revive your spirit. When you've ignored the Lord and become dirty from sin, He is the Fountain of living water to wash away your filth. Come to Him, get clean, and drink!

Holy Spirit, thank You for the constant invitation to drink.
I need Water. I want Water. I like Water. Here I come!

The Holy Spirit is *Rivers of Living Water*. Because He is God, He is the eternal Source of the spiritual refreshment and renewal that flow from the heart of God. When you have the Holy Spirit in your heart, you have it all. The Source of living water will flow from you out to others. But He is more than one River of water; He is multiple Rivers of water. How many? As many as you need, and more—enough for every person ever born again into the family of God. He is enough Water to satisfy all people, and He is living Water to satisfy all needs. Come and drink.

Holy Spirit, I bow to worship You for spiritual satisfaction. I come to
You to drink. Ah, this Water is good! Amen.

Reading: Isaiah 12
Key Thought: The Holy Spirit will satisfy your longings.

22 ▷ JESUS: A RANSOM FOR MANY

Even as the Son of man came not to be ministered unto, but to minister,
and to give his life a ransom for many.
MATTHEW 20:28, *KJV*

A ransom is the price paid to release someone who is captured or kidnapped. Satan tempted Eve to eat the fruit of the tree of the knowledge of good and evil; she gave it to Adam, and they both ate. In that act of disobedience, they were captured by Satan—both they and all their posterity. To release these captives, a price was paid. "You were not redeemed with corruptible things, . . . but with the precious blood of Christ, as of a lamb" (1 Peter 1:18-19). Jesus gave His life's blood to pay the ransom price; He was a *Ransom for Many*. Jesus is "the Lamb of God who takes away the sin of the world" (John 1:29). While His blood was the price for everyone in the world, it only applies to those who believe in Him and receive Him as Savior. It was a *Ransom for Many*, but it only applies to those who receive it.

Jesus, I love You because You first loved me. I will serve You
because You paid the ransom for me.

Jesus is the perfect example of a servant who ministers to others. He did not think of Himself—He thought of others. But He did more than think of us—He came and took the initiative. He gave His time, His strength and His life for our ransom.

Jesus, I will give my life for others because You have given Your
life for me. I will think of others, give my time for others and take
the initiative for others. Amen.

Reading: Matthew 20:20-34
Key Thought: Give your life for others, as Christ gave His life for you.

23 ⬥ JESUS: A REFINER'S FIRE

But who can endure the day of His coming? And who can stand when He appears? For He is like a refiner's fire and like fullers' soap.
MALACHI 3:2

Jesus is the *Refiner's Fire* to judge those who call themselves God's children. Jesus will return to separate true believers from those who only call themselves Christians. In Malachi's day, silver ore was crushed into small granules and then ground into powder. Water was poured over the powder to wash away the dross. The remaining silverlike powder was melted in a crucible. The more heat—*Refiner's Fire*—that was added, the more lead dross that came to the surface. By blowing hot air over the melted surface, lead dross was blown away, leaving pure silver. When Jesus returns, He will judge all to determine who are His true believers. His breath is the Word of God; it will blow away the dross.

*Lord Jesus, I'm not perfect, but I believe in You with all my heart.
I love You with all my heart, soul and strength.*

There is much ore that looks like silver, though it's not. In the same way, there are many who look like Christians, but are not. Sometimes, we are crushed by persecutions and ground to powder by trials; even then, true believers are not always identified. The water of the Word of God is poured over us in sermons and Bible readings, but even that doesn't single out true believers. Only the *Refiner's Fire* of judgment will identify those who truly belong to Christ.

*Lord Jesus, I know in my head that You exist. I know in my
experience that I've asked You to come into my life. I know in
my innate being that I'm Your child. Amen.*

Reading: Revelation 20:11-15
Key Thought: Jesus will judge all those who call themselves Christians in order to determine who is real.

THE TRINITY: THE GOD OF FORGIVENESS (*ELOHIM SELICHOT*)

24

But You are God, ready to pardon, gracious and merciful,
slow to anger, abundant in kindness.
NEHEMIAH 9:17

[handwritten: God's nature is to Forgive]

The Lord is *Elohim Selichot*, the *God of Forgiveness*. When you look at God through the Cross, you hear Him say, "Forgive them, for they do not know what they do" (Luke 23:34). How could God forgive those who crucified Jesus? He could because they didn't understand who they were killing or because they were just carrying out orders. Being vicious was just their nature. God knows all about us, and He knows all of us. If God didn't forgive any of us, none of us would be forgiven. But He forgave those who crucified Jesus, just as He'll forgive you. Just as the very nature of people is to sin, so the very nature of God is to forgive.

Lord, Your forgiving nature is just the opposite of my sin
nature. Thank You for forgiving my sin; I don't deserve it. Help me
walk today as a forgiven person.

God has two sides to His nature. God is just—*Elohim Mishpat*—which means He must punish those who break His laws. But God is also loving; He forgives any and all who say, "I'm sorry," and who come to Him through Christ. The Cross has two sides: The judgment side is God's punishing sin, and the loving side is God's forgiving your sins. Through the Cross, you obtained "redemption through His blood, the forgiveness of sins" (Ephesians 1:7).

Lord, I'm glad You don't kill me every time I sin. I will live
today as a forgiven saint. Thank You for Your forgiveness,
which daily changes my life. Amen.

Reading: Nehemiah 9:5-38
Key Thought: God's forgiveness will change you.

25 JESUS: A RIGHTEOUS MAN

> *Now when the centurion saw what had happened, he glorified God,*
> *saying, "Certainly this was a righteous Man!"*
> LUKE 23:47

Jesus was a *Righteous Man*, which means Jesus did right things in the right way. A righteous man is right in his desires and thoughts, in the things he does and in the way he does things. The centurion present at Jesus' crucifixion knew that the trial and execution of Jesus was not fair. He saw the Jewish leaders first accuse Jesus of blasphemy and then, when Pilate wouldn't recognize that as a legal indictment, charge Jesus with treason. The centurion heard Pilate say, "I find no fault in Jesus" (see Luke 23:4); yet the Jews crucified Him anyway. Jesus forgave His executioners and then told the repentant thief, "Today you will be with Me in Paradise" (v. 43). When the centurion saw the integrity of Jesus in the face of lies and dishonesty, he confessed, "This was a righteous Man" (v. 47).

> *Lord Jesus, I don't measure up to Your righteous standard.*
> *I don't always do the right things; forgive me.*

When the Jewish leaders and the Roman establishment schemed against Jesus, Heaven came to His defense. The bright noonday sun turned to darkness. When God couldn't look on the unfolding tragedy, the heavens became dark. As Jesus died, an earthquake rumbled over Jerusalem and the surrounding hills. God's Earth was protesting the despicable things done to God's Son. When the centurion had seen it all, he cried, "This was a righteous Man!" (Luke 23:47). Jesus was a *Righteous Man* because He was God incarnate in human flesh.

> *Lord Jesus, You always did the right things; I recognize You as a*
> *Righteous Man. I worship at Your feet. Amen.*

Reading: Luke 23:46-49
Key Thought: People recognized Jesus as a *Righteous Man* because He did all things right.

26 ❖ JESUS: A STAR OUT OF JACOB

*I see Him, but not now; I behold Him, but not near; a Star shall come
out of Jacob; a Scepter shall rise out of Israel.*
NUMBERS 24:17

Jesus is pictured as a *Star out of Jacob*. Just as mariners plot their course by
the stars, so the Lord wants to direct your life by the *Star out of Jacob*. Just
as stars give light in the black night, so Jesus, the *Star out of Jacob*, gives
light to a world darkened by sin. Just as stars tell the time and seasons
(see Genesis 1:14), so Jesus gives meaning to your appointment calendar.
Just as stars warn people that they have a limited amount of time left on
this earth, so Jesus, the *Star out of Jacob*, gives hope. Look to Him for
meaning in your life.

*Jesus, I look to You for direction this day. Guide me to make good choices
and help me shine Your light to those about me.*

Those who walk in darkness hurt themselves; they need Jesus, the
Star out of Jacob, to show them the way. Those who are lost in the black
night are cold and disoriented; they need the *Star out of Jacob* to point
them to the warmth of God's love. The *Star out of Jacob* reminds people
that the Father loves them and has a wonderful plan for their life. Carry
the light of Jesus to them (see John 8:12; Acts 2:1-4); He wants to light
the way of everyone coming into the world (see John 1:4).

*Jesus, I want to be guided by Your star. Keep me warm near the fire
and shine a reading lamp in my heart so that I can learn. Light my path,
and help me walk in the light. Amen.*

Reading: Numbers 24
Key Thought: Jesus gives light to help people find the right path.

27 ◆ THE FATHER: HIS NAME IS FATHER

I have come in My Father's name, and you do not receive Me; if another
comes in his own name, him you will receive.
JOHN 5:43

His Name is Father; this means that "Father" is more than a title. Men on Earth are called by the title "Father" because that is a description of all who sire children. But throughout eternity past, the first Person of the Trinity was known by His name "Father." He was called Father by His Son, Jesus Christ. Why is "Father" His name? The title reflects the intimacy of relationship that He had with Jesus and that He can have with you. The most important aspect of God is not His awesome power or His omniscient knowledge; the most important characteristic of God is His relationship with people—He is Father.

I worship You as My God because of Your almighty power. I magnify
You as my Lord because of all You've done for me. I follow You as my
Master because of Your wisdom and miracles. But I know You
intimately because You are my Father.

People did not pray to God in the Old Testament using the name "Father," so Jesus came to teach them to pray: "Our Father in heaven, hallowed be Your name" (Matt. 6:9). As a child goes to an earthly father with his needs, so you can take your requests and call Him by name.

My heavenly Father, hallowed be Your name in my thoughts,
actions and service. Father, I love Your name. It cheers me
when I am down. It gives me strength to serve when I am weak.
It guards me against evil when I'm tempted. Because I know You
by Your name, I come calling You Father. Amen.

Reading: John 12:27-50
Key Thought: Call Him by His name "Father."

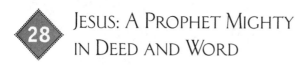

28   JESUS: A PROPHET MIGHTY IN DEED AND WORD

And He said to them, "What things?" And they said to Him,
"The things concerning Jesus of Nazareth, who was a Prophet mighty in deed
and word before God and all the people."
LUKE 24:19

God sent prophets to speak His message, but many times people wouldn't accept their message. So some prophets predicted the future to give them credibility; other prophets did miracles to get people to believe their message. The Bible describes these "prophets . . . who have . . . predicted signs or miracles" (Deuteronomy 13:1-2, *NLT*). Just as God's prophets in the Old Testament came with supernatural predictions and miracles, so Jesus came doing supernatural things as He preached to the multitudes. Jesus was a *Prophet Mighty in Deed and Word.*

Lord Jesus, I believe in the miracles recorded in the Bible. Lord Jesus,
I believe the truth You spoke in sermons. But I mostly believe because
You came into my heart and saved me.

Jesus did miracles for many reasons. He healed because He had compassion on those who suffered. He did supernatural acts to demonstrate His deity. Jesus did signs and wonders because the Old Testament predicted that the Messiah would do them. Jesus worked miracles so that His disciples and others would believe in Him. Jesus did miracles because it's only natural for God to do the supernatural. Today, let Jesus speak to you as a *Prophet Mighty in Deed and Word* who has God's message for you. Today, let Jesus do something supernatural for you.

Jesus, thank You for doing miracles while on Earth;
they give credibility to Your message. But thank You for the
miracles of my new nature and spiritual sight. Amen.

Reading: Luke 24:13-35
Key Thought: Jesus did miracles to give credibility to His sermons and His claims of deity.

29 JESUS: THE JUST ONE

*Which of the prophets did your fathers not persecute? And they killed
those who foretold the coming of the Just One, of whom you now have
become the betrayers and murderers.*

ACTS 7:52

Stephen preached a convicting sermon to those ready to kill him (see
Acts 7:1-53). The Jewish leaders stoned Stephen, just as they had been
responsible for the crucifixion of Jesus. Stephen said that the coming of
Jesus, the *Just One*, was foretold in Scripture. Stephen was suggesting
that Jesus was not guilty, but that He had been crucified unjustly. Jesus
did not die because He broke a law; rather, His death was a substitute for
everyone who had broken the Law. Jesus died on the cross so that people
wouldn't have to die eternally in Hell.

*Lord Jesus, You are the Just One, who died for me.
Thank You for taking my place.*

The title "Just" comes from the Greek word *dikaios*, which also can be
translated as "righteous." Jesus was always right—He never sinned. He
was right in character and actions. The Father made Jesus, who never
sinned, to become our sin, so we might have His righteousness (see
2 Corinthians 5:21). There is a double transfer in this verse. First, our
sins were transferred to the sinless One; and second, His righteousness
was transferred to us. It's not just enough to have your sins forgiven to
go to Heaven; you must be good—or in the words of this verse, you must
be righteous. In His substitution for us, Jesus, the *Just One*, did two
things: He took away our sin (subtraction), and He gave us His righteousness (addition).

*Lord Jesus, You came into my heart to take away my sins and give me
Your righteousness. You made me "good enough" for Heaven. Amen.*

Reading: Acts 7:51-60
Key Thought: Jesus makes us "good enough" to go to Heaven.

THE HOLY SPIRIT: THE BREATH OF THE ALMIGHTY

The Spirit of God has made me, and the breath of the Almighty gives me life.
JOB 33:4

The Holy Spirit is the *Breath of the Almighty;* He gives life to all living things. When Adam was originally created, God breathed into his physical lungs, and that clay body came alive. It was the Holy Spirit who entered into Adam's body. The Holy Spirit is life and gave Adam human life. Through the continual miracle of procreation, physical life was passed on to you. In the life of God, you live and move and have your being (see Acts 17:28).

*Holy Spirit, I thank You for physical life. Help me bring glory
to the Father, Son and Yourself this day. Keep my physical life strong
so that I can develop my spiritual life.*

The Holy Spirit is the *Breath of the Almighty* who first gave you spiritual life. When you became a Christian, He entered your life through the new birth (you were born again); now the Holy Spirit indwells your life. "Unless one is born of . . . the Spirit, he cannot enter the kingdom of God" (John 3:5). Now the Holy Spirit is present in your physical body to accomplish all the work that the Father and Son want to do through you. Will you yield to the Spirit's leading and let Him guide you today? Will you yield to His power and let Him work through you today?

*Holy Spirit, I am weak; I yield to Your power to overcome temptation.
I rely on Your power to live for You. Fill me with Your presence to
accomplish Your will this day. Amen.*

Reading: Genesis 2:1-7; Job 33:1-7
Key Thought: The Holy Spirit is God's Breath that gives me life.

31 JESUS: THE IMAGE OF THE INVISIBLE GOD

He is the image of the invisible God, the firstborn over all creation.
COLOSSIANS 1:15

Jesus is the *Image of the Invisible God* whom you can't see. Throughout history, people have asked to see God, but God has protected them. "No man shall see Me, and live" (Exodus 33:20), God told Moses. But there's another reason: You can't see God, because there's nothing to see. Jesus told the Samaritan woman, "God is Spirit" (John 4:24); and a spirit has no flesh or material substance to see. But still people want to see God. So they can see God by looking at Jesus. Read the pages of Scripture to see Jesus' character and miracles. See His acts of kindness. When you see Jesus in the Bible, you'll see God. You'll see how God in human flesh acted and reacted, for Jesus is God. He's the *Image of the Invisible God.*

Lord, in the pages of Scripture, I see kindness in Your
face. I feel the forgiveness of Your grace. When I can't see anything
else, the image of God I trace.

An image is an exact reflection. The original object can't move without the same movement in the image. Jesus is the Image of God; He is one with the Father—one in love, goodness and grace. Jesus said, "He who has seen Me has seen the Father" (John 14:9). To know the Father more intimately, look at Jesus; He is the *Image of the Invisible God.*

Jesus, I praise the Father in whose image You exist. One
look at You satisfies my curiosity about God. You are the
matchless beauty of deity. Amen.

Reading: Colossians 1:1-15
Key Thought: Jesus shows us how God would live and act in human flesh.

JUNE

JESUS: THE HOPE OF GLORY

To them God willed to make known what are the riches of the glory of this
mystery among the Gentiles: which is Christ in you, the hope of glory.
COLOSSIANS 1:27

Jesus is the *Hope of Glory*. All people will die, except for those who meet Jesus in the Rapture. No one looks forward to death; for most, it's a painful departure from this life. But when you walk through your personal valley of death, you won't have to be scared, because He will be with you (see Psalm 23:4). When you step into death, you'll come out on the other side in His presence. Yet some people have difficulty believing that there is life beyond the grave. To prove that the Lord will be with them in their death, He reminds them to look within their hearts at Christ's indwelling, because Christ is the *Hope of Glory*.

> *Lord, I'm grateful that You came into my heart. Now,*
> *I have confidence of my future home in Heaven.*

The indwelling of Jesus is your *Hope of Glory*. This assurance is your riches of glory (see Colossians 1:27). Don't spend this wealth on doubt. The unsaved can't understand this assurance; it's a mystery to them. Yet they would spend their life's savings to live beyond the grave. Heaven can't be bought with money, though; and confidence doesn't come from wealth. When you have Christ in your heart, you have the riches and *Hope of Glory*.

> *Lord, I know I'll live forever, but I don't look forward to*
> *the pain that is associated with death. Help me look beyond*
> *death to the Hope of Glory. Amen.*

Reading: Colossians 1:24-29
Key Thought: The indwelling Christ is your hope of enjoying the glories of Heaven.

THE FATHER: FATHER OF THE FATHERLESS

A father of the fatherless, a defender of widows, is God in His holy habitation.
PSALM 68:5

God is the *Father of the Fatherless*; He cares for the poor and needy. The Father cares for those who can't look after themselves and for all people who belong to Him. The orphans who walk with God can claim the Scripture that says, "When my father and my mother forsake me, then the LORD will take care of me" (Psalm 27:10). Many times God uses the Church to care for the needy, through homes, orphanages, hospitals, and so on. At other times, God cares for the needy through individual Christians. If you have plenty, let the *Father of the Fatherless* use your resources to care for someone in need. If you are in desperate conditions, call unto your heavenly Father for help.

> *Father, I am happy in Your presence. Although I have needs in my life,
> I am satisfied, because You are my Father. You have taken care of me,
> and I know You'll take care of me in the future.*

God is the *Father of the Fatherless*. Because He created the universe and mankind, He is the sovereign Father of all. Because believers have come to God through Jesus Christ, He is their personal heavenly Father. When God's children call unto Him, He is their intimate Father who provides for them. What can the Father supply for you today?

> *Father, I have no need when I look to You. But when I look at my
> schedule or I look out my window, I see needs everywhere. Thank You
> for taking care of me. Use me to meet the needs of the needy. Amen.*

Reading: Psalm 27:9-14
Key Thought: The Father in Heaven cares for the needy.

JESUS: THE HIDDEN MANNA

*He who has an ear, let him hear what the Spirit says to the churches.
To him who overcomes I will give some of the hidden manna to eat. And I will
give him a white stone, and on the stone a new name written which no one
knows except him who receives it.*

REVELATION 2:17

The rabbis taught that when the Messiah came, He would find the hidden Ark of the Covenant and feed the people the manna that was kept in the Ark. Since God supplied manna for Israel to eat in the wilderness, the people expected their Messiah to feed them in the same way. But Jesus corrected their false expectations with these words: "The bread of God is He who comes down from heaven and gives life to the world" (John 6:33). Then, to make sure all understood, He said, "I am the bread of life" (v. 35). Jesus was not going to give them physical bread to keep their bodies alive; He was going to give them spiritual bread. "If anyone eats of this bread, he will live forever" (v. 51).

*Lord Jesus, I have believed in You. I have eaten
Your bread, and You are good.*

When Jesus spoke of giving hidden manna, He was not talking about some stale bread left over from the wilderness wanderings. Nor was He talking about yesterday's day-old bread. The Jewish people were looking for a pot of old manna. It was as if they were looking for a huge pile of bread to last them the rest of their lives. Who wants a warehouse full of old bread when you have Jesus, the *Hidden Manna*? He says, "Whoever eats [of Me], . . . I will raise him up at the last day" (John 6:54).

*Jesus, I come daily to eat at Your table. Your bread is fresh and
good. I feel strong when I eat of You. Amen.*

Reading: Exodus 16
Key Thought: Jesus is the Manna that feeds.

4 JESUS: THE HEAD OF THE BODY

And He is the head of the body, the church, who is the beginning, the firstborn
from the dead, that in all things He may have the preeminence.
COLOSSIANS 1:18

Jesus is the *Head of the Body*; the One who gives direction to the Church.
Just as a head does the thinking for the human body, so Jesus can do
your thinking today. Just as the head makes choices, so Jesus can guide
your decision-making processes today. Just as the head sees the surrounding world and hears things and appreciates the aroma of good
things, so Jesus is your contact with the spiritual world. He knows what
has happened to you in the past, and He knows what will happen in the
future. Let Jesus—your Head—guide you today. He knows that good
encounters and evil experiences are headed your way. Look to Him—your
Head—for guidance this day.

Lord Jesus, I worship You for being the Head of the Body,
the Head of the Church. But I want more than knowledge about
You. Come be the Head of my life.

When the head is removed, the body dies; for the body can't work,
play, serve or worship without the head. You need Christ for everything
you do. You need Him more than once a week on Sundays and more
than once a day for revitalization. You need Jesus every minute of every
hour. Jesus, the *Head of the Body* is the secret of living.

Lord, be my eyes, so I can see spiritual things. Be my ears, so
I can hear the Father's voice; help me smell the sweet aroma of Your
presence. I crown You the Head of my life. Amen.

Reading: Revelation 22:1-5
Key Thought: Jesus must be the Head of your life.

5 ⬥ THE FATHER: THE FATHER OF SPIRITS

*Furthermore, we have had human fathers who corrected us, and
we paid them respect. Shall we not much more readily be in subjection
to the Father of spirits and live?*
HEBREWS 12:9

When you worship the Father, remember that "God is Spirit, and those who worship Him must worship in spirit and truth" (John 4:24). The Father is Spirit. That means He doesn't have a physical body; no one should make any images, idols or statues of Him. His nature is Spirit, but that doesn't mean He's like smoke or an illusion. The Father is a Person with the power of personality; that is, intellect, emotion and will. He has existence, and the Father is the powerful Creator, eternal Sustainer and infinite Judge of the universe. The Father is Spirit, the *Father of Spirits*.

*Father, come visit here, and let me feel Your presence. I bow before
You to worship You for Your awesome greatness. I pray to receive Your
personal care for me this day.*

The *Father of Spirits* is omniscient; He knows all things possible, so He knows all about you. The *Father of Spirits* is omnipotent; He has all power to do everything that is possible to do, so He can "work [all things] together for good" for you (Romans 8:28). The *Father of Spirits* is omnipresent; He is present everywhere at the same time, so He can be close to you and receive your worship. Therefore, worship Him in spirit, and He will hear your prayers.

*Father, I know You are here near me. You know all about me and You
know what I should do today; guide me. You have all power; work out
Your will in my life. Amen.*

Reading: Hebrews 12:6-15
Key Thought: The heavenly Father is near you to help you.

JESUS: THE HEAD OF ALL PRINCIPALITY AND POWER

6

And you are complete in Him, who is the head of all principality and power.
COLOSSIANS 2:10

Jesus is the *Head of All Principality and Power*, which means that laws and authority originally came from Him. Because He is righteous, He wants you to live by His righteous principles. These are the principles by which the Lord rules the world—principles (laws) of nature, the principles by which governments exist or the ethical principles that guide human conduct and human relationships. Also, the spiritual principles of peace and brotherly kindness come from the Lord. Commit yourself to learning all you can about the laws of this world (which come from God) so that you can understand how the Lord guides and controls all things.

> *Lord, teach me to live by Your principles so that I can*
> *please You and be like You. But I know my weakness;*
> *give me power to live by Your principles.*

Jesus is the *Head of All Principality and Power*. The power of laws and principles flowed into the natural world when He created everything in the beginning. The principles by which people live flowed into humanity when He created people in His image. The principles by which He sovereignly guides all things come from His power, for Jesus is the *Head of All Principality and Power*.

> *Lord, I want to live by Your principles because I don't know all things;*
> *teach me Your laws. Because I am weak, I need Your strength. Because I*
> *am needy, I come to You for help. Amen.*

Reading: Psalm 119:1-16
Key Thought: Know the Lord's principles, because they are the secret to successful living.

JESUS: THE LAMB SLAIN FROM THE FOUNDATION OF THE WORLD

All who dwell on the earth will worship him, whose names have not been written in the Book of Life of the Lamb slain from the foundation of the world.
REVELATION 13:8

As Israel faced the first Passover, "Moses called for all the elders of Israel and said to them, 'Pick out and take lambs for yourselves according to your families'" (Exodus 12:21). Each father placed his hands on the head of the lamb to confess the sins of each family member. Their sins were transferred to the lamb, and then the lamb was killed; the lamb died instead of the family. Jesus was "the Lamb of God who takes away the sin of the world" (John 1:29). Since Jesus is called God's Lamb, this suggests that God sent His Lamb—His Son—to die for the sin of the world. He is the *Lamb Slain from the Foundation of the World.*

Lord Jesus, thank You for dying for the world, but thank You most of all for dying for me.

It was a historical event when God's Son died on the cross. But God doesn't have a calendar and He doesn't keep time as humans. God is eternal, without time. He has always loved us and has always planned to give His Son to die for our sins. Jesus is the *Lamb Slain from the Foundation of the World.* At another place, the Bible reminds us, "You were not redeemed with corruptible things, like silver or gold, . . . but with the precious blood of Christ, as of a lamb . . . foreordained before the foundation of the world, but was manifest in these last times for you" (1 Peter 1:18-20).

Lord Jesus, thank You for planning my salvation from the foundation of the world. Thank You for coming to die on a cross for me. Amen.

Reading: Isaiah 53:1-7
Key Thought: The sacrifice of Jesus was planned in ages past but was accomplished on the cross.

THE HOLY SPIRIT: THE BREATH OF GOD'S NOSTRILS

The foundations of the world were uncovered at Your rebuke, O LORD, at the blast of the breath of Your nostrils.

PSALM 18:15

The Holy Spirit is the *Breath of God's Nostrils*. When God breathes judgment, the Holy Spirit executes His punishment. Sometimes in Scripture, God judged directly, such as when He struck a person with leprosy (see Numbers 12:9-12) or when He struck a person dead (see Acts 5:1-11). The Holy Spirit was God's direct instrument to carry out that punishment. Sometimes God judged indirectly, such as when He shut up Heaven so that it did not rain. Sometimes God sent a plague of locusts or used a storm or other natural means. The Holy Spirit was God's indirect instrument behind the apparent natural disaster. He can work good in your life, directly or indirectly. Or He can be the force of God's punishment, directly or indirectly.

Holy Spirit, if I'm doing anything that will lead to judgment, show me; I will repent and change. Breathe good things upon me.

The *Breath of God's Nostrils* controls nature. Sometimes disasters come upon you not because you sin or are disobedient. You may think you're being punished for something you did, but look behind the event. What you think is punishment may be God's classroom to instruct you about His grace. Remember, all things—including loss—will work together for good to those who love God (see Romans 8:28). Examine your loss to find what God is teaching you. Learn what He wants you to know, and then pray for the Breath of good things to blow upon you.

*Holy Spirit, let me feel Your breath of good things.
I don't pray for harmful consequences, but help me learn
from them when they come. Amen.*

Reading: Psalm 18:15-50
Key Thought: God controls the circumstances that control your life.

9 JESUS: THE LIFE

Jesus said to him, "I am the way, the truth, and the life.
No one comes to the Father except through Me."
JOHN 14:6

Jesus is the *Life*; He is the Source of life. He embedded the world with His life when He created it (see Colossians 1:16). The smallest building block of the universe is the cell, made up of protons, neutrons and electrons, all held together by the enormous power of Jesus who "holds all creation together" (v. 17, *NLT*). Jesus is also the Source of human life, for the first parents were made in God's image when God's life was breathed into Adam and he became "a living being" (Genesis 2:7).

Lord Jesus, I thank You for life in my physical body. I thank
You for food to eat, water to drink and air to breathe.
I thank You for mental and spiritual life.

Jesus is the Source of spiritual life. Jesus, the *Life* of God, was put to death, but He arose on the third day. He is "the resurrection and the life" (John 11:25). The apostle John was referring to Jesus when he stated, "The life was manifested, and we have seen, and bear witness, and declare to you that eternal life which was with the Father and was manifested to us" (1 John 1:2). Have you seen and received this life?

Lord Jesus, I have received Your life—eternal life—when
I was saved. I get enlightened from reading the Scriptures.
I experience renewed life when I fellowship with You in prayer.
I worship You for heavenly life. Amen.

Reading: John 3:22-36
Key Thought: You get the *Life* of Jesus when you receive Him into your life.

10 ◆ JESUS: THE LAWGIVER

There is one Lawgiver, who is able to save and to destroy.
Who are you to judge another?
JAMES 4:12

The Lord is the *Lawgiver*; He runs the world through natural laws such as the law of gravity. No one can break these laws without suffering consequences. He also runs the spiritual world through moral laws. Because no one has perfectly kept all laws, no one can enter Heaven. Jesus fulfilled the Law in His death; He nailed the law to His cross. No longer will broken laws keep you from going to Heaven (Colossians 2:14-15). Christianity is not about keeping rules or laws; it's about knowing Jesus. When you please Him, you satisfy all the laws, for Jesus created the laws; He is the *Lawgiver*.

Lord, it's sometimes hard to keep the laws, because I have a rebellious streak
in my heart. Help me submit to You. Help me live by Your principles.

Don't be just a law keeper; these people are called legalists. Look behind laws to see their purpose, because laws were given to point you to God. Jesus said the greatest law of all is to love the Lord your God with all your heart, and the second is to love your neighbor as yourself (see Matthew 22:37-40). When you follow the *Lawgiver* and live by the meaning of His laws, you will have a worthwhile life.

Lord, forgive me for just keeping laws for legalistic purposes.
Show me Your purpose behind Your laws. I love You with all
my heart, my soul and my mind. Show me the real meaning
behind Your laws, and give me the right attitude to live by
them. Give me the power to keep them. Amen.

Reading: Matthew 22:35-40
Key Thought: Focus on Jesus, not on impersonal laws.

11 ⬥ JESUS: A GOOD MAN

And there was much murmuring among the people concerning him: for some said, He is a good man: others said, Nay; but he deceiveth the people.
JOHN 7:12, *KJV*

As the Feast of Tabernacles approached, Jesus was the main topic of discussion. The people wondered whether Jesus would come to the feast, because there were rumors that the Jewish leaders would arrest Him. Jesus had broken their Sabbath laws, and He claimed to be God. Some said Jesus was a *Good Man*; others didn't think so. Some said Jesus was a prophet (see John 7:40); others knew He did miracles. Some thought Jesus was in fact their Messiah (see v. 41). During the life of Jesus, as in the world today, "there was a division among the people because of Him" (v. 43). Many theological liberals say that the Bible is not authoritative; if that were true, Jesus would be only a mere man. Some historians say that Jesus was only a good man; if that were true, they couldn't be saved by Him. The problem is that Jesus is the Lord God who demands our loyalty and total love.

Lord Jesus, I recognize that You are the Son of God, the second Person of the Trinity. I bow to worship You as my Savior.

To say that Jesus is a *Good Man* is a first step, but it's not enough to save you. It doesn't take much to acknowledge that Jesus is good, but it demands your total response to acknowledge that Jesus is Lord. What must you do? "For if you confess with your mouth that Jesus is Lord and believe in your heart that God raised him from the dead, you will be saved" (Romans 10:9, *NLT*).

Jesus, I confess that You are much more than a Good Man; You are the Lord of the universe; You are my Lord. Amen.

Reading: John 7:1-13
Key Thought: It's not enough to recognize Jesus as a *Good Man*; He must be your Lord.

12 JESUS: THE CONSOLATION OF ISRAEL

*And behold, there was a man in Jerusalem whose name was Simeon,
and this man was just and devout, waiting for the Consolation of
Israel, and the Holy Spirit was upon him.*
LUKE 2:25

Jesus was the *Consolation of Israel*. The word "consolation" means "comfort." Israel was waiting for God to send the Messiah to deliver them from oppression and suffering; they wanted the Messiah to give them comfort. Many Jews in Jesus' day were looking for political deliverance from Rome. They were oppressed financially, socially and, to some degree, spiritually. They expected the Messiah to free them from military bondage; then they would be comforted. Much of life is expectation and perception. Because the Jews expected the wrong kind of deliverance, they wrongly perceived who Jesus was and what He came to do.

*Lord Jesus, give me eyes to see You clearly, a clear mind to understand
You properly and a willing heart to follow You gladly.*

Jesus did not come the first time to sit on a military throne in Jerusalem. He came to sit on the throne of the heart of his followers. His consolation is not outward, but inward. Jesus came to rule people's thoughts and dreams and courage. When Jesus rules people's hearts, He conquers people from within. He is the inner *Consolation of Israel,* or the comforter of hearts. When He comes a second time, Jesus will conquer outwardly and will rule from Jerusalem.

*Lord Jesus, come rule my heart. You are the fulfillment of my dreams;
You are my comfort from oppression and suffering. Amen.*

Reading: Isaiah 40
Key Thought: Jesus offers inner comfort to us.

13 · JESUS: THE DELIVERANCE OF ZION

And it shall come to pass that whoever calls on the name of the LORD shall be saved. For in Mount Zion and in Jerusalem there shall be deliverance, as the LORD has said, among the remnant whom the LORD calls.

JOEL 2:32

The phrase *"Deliverance of Zion"* is a reference to Jesus and has a twofold application. First, it is a reference to the future physical deliverance of the nation of Israel. Armies shall come against Israel to destroy her, but when Israel calls upon the Lord Jesus, He will come to deliver the nation. Even though it's only a remnant that calls on Him, the Lord will be the *Deliverance of Zion*. If the Lord has promised to deliver His people in the future, don't you think He can come to deliver you in your present troubles?

*Lord, I know You are my Deliverer. I call on You today
to help me in my difficulties.*

The second application is to those who call upon the Lord today. On the Day of Pentecost, Peter quoted Joel 2:28-32 and applied it to those who were listening to him that day (see Acts 2:17-21). Your task is to call; the Lord's task is to deliver. Your call must be sincere; are you a seeking believer? Your call must be toward the Lord, not to a church, religion or any other cause. Have you called to the Lord? When you call, it must be outward, because the Lord wants your outward response. You don't have to shout; He can hear you if you whisper. The key is doing it—not thinking about it or planning to do it in the future. Call to Him now.

*I call out, Lord. I have thought about it, but now I do it.
I need You, Lord; come deliver me. Amen.*

Reading: Joel 2:28-32
Key Thought: The Lord delivers those who call on Him.

THE FATHER: THE ANCIENT OF DAYS

I was watching in the night visions, and behold, One like the Son of Man, coming with the clouds of heaven! He came to the Ancient of Days.
DANIEL 7:13

The Lord is called the *Ancient of Days*. He is eternal; He knows everything that is knowable. Nothing has happened in the past that escaped His knowledge; so He knows everything you have done in the past and everything you will do today. He knows what is best for you. Will you come to Him for direction this day?

Lord, You have all knowledge; I come seeking Your answers to the problems I face today. I need Your direction.

The Lord is called the *Ancient of Days* because He has always existed. He has great wisdom. He knows that you are trying to connect all the pieces of your life. But remember, the only "perfect" life is the one lived according to His will. To the *Ancient of Days*, yesterday is like tomorrow. Because He is God, He knows all things potential and "calleth those things which be not as though they were" (Romans 4:17, *KJV*). He knows what will happen to you if you do evil, and He knows what will happen if you do right. He has a perfect plan for you. Let Him guide you this day to do the right thing in the right way.

Lord, I accept Your will as the best plan for my life. I will do the right things, no matter what consequences I suffer for doing right. I will do right, because it is Your perfect plan for my life. I will put You first in all things. Amen.

Reading: Daniel 7:1-27
Key Thought: Because God knows everything, He has a perfect plan for your life.

15 JESUS: CLOUD

I don't want you to forget, dear brothers and sisters, what happened to our
ancestors in the wilderness long ago. God guided all of them by sending a
cloud that moved along ahead of them, and he brought them all
safely through the waters of the sea on dry ground.

1 CORINTHIANS 10:1, *NLT*

Jesus is a picture of the *Cloud* that led Israel through the wilderness (see Exodus 14:19). He knew what He was doing when Israel followed Him to a dead end at the Red Sea. There were mountains on both sides, and Pharaoh's army was chasing them from behind. There was no way across the sea. Why did Jesus put them in such a dangerous position? So His people would look to Him. Have you ever been at a dead end? Perhaps Jesus led you there to teach you the greatest lessons in life. You're never at a dead end by yourself. Don't fear, for He is behind you, keeping the enemy away. Don't panic, for He has a solution; you can leave a dead end as a victor.

Lord, too often I am problem focused, not victory focused. Teach me to
look beyond my dead-end situations to see You at work in my life.

When you get to a dead end, do what Israel did. First, wait on the Lord. Perhaps He's stopped your progress so that you can learn about your finiteness and His almighty power. Just as Israel didn't expect the Lord to roll back the sea, maybe you don't know yet how He'll solve your problems. Second, just as Moses lifted his rod for Israel to go forward, so Jesus wants you to walk forward through your obstacles. If Jesus doesn't test your faith, you'll not trust His guidance.

Lord, thank You for the dead ends of my life, which make me look to
You. Today, I look to You and call on Your power to see me through my
obstacles. It's good to get going again. Amen.

Reading: Exodus 14:19-22
Key Thought: Look for God's purpose when you come to a dead end.

16 JESUS: THE COMMANDER OF THE HOSTS OF THE LORD

So He [Jesus] said, "No, but as Commander of the army of the LORD I have now come." And Joshua fell on his face to the earth and worshiped, and said to Him, "What does my Lord say to His servant?" Then the Commander of the LORD's army said to Joshua, "Take your sandal off your foot, for the place where you stand is holy." And Joshua did so.
JOSHUA 5:14-15

Jesus is the *Commander of the Hosts of the Lord*. When Joshua was surveying the apparently impregnable Jericho before attacking the city, the Lord appeared to Joshua. Originally, Joshua thought the Lord was a soldier, so he asked, "Are You for us or for our adversaries?" (Joshua 5:13). The Lord was not on either side. The Lord simply answered He was the *Commander of the Hosts of the Lord*. Joshua fell on his face, calling him "my Lord" (v. 14). The answer to victory over Jericho was not Joshua's getting the Lord on his side but Joshua's getting on the Lord's side. When Joshua submitted to the Lord, he was given a divine strategy to win the battle (see 6:2-5).

Lord, too often I beg You for help in my plans. Teach me to submit my plans to You. I want to be on Your side.

When the Lord appeared to Joshua, it was a Christophany, an appearance of Christ in the Old Testament. Because the Commander is Lord, victory comes when you yield to His plans. Because the Commander is over the angelic host, victory comes when you get heavenly power on your side. The *Commander of the Hosts of the Lord* told Joshua to take off his shoes because he was on holy ground; likewise, you must worship to achieve victory.

Lord, I realize I'm in a spiritual battle. I want to join Your army; show me what to do. I want spiritual victory; send angelic hosts to help me. I want fellowship with You, so I worship You. Amen.

Reading: Joshua 5:13—6:21
Key Thought: Since Jesus is our Commander in battle, we must join His army.

THE HOLY SPIRIT: THE FULLNESS OF GOD

To know the love of Christ which passes knowledge; that you
may be filled with all the fullness of God.
EPHESIANS 3:19

The Holy Spirit is the *Fullness of God*. He is sent into your life by the Father and the Son to fill you with all the things you need to live for God. The Holy Spirit will fill you with spiritual power to withstand temptation, and He will fill you with wisdom so that you can live a godly life. He will fill you with spiritual understanding to interpret things in your life, and He will fill you with spiritual knowledge so that you will know what to do. What part of your life is empty? Let the Holy Spirit fill you with the *Fullness of God*.

Holy Spirit, I want to be more spiritual; fill me with Your Spirit.
I want to be more holy; fill me with Your holiness.

The Holy Spirit is the *Fullness of God*; when you have Him in your life, you are filled with the Godhead. You have Christ dwelling in your heart to ground your life in divine purpose (see Ephesians 3:17). You have the Father to strengthen you (see vv. 14-16). You have the Holy Spirit to help you comprehend the breadth, length, depth and height of the love of God (see vv. 18-19). Call on the Trinity today; they will fill your life with the *Fullness of God*.

Holy Spirit, I have a lot to do today; I need Your enablement. I am not
as godly as I want to be; make me holy. Fill me up; I am empty and I
need Your presence. Amen.

Reading: Ephesians 3:14-21
Key Thought: The Holy Spirit can fill your life with meaning.

18 ⬧ JESUS: I AM

Then—when He said to them, "I am He,"—they drew
back and fell to the ground.
JOHN 18:6

Jesus is the *I AM*, the eternal all-powerful Lord. Moses asked the Lord what His name was. The Lord answered, "I AM WHO I AM. . . . Thus you shall say to the children of Israel, 'I AM has sent me to you'" (Exodus 3:14). The name "Lord" comes from the Hebrew verb that means "to be"; it is first person, repeated twice. When you say "Lord," you are saying, "I AM I AM." God exists in Himself and by Himself.

Lord Jesus, You are the great I AM; You are without beginning and
without end. You exist by Yourself and of Yourself. You are the Lord.

Jesus used metaphors to tell people what He was like. Jesus said, "*I AM* the Bread," "the Light," "the Door," "the Good Shepherd," "the Resurrection," "the True Vine" and more. But when Jesus used these metaphors, He was saying more than that He was Bread that satisfied or the Way to Heaven. Jesus was telling His listeners that He was the Lord who was revealed in the Old Testament. When the soldiers came to arrest Jesus in the Garden of Gethsemane, Jesus asked them, "Whom are you seeking?" (John 18:4). They answered, "Jesus of Nazareth" (v. 5). When Jesus replied in return, "I am He" (v. 6), He pulled aside His humanity, and His glorious deity came bursting out. The soldiers fell backward to the ground in response. How will you respond to His awesome glory?

Lord Jesus, I bow myself to the ground. You are the Lord God of glory.
I worship You, the great I AM. Amen.

Reading: Exodus 3:1-15
Key Thought: Jesus is the great *I AM* of the Old Testament.

19 ❖ JESUS: GOD WITH US (*IMMANUEL*)

They shall call His name Immanuel, which is translated, "God with us."
MATTHEW 1:23

The angel told Joseph to name Jesus *Immanuel,* which means *"God with Us."* When Jesus was born, God visited humanity. He came to live with people and to die for their sins. Jesus was God, even though many did not recognize Him. Today, Jesus is still *Immanuel,* even when people don't feel His presence. Because Jesus is with you, you can get Him to help you face your problems. He's with you, even when you don't realize He's near. However, you must call on *Immanuel* to get His help. He is *Immanuel,* which means He'll be there when you need Him.

> *Immanuel, there are many times I can't feel Your presence. I want to feel Your nearness. I pray about my problems, but they're still here. I know You're by me. Manifest Yourself; help me make it through my day.*

Because He's *Immanuel,* you can win when you let Him direct your efforts. First, He will give you hope when you feel like giving up. Then He will give you a courageous spirit to carry you through the rough spots. Next, He will show you what to do and will guide your steps. Finally, He'll give you the tenacity to press on to victory. *Immanuel* is with you, but you must call on Him to get help.

> *Immanuel, I know You are with me. Help me feel Your guiding presence this day. Release Your indwelling power to do everything I'm supposed to do. I claim Your presence for victory today. Amen.*

Reading: Matthew 8:1-18
Key Thought: Jesus will be with you everywhere because He is God.

20 ◆ THE TRINITY: LEADER

The LORD is my shepherd; I shall not want. He makes me to lie down in green pastures; He leads me beside the still waters. . . . He leads me in the paths of right-eousness for His name's sake. Yea, though I walk through the valley of the shadow of death, I will fear no evil; for You are with me.

PSALM 23:1-4

The Lord is your Shepherd; He will lead you. Sometimes the Lord will lead you to still waters; at other times He will lead you through right paths. Because He is God, He knows the best path for you today. He knows the problems you will face today, so follow Him closely. He knows what troubles await you and may even lead you into some troubles to strengthen your faith. Just as the Father didn't deliver Jesus out of suffering, so He may not take away your pain. But remember, when the *Leader* leads you through the valley of the shadow of death, He will be with you.

Lord, I know You lead me, and I know suffering is inevitable in this life. But I don't like pain. Help me accept pain and learn from it.

Follow the *Leader* closely today. He knows when you should start walking, and He knows when you should stop. If you start walking when He says, "Stop," you may get into deeper trouble. If you obey the Lord, He will give you peace in the shadows of your dark valley; stay close to Him and obey Him. When the Lord, your *Leader*, says, "Stop," He may be keeping you from getting into severe trouble. But no matter what happens, He'll be with you.

Lord, I'll walk when You tell me, "Go," and I'll wait for You when You say, "Stop." I'll do what You tell me to do, because I want to be what You want me to be. Amen.

Reading: Psalm 103:1-14
Key Thought: Follow closely the Father's lead.

21 ◆ JESUS: JESUS CHRIST OUR LORD

*I thank God—through Jesus Christ our Lord! So then, with the mind
I myself serve the law of God, but with the flesh the law of sin.*
ROMANS 7:25

His name was Jesus. That's the name given to Him by Mary and Joseph. Throughout the Gospels, He is called Jesus. His office is Christ, much like people in the Body of Christ have the office of minister or teacher. The office "Christ" in the Greek language is the word "Messiah" in Hebrew, which comes from the root that means "to anoint." When you say, "Jesus Christ," you are saying, "Jesus, the Anointed One." People were inaugurated into office in the Old Testament by anointing; they had oil poured over them—a symbol of riches, prosperity and the Holy Spirit.

*Jesus, I come to You through Your earthly name. I thank You for
coming to Earth for me. Christ, I come to You through Your office;
You are the One who died for me.*

His title is "Lord." Just as the executive leader of the United States has the title "president," Jesus has the eternal title "Lord." With His title "Lord" goes ownership and control. Does Jesus have control over your life? Also, this title gives Him authority to direct people under Him and to punish those who disobey His laws. Have you let Jesus direct your life? He is *Jesus Christ Our Lord*; is He your personal Savior and Master?

*Thank You, Jesus, for coming into my life to save me.
Now I give You control of my life; I make You my Master.
Jesus Christ, You are my Lord. Amen.*

Reading: Romans 10:1-17
Key Thought: Jesus wants to be your Lord and Savior.

22 JESUS: JESUS OF GALILEE

Now Peter sat outside in the courtyard. And a servant girl came to him, saying,
"You also were with Jesus of Galilee."
MATTHEW 26:69

Jesus of Galilee was both His name and address. The angel told Mary to name Him Jesus. His name in Hebrew—*Yehoshua*—is a derivative of "Joshua" and means "Jehovah saves." Jesus, who came to save sinners, is from Galilee, so He was called *Jesus of Galilee*. The Old Testament predicted that the Messiah would come from Galilee: "by the way of the sea, beyond the Jordan, in Galilee of the Gentiles" (Isaiah 9:1). Did you see that Jesus' home area was called "Galilee of the Gentiles"? He was a Jew from the place where many Gentiles lived, because He is the Savior of all, both Jews and Gentiles.

Jesus, I know You came to Your people, but You died for all.
I thank You for dying for me.

The people of Jerusalem during Jesus' day were prejudiced against anyone from any other place. The servant girl sarcastically referred to Him as *"Jesus of Galilee"* (Matthew 26:69). Once before, some had questioned if their Messiah could come out of Galilee (see John 7:41). Another even claimed, "No prophet has arisen out of Galilee" (v. 52). Yet God had sovereignly arranged that His Son would be born in Bethlehem, the town of privilege, according to the prediction of Micah 5:2. Then Jesus grew up in Galilee in the city of Nazareth, fulfilling the prophecy, "He shall be called a Nazarene" (Matthew 2:23).

Jesus, I know Your earthly home was in Galilee, but now I want You to
make Your home in my heart. Amen.

Reading: Matthew 2:13-23
Key Thought: God prepared a specific location for Jesus' birth and home.

23 THE FATHER: THE FATHER

Behold what manner of love the Father has bestowed on us,
that we should be called children of God! Therefore the world does not
know us, because it did not know Him.
1 JOHN 3:1

The *Father* in Heaven is likened to an earthly father who loves his children before they are born. Your heavenly *Father* loved you long before you loved Him; He loved you before you were born. Just as an earthly father fellowships with his children, so your heavenly *Father* offers you His fellowship. Just as earthly children have access to their fathers, so you have access to Him through Jesus Christ. Just as earthly fathers guide their children in life's accomplishments, your heavenly *Father* wants to guide you today. And just as earthly fathers want their children to be like them, so your heavenly *Father* wants to conform you into His image.

Thank You, Father, for loving me. Help me learn about You and
become conformed to Your image. Help me know Your will and walk
according to it.

Your heavenly *Father* sometimes pushes you to walk, just as earthly fathers want their children to walk. Sometimes your heavenly *Father* wants you to run quickly when you are still growing. Why does He seemingly put more on you than you can bear? So you'll grow stronger and accomplish more. But learning is sometimes hard and discouraging. Sometimes you will want to give up, but your heavenly *Father* encourages you—just as an earthly father does—so you'll grow stronger and accomplish much with your life. Maybe the heavenly *Father* is allowing difficulties in your life so that you'll do more for Him.

Father, thank You for difficulties that make me stronger.
Thank You for your unending encouragement. Help me reach
the goals you set for me. Amen.

Reading: Ephesians 2:1-6
Key Thought: The *Father* encourages us to grow beyond our comfort level.

JESUS: JESUS OF NAZARETH

Philip found Nathanael and said to him, "We have found Him of whom Moses in the law, and also the prophets, wrote—Jesus of Nazareth, the son of Joseph."
JOHN 1:45

When you use the title *"Jesus of Nazareth,"* you are referring to both His name and His address, as you are when you use His title "Jesus of Galilee." Jesus came as a baby, so He had to be born somewhere—it was Bethlehem. Jesus was a child, so he had to grow up somewhere—it was Nazareth. He didn't grow up in Jerusalem near the Temple, even though Jesus called the Temple "My Father's house" (John 2:16). Corrupt priests, who eventually bribed Judas to betray Jesus, might have tried to corrupt the boy Jesus, if He had grown up there. Jesus grew up in a small, out-of-the-way town in Galilee. His main influences were His father and mother and the people of Nazareth. The word "Nazareth" comes from the Hebrew root *nazar*, meaning "separated." We know that Gentiles lived in the region, because it was known as "Galilee of the Gentiles" (Isaiah 9:1). But in this small town, Jesus was separated from outside influences, since the townspeople separated themselves from others. Nazareth was a perfect place for a Jewish boy to grow up and yet have a heart for all people and become "the Savior of the world" (John 4:42).

Lord, I praise You for perfectly guiding the childhood of Jesus so that He could become my Savior.

Jesus of Nazareth had a perfect childhood. Commit yourself to give your children or grandchildren the best possible conditions for them to grow "in the nurture and admonition of the Lord" (Ephesians 6:4, *KJV*).

Jesus, I know You love the children of the world. Help me to fulfill Your passion by loving all children, teaching them Your truth and leading them to salvation. Amen.

Reading: Deuteronomy 6:1-15
Key Thought: The boyhood of Jesus prepared Him to be your Savior.

25 JESUS: THE KING OF PEACE

To whom also Abraham gave a tenth part of all, first being translated "king of righteousness," and then also king of Salem, meaning "king of peace."
HEBREWS 7:2

Jesus is the *King of Peace*; no one can have peace apart from Him, because He is the original source of peace. While on Earth, Jesus could calm tremendous storms, for He had power over nature's violence. Jesus also calmed the disruptive demoniac of Gadera, because He had power over human nature. Jesus can give you peace when you're in the eye of a hurricane of circumstances. He can give you self-control and an inner calm when you receive His peace. When you let Him sit on the throne of your heart, the *King of Peace* works all things together for good. What do you need today?

Jesus, I look to You for inner peace. While I may not be responsible for all the troubles in my life, I am at least responsible for my reaction to them. Lord, help me react properly, the way You want me to react.

Satan is the author of confusion, strife and violence; but Jesus brings peace, and He rules by peace. When you're anxious and upset, you're not in the center of Jesus' will. But when Jesus controls your life, you'll experience self-control, and you can enter the center of His will. Will you invite King Jesus to sit on the throne of your heart today?

Jesus, teach me to look at trouble through Your eyes. Show me how to react when things around me are coming apart. I invite You to control my life and bring peace to my heart. Amen.

Reading: Psalm 62
Key Thought: You'll receive peace and self-control when Jesus controls your life.

26 THE HOLY SPIRIT: THE GIFT OF GOD

If you knew the gift of God, and who it is who says to you, "Give Me a drink,"
you would have asked Him, and He would have given you living water.
JOHN 4:10

The Holy Spirit is the *Gift of God*. He is the One who gave eternal life to you at salvation. He is called the Gift because salvation is a gift (see Ephesians 2:8-9). You cannot work for anything that He gives; you must receive the gifts freely from Him. When you let the Holy Spirit control your life, you have peace, wisdom, understanding, courage and a sound mind.

Holy Spirit, I receive You into my life. I take the gifts
You offer to me. Come into my life to empower the gifts You've
given me. Show me how to use the abilities I have.

The Holy Spirit is called the *Gift of God*, because He will give you spiritual gifts, or abilities, for your Christian service. He gives the spiritual gifts of evangelism, teaching, exhorting, managing, serving and showing mercy. The Holy Spirit gives you the enabling talents of faith and wisdom in order for you to be effective. Every good gift comes from the Father (see James 1:17) and is delivered to believers by the Holy Spirit (see 1 Corinthians 12:11). Do you know what your dominant spiritual gift is? Do you know how to use it? Ask the Holy Spirit to reveal your spiritual gifts to you, and then ask Him to help you use them in ministry.

Holy Spirit, I ask You to show me my spiritual gifts. Show me how to use
them properly. Give me power to use them. Amen.

Reading: Romans 12:1-8; Ephesians 4:7-16
Key Thought: The Holy Spirit is the *Gift of God* to us.

27 ◆ JESUS: A NAME FOR SALVATION

That believing you may have life in His name.
JOHN 20:31

The angel commanded, "Call His name JESUS, for He will save His people from their sins" (Matthew 1:21). The name "Jesus" originates from the Hebrew word *Yehoshua* (its shortened form is *Yeshua*), which means "Jehovah saves." "Yehoshua" is also translated as "Joshua," the name of the general who conquered the Promised Land for Israel. Many Jews were looking for their Messiah to be a soldier—a general who would drive the Romans out of their land. Jesus came to give personal redemption, not political victory. He offered Himself as their Savior from sin, not their deliverer from military tyranny. Salvation was not in military triumph; it was inward—"You must be born again" (John 3:7).

Just as the fishermen left their nets to follow You, I surrender all to You.
Because You said to take up my cross daily, I repent today of my sins.

The name "Jesus" is a *Name for Salvation.* "There is no other name under heaven given among men by which we must be saved" (Acts 4:12). You are saved through faith in His name (see Ephesians 2:8). But you do not receive salvation by merely repeating His name verbally. No! His name stands for the Person of Jesus, who came from God. His name stands for His death, which brings you forgiveness of sin. His name stands for His triumphant Resurrection, which gives you new life. His name saves you because "as many as received Him, to them He gave the right to become children of God, even to those who believe in His name" (John 1:12).

Lord Jesus, I believe in Your name. I now ask You into my heart.
Thank You for salvation. Amen.

Reading: Matthew 12:15-21
Key Thought: The name of Jesus represents His divine Person and His saving death.

28 JESUS: THE HOLY ONE AND THE JUST

But you denied the Holy One and the Just, and asked for a
murderer to be granted to you.
ACTS 3:14

The Jewish leaders rejected Jesus, the *Holy One and the Just.* They accused Jesus of being a blasphemer of God and a traitor to His nation. They called Him a liar, a winebibber and a hypocrite; and they said He did miracles by the power of Satan. But Jesus is the holy One, the second Person of the Trinity, the Son of God. Jesus was pure and separated from sin. He could do no sin, for He was God. When you sing three times, "Holy, holy, holy," you correctly repeat the word "holy" for each member of the Godhead. Jesus is the holy One, just as the Father and Spirit are holy. Will you worship His holiness?

Lord Jesus, I testify You are holy. You are holy in Your nature, Your
works, and Your dealings with all mankind.

Jesus is the just One; He never did anything unjustly. He did not treat the Jews unjustly, even though they lied about Him. He did not treat His Roman executers unjustly, even though they nailed Him to a cross. Just as He treated everyone justly in His earthly life, so He will treat you justly in all areas of your life. You can trust Him. Because His nature is just, Jesus will always do the right thing.

Lord Jesus, I have trusted You for eternal life. Now I trust You to guide
me and help me live this day. Help me to be holy as You are holy. Help
me treat all people justly, as You treat them. Amen.

Reading: Acts 3:1-16
Key Thought: Because Jesus is holy and just, He will always treat you fairly.

29 ◆ THE TRINITY: MY HELPER

So we may boldly say: "The LORD is my helper; I will not fear.
What can man do to me?"
HEBREWS 13:6

Hear, O LORD, and have mercy on me; LORD, be my helper!
PSALM 30:10

The Lord is your *Helper*; He is the One who comes alongside to assist you in doing what you can't do. In other cases, the Lord assists you in doing what you should do but don't want to do. All three Persons of the Trinity are your *Helpers*: Father, Son and Holy Spirit. First, the Father is your *Helper*. Psalm 30:8 describes, "I cried out to You, O LORD." The Lord did not ignore the cry, nor did the Lord leave that person unfulfilled when he cried, "LORD, be my helper!" (v. 10). Second, Jesus is your *Helper* in danger or trouble; He "will never leave you nor forsake you" (Hebrews 13:5). Since the Father and Son will help us, we should not fear what our enemies can do.

Lord, You are my Helper; I can't make it without You. Because You help
me through trouble and frustration, I will trust You.

Jesus promised us the Holy Spirit to help us (see John 14:16,26). The *Helper* helps us find salvation, regenerates us with the new birth, indwells us with His presence, baptizes us into the Body of Christ, seals us until the rapture and guarantees our eternal life. The Holy Spirit will convict us of sin, teach us what we need to know, guide us, give us gifts for service and fill us with power in our ministry.

Lord, thank You for sending the Holy Spirit to help me find
salvation. Thank You for the Holy Spirit, who helps me in Christian
service and uses me in ministry. Amen.

Reading: Psalm 30
Key Thought: The three members of the Trinity each have a role in helping my Christian life.

30 JESUS: HE WHO HAS THE BRIDE

He who has the bride is the bridegroom; but the friend of the bridegroom, who stands and hears him, rejoices greatly because of the bridegroom's voice.
JOHN 3:29

The Bride is the Church—born-again believers, those who have been saved. Jesus is the Bridegroom; it is *He Who Has the Bride.* In our society, the man usually courts the woman, just as Jesus is the One who seeks the lost. In our society, the man usually asks the marriage question, just as Jesus calls us to salvation. In our society, the man usually pays the price for the engagement ring, just as Jesus is the One who paid the ultimate price for our redemption. The man usually takes the initiative, "just as Christ also loved the church and gave Himself for it" (Ephesians 5:25). Because Jesus has done everything, it is *He Who Has the Bride.*

Jesus, when I hang on to You, it's good to know that You are hanging on to me. I know I belong to You.

Because the groom takes the initiative, the bride usually says yes. Have you said yes to Jesus? Because the groom first loves the bride, she usually follows his leadership. Have you followed Jesus? Because the groom protects his bride and seeks her welfare, the bride will go live with him. Have you let the Lord Jesus care and protect you? "For no one ever hated his own flesh, but nourishes and cherishes it, just as the Lord does the church. For we are members of His body" (Ephesians 5:29-30).

Jesus, I look to You for all my needs. I will obey You, love You and live for You. Amen.

Reading: Ephesians 5:22-33
Key Thought: Jesus is the Bridegroom who looks out for us, as well as for our needs.

JULY

JESUS: ROCK OF SPIRITUAL REFRESHMENT

And by a miracle God sent them food to eat and water to drink there in the desert; they drank the water that Christ gave them. He was there with them as a mighty Rock of spiritual refreshment.
1 CORINTHIANS 10:3-4, *TLB*

The Lord was in the Shekinah glory cloud that led Israel to Meribah (see Exodus 17:1-16); and when they arrived, the oasis was dry. The Lord knew there was no water even before He led them to a dry hole. He was not punishing them or frustrating them. He wanted Israel to do more than drink physical water; He wanted them to drink spiritually from Himself. The dry hole of Meribah revealed Israel's spiritually famished condition. Sometimes, He may lead you to a dry hole to help you see your spiritual emptiness, and then the Lord wants you to call on Him. Perhaps you'll be willing to drink of Him when He gives you water. Will you drink from the *Rock of Spiritual Refreshment* today?

Lord, now I know why there are dry holes in my life. Help me look beyond my troubles to see You in my life. I'm thirsty and need water. Quench my spiritual thirst.

Just as Israel had to repent and cry out for water, so you must turn to Jesus when you're spiritually thirsty. Just as Moses had to strike the rock in faith, so you must come to Jesus through Calvary, for it was there that He was smitten for you. Just as the Lord wanted to help Israel more than they sought Him, so He wants to give you a fresh drink of water today. When you drink from Christ, the *Rock of Spiritual Refreshment*, He'll satisfy the longings of your heart.

Lord, the dry holes in my life make me thirsty for nourishment and satisfaction. Ah, Your water is good. Amen.

Reading: Exodus 17
Key Thought: Jesus allows me to get thirsty so that I'll drink of Him.

2 THE FATHER: OUR SPIRITUAL FATHER

*Our earthly fathers correct us, and we still respect them. Isn't it even better
to be given true life by letting our spiritual Father correct us?*
HEBREWS 12:9, CEV

The Lord is called our *Spiritual Father*. All spirits in the universe are subject to Him. Also, all people have spirits, and they too are subject to the
Father. Just as an earthly father loves and directs his children, so our
Spiritual Father loves and directs His children on Earth (see Genesis 50:20;
Psalm 119:71; Romans 8:28). Will you let Him teach you today? An
earthly father provides protection and provision for his children, just as
the heavenly Father cares for you. Your *Spiritual Father* wants to demonstrate His protection and care of you. Will you accept them today?

*O Spiritual Father, I come to fellowship with You this day. I recognize Your
authority over my life. I want to please You, serve You and worship You.*

Because He is our *Spiritual Father*, He has the right to correct us.
People revere their physical fathers who corrected them; will you not
revere the Lord when trials come? Relationship is the key bond between
a father and his child. It is a relationship of love. Because a father loves
his children, he corrects them to bring out the best in them. Sometimes
a momentary correction in the long run is for the child's good. Your
heavenly Father corrects you because He loves you.

*You are my Father; I submit to Your correction. I accept Your plan in
my life. Help me learn from my affliction and become godlier. Amen.*

Reading: Matthew 7:25-29
Key Thought: Your *Spiritual Father* wants a relationship with you.

3 ⟩ JESUS: GOOD MASTER

And, behold, one came and said unto him, Good Master, what good thing shall I do, that I may have eternal life?
MATTHEW 19:16, *KJV*

The rich young ruler went to Jesus asking, "Good Master, what good thing shall I do, that I may have eternal life?" He wanted to go to Heaven and thought he had to do something to get there. He called Jesus *Good Master*, but Jesus turned away his acknowledgment, "Why do you call Me good?" (Matthew 19:17). Jesus didn't deny He was good, for He was God, who is good. Jesus used this question to impress upon the young man the seriousness of his request. To paraphrase Jesus' meaning: "Are you sure you know what 'good' means?" What the young ruler didn't realize was that it takes divine forgiveness to get to Heaven. Jesus said to him, "If you want to enter" (v. 17), which suggests he had not yet entered the kingdom of Heaven.

Lord, You are good, not because I said it, but because You are God.

Jesus told the young man to keep the commandments, which he claimed he had kept. So Jesus touched the young man's besetting sin—money—when He said, "Go, sell what you have" (Matthew 19:21). The man "went away sorrowful" (v. 22). The young man didn't just have money; his money had him. He was guilty of greed and financial lust. He had broken the tenth commandment, "You shall not covet" (Exodus 20:17).

Lord, I realize that just being good is not enough and that calling You good will not get me to Heaven. I call You my Savior; by grace, You have forgiven all my sin. Amen.

Reading: Matthew 19:16-26
Key Thought: Jesus must be more than a *Good Master*; He must be your Savior.

JESUS: THE GOOD SHEPHERD

I am the good shepherd. The good shepherd gives His life for the sheep.
JOHN 10:11

Jesus called Himself the *Good Shepherd*, because He does what good shepherds do: They give their lives for their sheep. They give up the pleasures of home to live outside in the pastures with sheep, just as Jesus gave up the glories of Heaven to come to Earth for His sheep. A good shepherd gives up his freedom to watch his sheep; Jesus gave up His eternal existence to take on the limitations of human flesh. A good shepherd gives up his sleep to search for lost sheep; Jesus came to Earth to search for the lost (see Luke 15:4-7). A good shepherd gives up his safety to brave the storm or fight a predator; Jesus came to Earth to be tempted, ridiculed and persecuted. A good shepherd will die protecting his sheep; Jesus gave His life on the cross for the world. Jesus said, "Other sheep I have which are not of this fold; them also I must bring" (John 10:16).

Jesus, You are the Good Shepherd, who gave Your life for the world. You are my Shepherd; I feel safe in Your presence.

Jesus is the *Good Shepherd* who asks you to become a shepherd for His sheep. He told Peter, "Take care of my sheep" (John 21:16, *NLT*). Just as Jesus is your Shepherd, you must become a shepherd to someone who needs your care. Peter wrote, "Care for the flock of God" (1 Peter 5:2, *NLT*).

Lord Jesus, You are my Shepherd; thank You for caring for me. I will give shepherd care to someone else. Amen.

Reading: 1 Peter 5:1-11
Key Thought: The *Good Shepherd* gives His life for you.

THE HOLY SPIRIT: THE GLORY OF THE LORD

But we all, with unveiled face, beholding as in a mirror the glory
of the Lord, are being transformed into the same image from
glory to glory, just as by the Spirit of the Lord.
2 CORINTHIANS 3:18

The Holy Spirit is the *Glory of the Lord*. He brings honor and prestige to the Father and the Son. When you look at God, you see the Holy Spirit. And the more you look at the Holy Spirit's glory to learn about God, the more you are transformed to be more godlike. When you look at His glory, you are elevated to a higher level of praising and exalting God. The Holy Spirit is the *Glory of the Lord* who brings out your best worship. When you look at Him, the mirror of God, you will be elevated to a higher level of worship.

Holy Spirit, when I see anew the Glory of the Lord, I begin
worshiping. I want to see more glory, so I can have more
intimacy in worship than ever before.

The Holy Spirit is the *Glory of the Lord* who wants to change your life so that you will become more like God. To be godlier, you must have a vision of what you want to be. Then you must aspire to have it. When you see the glory of the Holy Spirit, you will want to be more like God. So, look to the Holy Spirit in Scripture; look to the Holy Spirit in prayer; and look to the Holy Spirit in meditation.

Holy Spirit, make me godly. I will study about You in Scripture to learn
more about how You work in my life. When I see You in the mirror of
Your glory, I stretch myself to be more godly and to worship You. Amen.

Reading: 2 Corinthians 3:6-18
Key Thought: When you see the Holy Spirit, you will worship better.

6 JESUS: THE GREAT SHEPHERD OF THE SHEEP

Now may the God of peace who brought up our Lord Jesus from the dead, that great Shepherd of the sheep, through the blood of the everlasting covenant.
HEBREWS 13:20

There are many roles for the *Great Shepherd of the Sheep*. Jesus is the Shepherd who takes care of us (see Psalm 23:1). All that the sheep have to do to receive the Shepherd's care is to keep in good relationship with Him. Jesus is the Good Shepherd who gives His life for the sheep (see John 10:11). Just as a shepherd sacrifices his family time and the comforts of home to be with his sheep, Jesus gave up Heaven for us. Jesus is also the Great Shepherd who said, "I lay down My life" (v. 17).

Lord Jesus, You are my Shepherd who has died for my sins. You are my Shepherd who leads me daily and takes care of me.

Jesus is also called the *Great Shepherd of the Sheep* because He safely delivers His sheep to Heaven. The basis for the complete and final salvation of His sheep is first His blood, which forgives the sheep; and second, the resurrection of "our Lord Jesus from the dead" (Hebrews 13:20), which gives eternal life to the sheep. Because salvation is complete, the Shepherd can "make you complete in every good work to do His will" (v. 21). That means you can complete the Father's will. How can that happen? Because the *Great Shepherd of the Sheep* works "in you what is well pleasing in His [the Father's] sight" (v. 21).

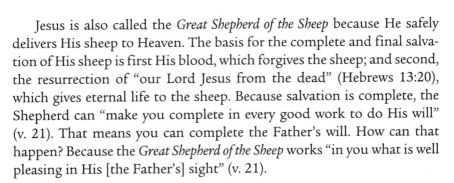

Lord Jesus, I am complete in You. You have taken away all my sins; You have given me eternal life; You have worked in my life to help me please the Father. Amen.

Reading: Hebrews 13
Key Thought: The *Great Shepherd of the Sheep* is great because He delivers me to Heaven.

7 JESUS: GREATER THAN JONAH

The men of Nineveh will rise up in the judgment with this generation
and condemn it, because they repented at the preaching of Jonah;
and indeed a greater than Jonah is here.
MATTHEW 12:41

Jonah was one of the greatest preachers. His preaching called the entire city of Nineveh to repentance. Nineveh contained "more than one hundred and twenty thousand persons" (Jonah 4:11). Jonah was also great because of the depth of the city's response: "So the people of Nineveh believed God, proclaimed a fast, and put on sackcloth, from the greatest to the least of them" (3:5). The king believed and published a command—"Let every one turn from his evil way" (v. 8)—and then asked, "Who can tell if God will turn . . . so that we may not perish?" (v. 9). Jonah began one of the greatest revivals in the Old Testament, yet Jesus is *Greater than Jonah* because the revival of Jesus broke out at Pentecost and went on to influence the whole world.

Lord Jesus, I know You are a great Preacher because of the influence of
Your message on others. But Your greatest preaching changed my life.

At first, Jonah didn't want to preach to Gentiles, so he sailed the opposite way. That's when God turned him around, through a storm and a great fish. Jonah instigated a great revival among Gentiles—an act unthinkable to the Jewish people of his day. Jesus is like Jonah because Jesus' message has reached beyond the Jewish world to that of the Gentiles. But, Jesus is *Greater than Jonah* because He loves the entire world and died for it.

Lord Jesus, thank You that the gospel was big enough for Jews—
God's chosen people—and for Gentiles. Amen.

Reading: Jonah 1; 3
Key Thought: Jesus is *Greater than Jonah* because He died for the entire world.

THE TRINITY: GOD OF MY PRAISE (*ELOHIM TEHILATI*)

Don't stand by silently, O God of my praise, while wicked people
slander me and tell lies about me.
SEE PSALM 109:1

David made it a habit to praise God all the time. David called the Lord the *God of My Praise*, a title that came from his daily experience. But David couldn't understand how God could let people criticize him and tell lies about him, especially since he consistently praised God. Maybe that's your question. You wonder why some people criticize you, especially when you have a good relationship with God. Even though you try to work hard and do right, some people stab you in the back. Even though you put God first in your life, some people seem to reject you.

Lord, I try to serve You and I continually praise You,
yet I have enemies. Why?

The law of unintended consequences says that your praise to God doesn't make people like you; rather, some people reject you because they reject God. Your goodness convicts them of their sins, and in anger they turn against you. Whenever you praise God, they reject God for the same reasons you serve Him. They don't want someone else—God—running their lives. They want to be the center of their lives; they don't want to put God there. So don't let their negative reactions ruin your good positive life; praise God anyhow. He is your Lord and Savior; make Him continually the *God of Your Praise*.

Lord, I will praise You when those around me criticize You. I will also
praise You when those around me join in worship. I will not let anyone
influence my worship of You. Amen.

Reading: Psalm 109
Key Thought: Make Him the *God of Your Praise*, no matter the circumstances.

JESUS: GREATER THAN OUR FATHER ABRAHAM

"Are You greater than our father Abraham, who is dead? And the prophets are dead. Who do You make Yourself out to be?" Then the Jews said to Him, "You are not yet fifty years old, and have You seen Abraham?" Jesus said to them, "Most assuredly, I say to you, before Abraham was, I AM."

JOHN 8:53,57-58

Abraham was one of the greatest patriarchs in the Old Testament. He is the father of Israel, for all Jews came from him. Of all Old Testament believers, Abraham perhaps had the greatest faith in God. He is known as the friend of God (see 2 Chronicles 20:7; James 2:23); and God called him, "My friend" (Isaiah 41:8). But Jesus is *Greater than Our Father Abraham* because Jesus is the great I AM; He is God.

Jesus, You are greater than the Old Testament fathers; You are greater than the angels. You are my Lord and Savior; You are the Lord God of the Universe.

The Jewish leaders rejected Jesus even though they witnessed His miracles. They refused to accept Jesus, even though He proved to them from the Scriptures who He was (see Matthew 21:23—22:46). The Jewish leaders called Jesus a sinner, accused Him of being born out of wedlock (see John 8:41), attributed His miracles to Satan (see Matthew 12:24) and said He had a devil (John 8:52). They sarcastically asked, "Are You greater than our father Abraham?" (v. 53). Jesus replied, "Your father Abraham rejoiced to see My day" (v. 56). They said, "You're not fifty years old; how could you see Abraham?" (see v. 57). Jesus answered, "Before Abraham was, I AM" (v. 58). In response, they picked up stones to kill Him. What is your response to the One who is *Greater than Our Father Abraham*? You must either pick up stones to cast at Him or fall at His feet to worship Him.

Jesus, I fall at Your feet to worship You. You are the great I AM, the Eternal God of the Ages. Amen.

Reading: John 8:37-59
Key Thought: Because Jesus is greater than Abraham, you must worship Him as the great I AM.

10 JESUS: GREATER THAN OUR FATHER JACOB

Are You greater than our father Jacob, who gave us the well, and drank from it
himself, as well as his sons and his livestock?
JOHN 4:12

The woman at the well asked Jesus if He was greater than Jacob. She was being sarcastic, assuming in her mind that Jesus could not be. Little did she know at the time that the answer to her question was yes! Even though Jesus came from the line of Jacob (see Matthew 1:2), He is much *Greater than Our Father Jacob* because He is the Son of God. The woman learned that Jesus is the I AM (see John 4:26) and that He indeed is "the Christ, the Savior of the world" (v. 42). What are your questions about Jesus?

Jesus, I believe You lived a perfect life and died a cruel death as a
substitute for my sin. Jesus, I believe You are the Son of God; but most
important, I believe You are my Personal Savior.

The woman at the well didn't understand what Jesus meant when He offered her living water (see John 4:10). At first she tried to tell Jesus that He didn't have a rope or bucket. When Jesus offered her water so that she would "never thirst" (v. 14), she again was wrong, thinking it was physical water (see v. 15). When she properly understood that Jesus is not only *Greater than Our Father Jacob* but also the Messiah, she ran to tell others: "Come, see a Man who told me all things that I ever did" (v. 29). Have you met Jesus in a personal experience, as did the woman at the well?

Jesus, You have answered my questions, just as You answered
those of the woman at the well. I will go tell others about You, just as
the woman at the well did. Amen.

Reading: John 4:12-29,39-42
Key Thought: Because Jesus is *Greater than Our Father Jacob*, He can meet our needs.

THE FATHER: OUR FATHER IN HEAVEN

Your Father knows the things you have need of before you ask Him.
In this manner, therefore, pray: Our Father in heaven.
MATTHEW 6:8-9

Not only were you born of an earthly father, but also you have a *Father in Heaven*. When you were born again of the Spirit, you received your heavenly Father's nature. Let your new divine nature control your life so that you can live above the old life. Also, you received the heavenly Father's life, and now you have eternal life. Let your earthly life reflect your heavenly Father's gift to you. You were given a new standing in Heaven; the heavenly Father's infinite resources are at your disposal. Since you are a child of the Father and a member of His family, you can call other believers your sisters and brothers, and you can receive their love as you love them.

Father, I am humbled to be Your child. I come to You in prayer,
just as a child comes to an earthly father, and ask for
Your blessing on my life today.

You have a heavenly Father; take time to fellowship with Him today. Enjoy your relationship with the Father. Take time to learn what He can do for you, so you can walk in His will. Take time to worship Him, remembering that the Father seeks worship (see John 4:23). When you worship and magnify your *Father in Heaven*, He in turn will enrich your life and bless you abundantly.

O Father in Heaven, thank You for giving me entrance into Your family.
I want to grow in my relationship with You and become more like You.
I will worship You today. Amen.

Reading: Matthew 6:6-15
Key Thought: Take advantage of the things you get from your heavenly Father.

JESUS: GREATER THAN SOLOMON

The queen of the South will rise up in the judgment with this generation and condemn it, for she came from the ends of the Earth to hear the wisdom of Solomon; and indeed a greater than Solomon is here.
MATTHEW 12:42

Solomon was one of the wisest men to ever live; yet Jesus is *Greater than Solomon,* because Jesus is the source of wisdom. Solomon was wise because he asked God for wisdom. At the beginning of his reign, Solomon confessed, "I am a little child" (1 Kings 3:7). So Solomon prayed, "Give to Your servant an understanding heart" (v. 9). Like Solomon, we can ask for wisdom. "If any of you lacks wisdom, let him ask of God, who gives to all, . . . and it will be given to him" (James 1:5). If you want to be wiser than you are, learn from the Bible about Christ. The more you know of Him, the wiser you'll be.

Jesus, I want to be wiser. I will master the Scriptures and will learn more about You. Take away my spiritual blindness, so I can see and learn.

Solomon wrote the book of Proverbs, the Song of Solomon, Ecclesiastes and some of the book of Psalms. He had a reputation for being greater than the wise men of Egypt and of the East, and he was an expert in zoology and botany (see 1 Kings 4:32-39). His greatest achievement was building Solomon's Temple, not because of its grandeur, but because God Himself came in a cloud to dwell in it (see 8:10). Solomon pointed us to Christ, who is *Greater than Solomon.*

Jesus, no one can be compared to You, for You are greater, wiser and more glorious than all humans, all angels—everything. Amen.

Reading: 1 Kings 3:5-28
Key Thought: We can get the wisdom of Solomon from Jesus.

13 JESUS: HE WHO COMES IN THE NAME OF THE LORD

Then the multitudes who went before and those who followed cried out,
saying: . . . "Blessed is He who comes in the name of the LORD!"
MATTHEW 21:9

On Palm Sunday Jesus rode victorious into Jerusalem on a donkey. The crowds spread palm branches and their coats on the road. They cried out, "Hosanna," and called Jesus Son of David, which meant they recognized that Jesus was heir to David's throne. The crowd recognized Jesus as their Messiah-Deliverer. They wanted Jesus to proclaim Himself to be the King of Israel, to raise an army and to drive the Romans into the sea. They recognized Jesus as *He Who Comes in the Name of the Lord*. Palm Sunday had everything to do with rightful ownership. Jesus owned the right to be their King. He had the royal rights to a kingdom on Earth, but He would not exercise His rights on Palm Sunday. Jesus would patiently wait until Good Friday to die for the sins of the world. Jesus wanted to first rule them internally, from within their hearts.

Jesus, You are Lord; thank You for coming to establish Your
kingdom in my heart. I yield to Your rule.

Jesus came the first time peacefully, upon a donkey, to establish His rule in the hearts of His subjects. Jesus will come a second time in war, riding upon a white horse to conquer His enemies. Then He will come in the name of the Lord to establish His earthly kingdom. He will institute social justice and set up world peace.

Jesus, I look forward to Your coming to establish justice and peace
in the world. Help me live for You in this present world, which has so
little peace and justice. Amen.

Reading: Matthew 21:1-11
Key Thought: Jesus came the first time to rule the hearts of people.

◆14◆ THE HOLY SPIRIT: HE

But the Helper, the Holy Spirit, whom the Father will send in My name, He will teach you all things, and bring to your remembrance all things that I said to you.
JOHN 14:26

The Holy Spirit is a Person. *He* is not like smoke, fog, a cloud or any other false idea that people have of Him. *He* is the third Person of the Godhead. Use the pronoun "He" when you pray to Him, because *He* is a Person. The Holy Spirit is a Person who has the ability to think infinitely; therefore, *He* knows all about you. The Holy Spirit is a Person who has the infinite capacities of emotion; therefore, *He* feels deeply for you. The Holy Spirit is a Person with the divine power of will; therefore, *He* can choose to do wonderful things for you when you obey the commands of Scripture. What would you like for the Holy Spirit to do for you today?

> *Holy Spirit, I realize that You know all about me, so forgive my shortcomings and errors. I feel Your love for me; help me love You in return. I want You to strengthen my will to live a godly life.*

The Holy Spirit is the third Person of the Trinity. *He* can be denied (see 2 Timothy 3:5), lied to (see Acts 5:3), resisted (see Genesis 6:3) and blasphemed (see Matthew 12:31). Because *He* is a Person, you can obey Him (see Hebrews 3:7-11), desire Him (see John 7:37-38) and follow Him (see Galatians 5:16,25). Call on Him today to help you glorify the Father.

> *Holy Spirit, I need Your help today. Come show me how to live in a more godly way. Come fill me with power to overcome temptation. Enter my life to make me holy like You, and make me spiritual like Your nature. Fill me today. Amen.*

Reading: Galatians 5:16-28
Key Thought: I should pray to the Holy Spirit as a Person.

15 · JESUS: HE WHO FILLS ALL IN ALL

Which is His body, the fullness of Him who fills all in all.
EPHESIANS 1:23

Jesus is *He Who Fills All in All.* Think of all you want to do for God; you can do it if you have faith to move mountains (see 1 Corinthians 13:2). Think of all your dreams to pray, to worship and to grow more godly; you can reach all of them if you pray properly, worship properly and learn properly. Jesus can help your dreams become a reality; He is *He Who Fills All in All.* Think of all your heartaches, your failures and your disappointments; you must confess them to Jesus. He can forgive your sins, help you forget your failures and cover up your mistakes. Will you let Jesus be All in All to you?

Lord Jesus, I need You now more than ever. I'm human, and I can't do it all; I can't be all I want to be. Help me.

Jesus will be your All in All. In all problems, look to Him. In all relationships, look to Him. In all endeavors, look to Him. In every area of your life, look to Him. When you focus completely on Jesus, He changes your selfish dreams into spiritual dreams. When Jesus is the aim of living, you get new goals and desires. Then He fills all in all.

Lord Jesus, I need You to be present in all areas of my life. I need You to give me new goals and dreams. Be my All in All. Amen.

Reading: Ephesians 1:15-23
Key Thought: Jesus gives you new goals and helps you reach them.

16 ◆ Jesus: Fullers' Soap

But who may abide the day of his coming? and who shall stand when he appeareth? for he is like a refiner's fire, and like fullers' soap.
MALACHI 3:2, KJV

Jesus is likened to fullers' soap, which was the best cleansing and whitening agent of its day. Before dyeing cloth, fullers' soap was used to completely clean the woven cloth of oily or gummy substances found on the natural, raw fiber. The cloth was soaked in water, spread out and sprinkled with powdered ashes (alkali or lye); then it was wrung and pounded so that the soap would penetrate every fiber. The cloth was thoroughly rinsed in a running stream to wash away the alkali or lye; then it was spread out to dry. Today's Scripture refers to the second coming of Jesus Christ, when He judges His people. Jesus is *Fullers' Soap*, which will penetrate every fiber of our being to determine the credibility of our faith.

Lord Jesus, I know You are coming back to judge all people. I know that You will judge rightly and that You will judge deeply. Cleanse me now, so I will be ready for judgment in the future.

Because Jesus will judge us like fullers' soap does, make sure you are cleansed from sin through and through. Only faith in Jesus will make us Christians. Make sure you are like those who will appear before God in Heaven, who have "washed their robes and made them white in the blood of the Lamb" (Revelation 7:14). No one can gain perfection by works and no one can live without sin. But all can be perfectly clean by His blood.

Lord Jesus, I know I have sinned and I am not perfect, but I have believed in You. Cleanse me from every sin. Amen.

Reading: Malachi 3:1-6
Key Thought: Jesus will thoroughly examine you for sin.

17 THE TRINITY: THE JUDGE OF ALL THE EARTH

*Far be it from You [God] to do such a thing as this, to slay the righteous
with the wicked, so that the righteous should be as the wicked; far be it from You!
Shall not the Judge of all the earth do right?*
GENESIS 18:25

The Lord God is the *Judge of All the Earth*. Abraham asked, "Will the judge
of all the Earth do right?" (see Genesis 18:25). The answer is yes. God will
always do right, because He has a righteous nature. The Lord has done
everything possible for the salvation of all. The Father revealed to the
wicked their lost condition through nature (see Romans 1:18-20),
through the conscience (2:14-16) and through the existence of law (2:12-
13). Jesus died for their sins. The Holy Spirit spoke to their hearts, draw-
ing them to salvation (Genesis 6:3). The Lord God has done the right
thing for everyone to be saved.

*Yes, Lord, I believe You are fair. Yes, Lord, I believe You are the Judge of
All the Earth, and everyone will appear before You. Yes, Lord, I know
You will always do the right thing.*

The Lord God is the *Judge of All the Earth*. Jesus will judge all believers
at the judgment seat of Christ to give His followers rewards (see
2 Corinthians 5:10). The Father will judge all unbelievers to find out if
their names are written in the Lamb's Book of Life and will punish them
according to their works (see Revelation 20:12-15). The Lord deals with
all people fairly, but it's grace we need—not judgment. The Lord can look
on the death of Jesus and forgive us, if we'll repent and trust Christ.

*Lord, I fully trust You now and will trust You in the Day of Judgment.
When You see my sin, look at the blood of Jesus, which forgives me. Look
on me through grace. Amen.*

Reading: Genesis 18:23-33
Key Thought: The *Judge of All the Earth* will always do the right thing.

18 ◆ JESUS: POTENTATE

He will manifest in His own time, He who is the blessed and only
Potentate, the King of kings and Lord of lords.
1 TIMOTHY 6:15

There are different kinds of power that Jesus has as a leader. A judge has judicial power, because the entire police force backs up his or her decision. A policeman has physical power to wrestle a suspect to the ground. A legislator has legal power to make laws to influence many. When Jesus is called *Potentate*, He is being described as a Soldier-King with omnipotent power to do great feats. The title *"Potentate"* comes from the Greek word *dunamai*, as in "the power of God to salvation" (Romans 1:16). Our word "dynamite" comes from the root for *"Potentate."*

Jesus, I look to Your leadership for guidance. I look to Your
power for help and protection today.

Jesus is described as the *Potentate*, the King of kings, which means He is like a fighting king who leads his army into battle. King Jesus is not like a weak old man who lets younger knights fight for him. He can wield a sword, as well as play out a winning strategy. As the King of your life, Jesus has a strategy to make you a winner; will you follow Him? As the mighty *Potentate*, Jesus can give you a new dynamic to resist sin or to win over addiction. Will you let Him do it? The title *"Potentate"* is used to describe Jesus when He returns in power and glory. It is then when He will lead the armies of Heaven to defeat the armies of Satan.

Lord Jesus, I know You have all authority, so I will follow Your
commandments. I know You have all mighty power, so I trust You to
give me strength to overcome sin and to live for You. Amen.

Reading: 1 Timothy 6:1-16
Key Thought: You need the mighty power of Jesus to live for Him.

19 ◈ JESUS: OUR PEACE

For He Himself is our peace, who has made both one, and has broken
down the middle wall of separation.
EPHESIANS 2:14

Most people think that peace is the cessation of war or that peace is doing something enjoyable, such as sitting by a lake or enjoying mountain scenery. These illustrations reflect only one kind of idyllic peace, but the word "peace" means "to join two opposing forces." Jesus is our *Peace* because He joined us to the Father. When you were opposed to the Father in selfish rebellion, Jesus joined you to Him. When the Father could not accept you because of your sin, Jesus was our *Peace* who turned the Father toward you and you toward Him.

Lord Jesus, You are my Peace. I've come to the Father through You.
Now I need to trust You to bring peace to my surroundings.
Come give peace to my world.

Jesus is our *Peace* who can give us an inner calm to deal with the pressures of this day. When you let "the peace of God rule in your hearts" (Colossians 3:15), you can adequately deal with circumstances. Invite Jesus to come control your life; He knows your future and what will happen. He can guide you, protect you and give you victory in the future. When you let Jesus control your life, He gives you inward peace; He calms your worries, and He gives you meaningful direction.

Lord Jesus, thank You for giving me peace with God so that
I am saved. Also, thank You for inner peace to control my thoughts and
life. I yield to Your will for today. Amen.

Reading: Philippians 4:1-8
Key Thought: Jesus gives you the peace of God.

THE FATHER: GOD AND FATHER

With it [the tongue] we bless our God and Father, and with it we curse
men, who have been made in the similitude of God.
JAMES 3:9

The Lord is both your *God and Father*. He's not just your God, who is powerful and far off. But He is also your Father, who is close to help you. Just as Adam was created in the image and likeness of the Lord, you are similar to your earthly father in your physical nature. You have the image of both your physical father and your heavenly Father through the miracle of procreation and birth. But Adam marred the image of God through disobedience, and that image is marred in you. Now you must take a journey back to God to become like Him. Your journey is to become godly like your heavenly Father.

Father, I have a desire to be like You; help me
conform myself into Your likeness.

The Lord is your *God and Father*; He created you with a rational mind to think. He put within you the capacity for deep emotional feelings, just as He has love for that which is good and hatred for that which is evil. The Father gave you the power of will. Just as the Father has the ability to choose, He allows you the opportunity to make choices in life. Your intellect, emotions and will are the power of personality. You have the power of personhood, just as God does. And what is the purpose of that power? The Father created you with the ability to know Him, to love Him and to choose to worship Him. He is your *God and Father*; you belong to Him just as an earthly child belongs to its human father.

I worship You, my God and Father, for Your awesome
creation power that formed me in Your image. I want to
be like You; I want to be godly. Amen.

Reading: James 3:1-12
Key Thought: You can become godly like God.

JESUS: THE PRIEST OF THE MOST HIGH GOD

For this Melchizedek, king of Salem, priest of the Most High God, who met
Abraham returning from the slaughter of the kings and blessed him.
HEBREWS 7:1

Melchizedek was a priest of the Most High God; and because he was a type of Jesus, Melchizedek's ministry was a foreshadow of Jesus' ministry. The title "Most High God" is *El Elyon*, which means "the God who rules Heaven and Earth." When people don't know what to call the Father or how to approach Him, at least they can come to Him as the Creator and Ruler of Heaven and Earth. Since no human can create the universe, all should recognize that there is only one Creator—God. Melchizedek recognized the legitimate God who ruled the Earth, and he prayed to Him. Melchizedek's prayer was a prototype of Jesus' ministry; He intercedes to El Elyon because Jesus is the *Priest of the Most High God*. Pray to the Father through Jesus today.

Lord Jesus, I know You stand in Heaven before the Creator God.
Remember me in Your intercession. I'm only one small person out of
6 billion people on this planet; please remember me.

Jesus is the Priest for all; He is your Priest. He will not forget you. Just as Melchizedek interceded for Abraham, so Jesus will intercede for you. Just as Melchizedek had bread and wine to feed Abraham when he was exhausted and hungry, so Jesus will feed you on heavenly things. Just as Melchizedek and Abraham fellowshipped together, so you can fellowship with Jesus today.

Lord Jesus, I look to You to intercede for me this day. Feed me
spiritually, and let me fellowship with You today. Amen.

Reading: Hebrews 7:1-3
Key Thought: Jesus is your Intercessor before the God of Heaven and Earth.

22 ❯ JESUS: PRINCE AND SAVIOR

Him God has exalted to His right hand to be Prince and Savior,
to give repentance to Israel and forgiveness of sins.
ACTS 5:31

After being released from prison, Peter told the Jewish leaders that Jesus was the *Prince* of salvation and the *Savior* of Israel. Peter understood his audience—the Jewish leaders—who were still looking for the Messiah. They had rejected Jesus. So Peter called Jesus *Prince*. A prince is one scheduled to be king but who is not yet ruling on the throne. That's a true picture of Jesus. He is not yet ruling on the throne of Israel. When Jesus returns to Earth in power and glory, He will be called King of kings, and He will rule on David's throne. When Jesus first came to Earth, He offered a kingdom of inward peace and righteousness. Jesus knew that the way to influence nations was to rule the hearts of individuals. Is Jesus your King?

Jesus, You are my King, and You rule my heart. I know that one day
You will rule the outward affairs of all people.

"Savior" is the second title used by Peter to describe Jesus. By calling Jesus *Savior*, Peter was pointing the Jewish leaders back to the accomplishments of the Cross. In His death, Jesus became the *Savior* of the world (see John 4:42). So in this quick description of Jesus, Peter gives the Jewish leaders both a backward and a forward look. In the past, Jesus was *Savior*; in the future, Jesus the *Prince* will become the King of Israel.

Jesus, I praise You for past salvation, and I worship You
as the coming King of all kings. Amen.

Reading: Zechariah 14:1-9
Key Thought: Jesus is the *Savior* and the coming King.

23 THE HOLY SPIRIT: HIS SEED

Whoever has been born of God does not sin, for His seed remains in him; and he cannot sin, because he has been born of God.
1 JOHN 3:9

The Holy Spirit is the *Seed* who was planted in your life when you were born again. It was His presence that delivered to you eternal life, as well as a new nature and new desires. Just as a seed planted in the ground will grow and bring forth its fruit, so the Holy Spirit is the *Seed* planted in your heart who will bring forth the fruit of righteousness and godliness. A seed has all the ingredients of what it will be when fully grown, and the Holy Spirit has everything you need to be completely godly and fully effective as a servant of God.

Holy Spirit, I know You were planted in my heart. Thank You for the good things that have grown there. I praise You for new desires and new character. Keep me growing to be like Christ.

God's *Seed* planted in your heart cannot bring forth bad fruit. The Holy Spirit cannot sin, nor can He tempt you to sin (see James 1:13). You were given a new nature, which is a divine creation; it cannot sin. Listen to the urges of your new nature, and follow it. Do not give in to the desires of your old nature, because it's the source of your temptations and problems. If you listen to the old nature, it will lead you astray. Listen to the Holy Spirit, and He will grow good fruit in your heart.

Holy Spirit, I want to be godly; grow the fruits of righteousness in my heart. I reject temptation and the lust of the old nature. Amen.

Reading: 1 John 3:1-10
Key Thought: The Holy Spirit is a *Seed* who grows good things in you.

24 JESUS: THE PRINCE OF LIFE

And killed the Prince of life, whom God raised from the
dead, of which we are witnesses.
ACTS 3:15

Before His death, Jesus was also called the *Prince of Life*. Because a prince is one who is waiting to ascend the throne, the name *"Prince of Life"* was a prediction of Jesus' coming resurrection. Because Jesus is Life, death could not keep Him in the grave. When He was raised from the dead, He was given new resurrection life. The predicted *Prince of Life* becomes the Resurrection and the Life to all who would believe. After His resurrection, Jesus ascended to His throne in Heaven and sat down at the right hand of God the Father. Now Jesus is more than the *Prince of Life*; He is the reigning King of Heaven. Today He wants to enrich your life.

Lord Jesus, when You died, my sins were nailed to the cross.
When You arose from the dead, I arose with you (see Galatians 2:20).
Now, let Your resurrection life flow through me.

Jesus gives eternal life to all who believe in Him, so they can live forever (see 1 John 5:12). He gives them abiding life, so they can be fruitful in Him, the Vine (see John 15:1-5). He gives them the power of resurrection life to overcome sin and temptation. He gives them satisfying life, so they can enjoy fellowship with Him. He gives them heavenly life, so they can worship Him. Will you worship the *Prince of Life* now?

Lord Jesus, I thank You for eternal life. I praise You for the power of
resurrection life and its victory over sin. Now I worship You for all you are.

Reading: Matthew 27:50—28:7
Key Thought: Jesus gives life to you.

25 ◆ JESUS: THE MAN CHILD

*And she brought forth a man child, who was to rule all nations with a rod of iron:
and her child was caught up unto God, and to his throne.*
REVELATION 12:5, *KJV*

Jesus is called the *Man Child* because He was born to live as a man and to die for the sins of the world. When Mary and Joseph first saw Jesus, He was a baby in the manger; but the heavenly Father always saw Jesus as a fully grown man hanging on the cross, because Jesus was born the *Man Child* to die for sins. But Jesus was more than one man who died; He was every man, because, on the cross, all mankind was identified in Him. Just as all died in Adam, so all were made alive in Christ (see 1 Corinthians 15:22). He was more than just one man hanging on the cross; Jesus was you, because He became your sin bearer. Your sins were on Jesus when He died.

*Lord, I thank You for being born as a child, growing to be a man and
then dying for me. Thank You for giving me eternal life.*

Satan knew that Jesus was the promised *Man Child* who would deliver the world, so throughout the Old Testament, Satan tried to eliminate the Jews so that Jesus wouldn't be born. He tried to prematurely kill Jesus so He wouldn't die on the cross. But Jesus prevailed for you, so today will you live for Him?

*Lord, You understand the pressures of life, because You lived as a man.
You were tried, hurt and disappointed. You know what it's like to be
tempted, because You overcame temptation. Help me overcome my
temptations and limitations today. Amen.*

Reading: Revelation 12
Key Thought: Because Jesus was a man, He understands your problems and is willing to help you.

26 ◆ THE TRINITY: SONG

The LORD is my strength and song, and He has become my salvation; He is my God, and I will praise Him; my father's God, and I will exalt Him.
EXODUS 15:2

You will want to sing when you see what God is doing in your life, because He is your *Song* of victory. Just as Israel recognized her helplessness in the face of an enemy, so you must realize you will face opposition from the world, the flesh and Satan. Just as Israel recognized that God gave her a great victory (see Exodus 15:1), so you will sing praises when you overcome your enemies. Just as Israel exalted the Lord after a victory, so you must praise Him in song when your enemy is defeated and when you win a great battle (see v. 2).

> *Lord, sometimes I sing triumphantly because You give me a great victory. Sometimes I sing reverently when I consider Your grace. Sometimes I sing worshipfully when I consider Your awesome presence.*

If you have no song to sing, it's because you don't see the Lord working in your life. When you are happy, the Lord is your *Song* of rejoicing. When sorrows break your heart, the Lord is your *Song* of consolation. When you meet the Lord in prayer, He is your *Song* of worship and adoration. There is no better theme to sing than to sing about the Lord. There is no better purpose to sing than to sing to Him.

> *Lord, my song exalts You for saving me, and my song blesses You for giving me victory. Amen.*

Reading: Exodus 15:1-21
Key Thought: Sing about the Lord and to the Lord.

27 JESUS: THE MAN

Then Jesus came out, wearing the crown of thorns and the purple robe.
And Pilate said to them, "Behold the Man!"
JOHN 19:5

Jesus is the *Man* whom the Jewish leaders brought to the Roman governor Pilate to be tried. They said that when Jesus claimed to be God, "He [had] spoken blasphemy!" (Matthew 26:65). Pilate interrogated Jesus but found no crime in Him. Still the Jews cried out for His blood. So Pilate had Jesus flogged with whips and sticks. The Roman governor wrongly thought that a brutal beating would satisfy the bloodthirsty crowd. Then Pilate presented Jesus to them, exclaiming, "Behold the Man!" (John 19:5). When he called Jesus the *Man*, perhaps Pilate thought that crowd would go way when they saw Him brutally beaten. But instead they cried, "Crucify Him!" What do you cry when you see Jesus the *Man*?

Lord Jesus, I repent of my sins when I see Your sufferings. I cry out for
forgiveness and mercy. You are the Son of God.

Jesus is the *Man* who was tried by a Roman court. Jesus is the *Man* who died for your sins. Jesus is the *Man* who intercedes for you at the right hand of the Father in Heaven. Jesus is the *Man* who will return from Heaven to judge the world. Jesus is the *Man* who also is God.

Jesus, I worship You for Your great divine glory, because I don't
understand why You would become a Man to die for me. I bow in
human amazement at your greatness. Amen.

Reading: John 19:1-6
Key Thought: The Son of God became a *Man* for us.

28 JESUS: THE MAN OF SORROWS

He is despised and rejected by men, a Man of sorrows and acquainted
with grief. And we hid, as it were, our faces from Him;
He was despised, and we did not esteem Him.
ISAIAH 53:3

Jesus is the *Man of Sorrows*. When the soldiers crushed a crown of thorns on His head, the crown left gashes on His forehead, and blood obscured His vision. When they scourged Jesus with a whip—39 times—the beating left Him in agony. They mocked Him, stripped Him of all dignity and made Him carry His cross to Calvary. Besides the physical torture, Jesus suffered His disciples' abandonment, Peter's denial and Judas's betrayal of Him. But Jesus suffered this all for you.

Lord Jesus, You have endured suffering for me; help me be faithful when
mocking and persecution come.

When soldiers nailed Jesus to the cross, Jesus knew it was only a matter of time before He would die. He cried, "I thirst!" (John 19:28). They pierced His side with a spear. But that was just physical torture. When Jesus took on the sins of the world, He suffered all the spiritual agonies of Hell and cried out, "My God, My God, why have You forsaken Me?" (Mark 15:34). The greatest suffering of all was for the Son of God to be separated from the heavenly Father. There was nothing beautiful in the *Man of Sorrows* on the cross—except the beauty of salvation it secured. There was nothing lovely—except the salvation of countless souls. There was nothing wonderful—except the praise of the ages to the Lamb who was slain for the sin of the world.

Lord Jesus, I worship You for being the Lamb who was slain for the sin of
the world. I praise You for being my Sin Bearer. Amen.

Reading: Isaiah 53
Key Thought: I must live for Jesus because of all He suffered for me.

29 ◆ THE HOLY SPIRIT: ONE SPIRIT

For by one Spirit we were all baptized into one body . . .
and have all been made to drink into one Spirit.
1 CORINTHIANS 12:13

The Holy Spirit is the *One Spirit* who baptized you into Christ Jesus. He placed you into Christ so that when Jesus died, you were identified in His death. When Jesus was buried, your sins were buried with Him. When Jesus arose from the dead, you were in Jesus, receiving new life (see Romans 6:3-4). The third Person of the Trinity is the *One Spirit* who baptized you into Christ with all other believers.

Holy Spirit, it is a privilege to be united with Jesus in His death, burial
and resurrection. Now I'm in Christ with all other believers.

The Holy Spirit is the *One Spirit* who gives us love for others. When you meet other believers—even for the first time—there's oneness, because you both love the same Lord. No other spirit can give you that feeling or common bond with other believers. You can pray with them, share your testimony or worship together, all because you are one in the Spirit. The Holy Spirit is the *One Spirit* who gives unity to the Body of Christ. "There is one body and one Spirit" (Ephesians 4:4). So realize that He works to give you and all other believers unity of heart and purpose. You should fellowship together, pray together, serve together and, when difficulties come, sacrifice and suffer together.

Holy Spirit, help me get along with other believers,
especially those I've had trouble with. Help me love other Christians
so that the world can see Jesus in us. Amen.

Reading: 1 Corinthians 12:12-27
Key Thought: The Holy Spirit gives unity to the Body of Christ.

30 JESUS: THE MEDIATOR

For there is one God and one Mediator between God and men, the Man Christ Jesus.
1 TIMOTHY 2:5

A mediator is a middleman between two persons or someone who acts on behalf of another before an organization or person of authority. Jesus is the *Mediator* to the Father for you. Just as a lawyer is a mediator who represents you before a judge, so Jesus is your *Mediator* who represents you before the Judge who forgives your sins. Just as a sales agent represents you in a business contract, so Jesus is your *Mediator* who presents your prayers to the Father. How can Jesus represent you today?

> *Jesus, I can't represent myself; I'm too imperfect to stand before the Father's throne to present my prayers to Him. I will pray through You because the Father will listen to You.*

A human mediator could never represent you to the Father. Another mediator would have to intercede for his or her own sin. Also, a human mediator would have his or her own fleshly agenda and wouldn't be concerned with your needs and problems. Because Jesus is God, He knows the Father's heart, and He can properly represent you to the throne. Because Jesus lived as a perfect man, He knows your human inclinations, and He can be a *Mediator* for you. Go to the Father through the *Mediator.*

> *Jesus, I am left alone and lost, if you are not my Mediator. Come to me, plead my case, forgive my sins, and deliver me to Heaven. Amen.*

Reading: 1 Timothy 2:1-8
Key Thought: Jesus is the only One who can be your *Mediator* to the Father.

31 ◆ JESUS: THE MIGHTY GOD

For unto us a Child is born, unto us a Son is given; and the government will be upon His shoulder. And His name will be called Wonderful, Counselor, Mighty God, Everlasting Father, Prince of Peace.

ISAIAH 9:6

Wonderful things happen to those who recognize Jesus as the *Mighty God* and who call on Him. When people refuse to recognize Jesus as their *Mighty God*, He cannot bless them, for they have shut the spiritual window of their lives. But to those who have yielded their lives to Jesus, He can be their *Mighty God*. Everything promised in Scripture can happen to you, because Jesus is mighty to bless those who have faith to receive it. What is your greatest desire today? "Delight thyself also in the LORD; and he shall give thee the desires of thine heart" (Psalm 37:4, *KJV*).

> *Lord, I recognize Your might, but my problem is outward. I don't have enough faith to trust You to do mighty things in my life. I believe in my head; overcome the unbelief of my heart.*

Jesus is the *Mighty God* to answer prayer. He is also the *Mighty God* to overcome bad habits and to give you strength to resist temptation. He is the *Mighty God* to give you peace in the middle of a storm. He can take you off of your wayward path and give you purpose in life. He transforms from the inside out. If you need a spiritual makeover, call on Jesus, your *Mighty God*.

> *Jesus, be mighty to discipline my thoughts. Be mighty to focus my emotions in worship to You. Be mighty to strengthen my will against temptation. Be mighty to use my body as Your temple. Amen.*

Reading: Mark 9:2-13
Key Thought: Jesus can change you from the inside out.

AUGUST

THE TRINITY: YOUR EXCEEDINGLY GREAT REWARD

After these things the word of the LORD came to Abram in a vision, saying,
"Do not be afraid, Abram. I am your shield, your exceedingly great reward."
GENESIS 15:1

The Lord God is your *Exceedingly Great Reward*; when you get to Heaven, He will give you spiritual treasures that He is holding for you. But it's not money or jewels you'll receive; the Lord is your treasure. "In Your presence is fullness of joy; at Your right hand are pleasures forevermore" (Psalm 16:11). Abraham fought a battle for the sake of righteousness (see Genesis 14:1-16), yet he refused to take the earthly treasures that were rightfully his (see vv. 17-24). Abraham received a reward greater than gold or silver. He enjoyed the happiness of Divine presence; the Lord was his reward. People on Earth strive for gold to make them happy, but they don't realize that the greatest happiness of all is found in the presence of God. If your life is empty, let the Lord fill it with His presence.

Lord, I confess I am empty. Fill me with Your presence.
Let me experience Your goodness today.

The Lord God is your *Exceedingly Great Reward*. Once you fix your love on Him, your money will have new meaning. You will get joy from donating to many righteous causes. All your work for the Lord will bring you greater pleasures, because you'll glorify Him in all you do. You won't use all your energy pursuing pleasures; you'll do the Lord's will, which will bring you the greatest happiness of all.

Lord, show me the path of life, and give me fullness of joy in Your
presence. Let me find pleasures forevermore at Your right hand. Amen.

Reading: Genesis 15:1-7
Key Thought: The Lord God is the greatest Source of reward and happiness in life.

JESUS: THE MINISTER OF THE HEAVENLY SANCTUARY

2

We have such a High Priest, who is seated at the right hand of the throne of the Majesty in the heavens, a Minister of the sanctuary and of the true tabernacle.
HEBREWS 8:1-2

Jesus is seated at the right hand of the Father to be your *Minister of the Heavenly Sanctuary*. Jesus is there to help you. Because you are in Christ and He indwells you (see John 14:20), you are as close to the Father as is Jesus. So don't worry about judgment, for Jesus has taken your punishment. Now your concerns are to please the Father and to worship Him. Do that through Jesus, for He will present your requests to the Father. Because the Father loves Jesus and accepts Him, you have immediate access through the Son; He is your *Minister of the Heavenly Sanctuary*.

> *Father, I am not worthy to enter Your presence, but in Jesus I stand perfect before You. My words are inadequate, but in Jesus my speech is perfect. My prayers are filled with doubts, but in Jesus I pray boldly.*

You have instant access to the Father through Jesus, who is your *Minister of the Heavenly Sanctuary*. Jesus is glorified when you pray through Him, for this is the fulfillment of His sacrifice. The Father is glorified by your worship, for that is the reason He sent Jesus to die for you.

> *Jesus, some of my prayers are selfish, and some are surrounded with fears. Search my true heart, and present those prayers to the Father that He should hear. Present my prayers in the way they should be offered. Because You are my Minister of the Heavenly Sanctuary, I pray with confidence. Amen.*

Reading: Hebrews 8:1-6
Key Thought: Jesus makes my prayers effective.

JESUS: THE FRIEND OF PUBLICANS AND SINNERS

The Son of man is come eating and drinking; and ye say, Behold a gluttonous man, and a winebibber, a friend of publicans and sinners!
LUKE 7:34

Jesus was called the *Friend of Publicans and Sinners*—not a complimentary term in His day. Jews especially hated publicans because publicans had "sold out" to the enemy, i.e., Rome. Roman officials "sold" Jewish citizens the right to collect taxes for Rome. These publicans bought the right to collect taxes, and then they added their profits or wages. If an unwilling Jewish taxpayer refused to pay his taxes, Roman soldiers were used to reinforce the publican's demands. Publicans were religiously unclean because they fellowshipped with Gentiles, and they were morally unclean for taking advantage of the poor and the innocent. Because the common people hated publicans, when Jesus went to eat with them, some observers questioned Jesus' motives—or at least His judgment. Jesus responded to this criticism: "Those who are well have no need of a physician, but those who are sick. I did not come to call the righteous, but sinners, to repentance" (Mark 2:17).

Lord Jesus, You did not come just for good people, but You came to save all kinds of sinners, including me.

The Jewish people also criticized Jesus for eating with sinners. There were people of Jewish blood who refused to keep the Jewish law, to attend the Sabbath observance and to honor God. The average Jew considered a sinner to be lost. But Jesus wanted everyone to know that He came into the world to save one and all—no matter if their behavior was righteous or sinful.

Jesus, You were the Friend of Publicans and Sinners while on Earth. Now You welcome all people to salvation.

Reading: Luke 5:27-32
Key Thought: Jesus loves and accepts any and all, no matter if their behavior is righteous or sinful.

4 ◇ THE HOLY SPIRIT: THE ANOINTING

But the anointing which you have received from Him abides in you,
and you do not need that anyone teach you; but as the same anointing teaches
you concerning all things, and is true, and is not a lie, and just as it has
taught you, you will abide in Him.
1 JOHN 2:27

The Holy Spirit is the *Anointing* who comes to give you spiritual insight. When you don't understand a Scripture, let Him anoint your spiritual eyes to see what the passage says. When you don't know where to go, let Him anoint your understanding so that you can choose the right paths. When you can't see Jesus working in your life, let Him anoint your spiritual perception. Remember, Jesus promised that the Holy Spirit would come to help believers glorify the Son (see John 16:14). Let the Holy Spirit magnify Jesus in your life today.

Holy Spirit, I want to glorify Jesus. Come anoint me with Your presence
so that I can see the work of Jesus in my life and glorify Him with my
praise. I need Your anointing today.

The Holy Spirit is the *Anointing* who comes to enlighten the Scriptures in your heart. But He doesn't work in a vacuum. You must read and memorize the Bible. You must study the Bible, comparing Scripture to Scripture. You must use commentaries and dictionaries. You must give time meditating on the Word of God. Then you must ask for Him to come help you understand spiritual things. When you seek enlightenment from the Holy Spirit, you are asking for the *Anointing* of the Holy Spirit. He will come shine light on your darkened understanding.

Holy Spirit, come shine Your light in my mind. Help me
see everything You want me to know, and then help me do all You want
me to accomplish. Come anoint me to know the Scripture. Amen.

Reading: 1 John 2:20-28
Key Thought: The Holy Spirit anoints you to understand the Bible.

5 JESUS: MY ANOINTED

Then I will raise up for Myself a faithful priest who shall do according to what is in My heart and in My mind. I will build him a sure house, and he shall walk before My anointed forever.

1 SAMUEL 2:35

The title *"Anointed"* in Hebrew is "Messiah"; in Greek it is "Christ." Jesus Christ is the *Anointed* One. He is Messiah. The heavenly Father calls Jesus My *Anointed*, because Jesus fulfilled the prophecy of the threefold anointed office of priest, prophet and king. Just as a priest was anointed with oil to sacrifice for sins, so Jesus was anointed with the Holy Spirit to offer a sacrifice for our sins. Just as a prophet was anointed to speak for God, Jesus was the Father's prophet who brought the message of grace. Just as a king was inaugurated into office by an anointing oil, so Jesus was the Father's *Anointed* One to rule the hearts of all people.

Jesus, I thank You for being the Anointed Priest to bring me salvation. I thank You for being the Anointed Prophet to deliver the word of God to me. I thank You for being the Anointed King to rule my heart. Anoint me for service today.

The anointing is for cleansing; let Jesus deal with your sin. The anointing is for victory; let Jesus deliver you from temptation and trouble. The anointing is for power; let Jesus use you today. The anointing is for joy; let Jesus, the *Anointed*, give you happiness today. Do you need a fresh anointing to face this day?

Jesus, it's hard to stay fresh; sometimes my daily life gets boring. Anoint my waiting soul. I'm walking through a hot, barren world. Let the oil of Your presence flow into every crack and crevice of my heart. Ah! Your oil feels good. Amen.

Reading: 1 Samuel 2:12-36; 4:10-22
Key Thought: The anointing of Jesus gives you a fresh start for a new day.

◆6◆ JESUS: DELIVERER

*But I am poor and needy; yet the LORD thinks upon me. You are my
help and my deliverer; do not delay, O my God.*
PSALM 40:17

There were many deliverers in the history of God's people: Noah delivered the human race from a judgmental flood; Moses delivered Israel from Egypt; Deborah delivered God's people from the Canaanites; Gideon, from the Midianites; and David, from the Philistines. But each time a human leader delivered them, God's people eventually drifted back into sin. The greatest *Deliverer* is Jesus. His past death delivered us from sin's penalty; He "forgives all your iniquities" (Psalm 103:3). His present indwelling delivers us from the power of sin; "Surely He shall deliver you from the snare of the fowler and from the perilous pestilence" (91:3). His future coming will deliver you from the presence of sin; He "delivers us from the wrath to come" (1 Thessalonians 1:10).

*Lord Jesus, I praise You for delivering Your people in the past. But most
of all, I praise You for delivering me.*

Jesus is your *Deliverer*. He saved you; He has "delivered us from so great a death" (2 Corinthians 1:10). You can have victory over addiction and habits; "He has delivered us from the power of darkness" (Colossians 1:13). He delivers from persecution (see 2 Timothy 3:11). And in the final day, He will deliver you to Heaven; "Jesus . . . delivers us from the wrath to come" (1 Thessalonians 1:10).

*Lord Jesus, I praise You because You saved me when I was in
sin. You brought me close when I was far away, and You delivered
me when I was in trouble. Amen.*

Reading: Psalm 40
Key Thought: Jesus will deliver you in many ways.

7 THE TRINITY: THE LORD MIGHTY IN BATTLE

Who is this King of glory? The LORD strong and mighty,
the LORD mighty in battle.
PSALM 24:8

Look to the *Lord Mighty in Battle* to give you victory in life. Battles are not easy; they're tough, threatening and tiring. Jesus went through many sufferings on Earth. His disciples left Him, Peter denied Him, and the Roman soldiers beat Him and then crucified Him on a cross. Though the enemy thought they won the battle by killing Jesus, it was in His death that the victory was won. Since the world hated Him, the world will oppose you. You will always have to fight the world, the flesh and Satan. Your enemies will be too strong for you, so you must look to the *Lord Mighty in Battle*. He will come to your rescue when you call on Him.

Lord, help me see my enemies through Your eyes. You defeated them on
the cross; give me faith to claim victory today.

When you think that sin will defeat you, remember that victory begins in your mind. You must want to win and look to His strength for victory. When you plan to win, remember that victory comes when you stand by the Lord. He will help you defeat the Enemy. When you're near Him, you can be victorious in His strength.

Lord, I'll not look at the strength of the Enemy; I'll look to Your might.
I know You defeated the Enemy on the cross, so I'll trust
You to win the victory today. Amen.

Reading: Psalm 60
Key Thought: Claim the victory of Jesus to win battles over sin.

8 JESUS: THE MYSTERY OF GOD

That their hearts may be encouraged, being knit together in love, and attaining to all riches of the full assurance of understanding, to the knowledge of the mystery of God, both of the Father and of Christ.
COLOSSIANS 2:2

Jesus wants you to have full assurance of your salvation. You can know that you are saved, and you can know how to please the Father. You can know these things because Jesus lives in your life and gives complete confidence to you. The world doesn't understand this mystery, but the Father and Jesus have taken the mystery out of your relationship with them. The fact that the Son indwells you is a mystery to the world, but you understand it because you originally asked Jesus into your heart when you were saved. The *Mystery of God* is the fact that Jesus indwells you to give you full assurance of sins forgiven and a future home in Heaven.

Lord, I want to know everything about my salvation.
Sometimes I just don't understand what You are doing in my life.
Sometimes things puzzle me.

Jesus is the *Mystery of God;* in Him are all the treasures of wisdom and knowledge (see Colossians 2:3). When you don't understand what's happening in your life, learn more about Jesus to find answers for your questions. When you are not sure what to do, come to Jesus for guidance. He can help you learn about the *Mystery of God.*

Lord Jesus, thank You for teaching me how to live the Christian life.
Thank You for new life and a future hope of Heaven. Help me learn
more about how to live for You. Amen.

Reading: Colossians 2:1-7
Key Thought: Knowing Jesus is the key to understanding the mysteries of God.

9   JESUS: A REPROACH OF MEN

But I am a worm, and no man; a reproach of men, and despised of the people.
PSALM 22:6

Over the centuries, the name of Jesus has come to be revered and respected by His followers. But there was a brief window of time when the followers of Jesus fled and hid themselves. The name "Jesus" was a reproach to them. When Jesus was arrested, "all the disciples forsook Him and fled" (Matthew 26:56). What would you have done? Peter ran away—but not too far, because he got entrance into the high priest's courtyard. A servant girl—the gatekeeper—recognized Peter and said, "You also were with Jesus of Nazareth" (Mark 14:67). Peter denied it three times in rapid succession; and the third time, "he began to curse and swear" (v. 71). Why? Because Jesus had been a Reproach to him. Has Jesus ever become a Reproach to you? Have you ever denied Him?

Lord Jesus, I am not perfect. I do not always speak up as a Christian, but You are not a Reproach to me. I will speak boldly in Your name in the future.

When Peter denied Jesus, he fulfilled the Old Testament prediction that Jesus would be a *Reproach of Men*. Hanging on the cross, Jesus was cursed, mocked, spat upon and rejected by the multitudes. But even in His rejection, a thief believed in Him; His mother and John were commissioned by Him; and at His death, the centurion recognized Jesus as a righteous man.

Lord Jesus, there are many who reject You in this world, but You are not a Reproach to me. I take the name of Christ; I am glad to be a Christian. Amen.

Reading: Mark 14:66-72
Key Thought: Jesus is either a Reproach to you or He is your Savior.

10 THE HOLY SPIRIT: THE BLESSING

I will pour My Spirit on your descendants, and My blessing on your offspring.
ISAIAH 44:3

The Holy Spirit is the *Blessing* you need. It's not help you need; it's the Holy Spirit. It's not money you need; it's the Holy Spirit. He is the *Blessing* you must have to fill up that hole in your life. Don't seek money or happiness or success; seek the Holy Spirit. It's not an ambiguous blessing you need; the Holy Spirit is the *Blessing* you need.

Holy Spirit, I will seek You so that I can have spiritual blessings in my life. I have occasional emergencies, but most of the time I just have pressures. Bless me with Your presence this day. Be with me in all that I do today. Bless my testimony to expand Your kingdom.

The *Blessing* you seek is the Holy Spirit. He will add value to all that you are and all that you do. He is the *Blessing*. He can bless you and keep you; He can make His face shine upon you and be gracious to you; He can give you peace" (see Numbers 6:24-25). The Holy Spirit is the *Blessing*. You must yield to His control so that He can bless your workplace and the work of your hands. The Holy Spirit is financial *Blessing*; you must yield the use of your checkbook to Him so that He can add financial value in your life.

Lord, You are my Blessing. I look to You and not to money, position or things. Add value to all I do, and help me be a blessing to others, as You have blessed me. Amen.

Reading: Mark 4:14-29
Key Thought: The Holy Spirit is the *Blessing* you need.

11   THE HOLY SPIRIT: THE SPIRIT OF THE LORD

The Spirit of the LORD came upon [Othniel], and he judged Israel.
He went out to war, and the LORD delivered Cushan-Rishathaim
king of Mesopotamia into his hand.
JUDGES 3:10

When the *Spirit of the Lord* came upon Othniel, it was the Holy Spirit—the third Person of the Trinity—who empowered him for service (Judges 3:10). When the *Spirit of the Lord* comes upon you, He will help you live a godly life and serve with power. Just as the *Spirit of the Lord* came upon Othniel to give him victory over a profane enemy, so He can fill every corner of your life with renewed energy. But He can't fill the empty parts of your life if you don't yield them to Him. Right now, stop your self-efforts. Cry out for the strength of the *Spirit of the Lord* to empower you.

Holy Spirit, I come to You for victory. Help me overcome
outward temptations. Give me the courage to overcome inner doubts.
Give me discipline to overcome my rebellion.

Just as the *Spirit of the Lord* strengthened Othniel to overcome a Syrian king, so the Holy Spirit can fill you with a power that you've never experienced before. But He will not fill a dirty vessel. Sin keeps the Holy Spirit from filling every crevice and cranny of your life. Deal with your rebellious attitude in a spiritual way so that the *Spirit of the Lord* can be poured out in full power.

Lord, I repent of my sin, and I turn to You. I confess my sin,
and I ask forgiveness. Holy Spirit, let Your power flow into my life.
Come, flow quickly into my life to fill every empty corner with
Your power. Flow, Spirit, flow. Amen.

Reading: Judges 3:1-12
Key Thought: You must prepare for the Holy Spirit before He will flow into your life.

12 JESUS: THE LORD GOD ALMIGHTY

Even so, Lord God Almighty, true and righteous are Your judgments.
REVELATION 16:7

When Jesus comes in judgment, He will come as the *Lord God Almighty*. Jesus will come as the Lord, the One who control all things. Today, the Lord allows evil rulers to make war, innocent victims to be killed, disease to run rampant in many places and crime to seem unstoppable. While it seems that Jesus is not in outward control, He is working inwardly to control the inner life of His followers. Will you let Him control your life? Jesus is the God who created all things; that means He has "eternal power" (Romans 1:20) to do all that God wills to do. But it seems that God is holding back His power—because Christians suffer, the Church is persecuted and evil thrives. But that is not true. God's power is not measured by what evil does or doesn't do. God allows evil in the world to test the obedience of His servants in order to determine if they will love Him more. Are you loving Him more? Jesus is also the Almighty, the One who exercises divine will, the One who works His plan in your life. Is He working His purpose in your life? In today's world, the *Lord God Almighty* is exercising divine patience until evil runs its course. At His second coming, Jesus will manifest Himself as the *Lord God Almighty*. He will directly control all things, and He will accomplish His almighty will.

Lord Jesus, come! I wait for Your return to Earth to rule everything. I wait for Your power to accomplish Your will. But until You return, come rule my life with Your power. Amen.

Reading: Revelation 16
Key Thought: Jesus has the power to control everything, and He will when He returns.

13 THE TRINITY: THE WINDOW OPENER

"Bring all the tithes into the storehouse, that there may be food in My house, and prove Me now in this," says the LORD of hosts, "If I will not open for you the windows of heaven and pour out for you such blessing that there will not be room enough to receive it."
MALACHI 3:10

The Lord is the *Window Opener* who will open the windows of Heaven and pour out blessings on all who bring the tithe to Him. It's not just money that the Lord wants from people; it's also their worship and obedience. When people give 10 percent of all of their increase (Deuteronomy 26:12), then the Lord responds by giving them the best of life, the provision for their needs; and the Lord will manifest His presence to them. Notice, the Lord does not give people everything they want; but He provides spiritual blessings for those who put Him first in their lives. People spend their money to find happiness or to provide for their needs. When we spend our money on God, we get the benefits for which others spend their money. God in Heaven sees what we do and gives us the blessings that we seek in life.

Lord, I acknowledge Your ownership over my life, including my time, talents and treasures. I will give You 10 percent of all I have, knowing that You will take care of my needs.

Heaven is stored with blessings and goodness for God's people. However, you can have them now by total obedience to God. When you do God's will and call upon Him, He will be the *Window Opener* and pour out His blessings for you in this life.

Lord, forgive me when I've not obeyed You. I commit myself now to giving financially to Your cause. I look forward to receiving Your blessings from the open windows of Heaven. Amen.

Reading: Malachi 3:7-11
Key Thought: God opens windows when you obey Him.

14 JESUS: THE LORD GOD OMNIPOTENT

*And I heard, as it were, the voice of a great multitude, as the sound
of many waters and as the sound of mighty thunderings, saying, "Alleluia!
For the Lord God Omnipotent reigns!"*
REVELATION 19:6

Jesus is the *Lord God Omnipotent*. Because Jesus is the God who created all things (see John 1:3), He has all power. What power do you need from Him today? Because Jesus is the Lord who controls all things by His laws and sovereignty, will you let Him control your life today? Because Jesus is omnipotent, He has the ability to do everything that is possible to do. Obviously, He will not make yesterday not happen, because that would mean God would have to deny that He existed. Nor will God make two times two equal three, for that denies truth. An omnipotent God can do anything He wills to do, but He will not go against what He has previously done. When Jesus comes to finally judge the world, He will have power to judge exactly as He wills. Therefore, you want to be in the center of God's will when He comes.

*Lord Jesus, be the Lord who controls my life. Be the omnipotent One,
whose will I do. Be the God who gives me power to accomplish Your will.*

Jesus will manifest Himself fully as the *Lord God Omnipotent* when He returns to Earth. Today, Jesus allows individuals to rebel against His control, deny His power and reject His will. But what about you? Will you yield to His control? Will you claim His power? Will you do His will?

*Lord Jesus, I want to glorify You with my life. I submit to Your control,
and I claim Your power; help me do Your will. Amen.*

Reading: Revelation 19:1-10
Key Thought: Jesus is the *Lord God Omnipotent* who wants to control your life.

15   Jesus: Lord Jesus Christ

My brethren, do not hold the faith of our Lord Jesus Christ,
the Lord of glory, with partiality.
JAMES 2:1

We usually think of Jesus as having three names: "Lord," "Jesus" and "Christ." But these three names are entirely different from the first, middle and last names that people have today. When you call Him Lord, that's His title. You are referring to His deity. No one gave Him the title "Lord," for He has eternally been Lord. When you call Him Jesus, you are referring to His humanity. The angel Gabriel told Mary to call Him Jesus, a Greek name that means "Jehovah saves." When you call Him Christ, you are referring to His anointed office. Just as prophets, priests and kings were anointed into their office, so Jesus came as Prophet to give the message of God, as Priest to bring salvation and as King to rule the hearts of His followers.

I worship You as Christ, who brought me salvation;
as Jesus, the virgin-born son of Mary; and as my King,
who sits on the throne of my heart.

Why does the *Lord Jesus Christ* have over 700 names, titles and descriptive metaphors? It's because He is and does a vast number of things. Similarly, men who do many things have many titles (dad, husband, uncle, boss, deacon and so on). But the names you call Him are not as important as your response to Him. He wants your love and obedience.

Jesus, You are my Redeemer, Intercessor, Guide, Protector and Friend.
You came to me as Light, Water, Bread, Shepherd, Vine and
Resurrection. But most of all, You are my Lord and my Savior. Amen.

Reading: 1 Timothy 1:1-2,12-17
Key Thought: Jesus has many names to elicit many responses.

"Your New Pathway (Part 2)"
Romans 7:6

<u>Introduction</u>

Pathway to Change: Old Way / New Way

Apart from Me you can do nothing.

The "New Way" (v. 6) *Stuck, you can't get anywhere.*

1. **Realize** your __brokenness__ and __inadequacy__ (Romans 7:5; John 15:5)
   Getting fed up w/ the old inadequate way.

2. **Recognize** the __indwelling Spirit of Jesus__ in you. (Romans 8:9, 11)

   Spiritual Life, begins when you accept brokenness.

3. **Refocus** __your faith__ on Jesus Christ. (Romans 8:4,6; Galatians 5:16, 25; Ephesians 5:18) *that's been our other things*

   "Make an adjustment on your life." Surrender

Putting it all together: *Talk to God in the empty chair*

REALIZE + RECOGNIZE + REFOCUS = CHANGE!

   What changes?

   • _____ with God (Romans 8:15-17)

   • _____ (Romans 8:6)

   • _____ (Romans 8:11)

   • Altered _____ and _____
     (Galatians 5:22-23)

they will start to flow through you into a new way.

Romans 7:5-6 (NASB) For while we were in *the flesh*, the sinful passions, which were aroused by the Law, were at work in the members of our body to bear *fruit for death*. 6 But now we have been released from the Law, having died to that by which we were bound, so that we serve in *new way of the Spirit* and not in the old way of the letter.

John 15:4-5 (NASB) "*Abide in Me, and I in you*. As the branch cannot bear fruit of itself, unless it abides in the vine, so neither can you, unless you abide in Me. 5 "I am the vine, you are the branches; he who abides in Me, and I in him, he bears much fruit; for *apart from Me you can do nothing*."

Romans 8:9, 11 (NASB) However, you are not in the flesh but in the Spirit, if *indeed the Spirit of God dwells in you*. But if anyone does not have the *Spirit of Christ*, he does not belong to Him. 11 But if *the Spirit* of Him who raised Jesus from the dead *dwells in you*, He who raised Christ Jesus from the dead will also give life to your mortal bodies through *His Spirit who indwells you*.

Romans 8:4 (NASB) in order that the requirement of the Law might be fulfilled in us, who do not *walk* according to the flesh, but *according to the Spirit*.

Galatians 5:16 (NASB) But I say, *walk by the Spirit*, and you will not carry out the desire of the flesh.

Ephesians 5:18 (NASB) And do not get drunk with wine, for that is dissipation, but *be filled with the Spirit*,

Romans 8:15-17 (NASB) For you have not received a spirit of slavery leading to fear again, but you have received a spirit of adoption as sons by which we cry out, *"Abba! Father!"* 16 The Spirit Himself bears witness with our spirit that we are *children of God*, 17 and if children, *heirs also*, heirs of God and fellow heirs with Christ

Romans 8:6 (NASB) For the mind set on the flesh is death, but the *mind set on the Spirit is life and peace*,

2 Corinthians 4:7 (NASB) But we have this treasure in earthen vessels, that the surpassing greatness of the power may be of God and not from ourselves;

The Holy Spirit points us to Jesus Christ saying follow me, learn from me, love me.

Intimacy w/ Jesus will help us not sin so much.

Everything therefore depends upon our maintaining union w/ Christ Charles Hodge

16 ♦ THE HOLY SPIRIT: THE BREATH OF GOD

As long as my breath is in me, and the breath of God in my nostrils.
JOB 27:3

The Holy Spirit is the *Breath of God*. When the Father wants to give life to something, the Holy Spirit is breathed into it. The Holy Spirit was the Breath that God blew into the nostrils of Adam, giving him life. The Holy Spirit was the *Breath of God* that hovered over the waters when life was given during Creation (see Genesis 1:2). The *Breath of God* blows like the wind over hills and oceans to give them life. The Holy Spirit is the *Breath of God*—the wind that blows where it wishes—to bring eternal life to those who believe in Jesus (see John 3:7-8). Let the Holy Spirit breathe new life into you today.

Holy Spirit, I need new enthusiasm to worship and serve You. Breathe new excitement and anticipation into me. Blow Your new life into me today.

The Holy Spirit is God's Breath. Just as you must breathe air to exist, so you must breathe the Holy Spirit to have eternal life. Breathe the Holy Spirit for illumination when you are spiritually blind. Breathe the Holy Spirit for guidance when you don't know what to do. Breathe the Holy Spirit for strength when you think you can't go on. Breathe the Holy Spirit for encouragement when things fall apart. Let the Holy Spirit be the Air that you breathe.

Holy Spirit, I breathe You into my cluttered lungs.
Clean out my selfish ways, and make me holy. Get rid of junk in
my schedule, and make me spiritual. Holy Spirit, make me holy
and make me spiritual, like You. Amen.

Reading: Job 27
Key Thought: The Holy Spirit breathes new enthusiasm into you.

17 JESUS: LORD (*KURIOS*)

You call Me Teacher and Lord, and you say well, for so I am.
JOHN 13:13

Jesus is the *Lord* of Heaven, the *Lord* of the universe and the *Lord* of the Church; but most of all, He should be your personal *Lord*. Just as a human can be the lord of a manor because he owns the house and directs its activities, so Jesus should be the *Lord* of your body—His Temple—because He provides for your needs and directs your activities. Jesus wants to be more than a guest in your home; He wants the title deed so that you belong to Him.

Jesus, enter my life as You might enter a home. Make my heart Your home. Live in my body.

If Jesus is your *Lord*, He should rest in the living room of your life. Jesus should feel comfortable in the recreation room, where you play and entertain yourself. Jesus should be invited into your dining room, where you eat and satisfy your appetite. He won't be happy if you eat the garbage of this world. Would Jesus rest comfortably in the bedroom of your life? Do you have a besetting sin hidden in the basement? When you invite Jesus into your home, He doesn't enter as a decoration or as a celebrity to give your home status. He doesn't come as a vacation guest or as a friend who pops in on the weekends. Jesus comes to be the *Lord* of your house.

Jesus, I give every room in my house to You. Enter each room, cleanse it, and make it Your own. I will make You Lord of my life. Amen.

Reading: John 13:1-17
Key Thought: Jesus will not be *Lord* at all unless He is the *Lord* of all.

18 JESUS: LORD OF LORDS

*He will manifest in His own time, He who is the blessed and only Potentate,
the King of kings and Lord of lords.*
1 TIMOTHY 6:15

Many in the world call Jesus Lord, but He is more; Jesus is *Lord of Lords.*
A lord holds vast properties and assets. Jesus is Lord because He owns
the world and rules the universe. A lord directs those under his rule.
Jesus is Lord because He holds the destiny of all people in His hand. A
lord is the absolute owner of all he surveys. Jesus is the Lord of everything because He created all things. Because He died for all people, all
will one day bow to His rule. Because He will come in the future to judge
all, you must be accountable to Him for how you live.

*Lord, there are many who do not recognize Your rule in their lives, but I
acknowledge You as my Lord. Teach me to adjust to Your rules. Let my
submission be a testimony to others.*

There are many lords in this world; they are called presidents, prime
ministers, governors, mayors and billionaires. They rule empires. While
they will not recognize the Lord's rule on Earth nor will they rule according to His righteous laws, one day they will acknowledge Jesus as King of
kings and *Lord of Lords.* Then every knee will bow, including theirs (see
Philippians 2:10-11).

*Jesus, I know that You will rule everything in the future, but I am
concerned about this day. Come take control of my heart, and be my
Lord. Be glorified in all that I do and say. Amen.*

Reading: 1 Timothy 6:15-21
Key Thought: Jesus will rule all things one day, so submit to Him today.

19 The Trinity: The Pillar of Fire

*And the LORD went before them by day in a pillar of cloud to lead
the way, and by night in a pillar of fire to give them light, so as to go
by day and night. He did not take away the pillar of cloud by day
or the pillar of fire by night from before the people.*
EXODUS 13:21-22

The *Pillar of Fire* that led Israel through the wilderness is a picture of the
Lord. It was more than a flame; it was His presence with His people.
Jesus is a Light to guide, to protect and to comfort His people. When
Isaiah went into the Temple, he saw the smoke from the sacrificial altar
drifting up into Heaven. That was the Shekinah glory cloud that symbolized God's presence. Then Isaiah cried out, "I saw the Lord" (Isaiah
6:1). Because the Lord is Light, He will give illumination, wisdom and
guidance.

*Lord, thank You for light in my life. Let me experience
Your presence today. I want to see You.*

The Lord manifested Himself in a *Pillar of Fire*; but if you were to take
away the smoke and the clouds, you wouldn't see anything, for there's
nothing to see. No one can see God, because God is Spirit (see John
4:24). But in order for people to know where God was located, He
appeared in a column of smoke or fire or in a thick cloud (see Exodus
40:34-35). God is invisible, so He can be everywhere present at the same
time. God is Spirit, so He can be near you and indwell you. Just as the
Lord led Israel by a *Pillar of Fire*, let Him lead you today.

*Lord, I feel comfortable in the fire of Your presence. Thank
You for light and direction. Lead me today. Amen.*

Reading: Exodus 13:20—14:20
Key Thought: The Lord can lead you today as He led Israel in the wilderness.

20 ◆ JESUS: MALEFACTOR

*They answered and said unto him, If he were not a malefactor, we
would not have delivered him up unto thee.*
JOHN 18:30, *KJV*

Those who had Jesus arrested called him a *Malefactor*, which means "evil-doer." They had to bribe their witnesses to lie, so Jesus' accusers knew that He was not a *Malefactor*. Still they accused Him, even though Jesus was perfect and without sin. He could say to the Jews, "Which of you can truthfully accuse me of sin?" (John 8:46, *NLT*). Pilate would testify, "I find no fault in Him" (19:6). Yet in the irony of this situation, the Jews accused an innocent man of being a *Malefactor*, when in actuality their lies made them the guilty ones. Jesus did not sin, but He was made to be sin for us (see 2 Corinthians 5:21). Jesus took on the sin of the Jews, the sin of the world and your sin.

*Lord Jesus, I know that You are the perfect Son of God. I also know that
You became sin for me. Thank You for Your death for my sins.*

The names that were given to Jesus reflect the roles that people projected onto Him. Jesus was a *Malefactor* in the eyes of those who hated Him. They hated Him because He attacked their dead religious rituals. Jesus was a rival "religious leader" because He gave the multitudes hope, which is something that the other religious leaders couldn't do. Jesus taught the truth, lived a perfect life and established a Kingdom of peace and righteousness.

*Lord Jesus, the world has called You a Malefactor, but
I call You my Savior. The world calls You an Evildoer,
but I call You my Redeemer. Amen.*

Reading: John 18:30-38
Key Thought: The world calls Jesus a *Malefactor*, but He is the Savior.

21 ◆ JESUS: MASTER (*EPISTATES*)

And Simon answering said unto him, Master, we have toiled all the night, and
have taken nothing: nevertheless at thy word I will let down the net.
LUKE 5:5, *KJV*

Jesus sat in Peter's boat and preached to a large crowd. When He finished, He told Peter, "Launch out into the deep and let down your nets for a catch" (Luke 5:4). Because Jesus knew all things, He knew that Peter had fished all night but didn't catch anything. Peter called Jesus *Master*, a title of respect that a worker would call a boss. Peter was respectful, but He replied, "I will let down the net" (v. 5). Did you see what Peter said? He would cast only one net, not all of the nets, as Jesus had originally commanded. Don't we do the same thing? Aren't we guilty of partial obedience to Jesus?

Jesus, forgive me for the times I have not completely obeyed You. Teach
me to completely obey Your commands.

Notice what happened when Peter let down only one net: "They caught a great number of fish, and their net was breaking" (Luke 5:6). Perhaps the singular net would not have been broken if Peter had let down all the nets. Isn't partial obedience full disobedience? When Peter saw his net breaking and the boat filled with fish, he fell at Jesus' feet, crying out, "O Lord!" (v. 8). Notice the change in titles. Jesus is no longer just respected as a boss; Jesus is now revered as *Master* and Lord. Do you just respect Jesus as your boss, or do you revere Him as your Lord?

Lord Jesus, I revere your miracle-working powers, but
I bow in worship because You are the Lord of the universe; You
are my personal Lord. Amen.

Reading: Luke 5:1-11
Key Thought: Jesus wants to be more than your *Master*; He wants to be Your Lord.

22 ▷ THE HOLY SPIRIT: A NEW SPIRIT

Then I will give them one heart, and I will put a new spirit within them, and take
the stony heart out of their flesh, and give them a heart of flesh.
EZEKIEL 11:19

The Holy Spirit is the *New Spirit* that enters a person's heart at salvation. He enters a hard heart and brings the love of God to soften it. When people realize how much the Father loves them and how much Jesus suffered for them on the cross, they'll soften in repentance and faith. The *New Spirit* will give them a new view of their sins, a new view of the gospel and a new view of salvation. But most of all, the *New Spirit* will give them a new heart to call upon God. Let the Holy Spirit give you a new life. Let the Holy Spirit show you what new things He can do for you today.

Holy Spirit, I need a new perspective on life. Give me a new focus
on my possibilities. Use me in a new way today.

The *New Spirit* is sent into your life to show you all the new things you get at salvation. You get peace (see John 14:27), guidance (see Galatians 5:25), assurance (see Ephesians 4:30), illumination (see 1 Peter 1:12); and you are filled with the presence of the Holy Spirit for new service (see Ephesians 5:18). When you get the fullness of the Holy Spirit, many new possibilities open up to you.

Holy Spirit, come touch me in a new way. I want all the new things You
have for me. Make this a wonderful day. Amen.

Reading: Ezekiel 36:25-36
Key Thought: The Holy Spirit gives new things to believers.

23 JESUS: MEEK

Take my yoke upon you, and learn of me; for I am meek and lowly in heart: and ye shall find rest unto your souls.
MATTHEW 11:29, *KJV*

Jesus called Himself *Meek* because He personified meekness. He calls us to a life of meekness instead of a life of arrogance and boastfulness. Because Jesus is humble, He calls us neither to serve ourselves nor to live for selfish advancement. Because Jesus was submissive to the Roman authorities and those over Him, His example calls us to meekness and surrender. We are to obey the rules, because God has put them over us. Jesus did not seek His own will; He testified, "I always do those things that please Him [the Father]" (John 8:29). But we are the opposite of Jesus; we seek our own fulfillment. "All we like sheep have gone astray; we have turned, every one, to his own way; and the LORD has laid on Him the iniquity of us all" (Isaiah 53:6).

Lord, I am human, and I follow my impulse to live for selfish purposes. Teach me to be meek like Jesus. Teach me to live for You.

Jesus is called *Meek* because He left His lofty position in Heaven, laid aside His glory and accepted a humble birth in a stable. When facing suffering, He prayed, "O My Father, if it is possible, let this cup pass from Me; nevertheless, not as I will, but as You will" (Matthew 26:39). Yes, Jesus meekly accepted the cross for you; what will you give up for Him?

Lord Jesus, thank You for Your sacrifice. Help me learn from Your meekness; help me to be like You. Amen.

Reading: Matthew 11:28-30; 26:36-46
Key Thought: You can learn meekness from Jesus.

24 ◆ JESUS: MERCY SEAT

*And above it [the Ark of the Covenant] were the cherubim of
glory overshadowing the mercy seat.*
HEBREWS 9:5

*And He Himself is the propitiation for our sins, and not for
ours only but also for the whole world.*
1 JOHN 2:2

The Lord has a throne in Heaven, but He did not let His people build
Him a throne on Earth. Rather, He instructed Moses to build the Ark of
the Covenant (the word "ark" meant "box"), where He would be present
(see Exodus 25:10). The lid of the box was called the mercy seat, because
that's where the Lord came to sit (see v. 17). The Lord's sitting on the
mercy seat is much like a human father sitting on a cedar chest (the
approximate dimensions of the ark). God came to sit on His box—the Ark
of the Covenant. It's ironic that the God of Heaven had to sit on a box
and not on a throne. Blood was sprinkled on the mercy seat once each
year, symbolic of God's covering Israel's sin. God wanted to sit where the
blood was sprinkled. The mercy seat was symbolic of forgiven sins.

*Lord Jesus, You are my Mercy Seat, for it was Your blood that redeemed
me. I worship You for salvation completed.*

The Shekinah glory cloud sat on the mercy seat. The glory of God—
His presence—was in that cloud as it filled the holy of holies. That's as
close as anyone will see God sitting on anything on this earth. Today,
invite Jesus' presence to fill your world and influence you, just as God's
glory came to sit on the mercy seat in the Old Testament.

*Jesus, You are the Propitiation—the Satisfaction—
for my sins. When You died for me, it was Your blood that was
sprinkled on the mercy seat. Amen.*

Reading: Hebrews 9:1-11
Key Thought: God sits on the mercy seat to forgive my sins.

25 THE TRINITY: EVERLASTING GOD (*EL OLAM*)

Then Abraham planted a tamarisk [oak] tree in Beersheba, and there called on the name of the LORD, the Everlasting God.
GENESIS 21:33

The Lord is *El Olam,* the God of mystery who is unknown to you. His name "Olam" means "secret" or "hidden." There are many things about God that are hidden in the clouds of eternity. You'll not be held accountable for the things you don't know about God—only for the things you know. These are the difficult challenges in life. The Lord is *El Olam*—the God of mystery. One day you'll understand the events of today—when you look back to see God's good plan for you. He is directing all things, even when you can't see what's happening.

El Olam, You made me human and finite. Teach me to trust You even when my path is cloudy. Teach me to follow You when I don't understand the events around me.

Abraham planted a grove of trees that would outlive his life in Beersheba, thereby symbolizing a relationship with God that would extend beyond his earthly life. *El Olam* is the God beyond this life. Even when you can't understand what's happening in your life, look beyond your circumstances to see His everlasting nature. Call on Him—the *Everlasting God*—to extend your influence into the future. And when you think your life is a mystery, remember that God has a plan for you and that one day it will be crystal clear to you.

O Everlasting God, accomplish Your plan in my life. Help me trust You when I don't know what You're doing. Help me follow You when I can't see where I'm going. Amen.

Reading: Genesis 20–21
Key Thought: Trust the *Everlasting God* who has a plan bigger than this life.

26 ▸ JESUS: MESSIAH

And after the sixty-two weeks Messiah shall be cut off, but not for Himself; and the people of the prince who is to come shall destroy the city and the sanctuary. The end of it shall be with a flood, and till the end of the war desolations are determined.

DANIEL 9:26

In the Old Testament, the people of God looked forward to the Messiah, their Deliverer. The title *"Messiah"* meant "anointed One." Just as David was anointed king and drove the unbelieving nations out of the Promised Land, so the Jews looked forward to their coming Messiah to drive the Romans into the sea. Just as prophets were anointed to speak God's message, so the Jews looked for their Messiah's coming with God's Word. Just as the priests were anointed to make sacrifices for sins, so the Jews looked for their Messiah to bring in universal peace and forgiveness of sins. Jesus was the *Messiah*, God's anointed One. He came fulfilling the threefold anointed office of prophet, priest and king.

Lord Jesus, thank You for being a Priest to forgive my sins. Thank You for being a Prophet to bring the message of love. Thank You for being a King to rule in my heart.

Jesus is the *Messiah*, the anointed One. He wants to anoint your mind to understand the Scriptures; so study the Word daily. He wants to anoint your prayer life for effective intercession; so bring your requests to God. He wants to anoint your quiet time with His presence; so seek Jesus now.

Lord Jesus, my life is empty; I need a fresh filling today. Pour Your presence into my life. Anoint me with Your power to live above temptations and trouble. Anoint me with peace and confidence to live for You this day. Amen.

Reading: Daniel 9:24-27
Key Thought: Jesus can anoint your life so that you can live above temptations and troubles.

27 JESUS: LORD AND SAVIOR

*For so an entrance will be supplied to you abundantly into the everlasting
kingdom of our Lord and Savior Jesus Christ.*
2 PETER 1:11

Jesus is both *Lord and Savior*. He is the Lord of the universe, because He
created everything. He is the Lord of the nations, because He created the
first humans. He is the Lord of nature, because He holds everything
together by His power. Jesus could have forced the first parents to be
obedient, but untested obedience doesn't glorify the Father. He had to
give Adam and Eve a free choice to love God or to rebel against Him.
When the first parents sinned, nature was cursed and humanity spun
out of control. Death reigned over all people. It was then that Jesus, the
Lord of all, had to become Savior of all. Jesus came to die so you could
live. Now Jesus is *Lord and Savior* of the world.

*Jesus, You are Lord and Savior, but everyone doesn't follow You.
However, You are my Savior and You are my Lord.*

Jesus has provided salvation to all, but many will not accept it. He is
neither their Savior from sin nor the Lord of their lives. Some have been
saved but will not obey Him. Jesus is only their Savior; He's not their
Lord. Today, Jesus wants to be both your Savior and your Lord. Will you
let Him direct your life? When you are yielded to Jesus, He'll be both
your *Lord and Savior*.

*Jesus, I want You to be both my Lord and Savior. I praise You for
forgiving my sins, and I give You the control of my life. Amen.*

Reading: 2 Peter 1:1-18
Key Thought: Jesus wants to be both your *Lord and Savior.*

THE HOLY SPIRIT: DIVIDED TONGUES AS OF FIRE

Then there appeared to them divided tongues, as of fire,
and one sat upon each of them.
ACTS 2:3

The Holy Spirit is *Divided Tongues as of Fire* that came upon the disciples in the Upper Room on the Day of Pentecost. They had been praying for 40 days when the Holy Spirit came upon them. The sign of tongues in the air was not illusionary; it was real. The Holy Spirit entered their lives and spoke through them with different languages. Jesus had told them to preach the gospel to all people: "Go therefore and make disciples of all the nations [ethnic groups]" (Matthew 28:19). So the Holy Spirit gave them different languages to speak to all people. This means that He can give you the ability to speak your language to those who are not Christians. But more than giving knowledge of a foreign language, the Holy Spirit, through their words, convicted of sin, exalted Jesus through their lives and drew people to salvation. Let the Holy Spirit speak through you today.

Holy Spirit, come fill my life with Your presence. Speak through my
words to my unsaved friends and associates.

The *Divided Tongues as of Fire* can purify you just as fire burns away impurities. The Holy Spirit can cleanse your tongue and clean up your thoughts. You can speak the pure Word of God from a clean heart. And just as fire burns everything it touches, the Holy Spirit can cause the message to burn in the hearts of those who listen to you.

Holy Spirit, I will testify to some unsaved people today.
When I speak, fill my words with fire. Help me bring
my friends to faith in Christ. Amen.

Reading: Acts 10:44-48
Key Thought: The Holy Spirit wants to use your words today.

29 ◆ JESUS: THE LIGHT OF MEN

In Him was life, and the life was the light of men.
JOHN 1:4

There are all kinds of light—sunlight, moonlight and the light from a fire or candle. Satan is an "angel of light" (2 Corinthians 11:14) who attracts people to sin and death. The original source of all light is Jesus, the Light who is the *Light of Men* (see John 1:4; 8:12). When people are lost in darkness, Jesus is the Light of salvation that directs people to Heaven. Just as light illuminates the right path so people won't get lost, so Jesus is the right path to Heaven. Just as a light will keep away dangerous predators, so Jesus is the Light that protects us on our journey. Just as a light makes it possible to read and explore things, so Jesus helps us learn and grow as Christians. Just as light makes us comfortable in the night, so Jesus gives us "the light of life" (8:12)

Jesus, shine light on me today.

There are several ways to walk in the light of Jesus, the Light of all people. Just as we hold light high to illuminate our surroundings, so we must hold Jesus high for all to see us as Christians. Just as we hold light in front of us to direct our steps, so we must let Jesus guide our attitudes, thoughts and actions. Just as we hold light near so that we can read and learn, so we must let Jesus into our hearts and minds through Bible reading, meditation and prayer.

Lord Jesus, You are the Light of my life. Keep me from
getting lost. Keep me from getting hurt. Keep me from the dangers of sin.
I will follow Your light. Amen.

Reading: Psalm 27:1-8
Key Thought: Jesus is my Light to guide me safely to God.

30   JESUS: KING OF THE JEWS

Where is He who has been born King of the Jews? For we have seen His
star in the East and have come to worship Him.
MATTHEW 2:2

Julius Caesar had put King Herod on the throne; so when Caesar was killed, Herod was threatened and ran quickly to Rome to have the Senate appoint him as the king of the Jews. That not only put Herod over Jerusalem and the surrounding territories, but it also gave Herod authority over Jews everywhere. No wonder Herod was "troubled" (Matthew 2:3) when wise men came looking for a baby who had been born *King of the Jews*. No wonder Herod sent soldiers to Bethlehem to kill all babies two years and under (see v. 16). Rome recognized Herod as the earthly king of the Jews, but the heavenly Father recognized Jesus as the eternal *King of the Jews*.

Lord Jesus, not only do I recognize You as the King of the Jews
and the King of my life, but I also recognize You as the King of
the universe and the King of Heaven.

Some men are made king because of their superior powers; others wait until their father dies before becoming king. Jesus was always King; and long before He ascends the throne of Israel in the coming millennium, He remains *King of the Jews*. Jesus was born with that title and lived with that title; and when He returns, all will recognize His title as King—*King of the Jews*. Jesus is King of kings and Lord of lords. Is He the reigning King on the throne of your heart?

Even so, come Lord Jesus; rule my life today. Amen.

Reading: Psalm 89:1-10
Key Thought: The *King of the Jews* wants to sit on the throne of your heart.

THE HOLY SPIRIT: FLOODS UPON THE DRY GROUND

31

For I will pour water upon him that is thirsty, and floods upon the dry ground:
I will pour my spirit upon thy seed, and my blessing upon thine offspring.
ISAIAH 44:3, *KJV*

The Holy Spirit is *Floods upon the Dry Ground*. He pours Himself out on you to give refreshment. Is your heart dry like cracked ground? Do you need Water? Just as water carries the nutrients of the soil into the plant to produce leaves and fruit, so the Holy Spirit is Water that brings new life to your life. Just as life-giving water upon dry ground brings fruit, the Holy Spirit can make you grow spiritually.

Holy Spirit, I need rejuvenation today. I feel like I'm drying up. The
heat of temptation has sapped my strength. The hot sun of opposition has
threatened my life. Pour life-giving Water on me.

The Holy Spirit is *Floods upon the Dry Ground*. Just as ground with life-giving nutrients is useless without water, so all the good things in your life are useless without the Holy Spirit's presence. Just as ground without water will crack, allowing the wind to blow it away, so your life without the Holy Spirit will deteriorate, and you'll begin to lose precious values and relationships. But water changes everything. It makes the ground soft. Let the Holy Spirit pour Himself into every empty crevice of your life. Let Him soften you. Let Him fill you. Let Him refresh you and make you grow. Ask for the Holy Spirit, and then wait for Rain.

Holy Spirit, I am dry and needy. Pour Your presence
into my life. Fill every crevice with life-giving liquid. Help me grow,
and help me bear fruit. Amen.

Reading: Isaiah 44:1-8
Key Thought: The Holy Spirit brings life to dry ground.

SEPTEMBER

1   JESUS: THE KING OF RIGHTEOUSNESS

To whom also Abraham gave a tenth part of all, first being translated "king of righteousness," and then also king of Salem, meaning "king of peace."
HEBREWS 7:2

Melchizedek had the title "king of righteousness," and Jesus is the prototype of Melchizedek. Jesus is the *King of Righteousness* for three reasons. First, Jesus is the *King of Righteousness* because He is the source of holiness and righteousness; both doing the right things and doing them rightly come from Him. Second, Jesus will rule in a righteous way, which means He will always do things right; yield to Jesus so He can direct your heart to do things right. Third, Jesus will rule over a righteous kingdom. That hasn't happened yet; but after His second coming, Jesus will rule over a righteous kingdom on Earth. You should live every day—including this day—in preparation for His return and the coming of His righteous kingdom.

Lord Jesus, in the past I have put You upon the throne of my heart. But for this new day, I again crown You King of my life. Help me live a righteous life.

If Jesus is your King, He wants you to live a righteous life today, which means you'll think right, decide right and act right. Jesus knows you're not perfect (see 1 John 1:8-10); but if you intend to always do the right thing, He'll forgive your sins (see v. 7), and you'll grow in grace. He'll bless you and use you.

Lord Jesus, I purpose to do the right thing this day. Help me think rightly and understand Your plan for my life. Help me make the right decisions, and give me strength to do the right thing in the right way. Amen.

Reading: Hebrews 7:4-10
Key Thought: To have a righteous life, you must give Jesus control.

2 ⬥ JESUS: A STONE OF STUMBLING

Therefore, to you who believe, He is precious; but to those who are disobedient,
the stone which the builders rejected has become the chief cornerstone, and a stone
of stumbling and a rock of offense.
1 PETER 2:7-8

Jesus is a *Stone of Stumbling* to the unsaved. The unsaved reject Christ because He demands that they live by His principles of Light, but they love darkness. They reject Christ because He demands that they walk the narrow way and enter Heaven by the straight gate (see Matthew 7:13-14), but they love the broad way. They reject Jesus, the only Cornerstone, because they don't want to build their lives on Him. Are you building your life on Jesus?

Lord Jesus, I know You were rejected, but I accept You. I realize that
those in the world don't want to build their lives and families on You,
but You are my Cornerstone.

Jesus is a *Stone of Stumbling*. The unsaved are blinded by their sin, and blind people stumble in the darkness. They treat Christ as if He never lived, but they can't ignore the truth. All creation points to a Creator; the existence of laws points to a Lawgiver; and the offended conscience points to the existence of right and wrong. Jesus is the Stone on which to build a life; but those who ignore Him will stumble over Him into Hell. Will you stumble over Him?

Lord Jesus, You are the Cornerstone of the universe; everything is built
on You. You are the Cornerstone of a good marriage; strong families are
built on You. You are the Cornerstone of personal integrity. I will not
stumble over Your demands; I will build my life on You. Amen.

Reading: 1 Peter 2:7-8
Key Thought: Build your lives on Jesus, the Cornerstone.

THE HOLY SPIRIT: A DEPOSIT

God, who sealed us has also given us the Spirit in our hearts as a
deposit that there are more good things coming.
SEE 2 CORINTHIANS 1:21-22

When you became a Christian, you received the Holy Spirit as the *Deposit* in your life to guarantee that there are more good things coming. When you got saved, you could not understand all God wanted you to know. So the Holy Spirit was placed into your life as a *Deposit*—a down payment—to let you experience some of the spiritual blessings that you will eventually receive. As a *Deposit*, the Holy Spirit wants you to be holy now, because you will be perfect in Heaven. As a *Deposit*, the Holy Spirit wants to give you spiritual understanding now, promising that you will know much more in Heaven. As a *Deposit*, the Holy Spirit wants to enrich your present life by giving you a foretaste of blessings to come in Heaven.

Holy Spirit, I know You have come into my life as a foretaste of the good
things to follow. I like the taste of it, but I want more.

The Holy Spirit is the *Deposit* to let you know some of the wonderful things that await you in Heaven. "Eye has not seen, nor ear heard, nor have entered into the heart of man the things which God has prepared for those who love Him" (1 Corinthians 2:9). But, don't get your eyes so fixed on the future that you forget today. Remember that what He'll do fully for you in the future, He'll begin to do today.

Lord, I want to know You better today because it will help me know You
more fully in the future. Get me started now! Amen.

Reading: 2 Corinthians 1:18-24
Key Thought: The Holy Spirit will give you some experiences now that you'll get in Heaven.

4 JESUS: BRIGHT AND MORNING STAR

I am . . . the Bright and Morning Star.
REVELATION 22:16

Jesus is the *Bright and Morning Star*; He shines in darkness to give all people hope. Just before the dawn, a bright star appears on the horizon where the sun will be rising. That last star of the night and the first star of the day is called the morning star. Jesus is the *Bright and Morning Star* who promises that the dark night of anxiety is almost over. The *Bright and Morning Star* announces the coming of the sun and a new day with new exciting possibilities.

Lord, my heart is cold; I need the warmth of Your light. You are a bright Star to my otherwise dark world; you are the Morning Star of hope. Help me forget my failures and troubles.

Jesus is the *Bright and Morning Star*. He brightens the dark morning sky after a long period of a black, frustrating night. When you are tired of blindness, look to the eastern horizon; He will come. His light will kindle optimism for a new day. Look to His light and forget the cold night. Jesus is the *Bright and Morning Star* who is already there in the sky long before you can see Him. He's been there waiting for you. Now the sun is coming; a new day approaches. Don't fear this day; Jesus is here to help you. Get up and go meet your challenges.

Morning Star, be even brighter for me this day; point me in the right direction. Star of hope, shine some light over here to give me hope. Amen.

Reading: John 7:14-36
Key Thought: Jesus is the *Bright and Morning Star* to give you optimism.

5 ◆ JESUS: SON OF MAN

No one has ascended to heaven but He who came down from heaven, that is, the
Son of Man who is in heaven. And as Moses lifted up the serpent in the
wilderness, even so must the Son of Man be lifted up.
JOHN 3:13-14

Jesus is the *Son of Man*. On Earth, Jesus called Himself by this title more than any other name or title. Why? Because Jesus had never been a human. He was eternal God and had always been Deity; but when He was born of a virgin, He became flesh to live among people and to die for their sins (see John 1:14). He became fully God and fully man, both at the same time, all the time. Jesus formed humankind, the highest expression of all God created, of the dust of the ground (see Genesis 2:7). After Adam and Eve, the first humans, had sinned, it was necessary for Jesus to come to redeem humankind. Just as Jesus created Adam in the image of God (see 1:27), Jesus then had to become flesh after their pattern. Now Jesus indwells those who believe in Him so that they can become like Him.

Thank You, Son of Man, for coming to give me an
example of how to live. Thank You for dying on the cross for me;
I worship You for Your purity and holiness.

Jesus, the *Son of Man*, will come again. His second coming is described in terms of His humanity: "When the Son of Man comes" (Luke 18:8). Jesus was the first human to enter Heaven—when He "led captivity captive" (Ephesians 4:8), making it possible for redeemed humanity to live with God. Jesus will return as the *Son of Man* with "authority to execute judgment . . . because He is the Son of Man" (John 5:27).

Lord, Jesus, I thank You for Your life and death, and
I look forward to Your return for me. Amen.

Reading: John 5:26-32
Key Thought: Jesus can help us because He became the perfect Man.

THE HOLY SPIRIT: THE SPIRIT OF SUPPLICATION

And I will pour on the house of David and on the inhabitants of Jerusalem the Spirit of grace and supplication; then they will look on Me whom they pierced.
ZECHARIAH 12:10

The Holy Spirit is the *Spirit of Supplication*. He receives your prayers and presents them to the Father. Many Christians feel as if they don't know how to pray as they ought or as if they don't properly phrase their prayers. But the Holy Spirit helps them pray, because "the Spirit Himself makes intercession for us with groanings which cannot be uttered" (Romans 8:26). He makes intercession for you too, and the Father hears Him because He prays "according to the will of God" (v. 27). So pour out your heart to the Father; the Holy Spirit will be right beside you as the *Spirit of Supplication*.

Holy Spirit, I know that You make intercession for believers and that You'll give people the Spirit of Supplication. Make my prayers effective. Come teach me to pray, and then pray through me.

In the future, the Holy Spirit will cause Israel to see Jesus as the Messiah they've rejected, so today He can help you see Jesus working in your life. The Holy Spirit can also give you a greater desire for prayer and actually help you pray. He can give you prayer requests and teach you the proper attitude of prayer. He can help you pray in Jesus' name (see John 14:13-14). The *Spirit of Supplication* can make your prayers effective. Claim His help today.

Holy Spirit, I want to learn how to be more effective in prayer. When I pray wrongly, convict me of my failures. When I pray rightly, confirm the way I should pray. Give me a spirit of supplication. Amen.

Reading: Zechariah 12
Key Thought: The Holy Spirit will help you pray.

7 ◆ JESUS: THE AMEN

And to the angel of the church of the Laodiceans write, "These things says the Amen, the Faithful and True Witness, the Beginning of the creation of God."
REVELATION 3:14

Jesus is the *Amen*, the final word on everything that is done by God. The *Amen* told the Laodiceans, "I know your works, that you are neither cold nor hot. So then, because you are lukewarm . . . I will vomit you out of My mouth" (Revelation 3:15-16). Compromise seems so innocent and so easy; all one has to do is do nothing. These Laodiceans were doing nothing good and nothing bad. Jesus told the Laodicean church—the compromising church—that He had the final word on their wayward life. They thought they were rich, but they didn't know that they were "wretched, miserable, poor, blind, and naked" (v. 17).

Lord, it's so easy to compromise. All I have to do is please myself, but I don't want to be a compromising Christian. Forgive my lukewarm heart; I don't want to be rejected by You.

Jesus is the *Amen*, the final word for your Christian life and success. "I counsel you to buy from Me gold refined in the fire" (Revelation 3:18). Jesus wants nothing but the best for you. However, the best is costly. The price is still total commitment to Him. "If anyone desires to come after Me, let him deny himself, and take up his cross daily, and follow Me" (Luke 9:23). Are you willing to give Him all?

Lord, I will do what You want me to do; I will go where You want me to go; I will be what You want me to be. I will pay the price. Amen.

Reading: Revelation 3:14-22
Key Thought: Jesus must have the final word in our life.

JESUS: THE ALMIGHTY

"I am the Alpha and the Omega, the Beginning and the End," says the Lord,
"who is and who was and who is to come, the Almighty."
REVELATION 1:8

Jesus' name *"Almighty"* comes from *El Shaddai,* which means "the One who satisfies all the yearnings of the heart." This name comes from *shad,* or "breast," the place where a crying baby goes for comfort. The breast of Jesus is the place for comfort and nourishment. If you are hurting or your spirit is crushed, the *Almighty* will comfort you. Come honestly to Him and let His sufficiency become your satisfaction. The name *"Almighty"* also stands for the chest, the symbol of strength. Jesus is the *Almighty,* the One who has power to look after Your needs and give You protection. Do you need His power today?

Jesus, I rest securely on Your strong breast, the place of
comfort and protection. It's good to know that You care for me,
and it's good to know that You can protect me. It's good to
be in Your presence; I don't want to leave.

Jesus is the *Almighty,* which means that He is the Strength-Giver, the One who knows your weaknesses. Look away from your weaknesses to Jesus; for when you want to give up, He can give you strength to keep on living and working. What do you need from the *Almighty* today?

Jesus, You are the almighty One; take control of my fitful
heart, and give it peace. Lord Jesus, sit upon the throne
of my heart to give it direction this day. I completely yield my will
to Your almighty sufficiency. Amen.

Reading: Mark 4:35-41
Key Thought: Jesus has strength to comfort and protect you.

9 THE HOLY SPIRIT: THE SPIRIT OF JEHOVAH

*The Spirit of Jehovah came mightily upon him, and the ropes
that were upon his arms became as flax that was burnt with fire,
and his bands dropped from off his hands.*

JUDGES 15:14, AMER. STD.

"Spirit of Jehovah" is an Old Testament phrase that describes the Holy Spirit. Whereas the name "God" tends to describe His absolute power in relationship to creation, the name "Jehovah," or "Lord," tends to describe His sovereign power in relationship to people. Just as the *Spirit of Jehovah* came upon Samson to loose him from the two new ropes that bound him (see Judges 15:13-14), so He can come upon you to give you victory over habits and addictions. Just as the *Spirit of Jehovah* came upon Othniel and Jephthah to give them victory in battle (see 3:9-10; 11:29), so He can give you victory over temptations and trials. Just as the *Spirit of Jehovah* enabled Gideon to call a courageous army together (see 6:34), so He can call all the forces of Heaven to your side. Call upon Him now.

*Holy Spirit, when I read the stories of great men and women, I realize
how little I do for You. Help me do more.*

The Holy Spirit is the *Spirit of Jehovah* who gave strength to the judges. He raised them up for leadership positions and gave them victory in battle. The judges were mere mortals, but the *Spirit of Jehovah* made the difference in their lives. What He has done for them, He can do for you.

*Holy Spirit, I know You are powerful. Flow Your power through me. I
know You have greatly used men and women in the past; use me today.
Flow Your power through me. Amen.*

Reading: Judges 15
Key Thought: The issue is not doing more for the Holy Spirit but letting the Holy Spirit do more through you.

10 ❖ JESUS: THE ADVOCATE

My little children, these things I write to you, so that you may not sin.
And if anyone sins, we have an Advocate with the Father, Jesus Christ the
righteous. And He Himself is the propitiation for our sins, and not for ours
only but also for the whole world.

1 JOHN 2:1-2

Jesus is the *Advocate*, the Defense Lawyer who will defend you against any accusations by Satan, "the accuser of our brethren" (Revelation 12:10). Let Him be your *Advocate*. Every time the Enemy points out a sin in you, Jesus will defend you, because "the blood of Jesus Christ . . . cleanses us from all sin" (1 John 1:7). Let your Lawyer handle your sin.

Jesus, thank You for being my Advocate. Satan discourages me. I admit
that I am not perfect, and I confess my sin (see 1 John 1:8-9). Jesus, defend
me against the Enemy. I claim Your promise that "there is therefore now
no condemnation to those who are in Christ Jesus" (Romans 8:1).

You can't plead ignorance or that you did not sin. If you say that you have not sinned, you make Christ a liar (see 1 John 1:10). Tell your *Advocate* what you've done. He is your Defense Lawyer. Let Him put together your defense and plead it to the Father. The *Advocate* will know how to defend your case. He will plead the blood, which satisfies all legal claims against you. Don't try to go it alone; you can get forgiveness for all your sin (see v. 7).

Lord, sometimes my biggest problem is myself; I can become guilt
ridden, or I get discouraged, or I want to just give up. Come, Advocate,
defend me from my doubts and self-incrimination. Help me
to be victorious in life. Amen.

Reading: 1 John 2:1-6
Key Thought: Jesus can defend you from the attacks of the Enemy.

11 JESUS: SACRIFICE FOR SINS

*But this Man, after He had offered one sacrifice for sins
forever, sat down at the right hand of God.*
HEBREWS 10:12

Jesus is the *Sacrifice for Sins*; you don't have to worry about sins again. When Jesus gave Himself for your sins, God completely forgave you. Why? Because Jesus was the perfect Sacrifice. Because God demanded a life for each transgression, Jesus gave His life for you. He took your punishment and was your substitute. Because God will not let us into Heaven with sin, Jesus wiped the slate clean. Today you stand forgiven before God. Why don't you thank Him for the *Sacrifice for Sins*?

*Thank You, Jesus, for Your life, which has been given for me. Thank You
for forgiveness of sins. Help me please You in all I do today.*

Jesus is your *Sacrifice for Sins*; you please the Father when you approach Him through the blood of Jesus. All your sins of the past have been forgiven. All your present imperfections and failures are forgiven. All your future transgressions are forgiven. Why? Because "the blood of Jesus Christ His Son cleanses us from all sin" (1 John 1:7). "All" means all past sins, all present sins and all future sins. Remember, Jesus "offered one sacrifice for sins forever" (Hebrews 10:12). Come to the Father through Him, because Jesus is your Intercessor at the Father's right hand.

*Jesus, I stand confidently before the Father in Your accomplishments of
Calvary. You are my Priest who stands at the Father's right hand. I pray
boldly to the Father through You. Amen.*

Reading: Hebrews 10:1-13
Key Thought: You come confidently to the Father through Jesus' sacrifice for sins.

THE HOLY SPIRIT: THE SPIRIT OF TRUTH

*And I will pray the Father, and He will give you another Helper, that He may
abide with you forever—the Spirit of truth, whom the world cannot receive,
because it neither sees Him nor knows Him; but you know Him,
for He dwells with you and will be in you.*
JOHN 14:16-17

The Holy Spirit is the *Spirit of Truth.* Jesus sent Him to indwell all believers to witness to them what is truth. There is much error in the world today in advertising, in business and in human relationships. Jesus sent the Holy Spirit into your life to reveal divine truth to you. People who refuse to believe in Jesus do not know the truth. They think they're right about spiritual things; yet because they deny Jesus, they don't know the truth. They may try to lead you astray, telling you they have the truth; but if they deny the Bible, they don't have the truth (see John 17:17). Some will mislead you intentionally about spiritual things, while others do it ignorantly. If they do not agree with Jesus, they don't have the truth. Jesus said, "I am . . . the truth" (14:6). When you are yielded to the *Spirit of Truth,* He will communicate truth to you. Will you let Him control your thoughts?

*Holy Spirit, be my Guide; I seek truth in the Bible
(see John 17:17) and I seek truth in Jesus (see 14:6).*

The *Spirit of Truth* is sent to live in you forever. He was not sent to help you occasionally, nor intermittently. Rely on the *Spirit of Truth* to guide you at any time, and all the time, no matter what issues you face. The *Spirit of Truth* will help you understand the Bible and Jesus.

*Holy Spirit, come guide my thought processes. Guide my reading and
listening so that I can know the truth. I yield to Your instruction. Amen.*

Reading: Mark 9:14-29
Key Thought: The Holy Spirit will lead you into truth.

JESUS: A PROPHET WITHOUT HONOR

So they were offended at Him. But Jesus said to them, "A prophet is not without honor except in his own country and in his own house."
MATTHEW 13:57

When Jesus returned to His hometown, the people did not receive Him; He was the *Prophet Without Honor*. The people of Nazareth knew Him as a boy growing up among them. As a young carpenter, Jesus worked among them. But when Jesus first returned and announced that He was fulfilling Scripture (see Luke 4:21), they rejected Him and "were filled with wrath" (v. 28). They ran Jesus out of town, and some tried to throw Him off a cliff (see v. 29). As a result, Jesus said, "A prophet is honored everywhere except in his own hometown and among his own family" (Matthew 13:57, *NLT*).

Jesus, I accept You, no matter who won't recognize You. I honor You, even though many reject You. You are my Lord and Savior.

How could those closest to the child Jesus end up rejecting Him? Some were spiritually blinded because of unbelief; they couldn't see the Child who didn't sin. Some were spiritually prejudiced; they were looking for a political Messiah to deliver them. Some were sinfully blinded; they looked at everything through their sinful lusts. As a result, "He did not do many mighty works there because of their unbelief" (Matthew 13:58).

Lord Jesus, I know You as my Savior from sin; come into my life. I know You as my Guide and Protector; come lead me today. I know You as my Friend and Helper; come dwell in my heart. I know You as my coming King; come, Lord Jesus, in power and glory. Amen.

Reading: Matthew 13:54-58; Luke 4:16-30
Key Thought: You must honor Jesus even when some will not.

14 JESUS: THE SEED OF THE WOMAN

And I will put enmity between you and the woman, and between your seed and her Seed; He shall bruise your head, and you shall bruise His heel.
GENESIS 3:15

Jesus is the *Seed of the Woman* who judged Satan. After Adam and Eve sinned, God promised them a seed (a child) who would judge the serpent who tempted them to disobedience. Their first child, Cain, was not the one who would crush the serpent's head. After many centuries, Jesus was born to the virgin Mary, the *Seed of the Woman*. Jesus was the promised Head Crusher. If you are tempted to sin, as were Adam and Eve, don't give in to the Evil One. Call on Jesus for help. Because He crushed the head of the serpent at the Cross, Jesus can save you in your hour of temptation.

Lord Jesus, thank You for Your victory on Calvary over Satan. I need Your help today. I trust Your power to help me overcome temptation. Give me victory.

Jesus is the *Seed of the Woman* who, on the cross, crushed Satan's domain (see Colossians 2:14-15). This is a past accomplishment. Look to Him for victory. Now He lives in your heart to give you daily victory over temptation and the power of sin (see 2 Corinthians 2:14). Yield to His power. In the future, Jesus will completely rid the earth of Satan's presence among mankind (see Revelation 20:1-3). Pray for that day to come.

Lord Jesus, thank You for Your past victory over Satan on the cross. Thank You for Your present deliverance over temptation. I look forward to the day when I will never be tempted again. May Your kingdom rule on Earth as You rule in Heaven. Amen.

Reading: Genesis 3
Key Thought: Jesus—the *Seed of the Woman*—has crushed the serpent's head so that we can have victory.

15 THE HOLY SPIRIT: THE WISDOM OF HIS SPIRIT

I pray that the great God and Father of our Lord Jesus Christ may
give you the wisdom of His Spirit. Then you will be able to understand
the secrets about Him as you know Him better.
EPHESIANS 1:17, *NLV*

The *Wisdom of His Spirit* is the Holy Spirit. He gives believers insight into the Word of God. Because some believers don't understand God's will, He helps them see and understand spiritual truths (see 2 Corinthians 4:3-4). Because unsaved people will not believe the Word of God, He convicts them of their sin (see John 16:9). Because some reject the Scriptures, He uses their conscience to enlighten them (see Romans 2:14-15). It is the task of the Holy Spirit to give all people the Wisdom of God.

Holy Spirit, I realize that I know very little about spiritual things. Show
me what I need to know and help me remember to use what You show me.

The theme of the book of Proverbs is "Get knowledge so that you can gain wisdom." Therefore, you learn the Word of God by acquiring facts or knowledge about God. The more facts you know about Scripture, the wiser you can become. Knowledge is learning Bible information; wisdom is understanding the meaning of the Bible and applying it to your life. That's where the Holy Spirit comes in. The *Wisdom of His Spirit* helps you understand the Bible and apply it to your life. The Holy Spirit gives you His wisdom as you study the Bible. When you yield to the Holy Spirit, He helps you understand the will of God.

Holy Spirit, I will study the Scriptures to master them. I want to know
everything You want me to know so that I can have wisdom. Enter my
mind, Wisdom of the Spirit, so I can grow spiritually. Amen.

Reading: 1 Corinthians 2:6-8
Key Thought: The Holy Spirit gives you wisdom as you learn the Scriptures.

16 ⬥ JESUS: THE SON OF THE BLESSED

But He kept silent and answered nothing. Again the high priest asked Him,
saying to Him, "Are You the Christ, the Son of the Blessed?"
MARK 14:61

During the trial of Jesus, the high priest asked Him, "Are You . . . the Son of the Blessed?" (Mark 14:61). The rabbis used the title "the Blessed" as a substitute for *Jehovah*; they didn't want to blaspheme the Lord's name by carnal speech. The sarcastic high priest didn't realize that Jesus was actually the *Son of the Blessed*; therefore, he didn't receive blessings from Jesus. The high priest didn't realize that Jesus was the Christ—the Messiah; therefore, he didn't believe in Him or worship Jesus.

Jesus, I recognize who You are. I accept You as Christ, who died for my
sins. I realize that You are the Son of God, so I worship You.

The high priest knew all about the doctrine of the Messiah in his head, but he rejected the Person of the Messiah when He stood before him. The Jewish leaders knew in their heads all the names of God; but when their Messiah stood before them, they were blinded by their unbelief. Doubt begins in the heart when we feed our appetites on sin. Corrupted belief comes from corrupted living. Keep yourself from outward evil so you that won't deny the Lord as the high priest did.

Jesus, I recognize that You are the Son of the Blessed.
Be honored in my life. Amen.

Reading: Mark 14:53-65
Key Thought: Jesus is the Son of God, who blessed us.

17 JESUS: THE BEGINNING AND THE END

"I am the Alpha and the Omega, the Beginning and the End," says the Lord,
"who is and who was and who is to come, the Almighty."
REVELATION 1:8

Jesus is the *Beginning and the End*; He was the Creator of all things, because nothing existed before Him—not the earth, not the throne, not even Heaven itself. "For by Him all things were created" (Colossians 1:16). He is the Beginning of time, of space, of matter, of human beings. Jesus initiated everything. Since Jesus began it all, He's in control.

Lord, I know You're the Creator, but the world is filled with chaos. I want to see Your plan unfolding in my life. Help me see Your purpose in the small details of my life.

Jesus is the *Beginning and the End*. What Jesus began, He will also finish. He will finish His plan and purpose on this earth. Nothing will keep Him from completing His perfect will—no dictator, terrorist, nuclear explosion or war. So don't worry about what will happen in your life today. Just because you can't see Jesus' overall plan for your life, it doesn't mean that there is no plan. Just because you don't understand events around you, it doesn't mean that Jesus doesn't know about them. Because Jesus is the *Beginning and the End*, He has absolute sovereignty over the broad sweep of history as well as the small details of your life. Jesus began history, and He will end history; so He can control everything in between.

Lord, open my eyes to see Your big picture. I am so small; help me see how I fit into Your big plan. Lord, I want to complete Your purpose for my life. Amen.

Reading: Acts 7:1-50
Key Thought: Jesus has a plan for your life.

18 THE HOLY SPIRIT: THE SPIRIT OF MIGHT

*The Spirit of the LORD shall rest upon Him, the Spirit of wisdom and
understanding, the Spirit of counsel and might, the Spirit
of knowledge and of the fear of the LORD.*
ISAIAH 11:2

The Holy Spirit is the *Spirit of Might*; He exercised great power in creation,
in the Resurrection, in judgment and in the supernatural miracles of the
Bible. He can forgive your sins, fix your life, guide you this day and keep
you from the Evil One. He can accomplish God's perfect plan in your
life. Will you let the *Spirit of Might* do it?

*O Spirit of Might, teach me Your power. Give me the necessary ability to
carry out the decisions that You lead me to make. I need greater faith in You.*

The secret of the Christian life is not to have great faith in God. Did
not Jesus recognize the smallness of belief when He said, "O you of little
faith" (Matthew 14:31)? The secret is to have faith in a great God. The
Holy Spirit is the *Spirit of Might*; when you realize His great strength and
the great things He can do for you, your faith will be strengthened to
believe in far greater things. Don't just pray for greater faith, pray for
understanding of God; then you can have greater faith. The One who can
give you that greater estimation of God is the *Spirit of Might* who already
dwells in your heart. Ask Him now for the faith you need for this day.

*O Spirit of Might, I pray with the disciples, "Increase our faith" (Luke
17:5). I recognize that You can do all You promise in the Scriptures;
now I claim that work in my heart today. Amen.*

Reading: Ephesians 4:1-16
Key Thought: You don't need greater faith; you need a greater understanding of God.

19 ⬥ JESUS: OUR HOPE

By the commandment of God our Savior and the Lord Jesus Christ, our hope.
1 TIMOTHY 1:1

Jesus is your *Hope* when things go wrong; He can change circumstances when you pray. Jesus is your *Hope* when you're in a hole and it seems you can't get out. He can transform you in the hole, or He can get you out. When your hole has you boxed in with no escape, Jesus can make a way of escape (see 1 Corinthians 10:13). Sometimes God lets you stay in your hole to learn lessons. And your hole becomes a classroom to teach you the perfect will of God. But even when you're laboring in difficulty, Jesus is your *Hope*, because He can change your attitude and outlook on life. He can teach you what you need to learn. Jesus can give you purpose and make the hole worthwhile.

> *Jesus, You are my Hope; I put all my trust in You to work all things together for good (see Romans 8:28). Teach me what I must learn from my circumstances. When I don't understand what's happening around me, give me hope for the future.*

Jesus is the *Hope* of future life for all believers, because all must die. But after our death, He will return to resurrect the bodies of all who believed in Him on Earth. You can have hope beyond the grave, for Jesus promises that you will live after death. You will live with Him forever in Heaven (see John 14:1-3).

> *Jesus, how can I be hopeless when I abide in You and You abide in me (see John 15:5)? You give me hope in this life, and You give me confidence beyond the grave. You are the only hope I have. Amen.*

Reading: 1 Timothy 1:15-20
Key Thought: You have hope when you have Jesus.

20 ◆ JESUS: PRAYING IN MY NAME

If you ask anything in My [Jesus'] name, I will do it.
JOHN 14:14

"Jesus" is the name through whom you get your prayers answered. God created humans to have daily needs; that way, they will depend on God and cry out daily to Him. "Your Father knows the things you have need of before you ask Him" (Matthew 6:8). Through your prayer, God will provide your needs; but you must ask in Jesus' name. "Whatever you ask in My name, that I will do" (John 14:13).

In Jesus' name I ask for strength to make it through this day.
In Jesus' name I ask for wisdom to make good decisions. In Jesus'
name I ask for guidance through my problems.

Why must you pray in Jesus' name? First, Jesus told you to ask in His name. Next, you come to the Father through Jesus' cleansing blood. Finally, Jesus is your Intercessor at the right hand of the Father; in Him you have "a new and living way . . . through the veil" (Hebrews 10:20). Therefore, ask in Jesus' name, because "There is one . . . Mediator between God and men, the Man Christ Jesus" (1 Timothy 2:5). Ask in Jesus' name, because no one is closer to the Father than Jesus Christ, and you are as close to the heart of God as His Son when you come in Jesus' name.

In the name of Jesus I ask for forgiveness of sins so that I can
intercede to the Father. Through the intercession of the Son,
I ask that You would hear me. Amen.

Reading: John 14:13-15
Key Thought: You must pray in Jesus' name to get answers to your prayers.

THE HOLY SPIRIT: THE SPIRIT OF THE FEAR OF THE LORD

The Spirit of the LORD shall rest upon Him, the Spirit of wisdom and understanding, the Spirit of counsel and might, the Spirit of knowledge and of the fear of the LORD.

ISAIAH 11:2

The Holy Spirit is the *Spirit of the Fear of the Lord*. He works in the hearts of people to revere the Father. When people take the Father's name in vain or sin against the Son, He convicts them of their transgressions and shows them where they fall short. He is the Holy Spirit, who convicts people of sin. He gives people a spirit of reverence to approach the Father.

> *O Spirit of reverence, I am blinded by my own good works. Many times I don't realize when I sin. Remind me any time I step out of line. Give me a sensitive spirit of obedience to the Father.*

The *Spirit of the Fear of the Lord* will shine light on your sinful habits to make you aware of them and to help you abstain from them. He will then change your attitudes that are offensive to the Father. He can give you a reverential heart. A spirit of reverence will keep you from evil and give you a thirst for godliness. The Holy Spirit is the *Spirit of the Fear of the Lord* who will show you when and how to pray.

> *Lord, I know that You punish sin in the lives of Your children and that You judge the transgressions of the unsaved. Teach me godly fear when I sin. Fill me with Your presence so that I won't sin again. I receive Your love; I stand in awe of Your power; and I receive Your Spirit of reverence. Amen.*

Reading: Exodus 33:1—34:9
Key Thought: The Holy Spirit teaches us to reverence the Father.

22 ◆ THE HOLY SPIRIT: THE SPIRIT WHOM HE HAS GIVEN US

Now he who keeps His commandments abides in Him, and He in him. And by this we know that He abides in us, by the Spirit whom He has given us.
1 JOHN 3:24

The Holy Spirit is the *Spirit Whom He Has Given Us*. He is the One that Jesus promised to give you (see John 14:17). There are no good works you can do to receive the Holy Spirit; He is a gift. Just as a gift is given without obligation, so the Holy Spirit is given freely to you. All you did was "believe on the name of His Son Jesus Christ" (1 John 3:23), and the Holy Spirit came into your heart to give you assurance of salvation. Because you have the Holy Spirit living in your life, you can know (have the assurance) that you are a child of God.

Holy Spirit, gratefully I receive You, as I would receive any gift. Thank You for entering my life. Thank You for assurance of salvation.

The Holy Spirit is a gift to all believers. When He was sent on the Day of Pentecost, He appeared as the sound of a mighty rushing wind and as cloven tongues of fire (see Acts 2:1-4). He was manifested with mighty symbols to tell all believers that He will do a mighty work when He enters their hearts. Just as the Holy Spirit came upon all believers in the Upper Room, so He enters all who are saved. As a matter of fact, Paul says, "If anyone does not have the Spirit of Christ, he is not His" (Romans 8:9).

Holy Spirit, thank You for indwelling my heart. Thank You for the spirit of confidence, which is greater than the spirit of anxiety. Thank You for giving me the assurance of eternal life. Amen.

Reading: 1 John 3:16—4:11
Key Thought: Everyone who is a Christian has the Holy Spirit.

23 JESUS: HE WHO IS HOLY AND TRUE

These things says He who is holy, He who is true.
REVELATION 3:7

Jesus is called "He who is holy" (Revelation 3:7). Great revivals in past centuries began when believers saw God's holiness. It was then that believers saw their sinfulness and cried out in repentance, seeking God's forgiveness. Revival is when God visits His people. It happens because God said, "I will pour out of My Spirit on all flesh" (Acts 2:17). Revival starts with God's holiness and grows when people experience His presence in their lives. Do you want revival?

Lord, I yearn for Your presence in my life. I want to feel Your atmospheric presence in the Church. Do for me what you did in the Early Church.

Jesus is also called "He who is true" (Revelation 3:7). True revival begins when you look at your life through God's truthfulness. No one is holy in comparison with God; everything pales in comparison to His truth. Jesus is *He Who Is Holy and True.* Jesus said to the Church, "See, I have set before you an open door, and no one can shut it" (v. 8). The door of opportunity is always open to God's people. We must look through the door to see the Lord's holiness, which is the first step of revival. Then we must act on the truthfulness of His promise. That's when His presence is poured out on us.

Lord, I want true godliness in my life; keep me from false spirituality. I want to serve You effectively; don't let my ignorant sin hold back Your blessings. Lord, send revival to Your Church, starting with me. Amen.

Reading: 1 Samuel 7
Key Thought: Jesus wants us to be holy and truthful.

THE HOLY SPIRIT: THE SPIRIT WHO DWELLS IN YOU

24

*But if the Spirit of Him who raised Jesus from the dead dwells in you,
He who raised Christ from the dead will also give life to your mortal bodies
through His Spirit who dwells in you.*

ROMANS 8:11

The *Spirit Who Dwells in You* is the Holy Spirit, the third Person of the Godhead. Long before the Holy Spirit indwelt you, He indwelt Jesus Christ. At the beginning of His ministry, Jesus was "filled with the Holy Spirit" (Luke 4:1). After the Holy Spirit led Him to the wilderness to be tempted by the Devil, Jesus "returned in the power of the Spirit to Galilee" (v. 14). Jesus said, "The Spirit of the LORD is upon Me" (v. 18). When Jesus faced death, the indwelling Spirit helped sustain His sufferings. When Jesus died, the Holy Spirit was with Him in the tomb. When Jesus was raised on the third day, the Holy Spirit brought Him back from the dead. Just as He was with Jesus, the *Spirit Who Dwells in You* will be with you in your hour of suffering and death.

*Holy Spirit, I can face problems when You are with me. I can even face
death because I have both You and Christ dwelling in my life.*

Christianity is much more than creeds, rituals and religious practices. Christianity is having the Holy Spirit dwell within you (see John 14:17). The Holy Spirit has many ministries in your life, but one of the most important is to raise you up in the day of Resurrection, just as He raised up Jesus. You can live triumphantly and die confidently because the Holy Spirit dwells in you.

*Holy Spirit, You give me great confidence to live on this earth because
I know what will happen at death. I submit to Your will, and ask that
You guide me through this life. Amen.*

Reading: Romans 8:1-11
Key Thought: The Holy Spirit can give you resurrected life, just as He gave to Jesus.

25 ◆ JESUS: I AM HE WHO LIVES

I am He who lives, and was dead, and behold, I am alive forevermore. Amen.
REVELATION 1:18

Jesus said, "I am He who lives" (Revelation 1:18), for in His death and resurrection He overcame sin and death. Even though you are a sinner (see Romans 3:23) and you will die, you can overcome sin and death when you live in Jesus. After Jesus went to the grave, He testified, "I am He who . . . was dead" (Revelation 1:18). Jesus died for your sin that you might not die. Now Jesus testifies, "I am alive forevermore" (v. 18). When you live in Christ, you too will live forevermore. Jesus breathes eternal life into the souls of those who trust Him for salvation. They will live as long as He lives. That will be forever, because He says, "I am alive forevermore."

Lord, I know You are alive forevermore, but I have a difficult time thinking about eternal life. I am a captive in this physical body, and all I can think about is the here and now. Help me understand my life. Help me find satisfaction and meaning in this world.

Not only does Jesus give duration of life—eternal life—but He also gives abundant life (see John 10:10). He can give you joy, fulfillment and fruitfulness. He can use you in His service, and your life can make a difference in the world. You can be happy and satisfied when you let Jesus, the great *I Am He Who Lives,* live His life through you. But you must ask for it and claim it.

Lord, I will yield my life to You. Fill me today with Your presence. Give me life—abundant life—to live for You. Amen.

Reading: Psalm 1
Key Thought: Jesus wants to put His abundant life in you.

26 ◆ JESUS: INTERCESSOR

*But He, because He continues forever, has an unchangeable priesthood. Therefore
He is also able to save to the uttermost those who come to God through Him, since
He always lives to make intercession for them.*
HEBREWS 7:24-25

Jesus is your *Intercessor*. When He was raised from the dead, He ascended
into Heaven to sit at the right hand of God the Father. As your
Intercessor, Jesus can present your prayers to the Father, as a lawyer pre-
sents a case to the judge. Just as a lawyer speaks on behalf of another, so
Jesus will present your case to the heavenly Father. You come to the
Father through Jesus.

*I need an intercessor because I feel so unworthy to pray. Jesus, be my
Intercessor; ask the Father to forgive my sin and cleanse me by Your blood.*

Maybe you've not received answers to your prayers because you've
asked for the wrong thing or you've asked with the wrong attitude or
you've asked at the wrong time. Come to the Father through Jesus; He
will be your *Intercessor* to communicate your prayers to the Father. He
will pray the right request at the right time with the right attitude. Jesus
can be your *Intercessor*, because He became flesh and lived among us as a
man (see John 1:14). As your high priest, He understands your weaknesses, for He faced the same temptations that you face yet did not sin.
Now you can come boldly to the throne of the heavenly Father through
Jesus (see Hebrews 4:15-16).

*Thank You for understanding me and forgiving me. Thank
You for correctly presenting my prayers to the Father. I feel confident
when You plead my case for me. Amen.*

Reading: Hebrews 7:14-28
Key Thought: As your *Intercessor*, Jesus can plead your case to the Father.

THE HOLY SPIRIT: THE SPIRIT OF KNOWLEDGE

*The Spirit of the LORD shall rest upon Him, the Spirit of wisdom
and understanding, the Spirit of counsel and might, the Spirit
of knowledge and of the fear of the LORD.*
ISAIAH 11:2

The Holy Spirit is the *Spirit of Knowledge*; it is His presence in the words of Scripture that helps you see what is true. It is His presence that inspires the accuracy of human authors as they wrote the Scriptures so that you can trust what you read in the Bible. It is His presence that fills each word in the Bible so that your heart will burn within you as you read the words of Scripture (see Luke 24:32).

*O Spirit of Knowledge, I have head knowledge of the Scriptures, but I
want my heart warmed with the Bible. I want the Word of God to
capture me and compel me to live for You today.*

The Holy Spirit is the *Spirit of Knowledge*; He can do much for you that you do not yet realize. "Eye has not seen, nor ear heard, nor have entered into the heart of man the things which God has prepared for those who love Him" (1 Corinthians 2:9). To fully understand, you must let the Holy Spirit teach you, because "God [the Father] has revealed them to us through His Spirit" (v. 10). Ask for the Spirit's indwelling presence to enter your understanding; then yield to His guidance.

*O Spirit of Knowledge, I will study the Word of God to learn more of
You. I will apply the principles of Scripture to my life so that I can
obey You. I will obey the commands of Scripture to follow You. I will
meditate on the words of Scripture to grow in Christ. Amen.*

Reading: 1 Corinthians 2
Key Thought: The Holy Spirit can give you correct knowledge.

28   JESUS: HIM WHO IS AND WHO WAS AND WHO IS TO COME

Grace to you and peace from Him who is and who was and who is to come.
REVELATION 1:4

Jesus is the One called *Him Who Is*. He is alive, and because He lives, you can enjoy His life. Are you afraid of something that might happen today? Don't look at your problems; look to Jesus. Jesus lives in the present tense; He is called *Him Who Is*. He can take care of you today because, while He knows the past and the future, He also knows today. Jesus also lives in the past tense; He is called *Him Who Was*. The past is the same to Jesus as the present. He knows what you did in the past; but remember, "the blood of Jesus Christ His Son cleanses us from all sin" (1 John 1:7). If He can cleanse the past, why can't you forget it?

Lord, I face my guilt from my past. I did some things I'd like to forget.
Come forgive me, cleanse me and help me forget.

Jesus is also called *He Who Is to Come*. He lives in the future. Jesus knows what will happen tomorrow and every day thereafter because He is eternal. You don't need to know the future; all you need to know is Him. Jesus is *He Who Is to Come*. He will be with you when you walk through the dark valley of the shadow of death. But perhaps you'll be part of that generation that will not die. Perhaps you'll meet Jesus in the Rapture. There you'll meet *He Who Is to Come*.

Lord, help me look beyond my small world. Lord, help me see You who
are, who was and who is to come. Amen.

Reading: Psalm 90
Key Thought: Jesus knows your past, your present and your future.

29 JESUS: A LIFE-GIVING SPIRIT

The first man Adam became a living being. The last Adam became a life-giving spirit.
1 CORINTHIANS 15:45

Jesus is a *Life-Giving Spirit* because He was victorious over death and the grave; He now has power to give life to everyone who believes in Him. Jesus submitted to the death of a cross and allowed them to bury Him in a tomb. On the third day, He overcame the power of the grave and arose victoriously. Because Jesus lives, now He can give life to His followers. You have received this life from Jesus; will you let it flow through you today?

> *Jesus, I believe in You. When You died, my sin died with You. When You were buried, I was identified with You in the grave. When You arose from the dead, I was in You, so now I have access to resurrection power. Give me power to serve You.*

Because Jesus is a *Life-Giving Spirit*, you now have life—eternal life. You'll never die. And your new life is victorious life; you can overcome temptation and sin. You can have an enlightened life; you can know the will of God and understand spiritual things. You can have a ministering life; Jesus can use your spiritual gifts to minister to others. Will you let Jesus live through you? Will you let His life flow through you?

> *Jesus, I want to live this day in the power of Your life. I want a victorious life over temptation, an enlightened life to experience Your leadership in my life and a ministering life to serve You. Amen.*

Reading: 1 Corinthians 15:45-58
Key Thought: Jesus gives life because of His death.

30 ⬧ The Holy Spirit: The Spirit of Counsel

*The Spirit of the LORD shall rest upon Him, the Spirit of wisdom
and understanding, the Spirit of counsel and might, the Spirit
of knowledge and of the fear of the LORD.*
ISAIAH 11:2

The Holy Spirit is the *Spirit of Counsel*; He can guide you in decision making and can show you where you must go. He can help you solve problems so that you will choose right paths for today.

*O Spirit of Counsel, I don't trust my ability to discern what I see.
Come help me make good choices today.*

The Holy Spirit is the *Spirit of Counsel*; He will help you understand the principles of Scripture, upon which you make decisions; but you must carefully study the Word to know what He wants you to do. He is the *Spirit of Counsel* to give you wisdom through the insights of other believers, but you must weigh carefully their motives and grasp of the situation before making decisions. He is the *Spirit of Counsel* who speaks to you through your common sense to make correct choices, but you must be yielded to His control. He can even guide you as you examine the lessons you've learned from past experiences; but in the final analysis, you must do what the Holy Spirit wants you to do.

*O Spirit of Counsel, I will carefully study the Scriptures to
know Your principles; help me see Your specific plan for my life. I will
listen to the counsel of mature believers; help me determine the best
action for my life. I will use the common sense You've given me; help me
remember what You've taught me in the past. I will apply my mind
to acquire as many facts as possible about my decisions so that
You can guide me to choose what is best. Amen.*

Reading: Proverbs 1
Key Thought: The Holy Spirit will help you make right decisions.

OCTOBER

1 ◆ JESUS: THE BRIDEGROOM

He who has the bride is the bridegroom; but the friend of the bridegroom, who stands and hears him, rejoices greatly because of the bridegroom's voice.
JOHN 3:29

Jesus is the *Bridegroom*. When you received Jesus Christ as Savior, you became His Bride. Just as a wife looks to a husband for protection, so you should trust Jesus, because He will guard you from the Evil One. He is the *Bridegroom* to keep you from sin. Just as a husband provides for the needs of his wife, so Jesus will provide for your needs. Look to Him when you lack anything. He will supply. If you have any needs, why don't you ask Him now?

Lord, I accept Your protection; keep me safe. I rest securely in Your presence; keep my mind focused on all You do for me. I need to love You more, and I need to feel Your love. You are my Bridegroom, so I know that You will provide for me.

Jesus is the *Bridegroom*, and He'll always be there for you. You don't have to worry that God has forgotten you or that He doesn't love you. Jesus loves you and cherishes you with the kind of love that husbands are commanded to love their wives. You belong to Him and He belongs to you. Nothing can take you away from the oneness you have with Jesus. Why don't you tell Him about your love now?

Lord, I love You for all You've done for me. But most of all, I love You for Yourself. You are the perfection of beauty and grace. You are my Bridegroom and I am Your Bride. Amen.

Reading: Song of Solomon 2:4–3:5
Key Thought: Jesus will take care of you because He loves you.

2 JESUS: THE DESIRE OF ALL NATIONS

"I will shake all nations, and they shall come to the Desire of All Nations, and I will fill this temple with glory," says the LORD of hosts.
HAGGAI 2:7

Jesus is the *Desire of All Nations*. At the present time, the nations do not look for Jesus; nor is He in their thinking. They do not desire Him. But there is coming a time in the future when the nations will desire Him. The prophet Haggai told the Jews who returned from captivity in Babylon to rebuild the Temple. The Jewish people felt defeated because their present circumstances were not as glorious or as spiritual as they were in the past. Haggai promised them that the *Desire of All Nations* would come into the Temple that they would build. That prophecy was first fulfilled when Jesus went into the Temple as a 12-year-old boy. But the Jewish people didn't know that Jesus was their Messiah; they had no desire to accept Him. The Jewish leaders desired political peace, but they refused the inner peace He offered. They desired a Jewish kingdom, but they refused His rule. Jesus was what they desired, but they were blind to His presence. Jesus will come at the end of time. His presence will come into the millennial Temple to fulfill what Haggai said: "I will fill this temple with glory" (Haggai 2:7). One day Jesus, the *Desire of All Nations*, will come. Then every nation will desire to come worship Him. The glory that Jesus will give to the future Temple, He can bring to your heart today.

Come, Desire of All Nations. Come into my heart, and fill me with the glorious experience of what You can do today. Come, Desire of All Nations. Come in your glorious appearing. Amen.

Reading: Haggai 1–2
Key Thought: One day every nation will desire to worship Jesus.

THE HOLY SPIRIT: THE SPIRIT OF ADOPTION

For you did not receive the spirit of bondage again to fear, but you received the Spirit of adoption by whom we cry out, "Abba, Father."
ROMANS 8:15

The Holy Spirit is the *Spirit of Adoption* who placed you in the family of God. The *Spirit of Adoption* facilitated your legal adoption by God the Father. Now that you have all the "rights" of God's children, you can call Him Abba, Father. Just as children are legal heirs of all their father's possessions, so you can inherit all the riches and benefits of your Father in Heaven. Because none of us is worthy to be God's children, our adoption is a gift of grace. It was through the death of Christ that our sins were forgiven, giving us a basis to become God's children.

Holy Spirit, thank You for making me a legal child of God; thank You for my adoption. Now help me please my Father and serve Him.

The *Spirit of Adoption* makes all the Father's wealth available to you. The Holy Spirit gives you a new nature (see Ephesians 4:22-24) and intercedes to the Father for you (see Romans 8:26-27). The Holy Spirit can show you all the glories of Heaven (see Ephesians 2:7) and give you Christian character (see Galatians 5:22-23). All that the Father wants to do for you, the Holy Spirit will deliver to you. But you must desire these benefits and claim them.

Holy Spirit, I was an alien from God, without hope and without promise (see Ephesians 2:12), but You drew me to salvation. You made it possible for me to be adopted into Your family. Thank You for this new relationship to the Father. Now help me live as a child of God should live. Amen.

Reading: 2 Samuel 9
Key Thought: The Holy Spirit adopted you into God's family.

4 ◆ JESUS: PROPHET

The LORD your God will raise up for you a Prophet like me from your midst,
from your brethren. Him you shall hear.
DEUTERONOMY 18:15

Jesus is called a *Prophet*; this was a title given to Him by Moses, who predicted Jesus' coming into the world. Not only did Moses give the Jewish people God's Law, but he also predicted that Jesus would be a *Prophet* to give them God's message. Jesus came with a message of hope and forgiveness for all. But He also has a message for you today. Will you listen to His message?

> *Lord, I need to hear from You today. I need some hope in my life,*
> *because the world seems hopeless. I need continual forgiveness of sins.*

Jesus is the *Prophet* who predicted the future. He can foretell God's message because He is eternal. Jesus knows what will happen to you in the future because He is God. He wants to guide your life because He knows what is best for you. Will you follow Him? Jesus is the *Prophet* who also forth-tells the message of God. Just as prophets aggressively told forth God's message in the Old Testament, Jesus boldly gave God's message while on Earth. The message of Jesus the *Prophet* has already been written in the pages of Scripture. If you want His message, you must study carefully the Scriptures, pray diligently and apply the Word of God to your life.

> *O Lord, my Prophet, tell me from the Scriptures what You*
> *want me to know. I look to You to lead me today. I accept*
> *Your message, and I will do it. Amen.*

Reading: Deuteronomy 18:15-23
Key Thought: Jesus has a message for you.

5 JESUS: GOD'S SON FROM HEAVEN

And to wait for His Son from heaven, whom He raised from the dead, even
Jesus who delivers us from the wrath to come.
1 THESSALONIANS 1:10

Jesus is *God's Son from Heaven*. Therefore, you should live a godly life, anticipating His return. Look at the example of the Thessalonicans; they turned from idols to serve the living and true God and to anticipate the return of God's Son, who will come from Heaven. Because Jesus is *God's Son from Heaven*, don't just spend your time waiting for His return, as if there were nothing to do. Serve Him with all of your might now. And yet, look to Heaven as if He'll come at any minute. If you think He may come at any moment, you will work longer and harder and smarter. You will adjust all of your life in light of His return.

Lord Jesus, I know in my heart that You can return in the next
minute; but since You haven't come yet, it's hard to keep on expecting Your
second return at any minute. How can I keep my anticipation sharp?

The key to keeping your anticipation of Christ's return sharp is relationship; if you love Jesus and are dedicated to serving Him, then you will keep your relationship to Him warm. You will want to develop a deeper fellowship with Christ each day. When *God's Son from Heaven* comes, you'll finally meet Him face-to-face, and that will consummate all the fellowship you've had on this earth.

Lord, I will look for Your return today, and I will live as though You'll
come in the next minute. But I'll also fellowship with You and plan my
work as if You're not coming in my lifetime. Amen.

Reading: 1 Thessalonians 1
Key Thought: Live as though Jesus will come at any minute.

6 THE HOLY SPIRIT: THE SAME SPIRIT OF FAITH

And since we have the same spirit of faith, according to what is written,
"I believed and therefore I spoke," we also believe and therefore speak.
2 CORINTHIANS 4:13

The Holy Spirit gave you the gift of faith when you believed in Christ for salvation (see Ephesians 2:8-9). The Holy Spirit is the *Same Spirit of Faith* who now builds up your daily faith to live the Christian life. The Scriptures instruct, "The just shall live by faith" (Romans 1:17). So He will give you strength and character to live by faith. If you want more faith, ask Him now, because He is the *Same Spirit of Faith*.

Holy Spirit, I want to walk daily by faith. Help me not to
rely on the flesh but to depend on Your power. Pick me up when I fall;
prod me when I slow down; and when I stray, pull me back
onto the straight and narrow path.

The Holy Spirit is the *Same Spirit of Faith* as He has always been. As He helped Abraham live by faith, so He can help you live above your temptations. As He helped Moses lead the multitude by faith, so He can help you follow the Lord today. As He helped David rule his kingdom by faith, so He can help you manage your life and tasks today. As He helped Paul evangelize, so He can help you share your testimony today. What is your greatest need? He is the *Same Spirit of Faith* who has worked in the past; He can give you faith to live today.

Holy Spirit, I am only average. Help me live above average
today. Help me do things above average today. Help me live
by faith and not by sight. Amen.

Reading: 2 Corinthians 4:7—5:7
Key Thought: The Holy Spirit will help you live by faith.

JESUS: HE WHO HOLDS THE SEVEN STARS IN HIS RIGHT HAND

These things says He who holds the seven stars in His right hand, who walks in the midst of the seven golden lampstands.

REVELATION 2:1

Jesus is *He Who Holds the Seven Stars in His Right Hand.* These stars were the seven messengers or pastors of the seven churches in Asia Minor (see Revelation 2—3). Just as Jesus protected and cared for these seven church leaders, so He will take care of you. You may think you're alone in the world; but you're not. You may think that Jesus has forgotten you in your troubles; but you're really in His hands. Trust Him.

Lord, I will do more. I will be victorious over sin and do exploits. Because I know that You're hanging on to me, I have more confidence to do more for You.

These seven churches and their leaders were weak and struggling. Some had even lost their first love for Christ. Some churches had sin in their midst, and some churches were enticed by false doctrine. Yet Jesus still held all of them in His hand, and He walked in the middle of them. Since He hung on to those struggling early churches, He can keep you safely in your struggles also. Remember that if you fall, you are not destroyed; nor are you permanently lost. Jesus has you in His hands. *He Who Holds the Seven Stars in His Right Hand* will hold you safely in His hand and will give you power to overcome (see Revelation 2:7).

Lord, give me a listening ear to hear Your instructions (see Revelation 2:7), and give me a ready will to obey Your voice. I will turn my back on sin (see v. 6) and will serve You (see v. 3). Amen.

Reading: Revelation 2:1-7
Key Thought: Hang on to Jesus, because He's holding on to you.

8 ❖ JESUS: HE WHO WAS DEAD AND IS ALIVE

These things says the First and the Last, who was dead, and came to life.
REVELATION 2:8

Jesus is *He Who Was Dead and Is Alive*; He will be with you in persecution because He understands suffering. He took the bitter drink of death for you. If you suffer, remember that He is suffering with you. Now you don't have to be afraid of death, because He was dead but now is alive. If God's enemies kill you, He will raise you up, just as He came back from the dead.

Lord, why do godly people have to suffer? I want everyone to like me. Why do I have tribulation and difficulties?

Because God's enemies persecuted Jesus, they will also attack you. Since they killed Him, they may even attempt to kill you. The world loves darkness rather than light, because its deeds are evil (see John 3:19). But "He who overcomes shall not be hurt by the second death" (Revelation 2:11). Jesus will be with you in persecution and trials, because He was persecuted and killed. He was dead and came back to life. Jesus says, "I know your works, tribulation, and poverty" (v. 9). Do not fear any of those things that you are about to suffer. He promises, "Be faithful until death, and I will give you the crown of life" (v. 10). Because *He Who Was Dead and Is Alive* has overcome death, He will crown you with eternal life.

Lord, be first in my life, and help me live for You until the end of my life. Because You have overcome death and are alive, I want You to live through me today. Amen.

Reading: Revelation 2:8-11
Key Thought: Because Jesus suffered, He knows your sufferings.

THE HOLY SPIRIT: THE POWER OF THE HIGHEST

*The Holy Spirit will come upon you, and the power of the
Highest will overshadow you.*
LUKE 1:35

The Holy Spirit is the *Power of the Highest*, the One responsible for the virgin birth of Jesus. The Holy Spirit is the active agent for the Father and the Son to accomplish the work of the Godhead in your world. Since the Holy Spirit generated the birth of Christ, He can do a mighty work in your life. He can give you new purpose, new desires, new attitudes and a new perspective. What do you want the Holy Spirit to do for you?

*Holy Spirit, I am weak and limited. There is so much I can't do. You are
the Power of the Highest; work in my life today.*

The Father is the Highest, and the Holy Spirit is His Power in the world. He can transform selfish people so that they put Christ at the center of their lives. He can open the eyes of spiritually blinded people so that they can understand the Scriptures. He can transform mean people into good people. He can break sin addiction in the lives of those trapped in a bad habit. He can solve problems in your life, unlock shut doors and work circumstances for the best. He can help you worship and glorify the Father. What would you like for the Holy Spirit, the *Power of the Highest*, to do for you today?

*Holy Spirit, help me do the things required of me this day. Help
me do everything appropriately, efficiently and on time. Help me
to do them to the glory of the Father. Amen.*

Reading: Luke 1:46-56
Key Thought: The Holy Spirit is the Power of God to help you.

10   JESUS: HE WHO HAS THE SHARP SWORD WITH TWO EDGES

These things says He who has the sharp two-edged sword.
REVELATION 2:12

Jesus is *He Who Has the Sharp Sword with Two Edges.* The Sword is the Word of God, which cuts two ways—it ministers to both believers and unbelievers. Jesus will use the Sword to help believers stand fast, even where Satan's seat is. (see Revelation 2:13). He will use the Sword to defend those who never deny their faith (even to martyrdom). Jesus says He will help us "hold fast to [His] name" (v. 13). The two-edged Sword also cuts to the heart of a matter to reward truth and faithfulness (see Hebrews 4:12). The Word of God is truth (see John 17:17), so it helps Jesus see accurately what His followers have done. "He who has an ear, let him hear what the Spirit says" (Revelation 2:17). Those who are overcomers will eat daily the hidden manna of the Word, and Jesus will have a new name for them when they reach Heaven (see v. 17).

Lord, what will happen to those Christians who compromise with the world and hold false doctrines? How will you judge them?

The sharp two-edged Sword of Jesus cuts the unsaved in judgment. It punishes the rebellious and the disobedient. Jesus says to those who compromise, "Repent, or else I will come to you quickly and will fight against them with the sword of My mouth" (Revelation 2:16).

Lord, forgive me for looking at the Enemy and for looking at the sins of other Christians. Lord, I will look to You for truth in judgment. Amen.

Reading: Revelation 2:12-17
Key Thought: The Lord uses the Bible to help Christians and to punish nonbelievers.

11 ⬥ JESUS: A STUMBLING BLOCK

But we preach Christ crucified, to the Jews a stumbling
block and to the Greeks foolishness.
1 CORINTHIANS 1:23

Jesus was a *Stumbling Block* to the Jews of His day. They should not have rejected Jesus because He was born a Jew, the Seed of Abraham and the Son of David. They were looking for military deliverance from Rome; Jesus came to deliver them from their bondage to sin. They wanted political peace; Jesus came to give them spiritual peace. They wanted prosperity; Jesus came to give them the riches of Heaven. They rejected Jesus, a *Stumbling Block,* because they were looking for the wrong kind of Messiah. Do you know people who are looking for the wrong things from God? How about you? When you seek God, are you looking for the right thing?

> *Jesus, I accept Your offer of spiritual liberty and forgiveness.*
> *You came into the world for sinners like me. I will not stumble*
> *over the good things You offer.*

Jesus is a *Stumbling Block* to the unsaved. They don't expect a humble Savior who submitted to crucifixion. They don't expect a suffering Servant who was tortured and finally died an ignominious death. They stumble over the idea of "Christ crucified" (1 Corinthians 1:23). But God's principle is always seen in its opposite expression. To be strong, you must yield. To get, you must give. Christ died that you might live.

> *Jesus, the world thinks that Your crucifixion was terrible, but I know*
> *that it was a triumph over the Evil One. They reject Your death as a*
> *defeat, but it was victory over sin. The world will reject Your crucifixion,*
> *but Your death led to my eternal life. Amen.*

Reading: Luke 23:27-38
Key Thought: The Jews were looking for the wrong kind of Messiah.

12 ◆ THE HOLY SPIRIT: THE OIL OF GLADNESS

You love righteousness and hate wickedness; therefore God, Your God, has anointed You with the oil of gladness more than Your companions.
PSALM 45:7

The Holy Spirit is the *Oil of Gladness*. When He is rubbed into your wounds, He will take away pain and hurt. Just as oil cleanses a wound and washes away impurities, so the Holy Spirit comes to deal with your sin and wash away all remembrances of your iniquities. Do you remember how good it feels when an ache quits hurting? When the Holy Spirit comes to wash away your transgressions, you'll feel good. The Holy Spirit is the *Oil of Gladness* to make you rejoice.

Holy Spirit, I need some laughter in my life. Thank You for reminding me of how much I used to hurt. Now it feels good to feel good! Thank You for putting a smile on my face.

The Holy Spirit is the *Oil of Gladness* to make Christians rejoice. When He convicts of sin, people agonize; but when He brings forgiveness, they rejoice. When people walk into dark shadows of death, they are terrified; but they are glad when they realize that the Holy Spirit is with them. When Satan has tempted people to sin, the Holy Spirit gives them victory. He is the Holy Spirit of gladness that pours the oil of happiness on your wounds.

Holy Spirit, come pour Your oil of gladness into my wounds to heal me. Take away my hurt and sadness. Flow into my life. I have been happy in the past, and I want to feel that way again. Make today a wonderful day. Amen.

Reading: Psalm 45
Key Thought: The Holy Spirit gives happiness.

13 JESUS: ALPHA AND OMEGA

"I am the Alpha and the Omega, the Beginning and the End," says the Lord,
"who is and who was and who is to come, the Almighty."
REVELATION 1:8

Jesus is the *Alpha and Omega*, the completeness of your salvation from the beginning of your salvation on the cross until His second return to take you to glory. Because Jesus is the *Alpha and Omega*, you don't have to worry about anything; He will take care of you.

Lord, there are so many little details in my life that I can't
think about them all. When I give too much attention to prayer,
I overlook Bible reading. When I give too much attention
to family time, I neglect witnessing.

Just as alpha is the beginning of the Greek alphabet, so Jesus helps all believers start their Christian life properly. And as omega is the last letter in the Greek alphabet, so Jesus will carry you safely through to completion. "He which hath begun a good work in you will perform it until the day of Jesus Christ" (Philippians 1:6, *KJV*). Jesus is the *Alpha and Omega*, the completeness of your daily sanctification; trust Him to work out all things. Jesus is not only the Beginning and the End; He is everything in between. He is the *Alpha and Omega*, the entirety of your salvation. When you have Him, you have everything you need.

Lord, I rest in Your completed work for me; it's
comfortable knowing that You've done everything that needs
to be done. I not only trust You for the big things, but I also trust
You for the little things in everyday life. Amen.

Reading: Philemon
Key Thought: Jesus begins salvation, and He will finish it.

14 ❖ JESUS: ANOTHER KING

There is another king.
ACTS 17:7

Jesus is a King not like any king of this world; He is another kind of King. He never came to rule an earthly kingdom. Why should He want outward obedience as given to the kings of this earth when He can rule inwardly the hearts of people? Earthly kings rule by laws and force. But Jesus rules inwardly by love. Earthly kings want their subjects to do things for them. But Jesus first loved us and died for our salvation; then He gave us all the blessings of Heaven and has given us the privilege of serving Him out of love and obedience.

Lord, You are my King; I love You because You first loved me. I come to worship You, because You first came to me.

Jesus is *Another King,* not like any other king on Earth. Some rule for ego or vanity, and some rule for greed or wealth. Others rule because they carry on the family heritage into which they were born. Jesus rules what He created, because He is God. Jesus rules those whom He redeems, because He is the Savior. Jesus rules what is yielded to Him, because He is the Lord. What will you let Him rule today?

Jesus, You are my Lord. You are unlike the lords of this world; come take my life. You are my King. You are unlike the rulers of this world; I will gladly let You rule my life. Come sit upon the throne of my heart and rule my life today. Amen.

Reading: Acts 17:1-9
Key Thought: Jesus rules His subjects unlike any other king.

THE HOLY SPIRIT: THE HOLY SPIRIT OF PROMISE

Having believed, you were sealed with the Holy Spirit of promise.
EPHESIANS 1:13

The third Person of the Trinity is the *Holy Spirit of Promise*. Jesus promised to send Him to the disciples: "When the Helper comes, whom I shall send to you from the Father" (John 15:26). Just as Jesus kept His promise and sent the Holy Spirit, so Jesus will keep every promise He's made to you. He promised to take away your sin (see 1:29), to give you peace (see 14:27), to guide you through dark places (see 8:12) and to give you assurance of salvation (see 5:24). Jesus has a track record of keeping His promises, so rest assured that the Holy Spirit will also keep His promises to you.

> *Holy Spirit, Your presence gives me confidence to keep on trying. I know that Jesus has begun to do a good work in me; I know He will complete it (see Philippians 1:6).*

The Holy Spirit has promised to bring power to your life so that you can witness to the unsaved (see Acts 1:8). Also, the Holy Spirit promised to give you victory in the hour of your temptation (see 2 Corinthians 2:14), to keep the Evil One from you (see Matthew 6:13), to guide your life (see Galatians 5:25), to give you spiritual ability for Christian service (see 1 Corinthians 12:1-7) and to produce Christian character in you (see Galatians 5:22-23). All these things the Holy Spirit has done for others. What He has done for others, He can do for you.

> *Holy Spirit, thank You for reminding me that these promises are mine. I believe them, and I will claim them. Thank You for keeping Your promise to believers. Amen.*

Reading: John 7:37-39
Key Thought: The Holy Spirit will keep the promises that He has made.

16 JESUS: AUTHOR OF ETERNAL SALVATION

He became the author of eternal salvation to all who obey Him.
HEBREWS 5:9

Jesus is the *Author of Eternal Salvation*; He is writing a story plot for your future. Just as an earthly author will know the content before writing, so Jesus knows what He wants to accomplish in your life. Just as an earthly author develops characters in the story, so Jesus knows what He wants you to become and how He wants you to live. He is the *Author of Eternal Salvation*; He has put the whole story of salvation together—from ages past to eternity future—so He is able to guide your life.

> *Lord, thank You for writing the great story of salvation. I have read Your Book, and I love its ending. I accept Your plot, and I will attempt to live my part of Your story. Come give me power to live for You today.*

Jesus is the *Author of Eternal Salvation*. Just as an earthly author lives through his or her writings, so Jesus is the living Salvation that He brings (see Luke 3:6). He wrote salvation's plan. Jesus came to bring salvation; and when we call upon Him, He gives us salvation (see Romans 10:13)—not partially or temporarily. Jesus has the ability to completely save those who come to Him, and He has the power to permanently keep them, because He gives them eternal salvation. Will you let Jesus finish writing the story of your life?

> *Lord, I am confident of this very thing: You have begun a good work in me, and You will complete it until the day You return (see Philippians 1:6). Amen.*

Reading: Hebrews 5:1-9
Key Thought: Jesus is writing the story of your life.

17 ◆ JESUS: THE BRANCH

I am bringing forth My Servant the Branch.
ZECHARIAH 3:8

Jesus is the *Branch*, an Old Testament title given to the Messiah. The name comes from the Hebrew word *tsemach*, which refers to a green shoot or a new sprout growing out of an old stump. When Nebuchadnezzar "chopped" down the kingdom of Israel in 587 B.C., the stump of the tree died—the kingdom ceased—but the roots did not die. The kingdom was renewed when Jesus was born King of the Jews (see Matthew 2:2). Jesus is the *Branch*—the new sprout from Jewish roots—demonstrating that God's kingdom will live again. When a fire devastates a forest, it looks like the end of beautiful, green woods. But wait! Look below the charred stumps to see life in the roots. Just as a burned area can become green again, so a new "branch" can spring from your blackened past. Jesus, the *Branch*, can give new opportunities to your life.

I come to You, Branch; sprout new life in me. Give me another new opportunity to serve You today.

Jesus is "the Man whose name is the Branch" (Zechariah 6:12), so He can identify with your needs. He is the righteous Branch (see Jeremiah 23:5) to help you do things right. Just as "the Branch of the LORD shall be beautiful" (Isaiah 4:2), so Jesus can make your life beautiful. And Jesus is the "Servant the Branch" (Zechariah 3:8) to serve you. Let Jesus, the *Branch*, bring new opportunities into your life.

Lord, give me new opportunities to live for You, and give me a new attitude towards life. Come grow new life in me. Amen.

Reading: Isaiah 4:1-6
Key Thought: Jesus offers another new beginning.

18 THE HOLY SPIRIT: THE PROMISE

You shall receive the gift of the Holy Spirit. For the promise is to you and to your children, and to all who are afar off, as many as the Lord our God will call.
ACTS 2:38-39

Peter, on the Day of Pentecost, promised that the Holy Spirit would come on those who believed in Christ. The fulfillment of that promise was the coming of the Holy Spirit on his listeners, just as the Holy Spirit came on the disciples in the Upper Room (see Acts 2:1-4). Peter promised that the Holy Spirit would come to do the work of the Father and Son in the lives of all Christians (see vv. 38-39). He has come into the world; and when you believed, He came into your heart (see John 15:26). Will you let the Holy Spirit work in your life today?

Holy Spirit, I have many spiritual needs. I yield my life to you; meet my needs. Fill me today; I need Your presence in my life (see Ephesians 5:18).

The Holy Spirit is the Fulfillment of the promises made by the Father and Son. He has regenerated you (see John 3:5); He has given you eternal life (see v. 36); He has given you a new nature (see 2 Peter 1:4); and He has guaranteed your home in Heaven (see Ephesians 4:30). Look at what the Holy Spirit can do in the future. He can give you peace (see John 14:27), Christian character (see Galatians 5:22-23), guidance (see v. 25) and spiritual gifts (see 1 Corinthians 12:7,11). These promises have been made to you; now you must claim them and act on them.

Holy Spirit, forgive my forgetful memory. I have forgotten the things You can do for me. Help me remember everything that You can do for me. Please help me claim them all. Amen.

Reading: Acts 1:1-14
Key Thought: The Holy Spirit is the Fulfillment of the promises made by Jesus.

19 ◆ JESUS: BREAD

And Jesus said to them, "I am the bread of life. He who comes to Me shall never hunger, and he who believes in Me shall never thirst."
JOHN 6:35

Jesus is the *Bread* who gives eternal life to those who believe in Him; you must believe in Him to get it. He is satisfying *Bread* who gives inner happiness; you must enjoy Him to get it. He is also strength-giving *Bread* to build you up and give you energy to serve God; you must learn of Him to get it. Jesus is resurrection *Bread* who gives you life now and life in the future. "Whoever eats My flesh . . . I will raise him up at the last day" (John 6:54). So, eat the *Bread* of Jesus; it will give you confidence, and in the future, you'll rise in the Resurrection. When you eat of Jesus, you'll find strength through your personal relationship with Him.

Lord, I'm weak; I need Bread to give me strength for today. Lord, when I get my eyes off You, I hunger for the things of this life. My unfilled desire makes me miserable. Teach me to eat the Bread of life so that I can experience spiritual satisfaction of the soul.

Jesus is supernatural *Bread*. Those who eat the *Bread* of Jesus are strengthened to run, work and wrestle (see Philippians 4:13). When you eat the *Bread* of Jesus, you have new purpose in your life to overcome obstacles and limitations. When you eat the *Bread* of Jesus, you have a supernatural life, because He will live in you and you'll live in Him. Are you hungry for Him today?

Bread of life, I am hungry; fill me. I am weak; strengthen me.
Come fulfill Your life through me. Amen.

Reading: John 6:32-59
Key Thought: Jesus is *Bread* to give you life.

20 ◇ JESUS: A NAME NO MAN KNEW

He had a name written that no one knew except Himself.
REVELATION 19:12

Jesus has a *Name No Man Knew*. This means that no one knows His hidden name, not even you. Even though you may want to know His secret name, you can't know it, because He has not told anyone—some things only God knows. At His return, there will still be a mystery about Jesus' nature that you cannot understand. Why? Because no finite human can comprehend the infinite God. So don't worry about what you don't know; rather, respond quickly to what you do know about Jesus' names. His name is "Wonderful, Counselor, Mighty God, Everlasting Father, Prince of Peace" (Isaiah 9:6)—and those are only a few of His names found in only one verse in the Bible.

*Jesus, I realize I can't know, nor will I ever know, all about You; but
I know I worship You as King of kings and Lord
of lords (see Revelation 19:16).*

Jesus has a *Name No Man Knew*. This means that there could be more than one name you don't know. Just as His names that you know reveal the unique characteristics of Jesus, His unknowable names reflect things about Him that you can never know. That's because Jesus is God and you are human. But trust what you know about Jesus, and obey what He wants you to do.

*Jesus, I don't know everything about You; but what I know, I love, I
trust, I worship. I will obey You as my Master. Amen.*

Reading: Revelation 19:11-12
Key Thought: Focus on what the names of Jesus tell us about Him.

THE HOLY SPIRIT: THE LORD OF THE HARVEST

21

The harvest truly is plentiful, but the laborers are few. Therefore pray the Lord of the harvest to send out laborers into His harvest.
MATTHEW 9:37-38

The Holy Spirit is the *Lord of the Harvest;* the harvest is His. Too often we think that the harvest is ours, but the Holy Spirit wants us to work for Him in the harvest of lost souls. Because there are many lost people, the fields are white for harvest (see John 4:35). When we tell lost people the good news of Jesus, the Holy Spirit will work in their hearts to convict them of sin. Then He will open their spiritually blinded eyes to see the gospel, and He will draw them to salvation. Will you work in the harvest today and let the Holy Spirit work through you? You can do that by sharing the gospel with a lost person.

Holy Spirit, I feel Your urging in my heart to be more active in evangelism. I will witness to someone today. Help me to communicate the gospel to someone. Work in the hearts of those to whom I witness.

The Holy Spirit is the *Lord of the Harvest.* When people believe in Jesus, the Holy Spirit regenerates their hearts (see John 3:5) and places eternal life in them. But most important, since it is His harvest, He preserves the fruit by indwelling the new believers with His presence to guarantee that they receive all the blessings that the Father has promised to them.

Holy Spirit, You are Lord of the Harvest! I cannot accomplish anything without Your working through me. I yield to Your leading. Use me today, as I testify to others of my salvation. Amen.

Reading: Matthew 9:35—10:26
Key Thought: The Holy Spirit works through you to win lost people to salvation.

22 ◆ JESUS: A PRICE

For you were bought at a price; therefore glorify God in your body
and in your spirit, which are God's.
1 CORINTHIANS 6:20

Jesus is the complete *Price* that was paid to redeem you from sin. Salvation was not free; He paid a price. His death was the price that gave you life. Salvation was not cheap; Jesus was humiliated and tortured, and He suffered for your sins. Your sin—and the sin of all others—had violated the perfection of God the Father. Sin had to be punished, so Jesus was punished for your violations. Instead of your paying the price, He paid it for you.

Jesus, thank You for paying the price for my sin. Now I am free from the
debt of sin. Help me to live in gratitude for what You've done.

Jesus is the *Price* big enough to cover all the sins of all people. He is the ultimate *Price*, enduring enough to cover all the sins committed in the future. He paid the price once for all. He forgave all sin—all past and all future sin. Now, if you walk in the light, the blood of Jesus Christ cleanses you from all sin (see 1 John 1:7). You don't have to feel guilty over your sin; instead, confess it and receive cleansing (see v. 9). Don't walk around in the darkness; rather, walk in the light of Jesus.

Jesus, it's easy to walk when there's light on the path. Keep me
from dark roads of sin and the valley of the shadow of death. Shine some
light over here; guide me today. Amen.

Reading: 1 Peter 1:18-25
Key Thought: Jesus paid the price to free you from sin.

23 ▸ JESUS: A SON OVER HIS OWN HOUSE

*But Christ as a Son over His own house, whose house we are if we hold fast the
confidence and the rejoicing of the hope firm to the end.*
HEBREWS 3:6

Jesus is the *Son over His Own House*. Just as Levi was the first priest
in Israel's genealogy, so Jesus is the first priest in New Testament
salvation. Just as Aaron was the first priest who interceded for Israel
in the Tabernacle, so Jesus is the High Priest who will intercede
for you in Heaven. All believers are members of Jesus' house, and He
will intercede to the Father for them. How can He intercede for you
today?

*Jesus, be my Intercessor to the Father. Every time I slip into sin,
intercede to the Father for my forgiveness. Every time the Evil One
comes to tempt me, protect me by Your intercession.*

Jesus is the *Son over His Own House*; "He is also able to save to the
uttermost those who come to God through Him, since He always lives to
make intercession for them" (Hebrews 7:25). So take your problems to
Jesus, trust Him, and let Him be your Intercessor. As your Intercessor,
Jesus "does not need daily, as those high priests, to offer up sacrifices"
(v. 27). He doesn't need to offer sacrifices daily for His sin because He is
"holy, harmless, undefiled, separate from sinners" (v. 26). He is the Son
forevermore (see v. 28). So come into His house for help to solve your
problems; let Jesus be your Intercessor.

*Lord, I know that "the blood of Jesus Christ . . . cleanses us from all sin"
(1 John 1:7), so I rest calmly in Your house. I know
You will intercede to the Father for me. Amen.*

Reading: Hebrews 3
Key Thought: Jesus intercedes for all those who belong to Him.

24 THE HOLY SPIRIT: THE HOLY SPIRIT OF GOD

*And do not grieve the Holy Spirit of God, by whom you were
sealed for the day of redemption.*
EPHESIANS 4:30

The *Holy Spirit of God* comes to you from God because the Holy Spirit is the third Person of the Trinity. The Father sent Him to help you become more like Himself. He wants you to become more holy, for He is the Holy Spirit. He wants to help you become more spiritual, for He is the Spirit of God. Will you yield to His work today?

*Holy Spirit, I come asking for an inward change. I want to live a pure
life, but I need help because I am weak. I want to be holy, but I need
Your strength. Sanctify me, and make me pure. Help me live a godly
life. Come live Your holy nature in my life.*

Don't grieve the *Holy Spirit of God* by allowing temptation or sin to settle down in your heart. Confess quickly and repent; then immediately begin living a pure life. Because the Holy Spirit lives in your life, don't even think about sin. Because He is holy, He is grieved when you allow sin to settle down in your mind. Because the Holy Spirit is God, He demands holiness in your life and in your thoughts. But He is also the Helper; ask Him to help you overcome temptation and distractions. Ask Him to make you holy and spiritual.

*Holy Spirit, come into my life. I want Your holiness to control my
thoughts and desires. I cannot separate myself from sin, for I am weak.
You are God; let Your holiness flow through me. Amen.*

Reading: Ephesians 4:17-32
Key Thought: The Holy Spirit was sent to make you godly.

25 ◆ JESUS: THE HOLY ONE

For You will not leave my soul in Hades, nor will You allow
Your Holy One to see corruption.
ACTS 2:27

Jesus is the *Holy One* of God. He was the Father's Representative sent to Earth to redeem the sinful race. When Adam sinned, all humanity was lost. Because the Father loved the people He created, He wanted to save them. How could the Father punish their sin yet allow people to go free? Since God the Father couldn't change His nature, He had to punish their rebellion and disobedience. So He sent Jesus to Earth to live a perfect life; Jesus was the *Holy One*. Jesus was the sinless One who was punished for the sins of the human race. He was the Father's Representative to give eternal life to those who would believe in Him.

Lord Jesus, I praise You for coming to Earth to die for my sins. I know
that You are the Holy One of God; thank You for Your sacrifice. Help
me live a godly life as a testimony for You.

Because Jesus was your Representative on the cross, He now wants you to be His representative to your non-Christian friends and relatives. He wants you to live a holy life before them. He wants you to share with them the plan of salvation. Since He has died for you, He wants you to live for Him.

Lord Jesus, I will be Your representative today. I will try to
live a holy life, but I need help. Come live in me and manifest
Yourself through me to others. Help me be a good example to
both saved and unsaved people. Amen.

Reading: Psalm 16
Key Thought: Jesus was the *Holy One*.

JESUS: THE FIRSTBORN FROM THE DEAD

And from Jesus Christ, . . . the firstborn from the dead.
REVELATION 1:5

Jesus was the *Firstborn from the Dead*, which means He was the first to be generated—or given life—from the dead. Jesus was a dead corpse but was given life by the Father; His body lived again. Also, Jesus was the *Firstborn from the Dead* in Resurrection. He was taken from among the dead, or from the location where the dead existed, and was taken to Heaven. Jesus can make life real to you today because He lives in you. Do you want it?

Lord Jesus, You arose from the dead so that You can come
into my heart with eternal life. Now You abide in me.
I praise You for giving life to me. Strengthen me for today's tasks.
I worship You as the Firstborn from the Dead.

Jesus was the *Firstborn from the Dead* and first in importance, because He became "a life-giving spirit" (1 Corinthians 15:45). This means that Jesus gave life to all. But Jesus was also the first in sequence; no one was raised from the dead before Him. Adam, Moses, David—all the Old Testament saints—He captured and led captive into heaven (see Ephesians 4:8). Jesus was the *Firstborn from the Dead* so that now all who believe in Him are "born again" from their spiritual death. All who believe in Him have His new life; they have eternal life. Why don't you thank Him.

Lord, You arose from the dead to fill my empty life with Your presence.
Give me happiness and meaning for life. Amen.

Reading: Matthew 28:1-10
Key Thought: Jesus can give you life because He was raised from the dead.

27 · THE HOLY SPIRIT: THE ETERNAL SPIRIT

*How much more shall the blood of Christ, who through the
eternal Spirit offered Himself without spot to God, cleanse your
conscious from dead works to serve the living God?*
HEBREWS 9:14

The Holy Spirit is the *Eternal Spirit*. He has always existed. He is the third
Person of the Trinity, who was active in creation (see Genesis 1:2) and
who worked throughout the Old Testament. Some people have mistakenly thought that He didn't come until Jesus promised to send Him into
the world (see John 15:26). But He is the *Eternal Spirit*. Now during the
Church Age, the Holy Spirit has a special relationship to believers. He
will indwell you, guide you, teach you, protect you and, when you are
weak, fill you with divine power. Do you want the Holy Spirit in your
life?

*Come, Eternal Spirit, and fill my life with Your presence.
I need to be holy; set me apart from sin. I need strength to obey
Scriptures; fill me with Your power.*

The Holy Spirit is the *Eternal Spirit*. He has always been the Spirit of
holiness, so He can make you holy. He has eternally been the Spirit, so
He can make you spiritual. The Father and Son have sent the Holy Spirit
to help you do what you're supposed to do. When the *Eternal Spirit* fills
your life, you'll sense God's purpose, and you'll realize that your life is
bigger than your everyday world. The *Eternal Spirit* will make you realize
that you're part of God's eternal plan.

*Holy Spirit, I want more than what I have in this world. Come,
Eternal Spirit. I want a touch of eternity in my life. Amen.*

Reading: Hebrews 9:12-22
Key Thought: The Holy Spirit will make you realize that you're part of
an eternal plan.

28   JESUS: THE FAITHFUL WITNESS

Grace to you and peace from Him who is and who was and who is to come, . . . and from Jesus Christ, the faithful witness.
REVELATION 1:4-5

Jesus is the *Faithful Witness*; He will give a faithful testimony to build you up. When you have doubts, He will come to build up your faith. When you are discouraged, He will come to give you divine confidence. Jesus can be a *Faithful Witness* to you every time you need it. But you must ask for His help.

I'm ashamed of my doubts, because my questions impugn Your integrity. Remind me again of Your faithfulness. Give me confidence in the promises You have made.

Jesus is the *Faithful Witness* who came to witness to the people of the world that the heavenly Father loves them. But they did not receive the testimony of Jesus. Even though He was a *Faithful Witness* and He demonstrated it with signs and wonders, the world wouldn't believe Him. Jesus told Pilate, "I . . . bear witness to the truth" (John 18:37); but Pilate rejected Him. Jesus faithfully declared the truth, but He was crucified because of what He said and did. Just as Jesus was faithful to the end, so He wants you to always be faithful—even if it costs you your life.

Jesus, You are my Faithful Witness; I receive you into my life as a sure evidence of truth. I believe what You said in Scriptures. I praise You for Your miracles and acts of kindness. I accept Your death as forgiveness for my sins. Thank You for Your faithful witness that gives me confidence and assurance. Amen.

Reading: John 19:7-15
Key Thought: Jesus will be faithful to tell you the truth.

29 JESUS: THE ROOT AND OFFSPRING OF DAVID

I am the Root and the Offspring of David.
REVELATION 22:16

Jesus is the *Root and Offspring of David*, the greatest king of Israel. Just as a tree gets strength and life from its roots, so David's accomplishments and strength came from Jesus. Just as David derived everything from Jesus, so your spiritual vitality comes from Him. You were born again when Christ came into your heart, so your spiritual life comes from Him.

*Lord, I know that my spiritual life comes from You; help me
never to forget where my strength lies.*

Jesus is the *Root and Offspring of David*. Jesus was not only David's source of strength, but He also was born into David's line. Jesus has the legitimate title to David's throne. Because of being born in the line of David, Jesus is qualified to fulfill all the Messianic prophecies for the salvation of every Israelite and for the nation as a whole. Look to Him for all your needs. Jesus is the *Root and Offspring of David*, which means that He was the "Son of David" (Matthew 1:1). When David wrote the Psalms, he called the coming Messiah "the Lord" (Psalm 110:1,5). Just as Jesus was the Lord of David, so He wants to be your Lord. Will you submit to Him today?

*Lord, You are the Root from which I get my life; I am Your offspring.
But more important, You are my Lord; I will serve You this day. Amen.*

Reading: Revelation 22:12-21
Key Thought: Will you submit to the lordship of Jesus, as David did?

THE HOLY SPIRIT: THE SPIRIT OF REVELATION

30

That the God of our Lord Jesus Christ, the Father of glory, may give to you the spirit of wisdom and revelation in the knowledge of Him.
EPHESIANS 1:17

Revelation is needed for the things you can't know until God reveals them to you. The Holy Spirit is the *Spirit of Revelation* who showed the writers of Scripture what to write and who guided them to write accurately the revelation of God. But the Bible is more than an accurate book; it is inspired (see 2 Timothy 3:16), which means that the Holy Spirit breathed His presence into its words. The Holy Spirit is embedded in the words of the Scriptures to minister to those who read it. So when you let the Word of God enter your life, the Holy Spirit enters your heart to influence you. Will you let the *Spirit of Revelation* show you from the Bible what God wants you to know?

> *Holy Spirit, I love the Word of God because it contains*
> *Your words. Speak to me through its pages so that*
> *I can know You better and do Your will.*

You don't know what the future holds, but the Holy Spirit knows both the coming joys and pains. Study the Bible to learn His instruction; He'll prepare you for all future eventualities. You don't know where you may go today, but the Holy Spirit knows God's will for you. Let Him guide you today. The *Spirit of Revelation* knows what is best for you; let Him help you find in the Bible God's will for your life.

> *Holy Spirit, I trust my future with You. I'll learn what You reveal to me*
> *from Scripture. I'll go where You lead me. Amen.*

Reading: 2 Timothy 3:14-17
Key Thought: The Holy Spirit can reveal God's will to you.

31 JESUS: THE KING INVISIBLE

Now to the King eternal, immortal, invisible, to God who alone is wise,
be honor and glory forever and ever. Amen.
1 TIMOTHY 1:17

Jesus is the *King Invisible*; you can't see Him, but He's there with you all day, every day. Just because He's invisible, it doesn't mean that He's not with you. While His body is sitting at the right hand of the Father in Heaven, His presence indwells our hearts. Because Jesus is God, the Spirit of Jesus is everywhere present at the same time. That He is invisible means that He exists everywhere in Spirit. Ask Him to help and protect you this day, because He's with you.

Jesus, thank You for being with me. Protect me today from dangers I
don't see, and help me through problems I haven't yet faced. Minister to
me in ways I don't know about. Help me be a godly person.

Jesus is the *King Invisible*; He rules the entire universe. He can be at all places at all times, because He is omnipresent. As Lord, Jesus rules the universe, and more important, He dwells in your heart (see Colossians 1:27). But He wants more than His presence living in your heart. He wants to rule your heart. As King, He wants to sit on the throne of your heart to rule your life today. Will you let Him do it?

Jesus, I want You to be Lord of my life and to rule me today.
May every word I speak glorify You. May every action I do further
Your kingdom. May every step I take be guided by You. Be with me
to protect me and to help me grow spiritually. Amen.

Reading: Matthew 14:22-36
Key Thought: Jesus is with you, even when you can't see Him.

NOVEMBER

1 ◈ JESUS: THE KING IMMORTAL

Now to the King eternal, immortal, invisible, to God who
alone is wise, be honor and glory forever and ever. Amen.
1 TIMOTHY 1:17

Jesus is the *King Immortal*. The word "immortal" means "not subject to mortality," and it also means "not subject to corruptibility." The *King Immortal* will never die; nor is there corruption in Him or in His rule. His laws are righteous; they were not made on selfish principles, nor were they enacted out of sinful purposes. Because He is the *King Immortal*, all His judgments are correct. Jesus has never made a mistake in enforcing His laws. Because Jesus is an immortal King, you can trust Him. He will not be corrupted; neither will His kingdom fall apart. Those under His rule cannot corrupt His standards. While some may corrupt themselves, no one can tarnish His laws.

Jesus, You are my immortal King. I bow to worship You because You
have always lived in the past, You will always live in the future and You
are alive today. Come sit on the throne of my heart; rule my life.

Jesus is the *King Immortal*. While on Earth, He did not sin, and Pilate found no fault in Him. Jesus died as the perfect Lamb who was the substitute for your sin. He was raised again on the third day to live forever. Death could not corrupt His perfect body. Jesus is the eternal King, which means that all people, of all ages, from all ethnic groups, must submit to His reign or be judged by His laws. He is the *King Immortal*, whose rule will not fail nor can it be overthrown.

Jesus, You are a righteous King. Everything You do is right.
I worship You for Your trustworthiness. I serve You because
You are my Savior. Amen.

Reading: Psalm 24
Key Thought: Jesus will not make any mistakes in your life.

2 THE HOLY SPIRIT: THE SPIRIT OF THE LORD

*The Spirit of the LORD shall rest upon Him, the Spirit of wisdom
and understanding, the Spirit of counsel and might, the
Spirit of knowledge and of the fear of the LORD.*
ISAIAH 11:2

The *Spirit of the Lord* is the Holy Spirit, who does the actual work in your heart for God the Father and God the Son. The *"Spirit of the Lord"* is a primary name of the Holy Spirit to reveal His character; in other words, who He is. When you think of the eternal nature of God, do not project onto Him human characteristics, as you would onto a physical being. Remember, "God is Spirit" (John 4:24), so the Holy Spirit is not limited. He can come minister to you anywhere, in any place and at any time.

*O Spirit of the Lord, come make this day wonderful. Help me bring
glory to the Father, Son and You, Holy Spirit.*

The *Spirit of the Lord* is with all believers, so He will be with you. He will fulfill what Jesus promised: "I will pray the Father, and He will give you another Helper, . . . the Spirit of truth; . . . He dwells with you and will be in you" (John 14:16-17). You must believe the promise of Jesus and act on it. You must receive the *Spirit of the Lord* if you want Him to work in your life; but He can energize only what You give Him, so yield to Him today what You want Him to use.

*O Spirit of the Lord, I give myself to You. Come fill me with a
new zeal to be holy. Give me a new desire to serve You. O Spirit of the
Lord, fill me completely, and use me. Amen.*

Reading: John 14:16-26
Key Thought: The Holy Spirit does God's work everywhere in all people.

3   JESUS: THE LAST ADAM

The first man Adam became a living being. The last Adam became a life-giving spirit.
1 CORINTHIANS 15:45

Jesus is the *Last Adam*. Just as Adam was the head of the human race, so Jesus is the Head of those He has redeemed. The first Adam, as head of the human race, disobeyed God, resulting in all becoming sinners. "Through one man sin entered the world" (Romans 5:12). Jesus, the *Last Adam*, made a decision to redeem the human race. He died for all. Jesus is the Head of a new race of all who are born again by the Spirit of God. Jesus arose the third day to give life to all who follow Him.

> *Lord Jesus, I come to you as my Ruler and Head, acknowledging Your leadership over my life. As I pray that others will let You rule their lives, I now surrender the control of my life to You.*

The first Adam was the first to sin, and by his disobedience, he plunged all humankind into eternal death. The death of Jesus—the *Last Adam*—delivered all who would believe in Him. Through His resurrection, He received the headship of a new race of believers. Now Jesus wants the headship of every area of your life—home, business, leisure, hobbies, vacations, amusements and so on. He wants you to serve Him with your time, talent and treasure. What will you give to Him?

> *Lord, I know that You are the Last Adam, the Head of the Body. Come, be the Head of my life and all my activities. I give my life to You. Amen.*

Reading: 1 Corinthians 15:35-45
Key Thought: Jesus, the Head of a new race, wants to be the Head of your life.

JESUS: THE ONLY BEGOTTEN SON

For God so loved the world that He gave His only begotten Son, that whoever believes in Him should not perish but have everlasting life.
JOHN 3:16

Jesus is the *Only Begotten Son*, an Old Testament title declaring that He was eternally generated from the Father. The Father said to Jesus, "You are my Son, begotten throughout eternity" (see Psalm 2:7). This does not mean that the Son was begotten at an event in eternity past; rather, it describes the eternal relationship of the Son to the Father. Both the Father and Jesus are equally eternal and equally God, but they have separate personalities. They are equal in nature. Jesus was not begotten at a time in the past, because that would mean the Son is not eternal. But the Father has eternally loved Jesus; and because the Father loved you and the world, He sent Jesus to die for your sins. When you receive Jesus as the *Only Begotten Son*, you have also believed in the Father.

Jesus, I worship You just as I worship the Father. You are both God, and I come into Your presence with thanksgiving for all You've done for me.

When you receive Jesus as Savior, you become a child of God (see Romans 8:14-16). The Father has only One Son who could die for the world, and because of that sacrificial death, the Father now has many "sons." You are a member of the family.

Jesus, I worship You as the Only Begotten Son. I praise You as the second Person of the Godhead. I thank You for coming into the world to die for my sins. Amen.

Reading: John 3:9-20
Key Thought: Jesus is the *Only Begotten Son* of the Father.

THE HOLY SPIRIT: THE SPIRIT OF UNDERSTANDING

The Spirit of the LORD shall rest upon Him, the Spirit of wisdom
and understanding, the Spirit of counsel and might, the
Spirit of knowledge and of the fear of the LORD.
ISAIAH 11:2

The Holy Spirit is the *Spirit of Understanding*; He can distinguish between the counterfeit and the real. Even though people use Christian words and gestures and claim to know God, He knows what is genuine and what is fake. He will help you take inventory of your spiritual life and show when you are sincere and when you are just being outwardly religious.

O Spirit of Understanding, expose any counterfeit motive in my life,
and help me be genuine in character and service. Help me worship the
Father authentically. I want to be like Christ. Give me real spiritual
power to live the Christian life.

The *Spirit of Understanding* recognizes a sincere heart in worshipers; that's why He gives them self-understanding. He encourages all those who want to be conformed to the image of Christ; that's why He gives them self-evaluation. He values all those who want to live an authentic Christian life; that's why He gives them self-direction for their daily walk. When the *Spirit of Understanding* rests upon you, then you can have self-assurance that you are doing the will of God. Then "the Spirit Himself bears witness with our spirit that we are children of God" (Romans 8:16).

O Spirit of truth, come show me my failures so that I can correct them;
show me my hypocrisy so that I can humbly walk with You; show me
Your will for my life, and help me do it. O Spirit of Understanding,
come give me assurance today. Amen.

Reading: Genesis 24
Key Thought: The Holy Spirit will show you what is real and what is fake.

6 JESUS: GOD MANIFESTED IN THE FLESH

God was manifested in the flesh, justified in the Spirit, seen by angels, preached among the Gentiles, believed on in the world, received up in glory.
1 TIMOTHY 3:16

Jesus was *God Manifested in the Flesh*. If you want to see what God is like, look at Jesus. You can see His life story in the pages of Scripture. As you study His life, you can see how God would react to situations. If you want to see how God would have you live, Jesus is your example. Will you follow His steps? Jesus is *God Manifested in the Flesh*. He was born in a stable in Bethlehem because people rejected Him at His arrival; there was no room in the inn (see Luke 2:7). How will you react to rejection? Because Jesus was born King of the Jews, Herod felt threatened and tried to kill Him (see Matthew 2:16). How will you handle persecution? The unsaved mind doesn't know what to make of Christ, because He was *God Manifested in the Flesh*.

> *Jesus, You are my Lord and God. I worship You for giving up the glories of Heaven to come to Earth to live in human flesh. I receive You, even though others reject You. I crown You King of my life, even though some tried to kill You. Thank You for becoming flesh for me.*

The greatest event in history was when God became flesh. The shepherds recognized what happened and worshiped Jesus as He lay in a manger (see Luke 2:15-16). The wise men worshiped Him with gifts of gold, frankincense and myrrh (see Matthew 2:11). Throughout history, believers have worshiped Him with the gift of their heart. What will you bring to Him today?

> *Jesus, I acknowledge that You are God Manifested in the Flesh. Jesus, I worship You with the gift of my heart; I have nothing greater to give You than myself. Amen.*

Reading: 1 Timothy 3:14-16
Key Thought: You must worship Jesus for becoming flesh.

7 ◆ THE HOLY SPIRIT: WELL OF WATER

*But whosoever drinketh of the water that I shall give him shall
never thirst; but the water that I shall give him shall be in him a
well of water springing up into everlasting life.*
JOHN 4:14, *KJV*

The Holy Spirit is a *Well of Water* to hot, thirsty travelers. Jesus said,
"Come to Me and drink" (John 7:37). He promised, "Out of [your] heart
will flow rivers of living water" (v. 38). He said that this Water is the Holy
Spirit: "This He spoke concerning the Spirit" (v. 39). That *Well of Water—*
living Water—is within you, so you'll never again have to search anywhere else for satisfaction. You'll never have to seek pleasure in sinful
activities. You'll not find thirst relief in the world, the flesh or the Devil.
That nagging thirst in your mouth is the Holy Spirit's own way of getting your attention. Look within your heart to find peace in Him. The
Holy Spirit is there when you're ready to drink.

*Holy Spirit, I know that You entered my heart when I was saved. Keep
me thirsty so that I'll turn to You when I need refreshing.*

The Holy Spirit is a *Well of Water* to renew your strength. When you're
too tired to go on, drink of Him. When you're out of spiritual energy, let
Him be your Strength. Maybe you need some cool shade and a little rest.
Drink some Water. Then you'll be ready to get back to the job that you
have to do.

*Holy Spirit, I need You today. The road is long, and I'm weary. The sun
is draining my energy, so I drink. Ah, Your water tastes good. Amen.*

Reading: John 4:1-14
Key Thought: The Holy Spirit refreshes you.

8   JESUS: HE WHO HAS THE SEVEN SPIRITS OF GOD AND THE SEVEN STARS

These things says He who has the seven Spirits of God and the seven stars.
REVELATION 3:1

Jesus is *He Who Has the Seven Spirits of God*. This is not a reference to seven different spirits sent by God; but rather, this is a reference to the One Spirit of God who will minister to you and to the Church in various ways. Jesus can send the Holy Spirit to do many things in your life. The Spirit can convict of sin, regenerate, indwell, baptize, seal, guide and give you spiritual gifts. Jesus can send the Holy Spirit to make you holy and to make you spiritual; receive what He sends.

*Lord, I receive all the various ministries of the Holy Spirit
into my heart. Work in my life today.*

Jesus is *He Who Has the Seven Stars*. These stars were churches (see Revelation 2:1). These churches were dear to Him, as are all churches and all believers in them. However, there were some problems in these churches. To the church in Sardis, He said, "You have a name that you are alive, but you are dead. Remember therefore how you have received and heard; hold fast and repent" (3:1,3). No matter how spiritual—or carnal—a church, Jesus knows, and He works in that church to make it godlier. Jesus is He that is coming as a thief in the night, in an hour when we do not expect Him (see v. 3). So walk faithfully before Him in love, because those who are overcomers will be clothed in white and their names will not be blotted out of the Book of Life (see v. 5).

*Lord, send the Holy Spirit to make me more godly. You are the coming
One; I wait for Your appearance. Amen.*

Reading: Revelation 3:1-6
Key Thought: Jesus knows us and works in us.

9 JESUS: THE RIGHTEOUS

My little children, these things I write to you, so that you may not sin. And if anyone sins, we have an Advocate with the Father, Jesus Christ the righteous.
1 JOHN 2:1

Jesus is the *Righteous*; no one can claim to be righteous, because the Bible says, "There is none righteous, no, not one" (Romans 3:10). A righteous person always does the right thing in actions, always has right thoughts and is right in attitude. When John baptized Jesus, it was "to fulfill all righteousness" (Matthew 3:15), which means that Jesus and John did the right thing in the right way. Jesus is the only righteous Person to ever live, for He always did the right thing and His character was perfect righteousness.

Lord Jesus, I know that You are perfect and that You never sinned (see 1 Peter 2:22), but what about me? How can I become righteous?

Jesus is the *Righteous*; when you enter the exchanged life, you identify with Jesus' position in Heaven, and He indwells you on Earth. Jesus said, "You in Me and I in you" (John 14:20). Because Jesus was perfect, the Father made Him to be your sin, and the Father gave His righteousness to you (see 2 Corinthians 5:21). The secret of the Christian life is that Jesus comes to live in you when you are saved. You are still a sinner—a forgiven sinner—but the righteousness of Jesus is accounted to you when you are saved. Now what you need is power to overcome sin. That happens when Jesus lives His life through you. Let the righteous One shine through your life today.

Lord, fill my imperfect life with Your righteousness. Live through me so that others can see Your perfection. Amen.

Reading: 2 Corinthians 5:14-21
Key Thought: The righteousness of Christ was applied to you when you were saved.

10 THE HOLY SPIRIT: YOUR GOOD SPIRIT

*You also gave Your good Spirit to instruct them, and did not withhold Your
manna from their mouth, and gave them water for their thirst.*
NEHEMIAH 9:20

The Holy Spirit is the *Good Spirit* of God. He is called good because that's
His nature. Goodness is the absolute personification of all positive
attributes. All that's good in the world comes from God. Creating the
world was a good thing to do, and when each aspect was completed,
"God saw . . . that it was good" (Genesis 1:4). The first parents spoiled
the good world through their sin, but God constantly came back to do
good things for the human race. This means that when you mess up, He
can come back to do good things for you. Ask God to fill you with good
things and to use you this day.

*God, You are great and You are good. Forgive me of my sins,
and come do good things for me today.*

The Holy Spirit is the *Good Spirit.* God is not made good by any good
thing in the world; but things are made good by Him. He will breathe
goodness upon the world when people allow Him to do so. He will touch
your life with goodness when you seek Him. Your good works will not save
you (see Ephesians 2:8-9), nor will they make you good. You become good
when you live in the Holy Spirit and let His goodness make you good.

*Holy Spirit, I choose goodness. I want the perfection of
Your divine nature to fill my heart and make me good.
I want to do the highest good today. Amen.*

Reading: Nehemiah 9:20-27
Key Thought: The Holy Spirit will do good things for you.

11   Jesus: The Son of God with Flaming Eyes and Feet Like Brass

And to the angel of the church in Thyatira write, "These things says the Son of God, who has eyes like a flame of fire, and His feet like fine brass."
REVELATION 2:18

Jesus is the Son of God, who is the judge of all humanity, of both believers and unbelievers. He judges all sin the same. Your sin was judged in the past at Calvary; the unsaved will be judged in the future. No one can hide from His flaming eyes of judgment; no one can run from His brass feet of judgment. The Son of God gave Himself for sin, but the unsaved won't come to Him for forgiveness, so they will meet Him in judgment. Also, the saved that keep on sinning will be judged by the One with flaming eyes.

O Son of God, I know I am forgiven, but sometimes I sin ignorantly. Forgive me now by Your blood (see Ephesians 1:7; 1 John 1:9).

The *Son of God with Flaming Eyes and Feet Like Brass* will see and understand the motives of all believers. You cannot hide from Him the fleshly sin of fornication or the doctrinal sin of heresy. He has all-seeing eyes, so He knows all about the iniquity in your life. Jesus has feet that run quickly to judge sin; you cannot get away with anything. You must deal with your sin before Jesus judges it.

Lord, daily I come to You, searching my heart for hidden sin. I confess my sin; forgive me. I repent and commit myself to live a godly life; cleanse me. I want to live a blameless life; help me. Give me wisdom to recognize temptation in my life, and give me strength to overcome it. I want to please You. Amen.

Reading: Revelation 2:18-29
Key Thought: Deal with your sin, because Jesus knows about it.

12 JESUS: THE SON OF ABRAHAM

The book of the genealogy of Jesus Christ, the Son of David, the Son of Abraham.
MATTHEW 1:1

Jesus is the *Son of Abraham*. Just as every Jew is a son of Abraham because Abraham was the first Hebrew, the father of all, so Jesus was a *Son of Abraham*. The Father in Heaven made great promises to Abraham—promises such as blessing him financially and making his name great. The Father in Heaven promised to bless those who blessed Abraham and to curse those who cursed Abraham. Then the Father in Heaven gave Abraham the greatest promise: that all the world would be blessed because a Jewish Messiah, who would deliver the world, would come through his seed. That's God's promise concerning Jesus Christ.

Lord Jesus, I know that Your birth was predicted and that, in the fullness of time, the Father sent You—born of a woman—to redeem all those who are lost (see Galatians 4:4-5).

Jesus is the *Son of Abraham*, yet the eternal Son of God. Jesus was born 2,000 years after Abraham, yet He lived during Abraham's life. Jesus said, "Abraham rejoiced to see My day and he saw it" (John 8:56). That happened when Abraham prayed to the Lord to save Sodom and Gomorrah (see Genesis 18:23-33); he was interceding to the One who would be his Seed in the future. Now you can pray to Jesus, just as Abraham did. Your prayers will be answered, just as Abraham's prayers were.

Lord Jesus, You answered the request of Abraham, so I know that You can answer my prayers. Teach me persistence in prayer so that I will not quit praying while You're still answering. Amen.

Reading: Matthew 1:1-17
Key Thought: You can get your prayers answered, just as Abraham did.

13 THE HOLY SPIRIT: MY WITNESS

Surely even now my witness is in heaven, and my evidence is on high.
JOB 16:19

But the Holy Spirit also witnesses to us.
HEBREWS 10:15

The Holy Spirit is the Father's *Witness* to your heart. When you don't know what to do, the Holy Spirit will let you know the Father's will, and He will tell you how to do it. When you have doubts, the Holy Spirit will give you assurance. Just as a witness must give an accurate testimony, so the Holy Spirit will tell you what the Father expects from you.

*Holy Spirit, thank You for speaking to my heart. Make me
wise enough to follow Your direction, strong enough to do Your
will and courageous enough to turn from the allurements of the
flesh and the world. Speak; I'm listening.*

The Holy Spirit is the *Witness* to the Father in Heaven. Just as a witness tells what he has heard, so the Holy Spirit will tell all of Heaven that He heard you pray to receive Christ. Just as a witness tells the court what he has seen, so the Holy Spirit will be your *Witness* and tell the Father that He saw your faithfulness and good works on Earth. Just as a witness must tell only what he has seen and heard, not adding his opinion to his testimony, so the Holy Spirit will accurately tell everyone all about you. Don't worry about being forgotten or overlooked in Heaven. The Holy Spirit is your *Witness*, who will testify for you in glory.

*Holy Spirit, thank You for living in my life. Thank You for being the
Witness from the Father to tell me what I should do on Earth. Amen.*

Reading: Hebrews 10:14-25
Key Thought: The Holy Spirit tells everyone in Heaven about your faithfulness.

14 ⬧ JESUS: A FLAG

In that day the offspring of Jesse [Jesus] will be a flag to which the people will rally.
SEE ISAIAH 11:10

Jesus is your *Flag*; rally to Him. The *King James Version* of the Bible calls Jesus an ensign; newer versions call Him a banner (see Isaiah 11:10). In battle, when warriors are separated from their fellow soldiers, they rally to their colors. There's strength and protection in numbers. When you're in a battle against the world, the flesh and the Devil, don't fight your brethren; just rally to Jesus for spiritual victory. Jesus is your *Flag*.

Lord, with so many Christians fighting each other, it's hard to keep my perspective. Help me look to You. Lord, I need eyes to clearly see the issues.

Jesus is a *Flag*; hold Him high so that people can see Him. Remember, Jesus said, "I . . . will draw all peoples to Myself" (John 12:32). You don't have to argue doctrine, baptism or anything else; just hold high the Jesus *Flag*, and He'll draw people to Himself. When the unsaved attack you or Christianity, Jesus is your *Flag*; lift Him up. His followers will rally with you to Him. Just as a flag stands for all the things that soldiers love about their country, so your Jesus *Flag* stands for all the things you love about Him. Sometimes, when warriors defend what they love, they become wounded and need help. Hold high the *Flag* so that the wounded can rally to Jesus. Those closest to the *Flag* can see it best; they will find protection near Jesus. So stay close to Him.

Lord, I will rally to You. I will defend You and the cause of Christianity. I will try to get others to join me and You, our Flag. Amen.

Reading: Psalm 60
Key Thought: Jesus is our rallying *Flag*.

15 ⟩ JESUS: CAPTAIN

For it became him, for whom are all things, and by whom are all things,
in bringing many sons unto glory, to make the captain of their
salvation perfect through sufferings.
HEBREWS 2:10, *KJV*

Jesus is the *Captain* of your salvation. *Archegos*, the Greek word from which this title originates, is also translated "author" and "prince," suggesting that Jesus is your Leader. He is the One who takes the lead in salvation; He died for you. He is the One who provided the complete forgiveness of sin. *THE MESSAGE* calls Jesus "Pioneer" in its translation of Hebrews 2:10. As a Pioneer, He went where no one else could go—He went into the grave of death for you. And He did what no one else could do—He returned alive. Call on your *Captain* today.

Lord Jesus, You are the Captain of my salvation; I owe
everything to You. Thank You for taking the initiative to obtain
my salvation and for making eternal life possible.

Jesus is the *Captain* of your salvation; He left Heaven to become flesh and to live among us. He took the initiative to show you the Father's love. He came to you before you could respond to His love. Now, since He is the *Captain* of your salvation, let Him work out His plan in your life. Just as His salvation is perfect, so He can guide you daily according to the "good and acceptable and perfect will of God" (Romans 12:2). Jesus knows the future, and He knows the plans God has for you (see Jeremiah 29:11). Will you follow your *Captain*?

Lord, I trust You as my Captain; lead my life today.
Help me understand Your will for my life, and then give
me strength to do it. I will obey You today. Amen.

Reading: Hebrews 2:1-10
Key Thought: As the *Captain* of your salvation, Jesus has taken the initiative.

16 THE HOLY SPIRIT: THE SPIRIT OF CHRIST

Searching what, or what manner of time, the Spirit of Christ who was in them was indicating when He testified beforehand the sufferings of Christ and the glories that would follow.
1 PETER 1:11

The Holy Spirit is sent to glorify Christ (see John 16:14). He is the *Spirit of Christ*, who explained in Old Testament times how Christ would come to suffer for sins and enter His glory. Since Christ's coming, the Holy Spirit has brought people to Christ for salvation. He is the Spirit that makes Christ real to you.

Holy Spirit, help me see all that Christ has done for me, and help me magnify Christ in a new and greater way.

The Holy Spirit is the One who is characterized as the *Spirit of Christ* because He delivers Christ's work on the cross to the hearts of people. It is the task of the Holy Spirit to bring people to salvation. In doing this, the Holy Spirit glorifies Christ (see John 16:14-15). Christ and the Holy Spirit are equal members of the Trinity—equal in power, authority, holiness and love. But they are separate Persons in the Godhead. The *Spirit of Christ* wants to magnify Jesus through all you do in your life. You allow the Holy Spirit to make you like Christ when you yield to Him. Because the Holy Spirit is holy, He will make you holy. Because the Holy Spirit is Spirit, He will make you spiritual.

Spirit of Christ, work in my life to bring glory to Jesus through all I do. My prayer is "For to me, to live is Christ" (Philippians 1:21) and "not I, but Christ" (Galatians 2:20, KJV). Amen.

Reading: 1 Peter 1:1-16
Key Thought: The task of the Holy Spirit is to apply the work of Christ to your life.

17 JESUS: CHRIST CRUCIFIED

But we preach Christ crucified.
1 CORINTHIANS 1:23

Jesus is *Christ Crucified*, the Jewish Messiah who was executed by the Romans on a cross. God's people—the Jews—rejected Christ. The Jewish leaders sent Him to be tried in a Roman court. When Pilate wanted to release Jesus, the Jews cried out, "Crucify Him!" (Luke 23:21). It was then that the Roman soldiers nailed Jesus to a cross and crucified Him. Six hours later, He died. Because the Jews allowed Rome to crucify Jesus, they actively rejected Him as their Messiah; yet Jesus died for them and for the world.

Jesus, Your pain was my gain. You died for my sin so that I might
be forgiven. While I'm horrified by the thought of crucifixion,
I worship You for being my Sin Bearer.

Being crucified did not catch Jesus by surprise. He came into the world to die for the world. The Old Testament predicted His crucifixion: "He who is hanged [on a tree] is accursed of God" (Deuteronomy 21:23; see Galatians 3:13). Jesus' death was necessary for Him to be "made a curse" for our sin (Galatians 3:13, *KJV*). When the curse was lifted from us, we were forgiven, we were free from punishment, we were acceptable to the Father. Christ was crucified for us.

Jesus, thank You for the ultimate sacrifice. I will live, because You died.
I will escape the judgment of Hell, because You suffered my judgment.
I will live forever with the Father in Heaven, because You left the Father
to come to Earth to suffer rejection and crucifixion for me. Amen.

Reading: John 19:16-30
Key Thought: Christ was crucified for me.

18 ◆ JESUS: THE POWER OF GOD

But to those who are called, both Jews and Greeks, Christ the
power of God and the wisdom of God.
1 CORINTHIANS 1:24

Christ is the *Power of God* to break the chains of iniquity, to forgive sin and to deliver souls from Hell. He is the *Power of God* to bind Satan, to open the doors of Hell and to take His followers to Heaven. What greater power is there in the world than the power that Christ has over the Evil One? Don't be concerned with those who have the power of money or position, for they can only do things in this life; you should fear God, who has power over the spiritual realm and over the next life.

Jesus, I bow in Your presence. I recognize Your eternal power
in the heavenlies. Forgive me for being so concerned with human
power that I didn't see Your power.

Jesus is the *Power of God*, who gives you great wisdom and insight into God's will for your life. He can give you victory over temptation and liberty over besetting sin. He can work all things together for your good (see Romans 8:28). He can use you in His service and give you the spiritual ability to lead unsaved people to salvation. You need His power in your life. You can release His power into your life today by seeking His presence and yielding to Christ when He comes to you.

Christ, I acknowledge Your presence in my life; it is the only power that
has eternal implications. Thank You for making Yourself available to
me; I claim the power of Your presence today. Amen.

Reading: 1 Corinthians 1:17-31
Key Thought: If you want the power of Christ, you must claim it.

19 THE HOLY SPIRIT: THE SPIRIT OF GLORY

*If you are reproached for the name of Christ, blessed are you, for the
Spirit of glory and of God rests upon you. On their part He is blasphemed,
but on your part He is glorified.*
1 PETER 4:14

The Holy Spirit is the *Spirit of Glory*, who rests on you when you suffer for
your faith. Remember, the Holy Spirit enters your life when you are
saved and helps you in Christian service. But the Holy Spirit has a special ministry when you are persecuted for your faith. He is the *Spirit of
Glory*, who helps you get through pain to experience God's glory. The
Spirit of Glory will help you see God's purpose for suffering. And when
you endure affliction with a victorious attitude, you bring glory to God.

*O Spirit of God, help me endure persecution when suffering comes. Bring
glory to the Father when I go through the valley of the shadow of death.*

The Holy Spirit will glorify the Father when you successfully overcome trials and temptations. He is the *Spirit of Glory*, who will minister to
you in your darkest hour. He is the Spirit of God, who rests upon all that
you do. Invite Him to direct your life today so that you will be ready when
the storms come. Yield to the *Spirit of Glory* so that you can worship today.

*Holy Spirit, guide me to the good things of life. When storms come,
keep me rejoicing and trusting You. Bring glory to the Father
through me, Spirit of Glory. Amen.*

Reading: 1 Peter 4:12-19
Key Thought: The Holy Spirit will give special help to you when you are
persecuted for your faith.

20 JESUS: COUNSELOR

For unto us a Child is born, unto us a Son is given; and the government will be upon His shoulder. And His name will be called . . . Counselor.

ISAIAH 9:6

Jesus is *Counselor*. Isaiah used this name for Jesus when he predicted His birth. It is Jesus' nature to give counsel to those who follow Him, because He knows all things. He can counsel you, because He knows what is best for you today. Jesus does not need to ask anyone what is best for you, because He is described as "wonderful in counsel and excellent in guidance" (Isaiah 28:29). He can show you what to do, if you will listen; and He can guide you, if you will obey.

Lord, I need Your direction today; "Guide me with Your counsel" (Psalm 73:24). You know all about me; I trust Your guidance.

Jesus is the *Counselor*, who will counsel you in many ways. He will guide you from the Scriptures. Study them well to find direction for your life. His solutions are not cookie-cutter answers, because He personally knows you and will apply the Scriptures to your life. Jesus has a plan for you individually; but to find it, you must know Him individually. You can find His counsel through prayer; talk to Jesus about your day. Jesus may also use wise counselors to guide you (see Proverbs 11:14). Then, Jesus may verify His counsel through the circumstances of your life. Jesus is your *Counselor*; what ways will He use to guide you today?

Lord, I will follow these guidelines to discover and follow Your counsel for my life. Amen.

Reading: Proverbs 8—9
Key Thought: Jesus can help us through His counsel.

21 JESUS: DAYSTAR

Ye do well that ye take heed, as unto a light that shineth in a dark place, until the day dawn, and the day star arise in your hearts.
2 PETER 1:19, *KJV*

Jesus is the *Daystar*. Just as the daystar is first seen after the night is ending, so Jesus was first seen after the long, dark night between the Old Testament and the New Testament. Jesus is the Light of the world, who brought salvation to all. When the dark night is filled with fear and discouragement, people lose their way in the dark; they stumble and fall. But the *Daystar* gives them optimism and hope. When hurting people see the first star of the morning, they fight their way through pain, because of the promise of a new day. Jesus is the *Daystar* who promises new opportunities for you this coming day.

Jesus, You are my Daystar of promise. I will not look back on the darkness of my failure. I will not give up in the blackness of despair. I know that help is coming; I will hang on.

Jesus is your *Daystar* who announces that the pain of the night is over. He comes to help you overcome your hurts and forget your defeats. He can forgive the sin of all your failure. He is the *Daystar* who introduces a new future. He can give you strength to be victorious in the day of new challenges.

Jesus, when I see You shining, I know that the night is almost over. I feel optimism from Your presence. Guide me, Daystar, to a better day. Amen.

Reading: 2 Peter 1:19-21
Key Thought: Jesus gives us optimism after a fearful night.

22 THE HOLY SPIRIT: THE SPIRIT OF GRACE

Of how much worse punishment, do you suppose, will he be thought worthy who has trampled the Son of God underfoot, counted the blood of the covenant by which he was sanctified a common thing, and insulted the Spirit of grace?
HEBREWS 10:29

The Holy Spirit is the *Spirit of Grace* who gives people the opposite of what they deserve. People deserve Hell because they have rejected the Father and the Son, but the *Spirit of Grace* offers them Heaven. People deserve misery and oppression because they chose sin, but the *Spirit of Grace* offers them the peaceful will of God. People deserve to be cut off from the Father because they turn their backs on Him, but the *Spirit of Grace* offers to fill them with God's presence and to enrich their lives. Grace is getting the good things of God instead of His judgment. The Holy Spirit wants people to be saved by grace and then to live by grace.

Holy Spirit, I don't deserve the good things of Heaven, but I accept them. I don't deserve grace, but I'm grateful for it.

The Holy Spirit is the *Spirit of Grace* who comes to give you the assurance of salvation so that you can live confidently. He gives you gifts to serve the Father, and He will guide your every step. The Holy Spirit gives you spiritual light to understand the Scriptures, and He will use you as you share the gospel with unsaved people. The Holy Spirit gives hope for life beyond the grave. What good thing do you want from Him?

Holy Spirit, I surrender to Your will; guide me this day. I accept all the good gifts You offer. Use me as I serve You this day. I like grace much more than legalism. Grace is a good way to live. Amen.

Reading: Hebrews 10:26-39
Key Thought: The Holy Spirit will give you much more than you deserve.

23 JESUS: DAYSPRING

The Dayspring from on high has visited us.
LUKE 1:78

The *Dayspring* is like the point on the horizon where the sun first shines. Jesus is the *Dayspring* who shines the light of salvation to your darkened heart. He is the first hope that help is on the way. Jesus is the *Dayspring* who brought you hope for a new life. Jesus can shine in your life to show you where to walk this day.

> *Lord, I need light on my path. If I knew what to do, I would do it. It's hard to have hope when the night is so scary. Shine light on my path today.*

Jesus is the *Dayspring*. Just as the early morning sun shines over the horizon and dispels the darkness of the night, so His light comes to dispel the darkness in our lives. Don't be afraid of last night's darkness that bred ignorance, doubt and despair. Look for the *Dayspring* on the horizon; you'll find His light compelling. Don't complain about darkness; look to the *Dayspring*, the beginning of light. When you originally looked to Christ, He gave you new hope. Just as the morning sun helps you understand your world, so He can enlighten this day's activities. And what the *Dayspring* can do today, He can do tomorrow and the next day. "The path of the just is like the shining sun, that shines ever brighter unto the perfect day" (Proverbs 4:18).

> *Dayspring, be the Sunrise of my life. There are so many paths; I need light to help me choose the right path for today. Amen.*

Reading: Psalm 84
Key Thought: Jesus is the Beginning of your optimism.

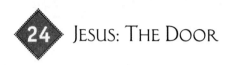

24 · JESUS: THE DOOR

*I am the door. If anyone enters by Me, he will be saved, and will
go in and out and find pasture.*
JOHN 10:9

Jesus is the *Door*, which means that individuals must go through Him to enter Heaven. But a door is also a barrier; it keeps intruders out. Those who reject Jesus cannot enter Heaven. He is the *Door* to keep hypocrites out of the Father's presence. "Not everyone who says to Me, 'Lord, Lord,' shall enter the kingdom of heaven" (Matthew 7:21), Jesus said.

*Lord, You are my Door; I have experienced salvation
through You. Today I have many choices to make. How can I know
which decisions—doors—to take?*

Jesus is the *Door* to salvation; those who come to Him have salvation, because "He who has the Son has life" (1 John 5:12). Some refuse to come to Jesus, believing that all religions are good; but "wide is the gate and broad is the way that leads to destruction, and there are many who go in by it" (Matthew 7:13). Not every door goes to Heaven, and not every door opens to eternal life. Jesus is the only *Door* to Heaven. He is a narrow *Door*; sometimes it's difficult to follow Jesus because "narrow is the gate . . . which leads to life, and there are few who find it" (v. 14). But when you choose according to the Scriptures, you have chosen the right path; you have chosen Jesus, the *Door* of countless opportunities.

*Lord, I walk through the doors that You open today. I will not
lag behind or run ahead of You. I will go where You lead.
You are my Door to life. Amen.*

Reading: Luke 9:23-26
Key Thought: Jesus is your *Door* of opportunity.

25 THE HOLY SPIRIT: THE SPIRIT OF HOLINESS

And declared to be the Son of God with power according to the Spirit
of holiness, by the resurrection from the dead.
ROMANS 1:4

The third Person of the Trinity is the *Spirit of Holiness*. His nature is pure and holy. He is separated from any fault or sin. The Holy Spirit is holy, just as the Father and Son are holy. No sinner can come before the Holy Spirit, because His holiness means that, like the Father and the Son, He is a consuming Fire that judges any sin in His presence. But because Jesus died to forgive your sin, you can live with the Holy Spirit forever. You can confess your sins and come into His presence with your prayers for this day.

I come to You, Spirit of Holiness, asking that You give me holy thoughts
and holy motives. I am only human and can't become godly in myself.

The *Spirit of Holiness* entered your life when you became a Christian. Because you are a finite human, you cannot be holy in yourself; but the presence of the Holy Spirit in your life makes you holy. Invite Him into your body today. When you yield to His control, you will develop holy values and attitudes. When you put the Holy Spirit first in your life, you can have holy thoughts. When you follow the leading of the Holy Spirit, you can have His power to live a holy life. Let the Holy Spirit fill your life with the *Spirit of Holiness*.

Holy Spirit, I want You to make me more godly. Fill me with Your
holiness, and make me spiritual. Amen.

Reading: Romans 7:23; 8:11
Key Thought: Only the Holy Spirit can make you holy.

26 JESUS: WISDOM

Christ . . . the wisdom of God.
1 CORINTHIANS 1:24

Jesus is *Wisdom*, the fountainhead of all truth. All knowledge began with Jesus, and any knowledge you have flows from Him into the world. As *Wisdom* flows into your life, will you share it with the world? Jesus is *Wisdom*; can He guide you because He knows what is best for you?

Lord, I need wisdom in my family relationships; there's so much I don't know. I need wisdom in my work; there's so much I have to do. I need wisdom just to keep my life on an even keel.

Jesus is *Wisdom*. He understands how people should relate to one another and treat each other. As *Wisdom*, He knows how you can perform the tasks that you face this day; let Him help you. As *Wisdom*, He knows where the bumps are located in your road; follow His direction.

As *Wisdom*, Jesus knows how the Enemy will tempt you; let Him protect you. Jesus is *Wisdom*; let Him show you the needs of this day, and let His wisdom solve your problems (see James 1:5).

Lord, I need wisdom to stand against the adversary; I face subtle temptations. I need wisdom to apply Your Word to my life. I confess my foolish pride, which thinks that I am smarter than You. I ask forgiveness for my stubborn will, for refusing to learn from You. I ask for wise guidance throughout this day. Be Wisdom to me. Amen.

Reading: Matthew 7:21-29
Key Thought: Let Jesus teach you what He wants you to know.

27 JESUS: THE SURETY OF A BETTER COVENANT

By so much more Jesus has become a surety of a better covenant.
HEBREWS 7:22

When two people make a contract or sign an agreement, the purchaser puts up a down payment, or surety, to guarantee there's more money to follow. Jesus is the Down Payment of the Father's agreement to redeem you; He is the Surety of the New Covenant. Under the Old Testament Covenant, the blood of a lamb or another substitute animal was the surety. The New Covenant was sealed with His blood; Jesus is the *Surety of a Better Covenant*. Because Jesus is the Son of God, His guarantee of salvation is much better than that of the Old Testament. Also, because Jesus lives in your heart and He stands before the Father for you, you can be sure of going to Heaven when you die.

Lord Jesus, I see You standing at the right hand of the Father for me. I praise You for Your death on the cross, which guaranteed my salvation.

The death of Jesus means much more than the Old Testament sacrifice of a lamb. The blood of lambs was an atonement. *Kaphar*, the Hebrew word translated as "atonement," also means "to cover." In the Old Testament, sins were only covered. "For it is not possible that the blood of bulls and goats could take away sins" (Hebrews 10:4). The death of Jesus took away your sin, and nothing can be charged against you—ever. Jesus is the *Surety of a Better Covenant*.

Lord Jesus, I walk confidently because You are my Surety. I pray with bold faith because You have guaranteed my salvation. I know that when I die, I'll go to see You in Heaven. Amen.

Reading: Hebrews 7:20–8:6
Key Thought: Jesus guarantees my salvation.

28 · THE HOLY SPIRIT: THE SPIRIT OF JUDGMENT

*When the Lord has washed away the filth of the daughters of Zion,
and purged the blood of Jerusalem from her midst, by the spirit
of judgment and by the spirit of burning.*
ISAIAH 4:4

The Holy Spirit is the *Spirit of Judgment* who convicts believers of sin and shows them the error of their ways (see John 16:8-11). Because He is the Holy Spirit, He is grieved when Christians allow sin to exist in their lives (see Ephesians 4:30). If they continue sinning, the Holy Spirit brings judgment and the consequences of sin. The Holy Spirit would rather do good things for the children of God, but as the *Spirit of Judgment*, He must deal with sin. So keep yourself from sin.

*Holy Spirit, I want to obey You and to become more godly. But
temptation is so subtle, and I am weak. Give me strength to live a godly life.*

The Holy Spirit does not warn you about judgment in order to terrify you or make you feel guilty. You don't grow as a believer by legalistically abstaining from sin. The Holy Spirit tells you of sin in order to protect you from harm and to help you live a good life. You grow in the Spirit as you love the Father and obey the Scriptures. But the *Spirit of Judgment* will punish you when you sin. He is also the Spirit of mercy, who forgives you when you cry out for mercy. Don't look to others to learn how the Spirit has judged sin; rather, look to Him alone for grace and mercy.

*Holy Spirit, thank You for both Your mercy and Your judgment in my
life. I look to You alone for Your grace and love. Amen.*

Reading: 1 Thessalonians 5:14-28
Key Thought: The Holy Spirit will judge the sin He finds in the lives of Christians.

29 ▸ JESUS: BLAMELESS

*He is the kind of high priest we need because he is holy and blameless,
unstained by sin. He has now been set apart from sinners, and he has been given
the highest place of honor in heaven.*
HEBREWS 7:26, *NLT*

Jesus was *Blameless*. He lived a blameless life. No one is able to point a finger to accuse Him of saying anything that was not true, nor of doing anything to hurt anyone. Jesus "knew no sin" (2 Corinthians 5:21), and He was "without sin" (Hebrews 4:15). Jesus lived a perfect life so that He could become a sacrifice without blemish for the sins of all (see 1 Peter 1:19). Now look to His life as a pattern for your life. Young people today ask, "WWJD?" (What would Jesus do?). You couldn't find a better example for your life. Let Him be your pattern for living.

*Lord Jesus, I love You for first loving me. Thank You for Your perfect life
and sacrificial death. Help me to follow Your example and live blamelessly.*

Some might think that Jesus was harsh because He accused the Pharisees of being hypocrites, graves and snakes (see Matthew 23:13-33); but what He said was true. Some might think that Jesus was cruel because He drove the moneychangers out of the Temple (see John 2:14-17), but He did what was right. He was *Blameless* in both speech and actions. But Jesus wants to be more than an Example to you of a blameless life; He wants to live in you and make His home in your heart. Jesus wants to give you power to live a blameless life. Begin each day by yielding to His guidance, and when you feel resentful and angry, yield to His control.

*Lord, I will learn about You and follow Your example. Help
me live a blameless life today. Amen.*

Reading: Mark 14:10-11; 43-46
Key Thought: Jesus' perfect life is our example.

JESUS: YOUR HOLY SERVANT

For truly against Your holy Servant Jesus, whom You anointed, both Herod and Pontius Pilate, with the Gentiles and the people of Israel, were gathered together.
ACTS 4:27

Jesus is the *Holy Servant*, whom the Father has anointed. Jesus assumed the threefold office of prophet, priest and king. Just as an Old Testament prophet was anointed before ministering a word of the Lord, so the Father anointed Jesus to deliver the message of salvation to the world. Likewise, as a Temple priest was anointed to make an offering for sin, so the heavenly Father anointed Jesus to make an offering for the sins of the world. Just as a king was anointed to rule his kingdom, so the Father anointed Jesus to enter the hearts of believers and to rule their lives. Did you know that the title "Christ" comes from the Hebrew root that means "anointed"? So Jesus' title is Christ, the anointed One.

Lord Jesus, You are my Prophet, Priest and King.
Come with the message of salvation and sit upon the throne
of my life to rule my thoughts and actions.

Jesus is the *Holy Servant* of the Father. The Father sent Jesus to do His will. He sent Jesus to live without sin among people. He sent Him to do mighty miracles and to demonstrate His love. He sent Jesus to die for all and to rise from the dead so that they might have life. Jesus was the *Holy Servant* of the Father for you.

Lord Jesus, just as You were the Holy Servant of the Father, so I want
to be Your servant. Just as You were anointed by the Father to do Your
work, I want Your anointing in my life. Come use me today.

Reading: Acts 4:23-31
Key Thought: Jesus was the Servant of the Father.

DECEMBER

1 THE HOLY SPIRIT: THE SPIRIT OF LIFE

For the law of the Spirit of life in Christ Jesus has made
me free from the law of sin and death.
ROMANS 8:2

The Holy Spirit is the *Spirit of Life* who gives eternal life to all who believe in Jesus Christ. Unsaved people will follow the law of sin because they are born with a sin nature (see Romans 3:23). But all those who are born again can be free from the law of sin (see 8:2). The Holy Spirit gives them this freedom when they claim His victory. All who put their trust in Christ Jesus should live by the new law of the *Spirit of Life.* Also, because laws come from God, the *Spirit of Life* gives you a new nature, which has new laws and new desires, to control your life. Don't follow the old laws of sin; follow the new laws of the Holy Spirit.

Holy Spirit, thank You for being the Spirit of Life in me. Thank You for
giving me new desires so that I can live above the law of sin and death.

The *Spirit of Life* has delivered you from the law of sin and death so that you don't automatically have to surrender to your old nature. Sin doesn't have to control your life. The *Spirit of Life* can give you power to overcome temptation. Also, the forces of sin and death cannot dictate your future. The *Spirit of Life* will deliver your soul to God at the moment of your death. You may die physically, but your body will be raised in the future, because of the *Spirit of Life* within you.

Holy Spirit, I yield to Your control of my life; live freely in
me. Give me Your power to overcome temptation and to live
a godly life for You. Amen.

Reading: Job 19:23-29
Key Thought: The Holy Spirit gives you life to overcome the law of sin and death.

2 Jesus: A Merciful and Faithful High Priest

Therefore, in all things He had to be made like His brethren, that He might be a merciful and faithful High Priest in things pertaining to God, to make propitiation for the sins of the people.
HEBREWS 2:17

In order to forgive our sins, Jesus was made flesh so that He could identify with us. The Bible says, "He had to be made like His brethren" (Hebrews 2:17), so that He could be a *Merciful and Faithful High Priest.* Jesus didn't forgive our sins without feeling or empathy. If He had done that, salvation would be impersonal and antiseptic. But when Jesus became human, He understood our temptations because He "was in all points tempted as we are, yet without sin" (4:15). Therefore, Jesus feels for us. He is merciful, not vindictive or judgmental. Because Jesus is a merciful High Priest, you can go to Him for help.

Lord Jesus, I come to You for forgiveness. Thank You for understanding my weakness.

Jesus did more than a human high priest did; He is faithful even when we are not faithful. Just as there are stories of priests in the Old Testament who were not faithful to their office, so the Scriptures describe Him as a faithful High Priest. He was human as we are, so He understood human weaknesses. Even though we may disappoint Him, He never once was a disappointment to Himself or to the Father. Because He is faithful, He was able to make propitiation (satisfaction) for our sins.

Lord Jesus, You have never disappointed me, even though I have disappointed You. Even in my weakness, You forgive my sins. I'm thankful for Your mercy and faithfulness. Amen.

Reading: Hebrews 2:17-18
Key Thought: Jesus became flesh so that He could be a *Merciful and Faithful High Priest* for my sins.

THE HOLY SPIRIT: THE SAME SPIRIT

But one and the same Spirit works all these things, distributing
to each one individually as He wills.
1 CORINTHIANS 12:11

The Holy Spirit is the *Same Spirit* who delivered salvation to you, and He is also the *Same Spirit* who gave you spiritual gifts. There's only one Holy Spirit (see Ephesians 4:4), and He is the *Same Spirit* who works in your heart. But He's also the *Same Spirit* who works in the heart of every believer all over the world. How can He be everywhere—equally—at the same time? He is omnipresent because He is God. He is the *Same Spirit* who's ministering in Heaven right now and the *Same Spirit* who wants to minister to you. Yield to His control.

Holy Spirit, forgive my limited view of who You are. Come stretch my
faith today. Teach me greater faith to see all You do.

The Holy Spirit is the *Same Spirit* who created the world (see Genesis 1:2) and the *Same Spirit* who formed you in the womb (see Psalm 139:13-16). He is the *Same Spirit* who gives the gift of faith to one and the *Same Spirit* who gives the gift of healing to another (see 1 Corinthians 12:9). He is "the same Spirit [who] works all these things" (v. 11). Look to Him for every spiritual need in your life.

Holy Spirit, thank You for reminding me of Your larger work in the
world and Your specific work in my life. Help me refocus my thoughts
on Your power so that I can do the things that I have to do today. Amen.

Reading: Psalm 139:7-16
Key Thought: The Holy Spirit does all the work of God.

4 JESUS: THE SAVIOR OF THE BODY

*For the husband is head of the wife, as also Christ is head of the
church; and He is the Savior of the body.*
EPHESIANS 5:23

Salvation means that you are in Jesus and He is in you. At your conversion, Jesus came into your heart to become a part of your life. At the same time, you were placed into His Body (the universal Church). "You in Me, and I in you" (John 14:20). All those in Christ are saved, because He is the *Savior of the Body*. If you are in Him, then you are saved. Have you invited Christ into your life?

*Lord, I have asked You into my heart, and You saved me. Thank You
for coming into my heart to become a part of my life. Also, I thank
You for placing me into Your Body to be a part of Your life.*

Jesus is the *Savior of the Body*. When you were placed into Him, you were saved from your past penalty of sin and from your future punishment in Hell. And today, you are being saved from servitude to sin. Jesus has a wonderful plan for each one in the Church. He wants you to love Him, serve Him and worship Him. Think about it. Jesus has a great and wonderful purpose for your life.

*Lord Jesus, thank You for a new, purposeful life. Because I am in You, I
will try to do Your will today. Because You are in Me, give me strength
to do Your purpose. I need Your power today. Amen.*

Reading: Isaiah 53:8-12
Key Thought: You are in Jesus, and He is in you.

5 | The Holy Spirit: The Spirit of Your Father

But when they deliver you up, do not worry about how or what you should speak. For it will be given to you in that hour what you should speak; for it is not you who speak, but the Spirit of your Father who speaks in you.
MATTHEW 10:19-20

Just as you have a spirit that is the intrinsic nature of who you are, so the *Spirit of Your Father* in Heaven has the same nature as the heavenly Father yet is a separate Person from the Father. The Holy Spirit is the third Person of the Godhead and is the *Spirit of the Father*. The Father sends the Holy Spirit to do His work. When you are persecuted, the Holy Spirit will indwell you to help you. When you don't know what to say to your oppressors, the Holy Spirit will speak through you. The *Spirit of Your Father* will give you "in that hour what you should speak" (Matthew 10:19).

> *Holy Spirit, I trust You to help me in my hour of trial. Help me to glorify the Father in all that I endure.*

The Holy Spirit was sent by the Father to give you boldness to speak when people reject your testimony. He will give you wisdom to know what to say and when to say it. At times, He will give you soft words that turn away wrath (see Proverbs 15:1) and, at other times, stinging words to convict of sin. But most of all, He will give you convincing words that will sink deep in the hearts of your listeners. The Holy Spirit will not speak of Himself; He will glorify Christ (see John 16:13).

> *Holy Spirit, fill my life with Your presence. Put words in my mouth that I need to speak, and use my testimony for Your glory. Amen.*

Reading: Matthew 10:5-42
Key Thought: The Holy Spirit will give you what to say when you are persecuted for your faith.

6 ◆ JESUS: THE LORD STRONG AND MIGHTY

Who is this King of glory? The LORD strong and mighty, the LORD mighty in battle.
PSALM 24:8

Jesus is the *Lord Strong and Mighty*. Come to Him when you're afraid and losing the battle. Lean on Him when you're weak. He knows that the battle is fierce, because He was mocked, beaten and finally crucified. The Lord knows how you feel in opposition, so come to Him for help. Let His wisdom guide you, and let His strength protect you. Don't give in to the Enemy, and don't give up. Draw energy from the Lord, for Jesus is the *Lord Strong and Mighty*. What do you need from Him?

Lord Jesus, I feel comforted when You are near. I get energy from You each day to face my problems. I feel secure in Your presence. Come help me face my problems today.

The world expects Christians to be weak and soft. That's because they've only seen one side of Jesus' personality. They've only heard about His gentleness toward those who suffer and His mercy to forgive. But Jesus has another side. He is the *Lord Strong and Mighty*. He will defeat the armies of Satan in the last battle. He will judge and condemn those who reject Him. So today, He will fight for you. When you are attacked, He will defend you. When the battle gets fierce, get close to Him. Jesus is the *Lord Strong and Mighty* in battle; call on Him for help right now.

Lord, I will not let the Enemy scare me; nor will I be afraid in battle. I look to You to fight my battles. Amen.

Reading: Psalm 7
Key Thought: Trust God's strength in your battles.

7 THE HOLY SPIRIT: THE HELPER

But the Helper, the Holy Spirit, whom the Father will send in My name, He will teach you all things, and bring to your remembrance all things that I said to you.
JOHN 14:26

The Holy Spirit is the *Helper* who was sent by Jesus for your assistance. Because Jesus couldn't remain in His physical body on Earth, He sent the Holy Spirit to indwell you. He can help you overcome sin and live a godly life. He can help you understand Scripture and give you power to live by its principles (see John 14:26). He can help you intercede to the Father so that your prayers will be answered (see Romans 8:26-27). He can guide your daily life and help you walk in righteous paths (see Galatians 5:16). If you need help in your Christian life, call on the *Helper* today.

> *Holy Spirit, I need You this day. I am weak; strengthen my will to follow You. I am limited; help me live above my weaknesses. I need Your help in every area of my life.*

The Holy Spirit is your *Helper*. Even though the Holy Spirit has many titles, *"Helper"* was Jesus' favorite name for Him, because it reflects what He does for us. The Holy Spirit helps people become Christians; then He helps them live godly lives. He helps them in Christian service. No matter what your need, call on the Holy Spirit today. He will help you.

> *Holy Spirit, I bow humbly, asking You for help. I need Your power to overcome temptation. I need Your light to understand Scriptures. I need Your guidance to walk the straight and narrow path. I need Your wisdom to solve my problems. I need Your presence to enrich my life and give me new purpose to live today. Amen.*

Reading: Romans 8:26-27
Key Thought: Jesus sent the Holy Spirit to help you live the Christian life.

8   JESUS: A MAN APPROVED BY GOD

Ye men of Israel, hear these words; Jesus of Nazareth, a man approved of God among you by miracles and wonders and signs, which God did by him in the midst of you, as ye yourselves also know.
ACTS 2:22, KJV

Jesus was a *Man Approved by God*. He was born of a virgin without a sin nature. He lived a perfect life without committing sin (see 1 Peter 2:22). But that doesn't mean He didn't have difficulties; He was tempted in all points as you are (see Hebrews 4:15), yet He didn't give in to temptation. Just as a sacrificial lamb had to be perfect to offer for sin, so Jesus lived a perfect life so that He could be a substitute for your sin. As the perfect Man, Jesus was approved by God to take your punishment and guilt.

Lord Jesus, I know that You became flesh for me. Thank You for Your human perfection. I worship You and cry out with other worshipers, "You are worthy, O Lord, to receive glory and honor and power" (Revelation 4:11). Yes, I say, "Worthy is the Lamb" (5:12).

Jesus was a *Man Approved by God*. Because God loved the world so much, He sent Jesus to redeem all people. Because Jesus is both the eternal God and the perfect Man, He qualified to be the Sin Bearer for all. Because He died, was buried and on the third day arose from the dead, the Father attested to His work and accepted all who believed on Him (see John 20:31).

Lord Jesus, I bow before You, thanking You for salvation. You were the only One who could have redeemed the sinful race. You are the One who redeemed me. Amen.

Reading: Acts 2:22-36
Key Thought: The Father approved the human life of Jesus.

9   THE HOLY SPIRIT: GENEROUS SPIRIT

Restore to me the joy of Your salvation, and uphold me by Your generous Spirit.
PSALM 51:12

The Holy Spirit is the *Generous Spirit* of God. He gives freely to you, because it's His nature to give. He gives eternal life, because Jesus died so that you can live forever. He gives abundantly, because the Scriptures promise life and life more abundantly (see John 10:10). He gives richly, because the riches of Heaven are His to give to you. He gives generously, because you have need of the generous blessings from Heaven. What do you want Him to give you today?

> *Holy Spirit, I am human flesh. I have earthly needs, but I also have spiritual needs. I have multiple problems, so I need Your power and guidance. Give me your generous blessings today.*

The Holy Spirit is the *Generous Spirit*. Some think that the Holy Spirit is a warehouse filled with blessings for Christians. But that is a wrong picture, because a warehouse can give out and become empty, but the Holy Spirit can never become empty or run out of blessings. Rather, the Holy Spirit is the Source of blessing. He is the *Generous Spirit* who gives eternally, because He is the unlimited Source of God's supply. He is the *Generous Spirit* who gives Himself freely to all believers. What more do you need than the Holy Spirit?

> *Holy Spirit, I need You more than the blessings I seek. I need You more than anything else. Fill my life with Your presence.*
> *Be generous; give me everything I can contain. Amen.*

Reading: Psalm 51
Key Thought: The Holy Spirit is the Blessing you need.

10   JESUS: A STONE CUT OUT OF THE MOUNTAIN

Inasmuch as you saw that the stone was cut out of the mountain without hands,
and that it broke in pieces the iron, the bronze, the clay, the silver, and the gold—
the great God has made known to the king what will come to pass after this. The
dream is certain, and its interpretation is sure.
DANIEL 2:45

When King Nebuchadnezzar saw the great image in a dream, he saw four coming, world-ruling empires: Babylon, Media-Persia, Greece and Rome (see Daniel 2:31-45). In the end times, the Roman Empire will be revived briefly. Then a stone will be cut out of the mountain to smash the revived Roman world empire. Jesus is the *Stone Cut Out of the Mountain* who will crush the kingdoms that oppose God; and then Jesus will rule the earth. Where earthly things look discouraging and you think that governments are out of control, remember that one day Jesus will rule the earth. But for now, His influence is exercised through individuals as He rules the hearts of people. Let Jesus influence your world by ruling your heart.

Lord Jesus, I want Your influence to flow through me today. Help me
feel Your presence, and help me experience Your power.

Until Jesus returns as a *Stone Cut Out of the Mountain*, He will not directly rule the world but will influence the world through secular rulers. The hearts of the rulers are in the Lord's hands, and He influences them concerning His will (see Proverbs 21:1). Most of the rulers of government do not recognize the Lord's authority over them, but without Him they could do nothing. Pray for the rulers over you so that the Lord can rule their lives and influence your nation for righteousness (see 1 Timothy 2:1-5). Your prayer for the rulers over you is your contribution to better government and a better life.

Lord Jesus, I pray for those who rule my nation; help them follow
principles of righteousness and justice. Amen.

Reading: Daniel 2
Key Thought: Now Jesus rules through the hearts of people, but one day He will rule directly.

11 THE HOLY SPIRIT: HIS VOICE

For He is our God, and we are the people of His pasture, and the sheep of His hand.
PSALM 95:7

Therefore, as the Holy Spirit says: "Today, if you will hear
His voice, do not harden your hearts."
HEBREWS 3:7-8

The Holy Spirit is the *Voice* of God. No matter how far you wander, He will call out to you. No matter how hard your heart, you can't block out His *Voice*. He could speak audibly, but He usually speaks directly from His heart to yours. The Holy Spirit doesn't want you to miss His *Voice* or misunderstand what He is saying. His message is simple: "The Father loves you, and the Son died for you; now the Holy Spirit is calling you back into fellowship with them."

Lord, You are my Shepherd, and I am Your sheep. You make me lie
down in green pastures; You lead me beside still waters. You restore my
soul. When I begin to stray, You call me back into Your fold. When I
wander out of sight, I hear Your Voice calling out for me. I strayed into
the valley of death, and I fell into a rocky pit. I thought that I would die
and You would never know what happened to me. Then in the night, I
heard Your Voice calling through the darkness. Forgive my hard heart;
come rescue me, and bring me back into your fold.

The Holy Spirit is the *Voice* of God. He will prepare a table full of food for you, and He will pour oil into your wounds for healing. He will take you where you can dwell in the house of the Lord forever.

Holy Spirit, I hear Your Voice; I want to come home to You. My pit is
deep; come lift me up and free me from the control of sin. I read that the
Shepherd put the straying lamb on His shoulder and returned home
rejoicing (see Luke 15:4-5). Lord, bring me home. Amen.

Reading: Psalm 29
Key Thought: The Holy Spirit calls you back to God.

12 ◆ JESUS: RULER

But you, Bethlehem Ephrathah, though you are little among the thousands of Judah, yet out of you shall come forth to Me the One to be Ruler in Israel, whose goings forth are from of old, from everlasting.

MICAH 5:2

Jesus is the *Ruler* in Israel. As *Ruler*, He has ownership of Israel, which means that He has authority and control over the nation. In His first coming to Earth, "He came to His own [the Jews], and His own did not receive Him" (John 1:11). The leaders rejected Jesus, telling Pilate, "We have no king but Caesar!" (19:15). Jesus had the biological right to be King, because of His birth. Jesus had the divine right, because He was sent from Heaven. Because the Jews only wanted outward peace and outward prosperity, they rejected Jesus' offer of inner peace and inward blessing. They did not want Jesus to rule their hearts.

Lord Jesus, even though the Jewish leaders rejected You, I accept Your rule in my life. Even though many still reject Your authority over them, I want You to rule my heart. I accept Your authority and control.

Jesus was born a *Ruler*, but He can't rule everyone unless He rules each one individually. And Jesus can't rule individuals unless His authority starts within the heart of each one. Jesus doesn't force outward conformity; He wants each one to give joyful obedience from the heart. Since Jesus' kingdom is peace and righteousness, He gives peace to those who willingly obey Him. He gives power to live righteously to those who love Him. Will you let Jesus be your *Ruler* today?

Jesus, I choose You to be my Ruler; come give me power to live a righteous life. I serve You out of love; give me inner peace and assurance. Amen.

Reading: Micah 4:1—5:4
Key Thought: Jesus must first rule inwardly before He will rule outwardly.

13 THE HOLY SPIRIT: THE SPIRIT OF WISDOM

*The Spirit of the LORD shall rest upon Him, the Spirit of wisdom
and understanding, the Spirit of counsel and might, the Spirit
of knowledge and of the fear of the LORD.*
ISAIAH 11:2

The Holy Spirit is the *Spirit of Wisdom*; He knows all things, actual and potential. He knows everything you do and all the thoughts you think. Nothing is hidden from Him. Let the Holy Spirit speak to your heart. He can help you discern the true nature of things in your life. The *Spirit of Wisdom* can teach you more about yourself. You can learn about truth, and you can get wisdom to understand things as they are. As you learn more about the Holy Spirit in the Scriptures, He'll take away your blindness.

*O Spirit of truth, I need Your presence to help me sort out the motives of
people around me. People take advantage of me and hurt me. I need to
look beneath the appearance of things for a better understanding of
what's happening in my world. I don't want to be deceived, but rather, I
want to be an efficient servant for You.*

The *Spirit of Wisdom* cannot be fooled by the images that people portray, nor can you hide anything from Him. He looks behind the masks that people use to cover their motives. He sees the real person. Let Him show you what He sees, and let Him transform you to be like Christ.

*O Spirit of Wisdom, help me be honest in all things. When You show me
my real self, don't overwhelm me with my weaknesses and sin. Give me
wisdom to accept myself. Give me wisdom to overcome my weaknesses
to be like Christ. Give me wisdom to live this day. Amen.*

Reading: Proverbs 2—3
Key Thought: The Holy Spirit will help you to honestly understand yourself.

14 JESUS: A SACRIFICE TO GOD

And walk in love, as Christ also has loved us and given Himself for us,
an offering and a sacrifice to God for a sweet-smelling aroma.
EPHESIANS 5:2

Jesus is a *Sacrifice to God* for the sins of the world. When He sacrificed His life for the entire world, it was the greatest gift that could be given. Jesus is the Son of the Father, but He sacrificed His position for you. Jesus is the second Person of the Trinity, but He sacrificed His rights for you. Jesus is the eternal Lord of the universe, but He sacrificed the riches of Heaven for you. Because He was a *Sacrifice to God* for you, He wants you to sacrifice your life to Him. He wants you to demonstrate your love for Him, just as He demonstrated His love for you.

Jesus, You gave up the royal palaces of Heaven to be born in a stable. You
gave up everything for me; I will not give You anything less than my heart.

Jesus is a *Sacrifice to God* and a sweet-smelling Aroma that pleased the Father (see Ephesians 5:2). He has given you the example of sacrificial love when He said, "I lay down My life. No one takes it from Me" (John 10:17-18). Jesus sacrificed Himself because He loved you; now He wants you to walk in love. "A new commandment I give to you, that you love one another; as I have loved you" (13:34).

Jesus, my love for You is shallow in comparison to
Your love for me. Forgive my weak love, and stir me to more
sacrifices for You this day. Amen.

Reading: Ephesians 5:1-8
Key Thought: Jesus sacrificed Himself for us because He loved us.

THE HOLY SPIRIT: THE HOLY SPIRIT SENT FROM HEAVEN

Those who have preached the gospel to you by the Holy Spirit sent from heaven.
1 PETER 1:12

The third Person of the Trinity is the *Holy Spirit Sent from Heaven*. He came upon the believers in the Upper Room on the Day of Pentecost; they had been praying for 10 days. When He came upon them in power, they witnessed to unsaved people, and more than 3,000 people believed in Jesus Christ and were baptized (see Acts 2:41). If you need power to witness, seek the *Holy Spirit Sent from Heaven*. He can fill you with His divine presence so that people will be saved through your influence.

Holy Spirit, come upon me today. Show me what I must do to win my unsaved friends to Christ. Use my testimony to draw people to Jesus Christ. Use my words to motivate people to salvation.

You need the power of the *Holy Spirit Sent from Heaven*. Just as the Holy Spirit used the witness of the disciples at Pentecost, so He can use you. But just as they were faithful in prayer, so you must intercede for your lost friends. Just as they searched their hearts to repent of secret sin to be effective vessels, so you must be clean and useable. The Holy Spirit was sent from Heaven to convict people of sin and to draw them to salvation. Let Him use you today as a witness.

Holy Spirit, show me anything that hinders my witness, and I will repent and receive cleansing by the blood of Jesus. I want to be used by You to bring people to Jesus. Amen.

Reading: John 15:26-27
Key Thought: The Holy Spirit was sent to use you in soul winning.

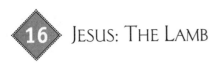

16 ⟩ JESUS: THE LAMB

*These will make war with the Lamb, and the Lamb will overcome
them, for He is Lord of lords and King of kings; and those who
are with Him are called, chosen, and faithful.*
REVELATION 17:14

Lambs provided three basic contributions to Jewish life. Lambs provided wool for clothing and food to eat, and they were the primary animals that Jewish people sacrificed as a symbolic substitution for their sins. Jesus was the ultimate Sacrifice, "the Lamb of God who takes away the sin of the world" (John 1:29). Lambs are gentle; they don't attack or hurt other animals, just as Jesus, the *Lamb*, was gentle to all. Lambs have no natural defense, such as teeth or claws; every other animal was given some form of protection. But Jesus was the defenseless *Lamb* who had no one to defend Him at His trials nor any warrior to protect Him from crucifixion. Lambs are meek, just as Jesus willingly submitted to death. Jesus said, "If My kingdom were of this world, My servants would fight" (18:36).

Lord, You are the meek Lamb slain for me. You are my gentle Savior.

Jesus, the meek *Lamb*, shall return a second time to destroy the evil works of Satan. In the book of Revelation, He is called *Lamb* 27 times to remind the readers that even though Jesus was gentle, He will return to judge evil. He will condemn those who rejected His salvation. The defenseless Jesus, the *Lamb*, will return to rule the world.

*Lord Jesus, You are the Lamb who died for the world. You will return as
the Lamb to judge the world. Amen.*

Reading: Revelation 7:9-17
Key Thought: Jesus, the meek *Lamb*, shall return to judge the world.

17 THE HOLY SPIRIT: THE VOICE OF THE LORD

The voice of the LORD is over the waters; the God of glory thunders; the LORD is over many waters. The voice of the LORD is powerful; the voice of the LORD is full of majesty. The voice of the LORD breaks the cedars, yes, the LORD splinters the cedars of Lebanon. The voice of the LORD divides the flames of fire. The voice of the LORD shakes the wilderness. And in His temple everyone says, "Glory!"
PSALM 29:3-5,7,9

The Holy Spirit speaks to people in many ways; He speaks through inner urges, through prophets and through miracles. The Holy Spirit speaks through the Scriptures. But constantly He speaks through the natural world, because the heavens and stars speak for Him (see Psalm 19:1-6). A powerful hurricane may be God's voice of judgment, or a powerful storm may be His classroom to teach you spiritual lessons. You may be facing financial storms, vocational storms, family storms or the storms of temptation. When the Holy Spirit allows troubling storms in your life, the storms can be the *Voice of the Lord.*

Holy Spirit, make me listen to Your voice in the rain and in the storms of life. Help me become sensitive to Your message; then help me do what You command.

The Holy Spirit speaks to you through intermediate agencies of tornadoes and floods. You don't know what trouble is heading your way, but the Spirit knows. You need to stay close to Him. He can prepare you for the coming storms, just as He can take care of you in the storms; and He can lead you out of the storms. He can make you victorious in spite of the storms. So when the winds begin to blow, don't struggle; listen for the *Voice of the Lord.*

Holy Spirit, I don't want storms in my life; but if they must come, I'd rather have a stormy day with You than a calm day without You. Amen.

Reading: Psalm 29
Key Thought: The Holy Spirit can speak to you through storms.

18 JESUS: LORD (*DESPOTES*)

> *But there were also false prophets among the people, even as there will be false teachers among you, who will secretly bring in destructive heresies, even denying the Lord who bought them, and bring on themselves swift destruction.*
>
> 2 PETER 2:1

Jesus is the Lord (*kurios*) who rules the hearts of those who willingly learn of Him. But Jesus is also the *Lord* (*despotes*) who will force submission on those who reject and deny Him. There are people who claim to know Jesus but who hold false beliefs about Him. Jesus is the Lord (kurios) who gave them the freedom to believe, but He is also the *Lord* (*despotes*) who will punish those who reject the truth of Scripture. That's because they have chosen to reject Him. The Bible describes their rebellion: "They willingly are ignorant" (2 Peter 3:5, *KJV*). Today you have the Scriptures; read its pages, learn of Him, obey its truth and know the Lord (kurios) intimately.

Jesus, I will open the pages of Scripture and learn its teachings. I will obey its truth, and I will submit to Your rule.

Jesus will be the Lord (kurios) to you, and He will bless you because you have yielded to His rule. Pray for those who reject the truth, that their hearts will be turned to righteousness. To those who reject Jesus, He will be the *Lord* (*despotes*) to judge them in the final day. Those who reject the rule of Jesus today will be forced to submit to His decisions and judgment in the future.

Jesus, I want to know doctrine as accurately as possible so that I'll have Your blessing. I want to know You as intimately as possible so that I can be as close as possible to the heart of God. Amen.

Reading: 2 Peter 2
Key Thought: You must recognize the lordship of Christ.

19 THE HOLY SPIRIT: THE WIND

The wind blows where it wishes, and you hear the sound of it, but cannot tell
where it comes from and where it goes. So is everyone who is born of the Spirit.
JOHN 3:8

Just as the Holy Spirit originally blew breath into the lifeless clay body
of Adam to give him physical life, so the Holy Spirit breathed eternal life
into you at salvation. Just as the body without breath is dead, so those
without the breath of the Holy Spirit are spiritually dead. Because you
must be born again to see the kingdom of God, the Holy Spirit breathed
His life into you so that you will have a spiritual rebirth (see John 3:5).
The Holy Spirit is the *Wind* that blows new life into those who believe in
Jesus Christ. Let the Holy Spirit—the breath of God—blow new life into
you.

> *Breathe on me, Wind of God. I'm hot and tired; a gentle, refreshing*
> *wind would feel good right now. The fire of opposition and the hot sands*
> *of this world have worn me out.*

The Holy Spirit is the *Wind* of God who constantly renews believers.
When you think you've walked too far and you feel too tired to go on, let
Him refresh you. For those who are out of breath, He is spiritual oxygen.
You can't see the Holy Spirit working in your life, just like you can't see
the blowing wind. But you can feel the results of an invigorating breeze,
just as you can feel the results of the Holy Spirit. Let Him renew your life.

> *Holy Spirit, You are the Breath of God that I need today.*
> *I can't make it spiritually without Your wind in my sails.*
> *Breathe on me, Breath of God. Amen.*

Reading: John 3:1-8
Key Thought: The wind of the Holy Spirit can renew your life.

20 JESUS: THE CHIEF CORNERSTONE

*Therefore it is also contained in the Scripture, "Behold, I lay in
Zion a chief cornerstone, elect, precious, and he who believes on Him
will by no means be put to shame."*
1 PETER 2:6

Jesus Christ Himself being the chief cornerstone.
EPHESIANS 2:20

Jesus is the *Chief Cornerstone*, the Foundation of Christianity and the Church. He is the *Chief Cornerstone* for your life. Just as a foundation is laid at the corner of a building and the superstructure is built upon it, so Jesus is the spiritual Foundation upon whom you must build your life. He will give you direction about how to live. Rest on Him; He can hold you up. He can give you a secure future. Don't worry; He can hold you steady in the storm. When pressures come, Jesus is a firm Foundation, the *Chief Cornerstone*. Do you need stability in your life today?

*Jesus, thank You for stability. I know I have weaknesses,
and I know where I fail. Thank You for never changing,
for never failing. I will rest on You today.*

Just as a cornerstone shows where the building will be built, so Jesus is the *Chief Cornerstone* who will show how to build your life. He has forgiven your sins, but the Christian life is much more than salvation. You must live for Christ and serve Him. You must build every part of your life on Christ. He will show how you should live and grow. Are you building on His foundation?

*Jesus, I need Your direction in my life. I try to follow You, but sometimes
I get sidetracked in the details of life. Show me what to do today and
what to say. I need help. Amen.*

Reading: 1 Peter 2:1-10
Key Thought: Jesus will give stability to your life.

21 THE HOLY SPIRIT: WATER

For I will pour water on him who is thirsty, and floods on the dry ground; I will pour My Spirit on your descendants, and My blessing on your offspring.
ISAIAH 44:3

The Holy Spirit is *Water* for thirsty people. Some people thirst because they have ignored the Lord. If that's you, drink of the Spirit. Some people need *Water* because they're going through hot, difficult troubles. If that's you, drink of the Spirit. Still others have dry, parched throats because they don't take time to stop for *Water*. Their minds are on other things—good things even—so they forget to drink of the Lord. They forget that spiritual *Water* is necessary, so they don't take time for the Holy Spirit or for the Scriptures, prayer and worship. Your human body can only go so long without water before you lose strength and faint or die. Only when they're thirsty do some people realize how important it is to drink regularly. Have you drunk spiritual *Water* today?

Holy Spirit, You are good Water; I need You daily. Remind me to heed my thirst and to come drink of You daily.

The Holy Spirit's water is more than life sustaining; His water is satisfying. Many people seek happiness through the lust of the flesh, the lust of the eyes and the pride of life; but pandering to the flesh or ego will not bring ultimate happiness. While some of these things will give momentary pleasure, there is nothing more satisfying than fellowshipping with your Creator. Come spend time with the Lord; drink deeply for the greatest experience in life. Aren't you thirsty?

Holy Spirit, I come for refreshing water; fill me. I come because I'll die if I don't drink; revive me. I come because I'm thirsty. Ah, how good Your water is! Amen.

Reading: Isaiah 12
Key Thought: The water of the Holy Spirit is refreshing.

22 Jesus: The Anointed of God

*Then I will raise up for Myself a faithful priest who shall do according
to what is in My heart and in My mind. I will build him a sure house, and he
shall walk before My anointed forever.*
1 SAMUEL 2:35
*The kings of the earth set themselves, and the rulers take counsel together,
against the LORD and against His Anointed.*
PSALM 2:2

Jesus is the *Anointed of God*. The word "anointed" comes from the same
Hebrew word that means "Messiah." When Jesus was born, the people of
Israel were looking for their Messiah-Deliverer to drive their enemies
into the sea. They longed for their Messiah to sit upon the throne of
Israel and to rule them in peace and righteousness. But Jesus didn't
come the first time as a Soldier-Messiah for political deliverance. He
came to rule the hearts of people and to give them principles by which
they could experience inner peace and righteousness. Any sensible king
would prefer to allow the inner compulsion of his subjects to rule them
rather than his using outward coercion. Let Jesus be your personal
Messiah, and let Him be your personal Deliverer. Let Jesus anoint you
this day for the task before you. Let Jesus rule your life.

*Lord Jesus, anoint me with Your strength to live this day; deliver me
from selfishness and temptation. Come sit upon the throne of my heart
to rule my thoughts, feelings and actions.*

Jesus is the *Anointed of God* who can anoint you with a fresh focus and
renewed strength. He can anoint you with confidence and a renewed
determination to live righteously. He can anoint you with His presence
so that you can enjoy His peace. Know Jesus more intimately this day;
that's your key to personal deliverance.

*Lord, I wait for Your anointing. Let the oil of Your presence flow into my
life. Heal me when I hurt, renew me when I'm exhausted, strengthen me
when I'm faint, and revive me when I've lost my vision. Amen.*

Reading: Psalm 2:1-5
Key Thought: The Lord's anointing can enrich your life.

23 ⬦ THE HOLY SPIRIT: THE VOICE OF THUNDER

*The voice of Your thunder was in the whirlwind; the lightnings lit up
the world; the earth trembled and shook.*
PSALM 77:18

The Holy Spirit speaks in the voice of thunder to warn of approaching storms. When lightning flashes, people in the distance see it and know that bad weather is coming. People who don't see lightning can hear the thunder's warning and seek shelter. Thunder is not loud to scare people; but rather, the opposite is true. It is loud to warn people to seek safety and comfort during a storm. The Holy Spirit is the *Voice of Thunder*, telling you that storms are coming to your life. There will be different kinds of storms for different people, such as financial storms, family storms, legal storms and, to others, storms of physical pain, religious persecution and job stress. Life will not always be easy; so listen to the Spirit's warnings. Prepare for difficulties by seeking the protection of His presence.

*Lord, I will listen for Your Voice, which warns me of coming
problems. I will be ready for all things—both the good days and
the bad. I will hide in Your presence.*

The *Voice of Thunder* tells of storms that are far off, when you don't see lightning on the distant horizon. These storms may take a long time to reach you, or they may go around you. So praise God both for sending the storms to teach and for keeping away other storms.

*Lord, I will hide in Your presence when the windstorm tears up my
outer life, and I will praise You when You keep them away. Amen.*

Reading: Psalm 77
Key Thought: The Holy Spirit warns us of coming danger so that we can prepare for it.

24 ▷ JESUS: HORN OF SALVATION

And has raised up a horn of salvation for us in the house of His servant David.
LUKE 1:69

The title for Jesus *"Horn of Salvation"* was a Hebraism that meant "a son" or "heir." When King Hezekiah had no male heir, there was no horn of salvation until God gave him 15 additional years and his first son was born in those years (see 2 Kings 20:5-6). Zechariah praised God for the coming Messiah—the *Horn of Salvation*—who would be the son and heir to David's throne (see Luke 1:69). Zechariah's son—John the Baptist—would introduce Jesus the Messiah to the world. Therefore Zechariah rejoiced and "was filled with the Holy Spirit" (v. 67).

> *Lord God, I praise You for sending Jesus, who was the Son of*
> *David. I praise You for sending Jesus, who is my Savior.*

The reference to "horn" comes from the utensils of that day. The people didn't have water bottles or canteens as we have. They carried liquid in the horn of an animal with the end plugged with soft wood, like a cork. In calling Jesus the *Horn of Salvation*, it is probably a reference to oil that was kept in a horn. Jesus was the oil of fruitfulness; that is, the son of David and the heir to his throne, whom all Israel expected. In application, out of the *Horn of Salvation* comes Jesus pours the oil of fruitfulness upon our lives, giving us spirituality and blessings.

> *Lord Jesus, I wait for You, just as Israel was waiting for her*
> *Messiah. Pour Your oil on my life. I need to experience*
> *Your presence and prosperity today. Amen.*

Reading: Luke 1:57-80
Key Thought: Jesus is the son of David and the heir to his throne, and He pours spiritual blessings on us.

25 JESUS: THE BABE

And this will be the sign to you: You will find a Babe
wrapped in swaddling cloths, lying in a manger.
LUKE 2:12

Jesus is the *Babe* born in Bethlehem, the One born to a virgin. He did not come in a spaceship, nor by some aberrant or bizarre entrance into the world. Jesus existed throughout eternity past, but He "became flesh" (John 1:14) and came as a little baby into the world. He needed a mother to care and love Him, just as any other child did. He played with other children and learned lessons at Mary's knee. Because Jesus was human, He knows your problems. Will you talk to Him about them?

Lord, because You became human, You know how weak I am. I need
strength to stand as a Christian in a non-Christian world. I need
strength to keep on living for You.

Jesus was the *Babe* who grew in "wisdom and stature, and in favor with God and men" (Luke 2:52), so He knows how you must grow both physically and spiritually. Because Jesus was the *Babe* of Bethlehem, He can identify with your weaknesses and help you overcome them. "He learned obedience by the things which He suffered" (Hebrews 5:8); therefore, He can help you through your pain and problems. Look to Jesus for help.

Lord, I have never been spat upon for being a Christian; nor
have I been beaten or nailed to a cross. But I face many hardships.
Life is difficult; can You help me? I look to Your human example;
I'm trusting Your inner strength. Amen.

Reading: Luke 2:1-20
Key Thought: Jesus understands my problems, because He was human.

26 JESUS: HE WHO SANCTIFIES

For both He who sanctifies and those who are being sanctified are all of one, for which reason He is not ashamed to call them brethren.
HEBREWS 2:11

Jesus is *He Who Sanctifies* you. The word "sanctify" means "to set apart." You are set apart to God and set apart from sin. The moment you get saved, Jesus begins sanctifying you. Jesus said, "You in Me, and I in you" (John 14:20). When you were saved, Jesus entered your life; He indwells your life. But also, you were identified with Jesus; you are in Him. This happened so that you might be sanctified, set apart from the world, the flesh and the Devil. He has already sanctified you in Heaven; now you must work it out in your daily life on Earth. You must set yourself apart from sin to live for Him.

Lord Jesus, I want to live a holy life, but it's hard. Help me! I want to experience Your presence daily, but I get distracted. Keep working Your sanctification in my life.

Jesus began a good work in you at conversion, and He will continue to work in your heart (see Philippians 1:6). Listen to His voice, heed His guidance, and let His indwelling presence work itself out in your daily activities. You will not reach perfection in your earthly life, but you can grow toward perfection when you let Jesus strengthen all that you do.

Lord Jesus, thank You for sanctifying me in Heaven.
I want my earthly life to reflect my heavenly position.
Work today in my life to make me like You. Amen.

Reading: Hebrews 2:5-12
Key Thought: I can grow to be like Christ.

THE HOLY SPIRIT: THE SPIRIT WHO IS FROM GOD

Now we have received, not the spirit of the world, but the Spirit who is from God,
that we might know the things that have been freely given to us by God.
1 CORINTHIANS 2:12

The Holy Spirit is the *Spirit Who Is from God*. On the Day of Pentecost, the Holy Spirit was sent to believers who were praying. He came with the sound of a mighty, rushing wind; and He appeared as divided tongues, like fire (see Acts 2:2-3). Just as He came in outward powerful manifestation at Pentecost, so He comes today in powerful inner workings of the heart. The world doesn't think that He's powerful, but who else can give great spiritual insight? Who else can transform a loser into a winner? Who else can break compulsive, addictive habits? Who else can restore harmony to ruptured homes? Who else can cause a self-serving young person to give up everything to minister among unreached tribes? Don't just look for outward manifestations; look for the the *Spirit Who Is from God* to manifest Himself powerfully in your inner person. What He's done for others, He can do for you.

Holy Spirit, I know that You've come from God into the world. Do a
supernatural work in my life; come manifest Yourself in me.

The Holy Spirit is sent from God. Today He comes to let you "know the things that have been freely given to us by God" (1 Corinthians 2:12). Examine all that the *Spirit Who Is from God* can do for you, and claim His work today.

Holy Spirit, come teach me about the blessings that are mine.
I want to walk in and serve with the life-changing power
that is available to me. Amen.

Reading: Acts 18:24-28
Key Thought: God sends the Holy Spirit to transform us.

28 ❖ JESUS: THE FRUIT OF MARY'S WOMB

Then she spoke out with a loud voice and said, "Blessed are you among women,
and blessed is the fruit of your womb!"
LUKE 1:42

Jesus is the *Fruit of Mary's Womb*. The Holy Spirit supernaturally conceived Jesus in the virgin Mary, and nine months later He was born in Bethlehem. Jesus was eternal: "In the beginning was the Word, and the Word was with God, and the Word was God" (John 1:1). He "came forth from the Father" (16:28). While Jesus' spirit and personality came from Heaven, His physical body came from Mary. Jesus can rightly be called the *Fruit of Mary's Womb*. When Mary watched Jesus grow, she saw her physical son developing. The Bible calls Jesus "her firstborn Son" (Matthew 1:25).

Lord Jesus, thank You for becoming flesh to live as
a human being. Thank You for limiting Yourself to be like finite
people so that You could die for them.

Jesus, the eternal God, became fully Man. Jesus, the Man, was fully God. He was the God-Man, always fully God and always fully Man. While we humans can't understand it, we read these apparent contradictions in the Bible and accept them both. They harmonize perfectly in Jesus. As a human, Jesus felt tired, hungry and thirsty. He didn't know who touched Him (see Mark 5:31); and He didn't know the date of His second coming (see Matthew 24:36), though He knew He was coming back. As God, Jesus raised the dead (see Mark 5:38-42), calmed a storm (see 6:47-51) and read people's thoughts (see 2:8). What wonderful *Fruit of Mary's Womb*!

Lord Jesus, thank You for coming to Earth to be born of Mary; I will try
to follow Your example as a Man; I will worship You as God. Amen.

Reading: Luke 1:36-45
Key Thought: From Mary, Jesus received His body, through which He fulfilled His task on Earth.

THE HOLY SPIRIT: THE SPIRIT OF HIM WHO RAISED UP JESUS

29

But if the Spirit of Him who raised Jesus from the dead dwells in you,
He who raised Christ from the dead will also give life to your mortal bodies
through His Spirit who dwells in you.
ROMANS 8:11

Did you see the Trinity in today's verse? First, the *Spirit of Him Who Raised Up Jesus* is the Holy Spirit. Second, the prepositional phrase "of Him" refers to the Father. When the Father decreed Jesus' resurrection, the Holy Spirit was the One who did it. And obviously, Jesus is the third Person of the Godhead. All three persons of the Trinity were active in the resurrection of Jesus, which provided new life for you.

Holy Spirit, thank You for the resurrection of Jesus from the dead, for it
demonstrates that my sins were forgiven. Let my new Christian life be a
testimony for You today.

You get many other benefits from Jesus' resurrection. You were raised with Jesus to a new position in the heavenlies (see Ephesians 2:5-6). You can claim God's blessings, for you are spiritually seated with Christ in glory. You are also indwelt with divine power to live a godly life (see Romans 1:4). Now you can call on the power of Christ for victory over sin. Finally, in the last day, the Father will raise our human bodies through the Holy Spirit, just as the Spirit gave life to the body of Jesus. Let the Holy Spirit work through you today.

Holy Spirit, thank You for the new resurrected life that is available
to me. I want resurrection power to overcome temptation and
adversity. I want my earthly life to reflect my new position in
the heavenlies. Thank You for the promise that my mortal body will be
raised with resurrection power in the last day. Amen.

Reading: Ephesians 2:1-10
Key Thought: The power of the Holy Spirit that raised up Jesus is available to you.

30   JESUS: HE WHO COMES DOWN FROM HEAVEN

For the bread of God is He who comes down from heaven and gives life to the world.
JOHN 6:33

Jesus is *He Who Comes Down from Heaven*; He is the only Person to ever have preexistence. He lived in Heaven before He was born. "I came forth from the Father and have come into the world. Again, I leave the world and go to the Father" (John 16:28), Jesus said. What does that mean to us? Because Jesus came from Heaven—the eternal City—He can give us heavenly life, eternal life. In addition, Jesus knows all about Heaven, because He lived there, so He can tell us how we will live in our future home. Also, Jesus lived with the Father, so He can tell us about going to live with the Father. Because Jesus came from Heaven, He can give us a little bit of Heaven on Earth. He promised that He and the Father would come to live in those of us who love Him and obey Him (see 14:23).

> *Lord Jesus, I worship You, the eternal One. You live from eternity*
> *past to eternity future. I thank You for coming to Earth*
> *to show us the Father, and to die for our sins.*

Jesus is *He Who Comes Down from Heaven* to tell us there's life and glory beyond the grave. If Jesus had not come, we'd live and die like the animals. We'd be without hope for this life and without hope of life after death.

> *Lord Jesus, thank You for giving me reason to live, and thank You for*
> *hope in the next life. Thank You for living in my life and giving*
> *me a little taste of Heaven on Earth. Amen.*

Reading: Revelation 22
Key Thought: Jesus came from Heaven to give us the assurance of going there.

JESUS: HEIR OF ALL THINGS

[God] has in these last days spoken to us by His Son, whom He has appointed
heir of all things, through whom also He made the worlds.
HEBREWS 1:2

Jesus is the *Heir of All Things*, because at the end of this age, all things will be given to Him. But right now, Satan is the god of this world (see 2 Corinthians 4:4). Right now, people are driven by the lust of their flesh, the lust of their eyes and the pride of life (see 1 John 2:16). The curse has hidden the ultimate beauty of nature (see Romans 8:20-21); and the Jews—God's people—are blinded to the gospel (see 2 Corinthians 3:14). But one day, the Father will reclaim all; He will control all things absolutely. And He will give everything to Jesus, because Jesus is the appointed *Heir of All Things*. Then Jesus will share it all with you, because you are His servant. Right now, His servants may suffer physical problems, and some are persecuted and martyred. Right now, it seems like Christians lose one battle for every one they win. Right now, Satan seems to have a strong hand. But one day, Christians will enjoy all things with their Lord.

Lord Jesus, I pray, "Your Kingdom come in my life."
I want You to rule my heart today.

You may not receive your rewards in this life, although you will enjoy many spiritual blessings. And you will not receive everything the moment you die. When Jesus, the Heir, receives all things at the end of the age, then you'll receive your proper reward.

Lord Jesus, I don't serve You for a reward. I serve You for the ultimate
experience of knowing and enjoying Your presence. Amen.

Reading: Revelation 20
Key Thought: At the end of the age, Jesus will receive all spiritual blessings, and He will share them with you.

JESUS

Names, Titles, Metaphors, Figures of Speech and Pictures of Jesus

Advocate with the Father (1 John 2:1)

Alien unto My Mother's Children (Psalm 69:8)

Alive for Evermore (Revelation 1:18)

All and in All (Colossians 3:11)

Almighty Which Is (Revelation 1:8)

Alpha and Omega (Revelation 1:8)

Altar (Hebrews 13:10)

Altogether Lovely (Song of Solomon 5:16)

Amen (Revelation 3:14)

Angel of God (Genesis 21:17)

Angel of His Presence (Isaiah 63:9)

Angel of the Covenant (Malachi 3:1)

Angel of the Lord (Genesis 16:7)

Anointed of God (1 Samuel 2:35; Psalm 2:2)

Another King (Acts 17:7)

Apostle of Our Profession (Hebrews 3:1)

Ark of the Covenant (Joshua 3:3)

Arm of the Lord (Isaiah 53:1)

Author of Eternal Salvation (Hebrews 5:9)

Author of Our Faith (Hebrews 12:2)

Babe of Bethlehem (Luke 2:12,16)

Balm in Gilead (Jeremiah 8:22)

Banner to Them That Fear Thee (Psalm 60:4)

Bearer of Glory (Zechariah 6:13)

Bearer of Sin (Hebrews 9:28)

Beauties of Holiness (Psalm 110:3)

Before All Things (Colossians 1:17)

Beginning (Colossians 1:18)

Beginning and the Ending (Revelation 1:8)

Beginning of the Creation of God (Revelation 3:14)

Beloved (Ephesians 1:6)

Beloved Son (Matthew 3:17)

Better (Hebrews 7:7)

Bishop of Your Souls (1 Peter 2:25)

Blessed and Only Potentate (1 Timothy 6:15)

Blessed for Evermore (2 Corinthians 11:31)

Blessed Hope (Titus 2:13)

Branch (Zechariah 3:8; 6:12)

Branch of the Lord (Isaiah 4:2)

Branch of Righteousness (Jeremiah 33:15)

Branch out of His Roots (Isaiah 11:1)

Bread of God (John 6:33)

Bread of Life (John 6:35)

Breaker (Micah 2:13)

Bridegroom of the Bride (John 3:29)

Bright and Morning Star (Revelation 22:16)

Brightness of His Glory (Hebrews 1:3)

Brightness of Thy Rising (Isaiah 60:3)

Brother (Matthew 12:50)

Buckler (Psalm 18:30)

Builder of the Temple (Zechariah 6:12-13)

Bundle of Myrrh (Song of Solomon 1:13)

Captain of the Hosts of the Lord (Joshua 5:14-15)

Captain of Their Salvation (Hebrews 2:10)

Carpenter (Mark 6:3)

Carpenter's Son (Matthew 13:55)

Certain Nobleman (Luke 19:12)

Certain Samaritan (Luke 10:33)

Chief Cornerstone (Ephesians 2:20; 1 Peter 2:6)

Chief Shepherd (1 Peter 5:4)

Chiefest Among Ten Thousand (Song of Solomon 5:10)

Child Born (Isaiah 9:6)

Child Jesus (Luke 2:27,43)

Child of the Holy Ghost (Matthew 1:18)

Chosen of God (Luke 23:35; 1 Peter 2:4)

Chosen out of the People (Psalm 89:19)

Christ (Matthew 1:16)

Christ a King (Luke 23:2)

Christ Come in the Flesh (1 John 4:2)

Christ Crucified (1 Corinthians 1:23)

Christ Jesus (Acts 19:4)

Christ Jesus Our Lord (2 Corinthians 4:5)

Christ of God (Luke 9:20)

Christ Our Passover (1 Corinthians 5:7)

Christ Risen from the Dead (1 Corinthians 15:20)

Christ the Lord (Luke 2:11)

Cleft of the Rock (Exodus 33:22)

Cloud (1 Corinthians 10:1)

Cluster of Camphire (Song of Solomon 1:14)

Column of Smoke (see Exodus 13:21)

Comforter (John 14:16-18)

Commander of the Hosts of the Lord (Joshua 5:14-15)

Commander to the People (Isaiah 55:4)

Conceived of the Holy Spirit (Matthew 1:20)

Consolation of Israel (Luke 2:25)
Corn of Wheat (John 12:24)
Counselor (Isaiah 9:6)
Covenant of the People (Isaiah 42:6; 49:8)
Covert from the Tempest (Isaiah 32:2)
Covert of Thy Wings (Psalm 61:4)
Creator (Romans 1:25)
Crown of Glory (Isaiah 28:5)

Darling (Psalm 22:20)
David (Matthew 1:17)
Day (2 Peter 1:19)
Daysman Between Us (Job 9:33)
Dayspring from on High (Luke 1:78)
Daystar (2 Peter 1:19)
Dear Son (Colossians 1:13)
Deceiver (Matthew 27:63)
Defense (Psalm 94:22)
Deliverance of Zion (Joel 2:32)
Deliverer (Psalm 40:17)
Desire of All Nations (Haggai 2:7)
Despised by the People (Psalm 22:6)
Dew of Israel (Hosea 14:5)
Diadem of Beauty (Isaiah 28:5)
Door (John 10:9)
Door of the Sheep (John 10:7)
Dwelling Place (Psalm 90:1)

Elect (Isaiah 42:1)
Eliakim (Isaiah 22:20)
Elijah (Matthew 16:14)
Emmanuel (Matthew 1:23)
End of the Law (Romans 10:4)
Ensign of the People (Isaiah 11:10)
Equal with God (Philippians 2:6)
Eternal God (Deuteronomy 33:27)
Eternal Life (1 John 1:2)
Everlasting Father (Isaiah 9:6)
Everlasting Light (Isaiah 60:19-20)
Everlasting Name (Isaiah 63:12)
Excellency (Job 13:11)
Excellency of Our God (Isaiah 35:2)
Excellent (Psalm 8:1,9)
Express Image of His Person (Hebrews 1:3)

Face of the Lord (Luke 1:76)
Fairer than the Children of Men (Psalm 45:2)
Faithful (1 Thessalonians 5:24)
Faithful and True (Revelation 19:11)
Faithful and True Witness (Revelation 3:14)
Faithful Creator (1 Peter 4:19)
Faithful High Priest (Hebrews 2:17)

Faithful Priest (1 Samuel 2:35)
Faithful Witness (Revelation 1:5)
Faithful Witness Between Us (Jeremiah 42:5)
Faithful Witness in Heaven (Psalm 89:37)
Father (Psalm 89:26)
Feast (1 Corinthians 5:8)
Fellow (Zechariah 13:7)
Finisher of the Faith (Hebrews 12:2)
First and the Last (Revelation 1:8)
First Begotten (Hebrews 1:6)
First Begotten of the Dead (Revelation 1:5; "Firstborn from the Dead," NKJV)
Firstborn (Hebrews 12:23)
Firstborn Among Many Brethren (Romans 8:29)
Firstborn of Every Creature (Colossians 1:15)
Firstborn Son (Luke 2:7)
Firstfruit (Romans 11:16)
Firstfruits of Them That Sleep (1 Corinthians 15:20)
Flag (see Isaiah 11:10)
Flesh (John 1:14)
Foolishness of God (1 Corinthians 1:25)
Foreordained Before the Foundation of the World (1 Peter 1:20)
Forerunner (Hebrews 6:20)
Fortress (Psalm 18:2)
Foundation Which Is Laid (1 Corinthians 3:11)
Fountain of Life (Psalm 36:9)
Fountain of Living Waters (Jeremiah 17:13)
Free Gift (Romans 5:15)
Friend of Publicans and Sinners (Matthew 11:9; Luke 7:34)
Friend That Sticketh Closer than a Brother (Proverbs 18:24)
Fruit of the Earth (Isaiah 4:2)
Fruit of Thy Womb (Luke 1:42)
Fullers' Soap (Malachi 3:2)

Gift of God (John 4:10)
Gin (Isaiah 8:14)
Glorious High Throne from the Beginning (Jeremiah 17:12)
Glorious Name (Isaiah 63:14)
Glory (Psalm 3:3; Haggai 2:7)
Glory as of the Only Begotten of the Father (John 1:14)
Glory of God (Romans 3:23)
Glory of His Father (Matthew 16:27; Mark 8:38)

God (Revelation 21:7)
God Blessed Forever (Romans 9:5)
God Forever and Ever (Psalm 48:14)
God in the Midst of Her (Psalm 46:5)
God Manifest in the Flesh (1 Timothy 3:16)
God of Glory (Psalm 29:3)
God of Israel (Psalm 59:5)
God of Jacob (Psalm 46:7)
God of My Life (Psalm 42:8)
God of My Mercy (Psalm 59:10)
God of My Righteousness (Psalm 4:1)
God of My Salvation (Psalm 18:46; 24:5)
God of My Strength (Psalm 43:2)
God Who Avengeth Me (Psalm 18:47)
God Who Forgavest Them (Psalm 99:8)
God with Us (Matthew 1:23)
Good Man (John 7:12)
Good Master (Matthew 19:16)
Good Shepherd (John 10:11)
Goodman of the House (Matthew 20:11)
Governor Among Nations (Psalm 22:28)
Great (Jeremiah 32:18)
Great God (Titus 2:13)
Great High Priest (Hebrews 4:14)
Great Light (Isaiah 9:2)
Great Prophet (Luke 7:16)
Great Shepherd of the Sheep (Hebrews 13:20)
Greater (1 John 4:4)
Greater and More Perfect Tabernacle (Hebrews 9:11)
Greater than Jonah (Matthew 12:41)
Greater than Our Father Abraham (John 8:53,57-58)
Greater than Our Father Jacob (John 4:12)
Greater than Solomon (Matthew 12:42)
Greater than the Temple (Matthew 12:6)
Guest (Luke 19:7)
Guide Even unto Death (Psalm 48:14)
Guide of My Youth (Jeremiah 3:4)
Guiltless (Matthew 12:7)

Habitation of Justice (Jeremiah 50:7)
Harmless (Hebrews 7:26; "Blameless," NLT)
He Goat (Proverbs 30:31)
Head of All Principality and Power (Colossians 2:10)
Head of Every Man (1 Corinthians 11:3)
Head of the Body (Colossians 1:18)
Head of the Corner (1 Peter 2:7)
Health of My Countenance (Psalm 42:11)
Heir (Mark 12:7)
Heir of All Things (Hebrews 1:2)

Helper of the Fatherless (Psalm 10:14)
Hen (Matthew 23:37)
Hidden Manna (Revelation 2:17)
Hiding Place (Psalm 32:7)
Hiding Place from the Wind (Isaiah 32:2)
High and Lofty One Who Inhabiteth Eternity (Isaiah 57:15)
High Priest (Hebrews 5:5)
High Priest After the Order of Melchizedek (Hebrews 5:10)
High Priest Forever (Hebrews 6:20)
High Tower (Psalm 18:2)
Highest Himself (Psalm 87:5)
Highway (Isaiah 35:8)
Holy (Isaiah 57:15)
Holy Child Jesus (Acts 4:27; "Holy Servant," NKJV)
Holy One (Acts 2:27)
Holy One and Just (Acts 3:14)
Holy One of Israel (Psalm 89:18)
Holy Thing Which Shall Be Born of Thee (Luke 1:35)
Holy to the Lord (Luke 2:23)
Hope (1 Timothy 1:1)
Hope of Glory (Colossians 1:27)
Hope of His People (Joel 3:16)
Hope of Israel (Acts 28:20)
Hope of Their Fathers (Jeremiah 50:7)
Horn of David (Psalm 132:17)
Horn of Salvation (Luke 1:69)
Horn of the House of Israel (Ezekiel 29:21)
House of Defense (Psalm 31:2)
Householder (Matthew 20:1)
Husband (Revelation 21:2)

I AM (John 18:6)
Image of the Invisible God (Colossians 1:15)
Immanuel (Isaiah 7:14)
Innocent Blood (Matthew 27:4)
Intercessor (Hebrews 7:24-25)
Isaac (Hebrews 11:17-18)

Jasper Stone (Revelation 4:3)
Jeremiah (Matthew 16:14)
Jesus (Matthew 1:21)
Jesus Christ (Hebrews 13:8)
Jesus Christ the Lord (Romans 7:25)
Jesus Christ, the Son of God (John 20:31)
Jesus of Galilee (Matthew 26:69)
Jesus of Nazareth (John 1:45)
Jesus of Nazareth, the King of the Jews (John 19:19)

Jew (John 4:9)
John the Baptist (Matthew 16:14)
Joseph's Son (Luke 4:22)
Judge of the Quick and the Dead (Acts 10:42; "Judge of the Living and the Dead," *NKJV*)
Judge of the Widows (Psalm 68:5)
Just One (Acts 7:52)
Just Person (Matthew 27:24)

Keeper (Psalm 12:15)
Kindness and Love of God (Titus 3:4)
King Eternal (1 Timothy 1:17)
King Forever and Ever (Psalm 10:16)
King Immortal (1 Timothy 1:17)
King in His Beauty (Isaiah 33:17)
King Invisible (1 Timothy 1:17)
King of All the Earth (Psalm 47:7)
King of Glory (Psalm 24:7-8)
King of Heaven (Daniel 4:37)
King of Israel (John 1:49)
King of Kings and Lord of Lords (Revelation 19:16)
King of Peace (Hebrews 7:2)
King of Righteousness (Hebrews 7:2)
King of Saints (Revelation 15:3)
King of Salem (Hebrews 7:2)
King of Terrors (Job 18:14)
King of the Jews (Matthew 2:2)
King Who Cometh in the Name of the Lord (Luke 19:38)
King's Son (Psalm 72:1)
Kinsman (Ruth 4:14)

Ladder (Genesis 28:12)
Lamb (Revelation 17:14)
Lamb of God (John 1:29)
Lamb Slain from the Foundation of the World (Revelation 13:8)
Lamb That Was Slain (Revelation 5:12)
Lamb Who Is in the Midst of the Throne (Revelation 7:17)
Last (Isaiah 44:6)
Last Adam (1 Corinthians 15:45)
Lawgiver (James 4:12)
Leader (Isaiah 55:4)
Life (John 14:6)
Life-Giving Spirit (1 Corinthians 15:45)
Lifter Up of Mine Head (Psalm 3:3)
Light (John 1:7)
Light of the City (Revelation 21:23)
Light of the Glorious Gospel of Christ (2 Corinthians 4:4)
Light of the Knowledge of the Glory of God (2 Corinthians 4:6)

Light of Men (John 1:4)
Light of the Morning (2 Samuel 23:4)
Light of the World (John 8:12)
Light of Truth (Psalm 43:3)
Light to Lighten Gentiles (Luke 2:32)
Light to the Gentiles (Isaiah 49:6)
Lily Among Thorns (Song of Solomon 2:2)
Lily of the Valleys (Song of Solomon 2:1)
Lion of the Tribe of Judah (Revelation 5:5)
Living Bread (John 6:51)
Living God (Psalm 42:2)
Lord *(despotes*; 2 Peter 2:1)
Lord *(kurios*; John 13:13)
Lord *(rabboni*; Mark 10:51)
Lord Also of the Sabbath (Mark 2:28)
Lord and My God (John 20:28)
Lord and Savior (2 Peter 1:11)
Lord Both of the Dead and Living (Romans 14:9)
Lord from Heaven (1 Corinthians 15:47)
Lord God Almighty (Revelation 16:7)
Lord God of Israel (Psalm 41:13)
Lord God of the Holy Prophets (Revelation 22:6)
Lord God of Truth (Psalm 31:5)
Lord God Omnipotent (Revelation 19:6)
Lord God Who Judgeth Her (Revelation 18:8)
Lord Holy and True (Revelation 6:10)
Lord Jesus (Romans 10:9)
Lord Jesus Christ (James 2:1)
Lord of All the Earth (Joshua 3:11)
Lord of Glory (1 Corinthians 2:8)
Lord of Hosts (Psalm 24:10)
Lord of Lords (1 Timothy 6:15)
Lord of Peace (2 Thessalonians 3:16)
Lord of the Vineyard (Matthew 20:8)
Lord of the Whole Earth (Psalm 97:5)
Lord Our God (Psalm 8:1,9)
Lord Strong and Mighty (Psalm 24:8)
Lord Who Is and Who Was and Who Is to Come (Revelation 1:8, *NKJV*)
Lord's Christ (Revelation 11:15)
Lord's Doing (Matthew 21:42)
Lowly in Heart (Matthew 11:29)

Magnified (Psalm 40:16)
Maker (Psalm 95:6)
Malefactor (John 18:30)
Man (John 19:5)
Man Approved of God (Acts 2:22)
Man Child (Revelation 12:5)
Man Christ Jesus (1 Timothy 2:5)
Man Gluttonous (Matthew 11:19)

Man of Sorrows (Isaiah 53:3)

Man Whom He Hath Ordained (Acts 17:31)

Man Whose Name Is the Branch (Zechariah 6:12)

Manna (Exodus 16:15)

Marvelous in Our Eyes (Matthew 21:42)

Master (*didaskalos*; John 11:28)

Master (*epistates*; Luke 5:5)

Master (*kathegetes*; Matthew 23:10)

Master (*rabbi*; John 4:31)

Master of the House (*oikodespotes*; Luke 13:25)

Meat Offering (Leviticus 2:1)

Mediator (1 Timothy 2:5)

Mediator of a Better Covenant (Hebrews 8:6)

Mediator of the New Covenant (Hebrews 12:24)

Mediator of the New Testament (Hebrews 9:15)

Meek (Matthew 11:29)

Melchizedek (Genesis 14:18)

Merciful and Faithful High Priest (Hebrews 2:17)

Mercy and His Truth (Psalm 57:3)

Mercy Seat (Hebrews 9:5; 1 John 2:2)

Messenger of the Covenant (Malachi 3:1)

Messiah (Daniel 9:26)

Messiah the Prince (Daniel 9:25)

Mighty (Psalm 89:19)

Mighty God (Isaiah 9:6)

Mighty One of Jacob (Isaiah 49:26; 60:16)

Minister of Sin (Galatians 2:17)

Minister of the Circumcision (Romans 15:8)

Minister of the Heavenly Sanctuary (Hebrews 8:1-3)

More Excellent Name (Hebrews 1:4)

Morning Star (Revelation 2:28)

Most High (Psalm 9:2; 21:7)

Mouth of God (Matthew 4:4)

Mystery of God (Colossians 2:2)

Nail Fastened in a Sure Place (Isaiah 22:23)

Name Above Every Name (Philippians 2:9)

Name for Salvation (John 20:31)

Name No Man Knew (Revelation 19:12)

Name of Jesus (Colossians 3:17)

Nazarene (Matthew 2:23)

New Name (Revelation 3:12)

Nourisher of Thine Old Age (Ruth 4:15)

Offering and a Sacrifice to God (Ephesians 5:2)

Offspring of David (Revelation 22:16)

Ointment Poured Forth (Song of Solomon 1:3)

Omega (Revelation 22:13)

One of the Prophets (Matthew 16:14)

Only Begotten of the Father (John 1:14)

Only Begotten Son (John 3:16)

Only Potentate (1 Timothy 6:15)

Only Wise God (1 Timothy 1:17)

Owl of the Desert (Psalm 102:6)

Passover (1 Corinthians 5:7)

Path of Life (Psalm 16:11)

Pavilion (Psalm 31:20)

Peace (Ephesians 2:14)

Peace Offering (Leviticus 3:1)

Pelican of the Wilderness (Psalm 102:6)

Perfect Man (James 3:2)

Person of Christ (2 Corinthians 2:10)

Physician (Luke 4:23)

Place of Our Sanctuary (Jeremiah 17:12)

Place of Refuge (Isaiah 4:6)

Plant of Renown (Ezekiel 34:29)

Polished Staff (Isaiah 49:2)

Poor (2 Corinthians 8:9)

Portion (Psalm 119:57)

Portion of Jacob (Jeremiah 51:19)

Portion of Mine Inheritance (Psalm 16:5)

Potter (Jeremiah 18:6)

Power of God (1 Corinthians 1:24)

Praying in My Name (John 14:14)

Precious (1 Peter 2:7)

Precious Cornerstone (Isaiah 28:16)

Preeminence (Colossians 1:18)

Price (1 Corinthians 6:20)

Price of His Redemption (Leviticus 25:52)

Priest Forever (Psalm 110:4)

Priest of the Most High God (Hebrews 7:1)

Prince and Savior (Acts 5:31)

Prince of Life (Acts 3:15)

Prince of Peace (Isaiah 9:6)

Prince of Princes (Daniel 8:25)

Prince of the Kings of the Earth (Revelation 1:5)

Prophet (John 7:40)

Prophet Mighty in Deed and Word (Luke 24:19)

Prophet of Nazareth (Matthew 21:11)

Prophet Without Honor (Matthew 13:57)

Propitiation (1 John 2:1-2)

Pure (1 John 3:3)

Purifier of Silver (Malachi 3:3)

Quick Understanding (Isaiah 11:3)

Quickening Spirit (1 Corinthians 15:45)

Rabbi (John 3:2)
Rabboni (John 20:16)
Rain upon the Mown Grass (Psalm 72:6)
Ransom for All (1 Timothy 2:6)
Ransom for Many (Matthew 20:28)
Red Heifer Without Spot (Numbers 19:2)
Redeemer (Job 19:25)
Redemption (1 Corinthians 1:30; Luke 21:28)
Redemption of Their Souls (Psalm 49:8)
Refiner's Fire (Malachi 3:2)
Refuge (Psalm 46:1)
Refuge for the Oppressed (Psalm 9:9)
Refuge from the Storm (Isaiah 25:4)
Refuge in Times of Trouble (Psalm 9:9)
Report (Isaiah 53:1)
Reproach of Men (Psalm 22:6)
Resting Place (Jeremiah 50:6)
Restorer of Thy Life (Ruth 4:15)
Resurrection (John 11:25)
Revelation of Jesus Christ (Revelation 1:1)
Reverend (Psalm 111:9)
Reward for the Righteous (Psalm 58:11)
Rich (Romans 10:12)
Riches of His Glory (Romans 9:23)
Riddle (Judges 14:14)
Right (Deuteronomy 32:4)
Righteous (1 John 2:1)
Righteous Branch (Jeremiah 23:5)
Righteous God (Psalm 7:9)
Righteous Judge (2 Timothy 4:8)
Righteous Lord (Psalm 11:7)
Righteous Man (Luke 23:47)
Righteous Servant (Isaiah 53:11)
Righteousness (1 Corinthians 1:30)
Righteousness of God (Romans 10:3)
River of Water in a Dry Place (Isaiah 32:2)
Rock (Matthew 16:18)
Rock of His Salvation (Deuteronomy 32:15)
Rock of Israel (2 Samuel 23:3)
Rock of My Refuge (Psalm 94:22)
Rock of Offense (Romans 9:33)
Rock of Our Salvation (Psalm 95:1)
Rock of Spiritual Refreshment (1 Corinthians 10:4, *TLB*)
Rock of Thy Strength (Isaiah 17:10)
Rock That Is Higher than I (Psalm 61:2)
Rod (Micah 6:9)
Rod out of the Stem of Jesse (Isaiah 11:1)
Root and Offspring of David (Revelation 22:16)
Root of David (Revelation 5:5)

Root of Jesse (Isaiah 11:10; Romans 15:12)
Root out of Dry Ground (Isaiah 53:2)
Rose of Sharon (Song of Solomon 2:1)
Ruler (Micah 5:2)

Sacrifice for Sins (Hebrews 10:12)
Sacrifice to God (Ephesians 5:2)
Salvation (Psalm 27:1)
Salvation of God (Luke 2:30; 3:6)
Salvation of Israel (Jeremiah 3:23)
Samaritan (John 8:48)
Same Yesterday, Today and Forever (Hebrews 13:8)
Sanctuary (Isaiah 8:14)
Sardius Stone (Revelation 4:3)
Saving Strength of His Anointed (Psalm 28:8)
Saviour (Titus 2:13)
Saviour of All Men (1 Timothy 4:10)
Saviour of the Body (Ephesians 5:23)
Saviour of the World (John 4:42; 1 John 4:14)
Scapegoat (Leviticus 16:8; John 11:49-52)
Sceptre of Israel (Numbers 24:17)
Sceptre of Thy Kingdom (Psalm 45:6)
Second Man (1 Corinthians 15:47)
Secret (Judges 13:18)
Secret of Thy Presence (Psalm 31:20)
Seed of Abraham (Galatians 3:16)
Seed of David (Romans 1:3; 2 Timothy 2:8)
Seed of the Woman (Genesis 3:15)
Sent One (John 9:4)
Separate from His Brethren (Genesis 49:26)
Separate from Sinners (Hebrews 7:26)
Serpent in the Wilderness (John 3:14)
Servant (Isaiah 42:1)
Servant of Rulers (Isaiah 49:7)
Servant the Branch (Zechariah 3:8)
Shadow from the Heat (Isaiah 25:4)
Shadow of a Great Rock (Isaiah 32:2)
Shadow of the Almighty (Psalm 91:1)
Shelter (Psalm 61:3)
Shepherd (Psalm 23:1; Isaiah 40:11)
Shepherd of Israel (Psalm 80:1)
Shield (Psalm 84:9)
Shiloh (Genesis 49:10)
Shoshannim (titles of Psalm 45; 69)
Sign of the Lord (Isaiah 7:11)
Siloam (John 9:7)
Sin (2 Corinthians 5:21)
Snare to the Inhabitants of Jerusalem (Isaiah 8:14)
Son (Matthew 11:27)

Son from Heaven (1 Thessalonians 1:10)
Son Given (Isaiah 9:6)
Son of Abraham (Matthew 1:1)
Son of David (Mark 10:47)
Son of God (John 1:49)
Son of Joseph (John 1:45)
Son of Man (John 1:51)
Son of Mary (Mark 6:3)
Son of the Blessed (Mark 14:61)
Son of the Father (2 John 3)
Son of the Freewoman (Galatians 4:30)
Son of the Highest (Luke 1:32)
Son of the Living God (Matthew 16:16)
Son of the Most High (Mark 5:7)
Son over His Own House (Hebrews 3:6)
Son Who Is Consecrated for Evermore (Hebrews 7:28)
Song (Isaiah 12:2)
Sower (Matthew 13:4,37)
Sparrow Alone upon the House Top (Psalm 102:7)
Spiritual Rock (1 Corinthians 10:4)
Star out of Jacob (Numbers 24:17)
Stay (Psalm 18:18)
Stone Cut out of the Mountain (Daniel 2:45)
Stone Cut Without Hands (Daniel 2:34)
Stone of Israel (Genesis 49:24)
Stone of Stumbling (1 Peter 2:8)
Stone Which the Builders Refused (Psalm 118:22)
Stone Which the Builders Rejected (Matthew 21:42)
Stone Which Was Set at Nought (Acts 4:11)
Stranger (Matthew 25:35)
Strength (Isaiah 12:2)
Strength of Israel (1 Samuel 15:29)
Strength of My Life (Psalm 27:1)
Strength to the Needy in Distress (Isaiah 25:4)
Strength to the Poor (Isaiah 25:4)
Strong (Psalm 24:8)
Strong Consolation (Hebrews 6:18)
Strong Lord (Psalm 89:8)
Strong Refuge (Psalm 71:7)
Strong Rock (Psalm 31:2)
Strong Tower (Proverbs 18:10)
Strong Tower from the Enemy (Psalm 61:3)
Stronger than He (Luke 11:22)
Stronghold in the Day of Trouble (Nahum 1:7)
Stumbling Block (1 Corinthians 1:23)

Sun of Righteousness (Malachi 4:2)
Sure Foundation (Isaiah 28:16)
Sure Mercies of David (Isaiah 55:3; Acts 13:34)
Surety of a Better Testament (Hebrews 7:22; "Surety of a Better Covenant," NKJV)
Sweet-Smelling Savor (Ephesians 5:2; "Sweet-Smelling Aroma," NKJV)

Tabernacle for a Shadow (Isaiah 4:6)
Tabernacle of God (Revelation 21:3)
Teacher (Matthew 10:25)
Teacher Come from God (John 3:2)
Temple (John 2:19)
Tender Grass (2 Samuel 23:4)
Tender Mercy of God (Luke 1:78)
Tender Plant (Isaiah 53:2)
Testator (Hebrews 9:16-17)
Testimony of God (1 Corinthians 2:1)
The Christ (1 John 5:1)
Treasure (2 Corinthians 4:7)
Trespass Offering (Leviticus 5:6)
Tried Stone (Isaiah 28:16)
Triumphant Lamb (Revelation 5:6)
Triumphant Son of Man (Revelation 1:12-13)
True Bread from Heaven (John 6:32)
True God (Jeremiah 10:10)
True Light (John 1:9)
True Vine (John 15:1)
True Witness (Proverbs 14:25)
Trustworthy Witness (Revelation 1:5, MLB)
Truth (John 14:6)

Undefiled (Hebrews 7:26)
Understanding (Proverbs 3:19)
Unspeakable Gift (2 Corinthians 9:15)
Upholder of All Things (Hebrews 1:3)
Upright (Psalm 92:15)
Urim and Thummin (Exodus 28:30)

Veil (Hebrews 10:20)
Very Great (Psalm 104:1)
Very Present Help in Trouble (Psalm 46:1)
Victory (1 Corinthians 15:54)
Vine (John 15:5)
Voice (Revelation 1:12)

Wall of Fire (Zechariah 2:5)
Wave Offering (Leviticus 7:30)
Way (John 14:6)
Way of Holiness (Isaiah 35:8)

Weakness of God (1 Corinthians 1:25)
Wedding Garment (Matthew 22:12)
Well of Salvation (Isaiah 12:3)
Wisdom (1 Corinthians 1:25)
Wisdom of God (1 Corinthians 1:24)
Wise Master Builder (1 Corinthians 3:10)
Witness (Judges 11:10)
Witness (Job 16:19)
Witness to the People (Isaiah 55:4)
Wonderful (Isaiah 9:6)
Wonderful Counselor (Isaiah 9:6)
Word (John 1:1)
Word of God (Revelation 19:13)
Word of Life (1 John 1:1)
Worm and No Man (Psalm 22:6)
Worthy (Revelation 4:11; 5:12)
Worthy Name (James 2:7)

Worthy to Be Praised (Psalm 18:3)

X (an unknown quantity; see Revelation 19:12)

Yokefellow (Matthew 11:29-30)
Young Child (Matthew 2:11)

Zaphnath-Paaneah (Genesis 41:45)
Zeal of the Lord of Hosts (Isaiah 37:32)
Zeal of Thine House (Psalm 69:9; John 2:17)
Zerubbabel (Zechariah 4:7,9)

Source: Elmer L. Towns, *The Names of Jesus* (Denver, CO: Accent Publications, 1987).

JESUS

Preeminent Pronouns of Jesus in Scripture

He That Cometh (Matthew 11:14; Luke 7:19)

He That Cometh After Me (John 1:15,27)

He That Cometh in the Name of the Lord (Matthew 21:9)

He That Cometh into the World (John 11:27)

He That Filleth All in All (Ephesians 1:23)

He That Hath the Bride (John 3:29)

He That Holdeth the Seven Stars (Revelation 2:1)

He That Is Higher than the Highest (Ecclesiastes 5:8)

He That Is Holy (Revelation 3:7)

He That Is True (Revelation 3:7)

He That Keepeth Israel (Psalm 121:4)

He That Liveth (Revelation 1:18)

He That Openeth (Revelation 3:7)

He That Sanctifieth (Hebrews 2:11)

He That Shutteth (Revelation 3:7)

He That Was Dead and Is Alive (Revelation 2:8)

He Who Brought Us Up (Joshua 24:17)

He Who Cometh Down from Heaven (John 6:33)

He Who Created (Revelation 10:6)

He Who Fighteth for You (Joshua 23:10)

He Who Hath His Eyes Like a Flame of Fire (Revelation 2:18)

He Who Hath His Feet Like Fine Brass (Revelation 2:18)

He Who Hath the Seven Spirits of God (Revelation 3:1)

He Who Hath the Sharp Sword with Two Edges (Revelation 2:12)

He Who Searcheth (Revelation 2:23)

He Who Sitteth in the Heavens (Psalm 2:4)

He Who Testifieth (Revelation 22:20)

He Who Walketh in the Midst of the Seven Candlesticks (Revelation 2:1)

Him That Bringeth Good Tidings (Nahum 1:15)

Him That Liveth Forever and Ever (Revelation 10:6)

Him That Loveth Us (Revelation 1:5)

Him That Sitteth on the Throne (Revelation 6:16)

Him That Was Valued (Matthew 27:9)

Him Who Is and Who Was and Who Is to Come (Revelation 1:4)

The One That Has the Key of David (Revelation 3:7)

This That Forgiveth Sins (Luke 7:49)

Thou Rulest the Raging of the Sea (Psalm 89:9)

Thou Who Hearest Prayer (Psalm 65:2)

Thou Who Liftest Me Up from the Gates of Death (Psalm 9:13)

Thou Who Saveth by Thy Right Hand (Psalm 17:7)

Who Art, and Wast and Shalt Be (Revelation 16:5)

Who Coverest Thyself with Light (Psalm 104:2)

Who Crowneth Thee with Lovingkindness (Psalm 103:4)

Who Dwelleth in Zion (Psalm 9:11)

Who Forgiveth All Thine Iniquities (Psalm 103:3)

Who Girdeth Me with Strength (Psalm 18:32)

Who Giveth Me Counsel (Psalm 16:7)

Who Hast Power over These Plagues (Revelation 16:9)

Who Healeth All Thy Diseases (Psalm 103:3)

Who Laid the Foundations of the Earth (Psalm 104:5)

Who Layeth the Beams of His Chambers in the Waters (Psalm 104:3)

Who Maketh His Angels Spirits (Psalm 104:4; Hebrews 1:7)

Who Maketh the Clouds His Chariot (Psalm 104:3)

Who Redeemeth Thy Life from Destruction (Psalm 103:4)

Who Satisfieth Thy Mouth with Good Things (Psalm 103:5)

Who Saveth the Upright in Heart (Psalm 7:10)

Who Stretchest Out the Heavens Like a Curtain (Psalm 104:2)

Who Walketh upon the Wings of the Wind (Psalm 104:3)

Whom Thou Hast Sent (John 17:3)

Source: Elmer L. Towns, *The Names of Jesus* (Denver, CO: Accent Publications, 1987).

THE FATHER

Preeminent Pronouns of the Father in Scripture

Abba Father (Mark 14:36)
Ancient of Days (Daniel 7:13)
Creator of the Ends of the Earth (Isaiah 40:28)
Father (1 John 3:1)
Father and the Son (1 John 2:22)
Father in Spirit (John 4:23)
Father, Lord of Heaven and Earth (Matthew 11:25)
Father of Glory (Ephesians 1:17)
Father of Lights (James 1:17)
Father of Mercies (2 Corinthians 1:3)
Father of Our Lord (Ephesians 3:14)
Father of Our Lord Jesus (Romans 15:6; 2 Corinthians 1:3; Colossians 1:3)
Father of Spirits (Hebrews 12:9)
Father of the Fatherless (Psalm 68:5)
Father Which Art in Heaven (Matthew 6:9)

God and Father (James 3:9, *NKJV*)
God and Our Father (Ephesians 1:2)
God, Even the Father (1 Corinthians 15:24)
God of My Fathers (Acts 24:14)
God Our Father (Romans 1:7)
God the Father (John 6:27)
Heavenly Father (Matthew 6:14)
His Name Is Father (John 5:43)
Holy Father (John 17:11)
Living Father (John 6:57)
My Father (Matthew 7:21; John 10:29-30)
My Father and Your Father (John 20:17)
My Father Is the Husbandman (John 15:1)
My Father Worketh (John 5:17)
One Father, Even God (John 8:41)
One God and Father (1 Corinthians 8:6)
Our Father in Heaven (Luke 11:2, *NKJV*)
Righteous Father (John 17:25)
Spiritual Father (Hebrews 12:9, *CEV*)
Very God of Peace (1 Thessalonians 5:23)
Witness of God (1 John 5:9)
Your Father in Heaven (Matthew 5:16, 45,48)

THE HOLY SPIRIT

The Names, Titles and Emblems of the Holy Spirit

Anointing (1 John 2:27)
Another Helper (John 14:16)
Blessing (Isaiah 44:3)
Breath (Ezekiel 37:9)
Breath of God (Job 27:3)
Breath of Life (Revelation 11:11)
Breath of the Almighty (Job 33:4)
Breath of the LORD (Isaiah 40:7)
Breath of Your Nostrils (Psalm 18:15)
Deposit (2 Corinthians 1:22)
Dew (Hosea 14:5)
Different Spirit (Numbers 14:24)
Divided Tongues, as of Fire (Acts 2:3)
Door-Keeper (John 10:3, *NEB*)
Dove (Mark 1:10)
Down Payment (see Ephesians 1:13-14)
Enduement of Power (see Luke 24:49)
Eternal Spirit (Hebrews 9:14)
Excellent Spirit (Daniel 5:12)
Finger of God (Luke 11:20)
Floods on the Dry Ground (Isaiah 44:3)
Fountain of Water (John 4:14)
Fullness of God (Ephesians 3:19)
Gatekeeper (John 10:3, *RSV*)
Generous Spirit (Psalm 51:12)
Gift of God (John 4:10; Acts 8:20)
Gift of the Holy Spirit (Acts 2:38)
Glory of the Lord (2 Corinthians 3:18)
God (Acts 5:4)
Good Spirit (Nehemiah 9:20)
Guarantee of Our Inheritance (Ephesians 1:14; see 2 Corinthians 5:5)
Hand of God (2 Chron. 30:12)
Hand of the LORD (Job 12:9; Isaiah 41:20)
Hand of the Lord GOD (Ezekiel 8:1)
He/Himself (John 14:16,26; Romans 8:16,26)
Helper (John 14:26)
His Holy One (Isaiah 10:17)
His Holy Spirit (Isaiah 63:10)
His Spirit (Numbers 11:29)
Holy One (Job 6:10)
Holy Spirit (Luke 11:13)
Holy Spirit of God (Ephesians 4:30)
Holy Spirit of Promise (Ephesians 1:13)

Holy Spirit Sent from Heaven (1 Peter 1:12)
Holy Spirit Who Dwells in Us (2 Timothy 1:14)
Holy Spirit Who Is in You (1 Corinthians 6:19)
Lord (2 Corinthians 3:17)
Lord of the Harvest (Matthew 9:38)
Mighty Voice (Psalm 68:33)
My Spirit (Genesis 6:3)
New Spirit (Ezekiel 11:19)
Oil (Hebrews 1:9)
Oil of Gladness (Psalm 45:7; Hebrews 1:9)
One Spirit (1 Corinthians 12:13; Ephesians 2:18; 4:4)
Power of the Highest (Luke 1:35)
Promise (Acts 2:39)
Promise of My Father (Luke 24:49)
Promise of the Father (Acts 1:4)
Promise of the Holy Spirit (Acts 2:33)
Promise of the Spirit (Galatians 3:14)
Rain (Psalm 72:6)
Rivers of Living Water (John 7:38)
Same Spirit (1 Corinthians 12:4,8-9,11)
Same Spirit of Faith (2 Corinthians 4:13)
Seal (John 6:27; 2 Timothy 2:19)
Seal of God (Revelation 9:4)
Seal of the Living God (Revelation 7:2)
Seed (1 John 3:9)
Seven Eyes (Zechariah 3:9; 4:10; Revelation 5:6)
Seven Horns (Revelation 5:6)
Seven Lamps of Fire Burning Before the Throne (Revelation 4:5)
Seven Spirits of God (Revelation 3:1; 4:5)
Seven Spirits of God Sent Out into All the Earth (Revelation 5:6)
Seven Spirits Who Are Before His Throne (Revelation 1:4)
Showers That Water the Earth (Psalm 72:6)
Sound from Heaven (Acts 2:2)
Spirit (Numbers 27:18)
Spirit of
 a Sound Mind (2 Timothy 1:7)
 Adoption (Romans 8:15)
 Burning (Isaiah 4:4)
 Christ (Romans 8:9; 1 Peter 1:11)
 Counsel (Isaiah 11:2)
 Deep Sleep (Isaiah 29:10)
 Elijah (2 Kings 2:15; Luke 1:17)
 Glory (1 Peter 4:14)
 God (Genesis 1:2)
 Grace (Zechariah 12:10; Hebrews 10:29)

Him Who Raised Up Jesus (Romans 8:11)

His Son (Galatians 4:6)

Holiness (Romans 1:4)

Jehovah (Judges 15:14, *Amer. Std*)

Jesus (Acts 16:7, *NIV*)

Jesus Christ (Philippians 1:19)

Judgment (Isaiah 4:4)

Knowledge (Isaiah 11:2)

Life (Romans 8:2)

Love (2 Timothy 1:7)

Might (Isaiah 11:2)

My Understanding (Job 20:3)

Our God (1 Corinthians 6:11)

Power (2 Timothy 1:7)

Prophecy (Revelation 19:10)

Revelation (Ephesians 1:17)

Stupor (Romans 11:8)

Supplication (Zechariah 12:10)

the Fear of the LORD (Isaiah 11:2)

the Holy God (Daniel 4:8-9,18; 5:11)

the Living Creatures (Ezekiel 1:21)

the Living God (2 Corinthians 3:3)

the LORD (Judges 3:10)

the Lord GOD (Isaiah 61:1)

the Prophets (1 Corinthians 14:32)

Truth (John 14:17)

Understanding (Isaiah 11:2)

Wisdom (Exodus 28:3; Deuteronomy 34:9; Isaiah 11:2)

Your Father (Matthew 10:20)

Spirit Who Dwells in You (Romans 8:11)

Spirit Who Is from God (1 Corinthians 2:12)

Spirit Whom He Has Given Us (1 John 3:24)

Steadfast Spirit (Psalm 51:10)

Voice (Psalm 95:7; Hebrews 3:7)

Voice of the Almighty (Ezekiel 1:24)

Voice of the LORD (Psalm 29:3-5,7-9)

Voice of Thunder (Psalm 77:18)

Water (Isaiah 44:3)

Well of Living Waters (John 4:14)

Wind (John 3:8)

Wisdom of His Spirit (Ephesians 1:17)

Witness (Job 16:19; Hebrews 10:15)

Your Holy Spirit (Psalm 51:11)

Your Spirit (Psalm 104:30)

Source: Elmer L. Towns, *The Names of Jesus* (Denver, CO: Accent Publications, 1987).

THE TRINITY

The Names of the Lord (*Jehovah*) in the Old Testament

Adonai Jehovah—The Lord GOD (Genesis 15:2)

Hamelech Jehovah—The LORD, the King (Psalm 98:6)

Jehovah—The LORD (Exodus 6:2-3)

Jehovah Adon Kol Ha'arets—The LORD, the Lord of All the Earth (Joshua 3:13)

Jehovah Bore—The LORD Creator (Isaiah 40:28)

Jehovah Eli—The LORD My God (Psalm 18:2)

Jehovah 'Elyon—The LORD Most High (Psalm 7:17)

Jehovah Gibbor Milchamah—The LORD Mighty in Battle (Psalm 24:8)

Jehovah Go'el—The LORD Thy Redeemer (Isaiah 49:26; 60:16)

Jehovah Hashopet—The LORD the Judge (Judges 11:27)

Jehovah Hoshe'ah—The LORD Save (Psalm 20:9)

Jehovah 'Immekha—The LORD Is with You (Judges 6:12)

Jehovah 'Izuz We Gibbor—The LORD Strong and Mighty (Psalm 24:8)

Jehovah Jireh—The-LORD-Will-Provide (Genesis 22:14)

Jehovah Kabodhi—The LORD My Glory (Psalm 3:3)

Jehovah Keren-Yish'i—The LORD the Horn of My Salvation (Psalm 18:2)

Jehovah Khereb—The LORD . . . the Sword (Deuteronomy 33:29)

Jehovah Machsi—The LORD My Refuge (Psalm 91:9)

Jehovah Magen—The LORD, the Shield (Deuteronomy 33:29)

Jehovah Maginnenu—The LORD Our Defence (Psalm 89:18)

Jehovah Makheh—The LORD That Smiteth (Ezekiel 7:9)

Jehovah Ma'oz—The LORD . . . My Fortress (Jeremiah 16:19)

Jehovah Ma'oz Khayyay—The LORD the Strength of My Life (Psalm 27:1)

Jehovah Melek 'Olam—The LORD King Forever (Psalm 10:16; Isaiah 6:5)

Jehovah Mephalti—The LORD My Deliverer (Psalm 18:2)

Jehovah Meqaddishkhem—The LORD Our Sanctifier (Exodus 31:13)

Jehovah Metsudhathi—The LORD . . . My Fortress (Psalm 18:2)

Jehovah Misgabbi—The LORD My High Tower (Psalm 18:2)

Jehovah Moshi'ekh—The LORD Thy Savior (Isaiah 49:26; 60:16)

Jehovah Nissi—The LORD Our Banner (Exodus 17:15)

Jehovah 'Ori—The LORD My Light (Psalm 27:1)

Jehovah 'Oz-Lamo—The LORD the Strength of His people (Psalm 28:7)

Jehovah Qanna—The LORD, Whose Name Is Jealous (Exodus 34:14)

Jehovah Ro'i—The LORD My Shepherd (Psalm 23:1)

Jehovah Rophe—The LORD That Healeth (Exodus 15:26)

Jehovah Sabaoth—The LORD of Hosts (1 Samuel 1:3)

Jehovah Sal'i—The LORD My Rock (Psalm 18:2)

Jehovah Shalom—The LORD Our Peace (Judges 6:24)

Jehovah Shammah—The LORD Is There (Ezekiel 48:35)

Jehovah Tsidqenu—The LORD Our Righteousness (Jeremiah 23:6)

Jehovah Tsuri—O LORD, My Strength (Psalm 19:14)

Jehovah 'Uzam—The LORD Their Strength (Psalm 37:39)

Source: Elmer L. Towns, *The Names of Jesus* (Denver, CO: Accent Publications, 1987).

THE TRINITY

The Names of the Lord God (*Jehovah Elohim; Kurios Ho Theos*) in Scripture

Holy LORD God (1 Samuel 6:20)

LORD God (*Jehovah Elohim*; Genesis 2:4)

LORD God . . . Abounding in Goodness (Exodus 34:6)

LORD God . . . Abounding in Truth (Exodus 34:6)

Lord God Almighty (Revelation 4:8)

LORD God . . . Gracious (Exodus 34:6)

LORD God, Judge of All the Earth (Genesis 18:25)

LORD God . . . Long-suffering (Exodus 34:6)

LORD God Merciful (Exodus 34:6)

LORD, God Most High (*Jehovah El Elyon*; Genesis 14:22; Psalm 18:13)

LORD God of Abraham, Isaac, and Israel (1 Kings 18:36)

LORD God of Elijah (2 Kings 2:14)

LORD God of Gods (*El Elohim Jehovah*; Joshua 22:22)

LORD God of Heaven (Genesis 24:7)

LORD God of Hosts (*Jehovah Elohim Tseba'oth*; 2 Samuel 5:10)

LORD God of the Hebrews (Exodus 3:18)

Lord God of the Holy Prophets (Revelation 22:6)

LORD God of Israel (*Jehovah Elohe Yisra'el*; Exodus 5:1)

LORD God of My Lord the King (1 Kings 1:36)

LORD God of My Master Abraham (Genesis 24:12,27,42,48)

LORD, God of My Salvation (*Jehovah Elohe Yeshu'athi*; Psalm 88:1)

LORD God of Truth (*Jehovah El 'Emeth*; Psalm 31:5)

LORD God of Your Fathers (*Jehovah Elohe 'Abothekhem*; Exodus 3:15)

Lord God Omnipotent (Revelation 19:6)

Lord God Who Judges Her (Revelation 18:8)

LORD Is a God of Justice (Isaiah 30:18)

LORD Is God of the Hills (1 Kings 20:28)

LORD Is . . . God of the Valleys (see 1 Kings 20:28)

LORD Is My Helper (Hebrews 13:6; Psalm 32:7)

LORD Is My Strength and Song (Exodus 15:2)

LORD Is the God of Knowledge (1 Samuel 2:3)

LORD Is the God of Recompense (*Jehovah El Gemuloth*; Jeremiah 51:56)

LORD Is the Great God (Psalm 95:3)

LORD, Mighty in Battle (Psalm 24:8)

LORD, Pillar of Fire (Exodus 13:21-22)

LORD, the Everlasting God (*Jehovah El Olam*; Genesis 21:33)

LORD, the God of All Flesh (Jeremiah 32:27)

LORD, the God of David Your Father (2 Kings 20:5)

LORD, the God of Heaven and the God of Earth (Genesis 24:3)

LORD, the God of Shem (Genesis 9:26)

LORD, the God of the Spirits of All Flesh (Numbers 27:16)

LORD, the Window Opener (see Malachi 3:10)

LORD, Thy Exceedingly Great Reward (Genesis 15:1)

Source: Elmer L. Towns, *The Names of Jesus* (Denver, CO: Accent Publications, 1987).

THE TRINITY

The Names of God (*Elohim*) in Scripture

Almighty God (*El Shaddai*; Genesis 17:1)

Eternal God (Deuteronomy 33:27)

Everlasting God (Isaiah 40:28)

Faithful God (*El Emunah*; Deuteronomy 7:9)

Father to Those Who Have No Father (Psalm 68:5)

God (*Elohim*; Genesis 1:1)

God Almighty (Genesis 28:3)

God in Heaven (*Elohim Bashamayim*; Joshua 2:11)

God Is a Refuge for Us (*Elohim Machaseh Lanu*; Psalm 62:8)

God Is My Helper (*Elohim 'Ozer Li*; Psalm 54:4)

God Most High (*El 'Elyon;* Genesis 14:18)

God Most High (*Elohim 'Elyon*; Psalm 57:2)

God My Exceeding Joy (*El Simchath Gili*; Psalm 43:4)

God, My King (*Eli Malki*; Psalm 68:24)

God My Rock (*El Sela'*; Psalm 42:9)

God of Abraham (Genesis 31:42)

God of All Comfort (2 Corinthians 1:3)

God of All Grace (1 Peter 5:10)

God of All the Families of Israel (Jeremiah 31:1)

God of Bethel (Genesis 31:13)

God of Daniel (Daniel 6:26)

God of Forgiveness (*Elohim Selichot*; Nehemiah 9:17)

God of Glory (*El Hakabodh*; Psalm 29:3)

God of Gods (Deuteronomy 10:17)

God of Heaven (Ezra 5:12)

God of Heaven and Earth (Ezra 5:11)

God of His Father David (2 Chronicles 34:3)

God of Hope (Romans 15:13)

God of Hosts (*Elohim Tsaba'oth*; Psalm 80:7)

God of Isaac (Genesis 28:13)

God of Israel (*Elope Yisra'el*; Exodus 24:10)

God of Jacob (*Elope Ya'akob*; 2 Samuel 23:1)

God of Jerusalem (2 Chronicles 32:19)

God of Jeshurun (Deuteronomy 33:26)

God of Judgment (Malachi 2:17)

God of Love (2 Corinthians 13:11)

God of My Father (Genesis 31:5)

God of My Life (*El Khayyay*; Psalm 42:8)

God of My Praise (Psalm 109:1)

God of My Righteousness (*Elohe Tsidqi*; Psalm 4:1)

God of My Salvation (*Elohe Yish'i*; Psalm 18:46)

God of My Strength (*Elohe Ma'uzi*; Psalm 43:2)

God of Nahor (Genesis 31:53)

God of Our Lord Jesus Christ (Ephesians 1:17)

God of Patience (Romans 15:5)

God of Peace (Romans 15:33)

God of Shadrach, Meshach and Abednego (Daniel 3:29)

God of the Armies of Israel (1 Samuel 17:45)

God of the Beginning (see Deuteronomy 33:27)

God of the Earth (Revelation 11:4)

God of the Gentiles (Romans 3:29)

God of the Hebrews (Exodus 5:3)

God of the House of God (*El Bethel*; Genesis 35:7)

God of the Jews (Romans 3:29)

God of the Land (2 Kings 17:26)

God of the Living (see Matthew 22:32)

God of Truth (Deuteronomy 32:4)

God of Your Father Abraham (Genesis 26:24)

God, the God of Israel (*El Elohe Israel*; Genesis 33:20)

God Who Avenges Me (*El Nekamoth*; Psalm 18:47)

God-Who-Forgives (*El Nose'*; Psalm 99:8)

God Who Is Near (Jeremiah 23:23-24)

God Who Judges the Earth (*Elohim Shophtim Ba'arets*; Psalm 58:11)

God-Who-Sees-Me (*El Roi*; Genesis 16:13)

Great God (Deuteronomy 10:17)

Holy God (*Elohim Qedoshim*; Joshua 24:19)

Jealous God (*El Qanna*; Exodus 20:5)

Living God (*El Khay*; Joshua 3:10)

Merciful God (*Elohe Khasdi*; Psalm 59:10)

Mighty God (*El Gibbor*; Jeremiah 32:18)

Unknown God (Acts 17:23)

Voice (Psalm 18:13)

Source: Elmer L. Towns, *The Names of Jesus* (Denver, CO: Accent Publications, 1987).

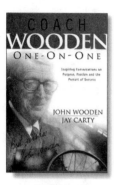
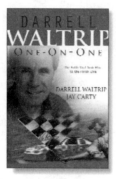

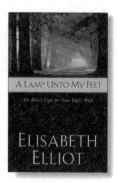

1 Samuel 17

Killing A Giant

David + Goliath

1.) Choose Your Side

2.)

3.) Pick your fights/battles.

4.) Keep God in it!

5.)

6.) Cut the head off!

Satan wants us to lose energy - fighting, sinning.

"People shouldn't strive themselves or others to be spiritual, but to BE HONEST"